ASPECTS
OF
LANGUAGE

Third Edition

DWIGHT BOLINGER
Emeritus, Harvard University

DONALD A. SEARS
California State University, Fullerton

HARCOURT BRACE JOVANOVICH, INC.

New York   San Diego   Chicago   San Francisco   Atlanta
London   Sydney   Toronto

To two dedicated public servants who hold our
admiration and love

Bruce Bolinger, Clerk Recorder,
Nevada County, California

Oretta Ferri Sears, Judge, Superior Court,
Orange County, California

ISBN: 0-15-503872-9

Library of Congress Catalog Card Number: 80-82013

Printed in the United States of America

PREFACE

A new edition benefits—one always hopes—from the comments by users of the earlier book. Since 1975, courses in linguistics or courses with a definable linguistic content have increasingly taken their place in the curriculum, and as a result a clearer agreement about the content of introductory courses has taken shape. The Second Edition of *Aspects of Language,* which reflected the explosion of linguistics during the sixties and early seventies, had expanded to the point of being too heavy a diet for many. In streamlining and focusing this new edition, the authors have benefited from the comments—frank and detailed—that they sought not only from instructors but from the true users, the students who were assigned the text.

So the Third Edition appears as a slimmer book, but one no less rigorous. There has been no sacrifice of careful grounding in the scholarship of language study. The authors believe that many textbooks err by setting too low a value on the undergraduate mind. Young adults deserve a test of intellect suitable for adults; an overplus is not to be justified, but a sense of the important and the unimportant is absolutely necessary. Above all, the beginner in linguistics needs to be guided into a new way of seeing language, a way that turns language inward upon itself to make conscious and tangible those subtle and almost automatic uses that escape the speaker's notice until someone discovers them and holds them up to view.

When the book and the course succeed, one is rewarded with comments like this, from a student at end of term:

> For all of my years of school I never felt that I fully grasped grammar. I feel that most of the time I can write fairly well-constructed papers, yet I always had a difficult time understanding my teacher's explanation of sentences, and syntax, and all of the rest. However, I must say, my growth this last semester has been tremendous. I feel that the material was finally presented in a way that I could understand.

This student was groping to explain her insights into the ways in which language operates. In her introduction to linguistics she had followed the path of training that the Foreword to the First Edition had hopefully enunciated:

> To read the typical book on the wonderful world of words is hardly to see in the spectacle any particular relevance to oneself. Yet there is no science that is closer to the humanness of humanity than linguistics, for its field is the means by which our personalities are defined to others and by which our thoughts are formed and gain continuity and acceptance. Until linguists can bring their point of view clearly and palatably before the student in the language classroom and the reader at large, they will have only themselves to blame for what one linguist has called the towering failure of the schools to inform ordinary citizens about language. Of no other scientific field is so much fervently believed that isn't so. And not only believed but taught.
>
> We do not need to travel abroad nor back in time to discover the facts of language. They lie all about us, in our daily writings and conversations, open to interpretation and uninhibited by rules of what should or should not be written or said. Almost nothing of interest to the linguist goes on anywhere that does not go on in our communication here and now. This book invites all of us to see within ourselves and around ourselves the objects of a science and to glimpse how the scientist interprets them. It is intended to help the users of language detect the inner spark that created the most wonderful invention of all time.

In its presentation, the Third Edition remains eclectic. It tries to speak for an enlightened traditionalism. Its attitude toward usage is not puristic, but it sees purism as one of the inevitable forces that maintain stability. Its attitude toward theory is not transformationalist, but it recognizes transformationalism as the particular species of formalism in linguistics that has channeled discussion for over two decades. Now that the tide seems to be ebbing somewhat, the reader looking for alternatives need not feel left out. Other viewpoints are given their place, and there is plenty of variety for the individual taste.

Responding to the newer subdisciplines of sociolinguistics and psycholinguistics, the book pays due attention to language in its social and socializing aspects. A freshly integrated chapter, "Growth: The Child and the Race," brings together the somewhat parallel ways in which language seems to have been acquired by humankind and by the individual child. The other chapters have been extensively rewritten to hold a straight course and resist the temptation of detours and side alleys however inviting. In keeping with this purpose, three chapters have been dropped: "Schools and Theories," which is for the specialist and specialist-to-be; "Style," which is better suited to a course in writing; and the greater part of "Variation in Time," which is too technical for the beginning student.

The aim is to make the student think about language in a scientific way, using the logical tools that linguistics provides. In each chapter, following the text, there is material to help integrate the matters presented. A list of Key Terms and Concepts—arranged in the order of appearance—gives a means of ready review. A list of Further Reading comprises a brief selection of the most available and readable books for a deeper look into certain topics. Each chapter concludes with Applications—exercises and thought questions to prepare the student for informed classroom discussion.

We wish to thank the many wise and generous persons who helped us shape this new edition: William A. Pullin of Harcourt Brace Jovanovich, who was closely associated with both previous editions, conferred with us for many hours. Harold B. Allen, University of Minnesota; Donald C. Freeman, Temple University; Jeffrey Kaplan, Northeastern University; Joseph B. Monda, Seattle University; and Elizabeth Traugott, Stanford University, provided detailed and stimulating suggestions, which would have cost us dearly to do without. Natalie Bowen with Yankee shrewdness raised the right questions as she edited the various drafts. Roberta C. Vellvé focused meticulous care on the preparation of the final copy. And many others, acknowledged throughout the text, made suggestions and gave freely of information that we found invaluable.

Dwight Bolinger
Donald A. Sears

INTRODUCTION

Thomas A. Edison is supposed to have parried the question of a skeptic who wanted to know what one of his fledgling inventions was good for by asking, "What good is a baby?" Appearances suggest that a baby is good for very little, least of all to itself. Completely helpless, absolutely dependent on the adults around it, seemingly unable to do much more than kick and crawl for the greater part of nine or ten months, it would seem better off in the womb a little longer until ready to make a respectable debut and scratch for itself.

Yet if the premature birth of human young is an accident, it is a fortunate one. No other living form has so much to learn about the external world and so little chance of preparing for it in advance. An eaglet has the pattern of its life laid out before it hatches from the egg. Its long evolution has equipped it to contend with definite foes, search for definite foods, mate, and rear its young according to a definite ritual. The environment is predictable enough to make the responses predictable too, and they are built into the genetic design. With human beings this is impossible. The main reason for its impossibility is language.

We know little about animal communication, but enough to say that nowhere does it even approach the complexity of human language. By the age of six or eight a child can watch a playmate carry out an intricate series of actions and give a running account of it afterward. The most that a bee can do is perform a dance that is related analogously to the direction and distance of a find of nectar, much like what we do in point-ing a direction to a stranger. The content of the message is slight and highly stereotyped. With the child, the playmate's actions can be as unpredictable as you please—they will still be verbalized. Attaining this skill requires the mastery of a system that takes literally years to learn. An early start is essential, and it cannot be in the womb. Practice must go on in the open air where sounds are freely transmitted, for lan-guage is sound. And if language is to be socially effective it cannot be acquired within a month or two of birth when the environment is limited to parents and crib but must continue to grow as the child becomes stronger and contacts widen. Human evolution has ensured that this will happen by providing for a brain of such extraordinary size that the head, if allowed to mature any further before birth, would make birth impossible—a brain, moreover, in which the speech areas are the last to reach their full development.[1] So we might say to the skeptic's question that a baby is good for learning language.

All that a child can be born with is instincts for language in general, not for any particular language—exactly as with an instinct for walking but not for walking in a given direction. This is another reason why an early beginning is necessary: languages differ, and even the same lan-guage changes through time, so that an infant born with patterns already set would be at a disadvantage. One still hears the foolish claim that a child born to German parents ought to be able to learn German more easily than some other language. Our experience discredits this. Ancestry makes no difference. Children learn the language they hear, one about as easily as another, and often two or more at the same time. Complete adaptability confers the gift of survival. Children do not depend on a particular culture but fit themselves to the one into which they are born —one that in turn is maintaining itself in a not always friendly universe. Whatever success that culture has is largely due to the understanding and cooperation that language makes possible.

Another reason for an early beginning and a gradual growth is *perme-ation*. The running account that a child is able to give after performing a series of actions or seeing one performed betokens an organized activity that is not enclosed within itself but relates at all times to something else. It would seem absurd to us to be told that every time we stood up, sat down, reached for a chocolate, turned on a light, pushed a baby carriage, or started the car we should, at the same time, be twitching in a particu-lar way the big toe of our left foot. But just such an incessant accom-paniment of everything else by our speech organs does not surprise us at

---

[1] Lamendella 1975, Ch. 2, p. 2; Carmichael 1966, pp. 17–19.

all. Other activities are self-contained. That of language penetrates them and almost never stops. It must be developed not separately, like walking, but as part of whatever we do. So it must be on hand from the start.

And it continues through life. A language is never completely learned. There is always someone who knows a bit of it that we do not know.[2] In part this is because with the experimental and inventive way in which learning is done, no two people ever carry exactly the same network of shapes and patterns in their heads. A perfect command eludes us because as we catch up it moves off—"the language" exists only as imperfect copies, with original touches, in individual minds; it never stays exactly the same. All we can say is that interplay is so fast, frequent, and vital that great differences are not tolerated, networks are forced to acquire a similar weave, and all networks within cooperating distance tend to share the same grammars and vocabularies.

---

[2] Including parts of grammar as well as vocabulary. One study has shown that ninth and tenth graders get almost as many sentences wrong as they do right in their written compositions. Another has shown definite effects of education on adult speakers. See Bateman 1966, and Gleitman and Gleitman 1970.

CONTENTS

3

SOUNDS AND WORDS   36

4

WORDS AND THEIR MAKE-UP   52

5

THE STRUCTURE OF SENTENCES   74

6

MEANING   108

7

MIND AND LANGUAGE   134

8

GROWTH: THE CHILD AND THE RACE   158

9

VARIATION IN SPACE   191

10

VARIATION IN TIME   231

11

WRITING AND READING   273

12

LANGUAGE AND THE PUBLIC INTEREST   300

SOME TRAITS OF LANGUAGE 1

Five thousand is a fair guess as to how many languages are in active use in the world today—in Colombia, for example, almost two hundred separate languages and dialects have been identified.[1] But "dialect" is a key word—what is "a language" really? Swedish and Norwegian have a high degree of mutual intelligibility, but we count them as two. "One language," Chinese, includes Cantonese and Mandarin, which are about as dissimilar as Portuguese and Italian. To be scientific we have to ignore politics and forget that Sweden and Norway have separate flags and mainland China one. True differences are quantitative: how much should we allow before graduating X from "a dialect of Y" to "a language, distinct from Y"?

However this is reckoned, the number of different languages is formidable and awesome if we include the tongues once spoken but now dead. Languages are like people: for all their underlying similarities, great numbers mean great variety. Variety confronts us with these questions: Do we know enough about languages to be able to describe language? Can we penetrate the differences to arrive at the samenesses underneath?

The more languages we study, the more the answer seems to be yes. Variety is enormous, but similarities abound, and we can even attempt a

---

[1] Arango Montoya 1972.

definition—something like "Human language is a system of vocal-auditory communication, interacting with the experiences of its users, employing conventional signs composed of arbitrary patterned sound units and assembled according to set rules." However we word it—and obviously no one-sentence definition will ever be adequate—there is enough homogeneity to make some sort of definition possible.

LANGUAGE IS HUMAN

Languages are alike because people have the same capacities everywhere. All infants babble—even those deaf at birth. The incredibly complex system that constitutes every known language is largely mastered before a child learns to divide ten by two. No one knows yet how far the great apes may progress in communicating with people and with other apes using human sign language, but for all their skill in using it, they did not invent it (see page 177).

LANGUAGE IS THOUGHT AND ACTIVITY

A language can disappear without a trace when its last speaker dies. This is still true of the majority of the world's languages, in spite of the spread of presses and tape recorders. Written and spoken recordings do endure, and writing in particular has evolved to some extent independently; but the essence of language is a way of thinking and acting. Our habit of viewing it as a *thing* is probably unavoidable, even for the linguist, but in a sense it is false.

What *is* something thing-like, because it is transmitted from speaker to speaker, is the system that underlies the thinking and acting: the *competence* each of us acquires that enables us to *perform* at any given moment. Competence is to performance as a composer's skill is to an improvisation or the writing of a musical work. This is what makes language so special, so different from inborn abilities like breathing, grasping, and crying. With language, all we are born with is a highly specialized capacity to learn. As the child acquires language, the system is probably engraved somehow on the brain; if we had the means to make the system visible we could interpret it. For the present we can only listen to our thoughts and observe how others act, and linguists are useful because, since we are not mind readers, we need specialists to study the behavior and infer the system.

THE MEDIUM OF LANGUAGE IS SOUND

All languages use the same channel for sending and receiving: sound waves, the vibrations of the atmosphere. All set the vibrations moving by the activity of the speech organs. And all organize the vibrations in essentially the same way, into small units of sound that can be combined and recombined in distinctive ways. Except for this last point, human communication is the same as that of many other warmblooded creatures that move on or over the earth's surface.

What sets human speech apart also sets it above dependence on any particular medium: the capacity for intricate organization. The science of *phonetics*, whose domain is the sounds of speech, is to linguistics what numismatics is to finance: it makes no difference to a financial transaction what alloys are used in a coin, and it makes no difference to the brain what bits of substance are used as triggers for language—they could be pebbles graded for color or size, or, if we had a dog's olfactory sense, a scheme of discriminated smells. The choice of sound is part of our human heritage, probably for good reason. We do not have to look at or touch the signaler to catch the signal, and we do not depend on wind direction as with smell; nor, as with smell, are we unable to turn it off once it is emitted.[2] Most important, we can talk and do other things at the same time. This would be difficult if we could only make signs with our hands.

Language is sound in the same sense that a given house is wood. We can conceive of other materials, but it is as if the only tools we had were woodworking ones. If we learn a language we must learn to produce sounds. Other mediums are used only as incidental helps, except among the deaf, whose sign language rivals spoken language in intricacy and efficiency. So part of the description of language must acknowledge that the sound that enters into the organization of language is as indispensable as the organization itself.

LANGUAGE IS HIERARCHIC

Though fluent speakers may seem to talk in a continuous stream, language is never truly continuous. To convey discrete meanings there have to be discrete units, and the first task in breaking the code of a new language is finding what they are. At the lowest level are bits of distinctive sound meaningless in themselves—the hum of an *m* or the explosion of a *p*,

---

[2] Sebeok 1962, p. 435.

which occur in clumps that we call syllables. A *syllable* is the smallest unit that is normally spoken by itself. It is the poet's unit, the unit of rhythm and audibility.

Above the level of meaningless sounds and syllables are the levels that are segmented both for sound and for meaning. First are words and parts of words that we recognize as having meaningful shape, such as the prefix **trans-** or the suffix **-ism**. Above the word level is the level of syntax, itself a complex of levels, since the unit that we call a sentence is often made up of a combination of simpler sentences, usually in some abbreviated form; and these in turn contain smaller units termed phrases, such as the prepositional phrase **to the west** and the verb phrase **ran fast**. Still higher units have to be recognized—question-and-answer, paragraph, discourse —but the larger they get, the harder it is to decide just what the structure is supposed to be. Most linguistic analysis up to very recently has stopped with the sentence.

Stratification—this organization of levels on levels—is the physical manifestation of the "infinite use of finite means," the trait that most distinguishes human communication and that provides its tremendous resourcefulness. Dozens of distinctive sounds are organized into scores of syllables, which become the carriers of hundreds of more or less meaningful segments of words, and which in turn are built into thousands of words proper. With thousands of words we associate millions of meanings, and on top of those millions the numbers of possible sentences and discourses become astronomical. One linguist calls this scheme of things "multiple reinvestment."[3]

Underlying multiple reinvestment is the "structural principle," whereby instead of having unique symbols for every purpose, which would require as many completely different symbols as there are purposes, we use elementary units and recombine them. With just two units at the word level, **brick** and **red,** plus a rule of modification, we can get four different meanings in answer to the request **Describe the house:**

It's brick.　　　It's brick red.
It's red.　　　　It's red brick.

LANGUAGE CHANGES TO OUTWIT CHANGE

Every living language is in a state of dynamic equilibrium. Infinitestimal changes occur in every act of speech and rarely make an impression— they are not imitated or perpetuated, because hearers ignore them (for

---

[3] Makkai 1973.

example, the fumbling of someone who talks in a hurry or coughs in the middle of a word). Now and then a scintilla is captured and held. We hear a novel expression and like it. It is adaptive—fits a style or names a new object or expresses an idea succinctly. Others take it up and it "becomes part of the language." The equilibrium is temporarily upset but reestablishes itself quickly as the new expression marks out its territory, and the older inhabitants defend what is left of theirs.

The vast open-endedness of language that results from multiple reinvestment makes it both systematic and receptive to change. The parts are intricately interwoven, and this maintains the fabric; but they are also infinitely recombinable, and this makes for gradual, nondestructive variation. The linguistic code is like the genetic code—so much so that geneticists refer to "the syntax of the DNA chain." The hierarchical organization of meaningful units in language—from words through phrases and sentences and on up to discourses—is paralleled by ranks of genetic sequences with their inherited messages that control growth and development. Underlying both codes are meaningless subunits, called phonemes in language and nucleotide bases in genetics.[4] Changes in language and mutations in genetics serve a similar purpose: to outwit the random changes in society and in nature. One cannot predict an accident, but one can provide enough variety to ensure that at least one variant of a living form will be resistant enough to survive. This is no guarantee against disaster, and languages as well as species do perish. But it suffices to cope with the normal rate of random intrusions.

LANGUAGE IS EMBEDDED IN GESTURE

If language is an activity, we cannot say that it stops short at the boundary of *verbal* speech activity, for human actions are not so easily compartmentalized. In a primary language encounter—face-to-face speech—the language is reinforced by both *audible* and *visible gestures*. Even when speaking on the telephone a person may sneer, and we will hear the sneer because the sound wave is distorted in characteristic ways.

Audible and visible gestures are usually termed *paralanguage* and *kinesics*, respectively.[5] *Body language* is another word for kinesics, but is generally reserved for movements that communicate without being part

---

[4] See Jakobson 1970, pp. 437–40.

[5] A method for recording visible gestures was developed by Ray L. Birdwhistell as early as 1952. See his *Kinesics and Context* (Philadelphia: University of Pennsylvania Press, 1970), pp. 257–302.

of a clearly established social code—we might say that they are unconscious. For instance, when one is seated, just crossing the legs may
convey a meaning—nonchalance, perhaps. Even when nothing appears
to be going on at all, *something* may be communicated—there is a
language of silence.[6] Skilled comedians know exactly when and for how
long to pause to let a point sink in; spoken language demands time for
decoding as well as time for speaking. But silence is effective only when
one commands the field and fends off would-be interrupters. To avoid
being interrupted while gathering their thoughts, speakers use a kind
of audible gesture called a *hesitation sound,* usually a low-pitched **uh** or
unh. Sometimes words are employed for the same purpose: **well** or **ya
know** in English, **este** ('this') in American Spanish. If you are asked what
time it is and you know, you will reply without hesitation. But if you have
to look at your watch, you may say **It's now-w-w ten-fifteen,** using a
drawled **now** to keep command of the situation. The amount of verbalized
makeweight with which a speaker packs a conversation gesturally to
keep from yielding the floor is incalculable. This is one of the great
stylistic differences between spoken and written language, and is why the
latter appears so carefully pruned.

Gesture may occur alone as when we nod assent, or may accompany
verbal speech. If the sentence **Still, he did his best** is accompanied by a
pouting lower lip and a shrug of the shoulders, visible gesture turns the
words into an ironic apology. If **Oh, Jack's all right, but hell** . . . is spoken
with a deprecatory grimace on the last two words and with a drop of
pitch on **hell,** the result is a trio of verbal language, visible gesture, and
audible gesture.

Gestural systems that are substitutes or virtual substitutes for spoken
language are a study in themselves. The American Sign Language used
by the deaf and the sign language of the Plains Indians are the best-
known examples. Whistle languages and African drum languages
are based in their own peculiar ways on speech, and telegraphic and
semaphoric signaling are based on writing—that is, on spelling. The
finger-spelling used by the Japanese is similar, but is used along with
speech to clear up ambiguities caused by the many sound-alike words in
that language (like the English **deign** and **Dane**).

The gestures, both audible and visible, that accompany ordinary speech
are of two main types and four subtypes. The first main type is *learned*
gestures. These are acquired as part of a speaker's culture, just as words
are; and those of the first subtype, which can be called *lexical,* resemble
words closely enough to have standard spellings: **uh-huh** for 'yes,' **huh?**

---

[6] Bruneau 1973; Edward T. Hall, *The Silent Language* (New York: Doubleday &
Company, 1959).

for 'what?' *hmm* for 'I wonder,' *tsk-tsk* for the click of the tongue used to show disapproval. Visible gestures in this subclass include waving the hand for 'good-bye,' holding both hands out with palms up and shoulders raised for 'I don't know,' and putting the index finger against the lips for 'Be quiet' (often accompanied by the audible lexical gesture *shhh*). Other cultures may use entirely different lexical gestures, or similar ones with different meanings. Our gesture for 'Come here' is holding the hand out cupped palm up with the fingers beckoning; in some other areas—for example, Mexico—it is the same except that the hand is cupped palm down.

The second subtype of learned gestures is *iconic:* the communicator *imitates* some aspect of the thing signified. An audible gesture for 'sound of a bee' is *bzzzz.* For 'machine gun fire' a favorite of small children is *ah-ah-ah-ah-ah-ah,* with a glottal stop. A visible gesture for 'round' is a circle described by the fingers; one for 'so-high' is the hand held at the indicated height above the ground. And a speaker who says *I pushed him away* is apt to make a pushing motion with the hand at the same time. Most descriptions of actions are thus embellished. Iconic gestures tend to be *analog*—more of something can be shown by more of the gesture, less by less (*bzz* for a short buzz, *bzzzz* for a longer one); lexical gestures, on the other hand, are *digital*—more of them may add emphasis, but does not mean more of what they signify—*shhhh* is not quieter than *shhh* but is a more vigorous command to be quiet.

The second main type of gesture is *instinctive*, with subtypes *involuntary* and *voluntary*. No one has to learn to laugh or smile or cry or dodge a blow or blink when an object comes unexpectedly toward the eyes. These actions are controlled by the autonomous nervous system and frequently cannot be avoided even with practice. People who blush easily betray embarrassment in spite of themselves. But the line between involuntary and voluntary is a shifting one. In human beings the limbic system of the brain, which controls involuntary actions, is overlaid by higher systems, and this leads to some measure of voluntary control of reactions that in other animals are purely automatic.[7] A sign of adulthood is the "insincerity" of originally autonomous actions. A smile may no longer be a symptom of feeling but a purposive act intended to please. The hollow laugh and the crocodile tear are instinctive gestures that have become part of etiquette. In the long run all instinctive gestures acquire a social significance and take on local modifications, one reason why members of one culture may behave awkwardly when transplanted to another.

All gestures, but instinctive gestures especially, cooperate with language in a total communicative act. While we can usually guess a

---

[7] Lamendella 1975, Ch. 2, pp. 23, 24, 33.

Table 1–1
Summary of Gesture Types

		Audible	*Visible*
LEARNED	*Lexical*	uh-huh shhh	nod of head finger to lips
	Iconic	bzzz	hand indicates height from ground
INSTINCTIVE	*Involuntary*	cough sneeze	blink of eye blush
	Voluntary	cough for getting attention	smile (to please)

speaker's intent, we may be unsure if the gestural part is extracted. In the following utterance,

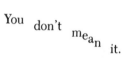

everything can remain the same, yet with one's head held slightly forward, eyes widened, and mouth left open after the last word, the result is a half-question ('You surely don't mean it, do you?'), while with head erect, eyes not widened, and mouth closed afterward, it is a confident assertion. In the first case, cooperation is a kind of competition—the words declare, but the gesture asks. When this happens the gestural meaning is usually closer to the heart of the matter than the meaning of the words and syntax—a sentence like *He's a great guy* can be reversed in meaning by a knowing look (we call such remarks *ironic*). Gestures of pointing are often indispensable. The sentence *He doesn't know you're on my side* immediately preceded by a sidewise toss of the head in the direction of the person referred to makes it clear, by pointing, who *he* is. Gestures of the hands and head are also used to reinforce the syllables on which an accent falls. A person too far away to hear a conversation can often tell what syllables are being emphasized by the way the speaker hammers with a fist or jabs downward with the jaw.

In most accounts of language, gesture has been underrated or ignored.

Body language,[8] along with other bodily functions, has been a partially tabooed subject; even today we would feel embarrassed by saying to someone, "Why did you thrust your head forward when you said that?" though a question like "Why did you say *absolutely* when you weren't sure?" is commonplace. As a reflection of this, linguists have traditionally concentrated on the language of information—propositional language— which is the only kind that *writing* can convey with a high degree of efficiency. But even this kind of language, when spoken, is signaled as true or false, positive or doubtful, welcome or unwelcome, by gesture; and all other forms of language—questions, commands, wishes, exclamations, denials—are heavily dependent on it.

LANGUAGE IS BOTH ARBITRARY AND NON-ARBITRARY

If people are to cooperate they must understand one another by sharing values. Sometimes we deliberately agree to agree, as in learning the mathematical formula $c = \pi r^2$ or the symbols H_2O for water. In such a case the arbitrariness and conventionality of the symbols and their relation to reality stand out boldly.

Language is similarly conventional and arbitrary. There is no need for us to worry about our different perceptions of what a dog looks like, feels like, or sounds like, in order to refer to one. If we are agreed on calling it *dog* we can give socially vital warnings like *Mad dog!* with assurance. *Dog* has an arbitrary, conventional value in our society, as do most of the words in any language.

The obvious exceptions are few. If there were always a close connection between the sound of a word and its meaning, we would not need to know the language to guess the word if we knew the meaning and guess the meaning if we knew the word. Now and then we can do this: *meow* in English and *miaou* in French sound the same and mean the same. Yet even with words that imitate sounds this seldom happens (*to caw* in English is *croasser* in French; *to giggle* in English is *kichern* in German). With other words it is practically never found: *square* and *box-shaped* have similar meanings but no resemblance in sound.

Arbitrariness comes from having to code a whole universe of meanings. The main problem with such vast quantities is to find not resemblances but differences, to make a given combination of sounds sufficiently unlike

---

[8] The subject has been popularized by Julius Fast, *Body Language* (New York: M. Evans, 1970; Pocket Books, 1975).

every other combination so that no two will be mistaken for each other.[9] It is more important to make *wheat* and *barley* sound different than to use the names to express a family relationship as a botanist might do.

Syntax—the grammar of arrangement—is somewhat less arbitrary than words, especially in the order of elements. We say *He came in and sat down* because that is the sequence of the actions; if we said *He sat down and came in* it would have to mean that the opposite sequence occurred —perhaps he decided to get into his wheelchair to propel himself into the room. To reverse the order we need a specific grammatical instruction, say the word *after: He sat down after he came in.* But arbitrariness lingers even without such traffic signs: *ground parched corn* has *first* been parched and then ground.

The most rigidly arbitrary level of language is that of the distinctive units of sound by which we can distinguish between *skin* and *skim* or *spare* and *scare.* It was noted earlier that using sound for this purpose, while practical, was not necessary for the system. And even when sound became the medium, *particular* sounds did not matter so long as they could be told apart. What distinguishes *skin* from *skim* is the sound of [n] versus the sound of [m], but could just as well be [b] versus [g]— there is nothing in the nature of skin that decrees it shall be called *skin* and not *skib.* The only "natural" fact is that human beings are limited by their speech organs to certain dimensions of sound. But given the sets of sounds we *can* make (not identical, of course, from one language to another, but highly similar), arbitrariness frees us to combine them at will. The combinations do not have to match anything in nature, and their number is therefore unlimited.

Still, arbitrariness has its limits. Whenever one thing stands for another —as pictures, diagrams, and signals do—it is normal to look for resemblances. A wiring diagram for a television set represents each part and connection in detail. If someone asks directions and the person asked points to the right, the direction of travel is also to the right. Most gestures have at least an element of guessability about them; the lexical gesture for 'I don't know' described earlier uses empty hands to mean 'I have no information.'

Even the distinctive units of sound are not always arbitrary. There seems to be a connection, transcending individual languages, between the sounds of the vowels produced with the tongue high in the mouth and to the front—especially the vowel sound in *wee, teeny*—and the meaning of 'smallness,' while those with tongue low suggest 'largeness.' The size of the mouth cavity—this *ee* sound has the smallest opening of all—is

---

[9] What happens when two words come to sound the same is treated in Chapter 10.

matched with the meaning. We *chip* a small piece but *chop* a large one; a *slip* is smaller than a *slab* and a *nib* is smaller than a *knob.* Examples crop up spontaneously—"A *freep* is a baby *frope*," said a popular entertainer in a game of Scrabble.

The curious thing about the balance between arbitrariness and its opposite is that, given language (or anything else) as a fact of life, much of the arbitrariness falls away. We can say that the shape of an apple is arbitrary because it "might as well" be square. But apples are a fact of life, and they are not square; and this relates them, non-arbitrarily, to the other fruits in the universe of fruit. The letter F "might as well" have the shape *L*, but it does not, and this relates it non-arbitrarily to the other shapes of the same letter, *f* and f. If we accept the initial arbitrariness of the existence of almost anything, non-arbitrariness follows in most of its subsequent connections. The English language seems inexcusably arbitrary to the speaker of French, yet it is a world to itself, and within that world there are countless more or less self-evident relationships. For example, given the set of words *bolt* (of lightning), (frisky) *colt,* and *jolt,* it is natural to tie a similar jarring meaning to *volt* (named for Alessandro Volta). The more volts the bigger the jolt.[10]

Almost nothing about language is arbitrary in the sense that some person sat down on some occasion and decided to invent it, for virtually everything in language has a nonarbitrary origin. Some things evolve toward greater arbitrariness, others toward less.

LANGUAGE IS VERTICAL AS WELL AS HORIZONTAL

When we hear or look at a display of speech or writing, the dimension we are most conscious of is a horizontal one—the stream of time in speech, the span of lines in writing. Almost everything that we put in a message has to go to the right or left of something else. Much that happens when a language changes is due to collisions or confusions along this course. It may be only a lapse, as when a speaker, intending to say *discussing shortly,* says *discushing,* bringing a sound that belongs on the right over to the left. Or it may be permanent, as in *horseshoe,* in which everybody sounds the *s* of the first element so that it disappears into the *sh* of the second.

---

[10] For a discussion of the relativity of arbitrariness according to the linguist Ferdinand de Saussure, see Wittmann 1966, pp. 88–90. See below, pages 130–31, for *phonesthemes.*

If people merely parroted and never assembled utterances on their own, language might have just a single dimension. But they do assemble, and the question is, where do they go for the parts? It must be to a stockroom of some sort. And stockrooms require a scheme for storage, or we could never find what we are looking for. This is the vertical dimension of language. It is everything that our brains have hoarded since we learned our first syllable, cross-classified in a wildly complex but amazingly efficient way. Nothing less depends on it than the means to summon whatever we need the instant we are framing our ideas for the next phrase and probably still uttering the last one. This vast storehouse of items, categories, and connections is the *competence* that we identified earlier. When we utter a sentence, we choose from a sort of vertical array of words:

$$
\text{The} \begin{bmatrix} \text{small} \\ \text{tiny} \\ \text{miniature} \\ \text{toy} \\ \text{etc.} \end{bmatrix} \text{dog} \begin{bmatrix} \text{leaped} \\ \text{jumped} \\ \text{hopped} \\ \text{flew} \\ \text{etc.} \end{bmatrix} \text{into my lap.}
$$

The number of vertical sets runs into the thousands, and the classes they represent may be small, tight, highly structured ones whose alternation follows some fairly strict grammatical rule, or loose and partially open semantic ones that may even cause speakers to hesitate at times in making a selection. An example of the former is the set of possessives that are used as nouns, which fill the slots in *I had mine, You had* _____, *We had* _____, and *They had* _____. An example of the latter is the set of "coins" (*penny, nickel, dime, quarter*) versus the set of "values" (*eight cents, two bits, a dollar seventy-five*).

The horizontal dimension of language is the domain of *syntax,* which is literally a "putting together." The vertical dimension is the domain of *paradigms,* any of the vertical sets that we have just discussed, as well as the sets that are tied together by some grammatical rule, such as pronouns with their cases, or verbs with their inflections for number, tense, and person.

LANGUAGES ARE SIMILARLY STRUCTURED

Languages can be related in three ways: genetically, culturally, and typologically. A genetic relationship is one between parent and child or between two siblings or cousins: there is a common ancestor somewhere in the family line. A cultural relationship arises from contacts in the real world at a given time; enough speakers command a second language to adopt some of its features, most often terms of cultural artifacts but sometimes other features as well (the borrowed words may contain unaccustomed sounds, which are then domesticated in the new language if conditions are favorable). A typological relationship is one of resemblances regardless of where they came from. English is related genetically to Dutch through the common ancestry of Germanic and Indo-European. In the United States it is related culturally to North American Indian languages, from which it has taken many place names and terms *(Wisconsin, moose, squash, sequoia).* And it is related typologically to Chinese, which it resembles more than it resembles its own cousin Latin in the comparative lack of inflections on words.

Though genetic and cultural relationships tend to parallel typological ones, it often happens that languages of the same family diverge so radically in the course of time that only the most careful analysis will demonstrate their kinship. The opposite happens too: languages unrelated genetically may "converge" to a high degree of similarity. Typological resemblance reveals traits that are universal to all humankind. If we find that languages in scattered parts of the world, which could hardly be related historically, use the pitch of the voice to distinguish questions from statements, or show a predilection for certain vowel sounds over others, or manifest without exception a class of thing-words that may be called nouns, we can be fairly sure that this somehow reflects the physical and mental equipment that all speakers are born with, regardless of their linguistic heritage.

Typological similarities can be found at all levels; the degree and number of them make it possible to classify languages by types. We can match them in terms of the numbers and kinds of distinctive sounds that they have, the way they build words, and the way they arrange sentences. The second of these three methods was long the favorite; languages have been classified as *analytic* (modifications of meaning expressed by separate words: English *I will go* versus French *j'irai*); *synthetic* (modifications built in: English *went* or *departed* versus *did go* or *did depart*); and *polysynthetic* (extremely complex internal structure, roughly as in English *antidisestablishmentarianism*). Cutting across these categories are others depicting how modifications of meaning are handled: *isolating* (arrangement alone distinguishes relationships, as in English **Show me Tom** versus **Show Tom me**); *agglutinative* (relationships are shown by attaching elements that nevertheless retain a clear identity, as in **greenish**); *fusional* (elements are attached that virtually lose their identity in the process, as in *dearth* from *dear + -th; darling* from *dear + -ling*); and *modulating* (internal changes are made without the addition of anything readily seen as having an identity of its own, as in *steal, stole*). It is significant that examples of all these types of structure can be found in English. They are useful as statistical generalizations: most languages are typically more one than another—for example, Chinese is isolating and analytic, Latin fusional and synthetic—but all are mixtures to some extent.[11]

More recently, interest has shifted to sentence structure, in particular the sequence of subject, verb, and object in simple declarative sentences. Languages are classed as SVO, SOV, or VSO.[12] These arrangements are somehow basic, since other facts of structure can be predicted from them. For example, taking V and O as the most essential elements, it generally happens that a qualifier will use whichever one of these two elements it qualifies as a fulcrum and will occur on the side opposite the other element. A negative, for example, which primarily modifies the verb will occur opposite the object, so that V is between: NegVO or OVNeg. An adjective uses the noun (the object) as a fulcrum, resulting in the order AdjOV or VOAdj.[13]

These are some of the large-scale generalizations that can be made about similarities in structure. There are small-scale ones as well. For example, it is predictable that even if a language has a linking verb, young children will not use it; they will say **Daddy here,** not **Daddy is here.**

LANGUAGE IS HEARD AS WELL AS SPOKEN

Though every speaker is also a hearer, the psychology of one role is not always the same as that of the other. The principle of least effort decrees that speakers will work no harder than they have to in order to make themselves understood. This form of laziness results in the blurring of sounds. But the same principle decrees that listeners will work no harder than they have to in order to understand. And this form of laziness compels speakers to use care if they expect cooperation and if they do not want to have to repeat themselves. These are the radical and the conservative forces in language, which account for change and for resistance to change. As they are never quite evenly balanced at any one time, changes do occur, but then the conservative force steps in and reestablishes a norm.

---

[11] For these classifications see especially Sapir 1921, Ch. 6.

[12] The orders VOS, OVS, and OSV do occur, but generally for special purposes, as in **The corn we ate but the beans we threw away,** where the objects have replaced the subjects as the topic.

[13] Lehmann 1973.

Key terms and concepts

competence

performance

phonetics

syllable

paralanguage

  kinesics (body language)

  gesture

arbitrariness vs. non-arbitrariness

syntax, syntagmatic

paradigm, paradigmatic

types of languages

  analytic

  synthetic

  polysynthetic

  isolating

  agglutinative

  fusional

Additional remarks and applications

1. Can the sense of touch be used for communicating in language? Consider the reading of Braille. Can the temperature sense be so used? If not, why?

2. What type of gesture is a handshake? Could one male be sure, if he held out his hand to a male member of some unknown culture, that the other male would not take it as a challenge to a wrestling match?

3. Is the supposed "cooperation" between language and gesture sometimes contrapuntal, in that one says one thing and the other says the opposite? Think of some examples.

4. A gesture may imitate an actual event. In kissing, for example, we have the real thing; then the perfunctory kiss; then the kiss in the air, which may be "tossed." Think of another example.

5. If we think of families of words related in meaning as being less arbitrary if the relationship shows somehow in the word form, how do the two families *inch, foot, yard, rod, mile* and *millimeter, centimeter, meter, kilometer* compare? List two other opposing series like these (say, the popular versus the scientific names for a family of plants).

6. A story by Robert Louis Stevenson contains the sentence *As the night fell, the wind rose.* Could this be expressed *As the wind rose, the night fell?* If not, why? Does this indicate a degree of nonarbitrariness about word order?

7. Consider the two headlines *Woman Running Across Street Killed* and *Woman Killed Running Across Street.* Does syntax tend to be non-arbitrary in terms of putting together things that belong together?

For further reading

Allen, Harold B. 1977. *Linguistics and English Linguistics,* 2nd ed. (Arlington Heights, Ill.: AHM Publishing Company).

Crystal, David. 1971. *Linguistics* (Harmondsworth, England: Penguin Books).

Fast, Julius. 1975. *Body Language* (New York: Pocket Books).

Firth, J. R. 1964. *The Tongues of Men* (1937) and *Speech* (1930) (London: Oxford University Press).

Hall, Edward T. 1959. *The Silent Language* (New York: Doubleday).

Hartmann, R. R. K., and F. C. Stork. 1976. *Dictionary of Language and Linguistics* (New York: John Wiley).

Sapir, Edward. 1921. *Language* (New York: Harcourt Brace Jovanovich).

Whatmough, Joshua. 1957. *Language* (New York: New American Library), pp. 13–55.

LANGUAGE AS DISTINCTIVE SOUND 2

Most English-speaking children by the age of five or six know the word *picture.* Few know such relatable words as *pictorial, depict,* and *pigment*—"cognates" of *picture,* to the etymologist. Like all other words in the child's early vocabulary, *picture* is a unique combination of sounds contrasting with all other combinations. This chapter is about the relatively uncomplicated sounds of that first stage, typified by *picture.* The *picture–pictorial–depict* stage will be described later.

How do the two stages differ? Besides *picture,* our child knows such words as *pin, pillow, pound,* and *pie,* all containing a sound that distinguishes them from *tin, willow, round,* and *die.* Most early learned words are like these—simple in structure, usually native to English (not many Latinisms), and starkly independent—that is, unburdened with the connections that the child learns to make later: *love–lovely–loveliness–beloved, question–quest–request–inquest–query–inquiry–inquisitive–questionable–questionnaire.* The simple stock of early words, all maximally different, demands a sound system that will set *difference* above any other requirement. Sounds have but one purpose: to help tell words apart.

So it happens that as a byproduct of the early words, the child comes to identify the distinctive sounds that make each word different from the rest. One by one the *p* sound of *pin,* the *s* of *house,* the *m* of *animal,* and the *t* of *toy* are picked out and take on a life of their own. *House* is distinguished from *mouse* by the contrast of *h* and *m,* and *much* from *chum* by reversing the positions of *m* and *ch*. The relationship among the sounds at this stage is one of simple *opposition*. Though some may resemble each other more than others (*d* is more like *t* than like *ch*), in their function all are totally different: *dip* is as different from *tip* as it is from *chip*.

PHONETICS AND PHONOLOGY

The distinctive sounds come wrapped in an envelope of other disturbances of the air that convey such information as whether the speaker has a cold or has been eating or feels angry or is a long way off or is an adult rather than a child. Only part of the sound wave corresponds to the central organization, a narrow and precisely limited set of contrasts between various combinations of pitches, durations, loudnesses, and voice and whisper, which are the audible results of the ways we exercise our speech organs. Though no two languages are identical, these ways are similar enough to generalize about them.

We are so accustomed to look at print with its tightly formed letter symbols and neat spaces that we tend to think of "units" of sound in the same way. But clear separations of sound are rare: though we can hear a hissing segment followed by a nasal segment in the word *smell*, generally things are rather badly smeared together—as we can tell with a word such as *arm* by trying to imagine where the *ar-* part ends and the *-m* part begins. Most speakers will say *arm* with the nasal passage open during the whole word—the nasality of the *m* is heard throughout. Furthermore, the sound of the *r* overlaps the vowel, and the tongue remains in the *r* position while lips negotiate the *m*. These are no beads on a string, but a jumble that the brain must somehow keep track of.

Of course the important thing is to recognize the *word*—missing part of a sound or two will probably make no difference. Sometimes one can miss the whole word and still guess it—*He held me at _____ length* begs for the word *arm's*. The redundancy—surplus information—that overflows most things we say enables us to get away with sloppy pronunciation much of the time. Listeners can make sense even if what they hear is deliberately distorted.[1] The result is that "distinctive sounds" do not have to be precise: they represent a range rather than a point. Though we can idealize each range and treat it like a point (a bull's-eye on a target) so long as the targets themselves are far enough apart, anything but a clean miss will count as a hit. The distinctive sounds thus

---

[1] Subjects required to react to question-and-answer pairs in which the answer does not fit the question tend to reinterpret them so that they will agree. See Fillenbaum 1971.

carve up a continuum, each with its proper zone or target area, and with unused buffer zones between.

The vowel sounds provide a clear example. Take a language that has a system of just three vowels, the *ee* of *meet,* the *a* of *father,* and the *u* of *blue,* as happens with the Tagalog language spoken in the Philippines. A speaker could "mispronounce" *meet* as *mit* and still be heard to say *meet,* because the *i* of *mit* is closer to *ee* than to *a* or to *u.* English has more than three vowels and accordingly makes a distinction between *meet* and *mit* that would not be found in the three-vowel language. This means that English speakers have learned to be a bit more discriminating in this one zone. But in any language there is still enough room within phonetic space for vowels to be kept apart without at the same time requiring that they be exactly on center target every time.

The idealization that represents each target area of distinctive sound is the *phoneme.* A phoneme is not a sound but an abstraction, just as a word is an abstraction: we can utter the sounds of *please,* but that set of single utterances is not the word *please,* for if it were, by saying it we would use it up and never be able to say it again. It goes on, as a trace in our minds, or nervous systems, or wherever. But hearing *please* over and over, used appropriately, is what put the trace there in the first place, and the same goes for the phonemes. This makes it possible to describe phonemes as if they really were sounds. There is no danger so long as we remember that no two languages carve up the continuum in exactly the same way, and what is distinctive in one may not be distinctive in another. Some targets are big enough to include the range of two targets in another language; or two targets in two languages may be the same size, but overlap. From years of selective listening the speakers of a language simply do not hear what is not significant for them. This poses a problem when they try to learn another language. The Japanese confuse *r* and *l* in English because in Japanese there is a single sound where English has two. English speakers learning German sometimes substitute *k* for the sound of *ch,* as in *ach* (which can be heard in the English *pack-horse* spoken rapidly). In this case it is German that has two sounds, which contrast in *Acht* 'ban' and *Akt* 'act,' and English that has one.

The study of sounds is *acoustics;* that of speech sound is *phonetics.* The systematic use of sound in language is the field of *phonology. Articulatory phonetics* looks at how speech sound is produced, *acoustic phonetics* looks at the wave form: its shape, intensity, periodicity versus noise, presence of overtones, and so on.

ARTICULATIONS

All languages use certain articulations that interrupt the stream of voiced sound and others that let it flow freely. The first are typically the consonants, the second the vowels. Alternating them is essential to get the variety needed for a large enough set of signaling units. The two depend on each other: the consonants separate the vowels and the vowels help the speech organs to get from one consonant position to the next.

Consonants are made either by shutting off the air completely (*stop consonants*) or constricting it so that it comes through noisily (*fricative consonants*). The stopping or constricting can occur at any point that our speech organs permit, from the lips all the way back and down to the vocal cords. This makes for a good deal of variety in the particular sounds that different languages adopt. English uses the following:

1. The lips. The [p] and [b] in **pane** and **bane** are *bilabial* ('two-lip') stops: the lips are closed and then abruptly parted. The [f] and [v] in **feign** and **vane** are *labiodental* ('lip + teeth') fricatives: the air keeps coming through with friction.

2. The tongue tip on the upper front teeth. English has two fricatives (but no stops) made this way: [θ] (called *theta*) and [ð] called *eth*)—the initial sounds in **thin** and **that.** These and most of the remaining English consonants are classed by the position that the tongue touches or approaches: [θ] and [ð] are *dentals.*

3. The tongue tip on the alveolar ridge directly behind the upper front teeth. These *alveolar* sounds are the stops [t d] and the fricatives [s z] in **to, do, seal, zeal.**

4. The whole front of the tongue on the palate (roof of the mouth). The *palatals* include two fricatives [š ž] and two affricates (see below) [č ǰ]—the sounds at the ends of the words **ash, rouge, rich,** and **gouge.**

5. The rear of the tongue backed against the velum (soft palate), the fleshy part of the roof of the mouth at the rear. The *velars* include two stops, [k g], as in **caw, go.** English has no velar fricatives (except in borrowed words like Scottish **loch** and German **Achtung**).

Other sounds are possible and many are found in other languages. Many languages use a *glottal stop* [ʔ], which English uses in just a few expressive words—the warning **uh-oh!** ('look out, you're about to make a mistake!') and the negative **hunh-uh** or **unh-uh.** Some languages produce certain stops with an intake of air like the smack of a kiss or the expressive **tsk! tsk!** used in English to mean disapproval.

The stops and fricatives are the two chief *manners* of manipulating the air at the various contact points. But there are other ways. One is by tapping the point of the tongue on the alveolar ridge, as in the Spanish [r] of *cara* ('face'), or the English [t] of *gotta.* This is called a *flap,* and when it is repeated it is a *trill,* as in Italian *rosa.* (The uvula is also loose enough to produce a flap or trill: French and German have such *uvular* sounds.) Another manner combines stop and fricative: instead of breaking the contact crisply, these *affricate* sounds are made by withdrawing the tongue gradually. English has two palatal affricates, [č ǰ], as in *itch* and *age* (plus a borrowed alveolar affricate in words such as *Tsar* and *tsetse*). Still another manner affects the direction of the air: when diverted through the nose before or instead of being released from the mouth, the result is one of the *nasals:* labial [m] in *ram,* alveolar [n] in *ran,* and velar [ŋ], called *angma,* in *rang.* If the air passes around the sides of the tongue instead of along the median line, a *lateral* results: the alveolar lateral [l], as in *Lee.*

Three sounds, the *semivowels* [y w r], are as much like vowels as consonants. Their constriction is fairly tight but less so than for fricatives. They are used in *diphthongs* (to be discussed shortly).

The most fundamental contrast in English is that of voice and voicelessness. Making the vocal cords vibrate produces a *voiced* sound, as in [v] (prolong the [v], put a finger on your Adam's apple, and you will feel the vibration). If the air passes the vocal cords without vibration, the result is a *voiceless* sound, as in [f]. Voiceless and voiced sounds usually come in pairs for each position and manner: [p b], [f v], [θ ð], [t d], [s z], [š ž], [č ǰ], [k g]. Vowels are typically voiced, but English has a consonant that is like a vowel without voice: the [h] of *heat, hope, hail, hoot,* and so on, is made by starting the sound of the following vowel without voice.

These descriptions do not necessarily hold for other languages, or even among all varieties of English. For example, many speakers make the hiss of an [s] not with the tongue tip but by bunching the blade or flat part of the tongue up against the alveolar ridge, letting the tip curl down behind the lower front teeth. There may be subtle differences among sounds otherwise quite similar. English voiceless stops are *aspirated* at the beginning of a word—the voicing of the vowel is delayed so that we hear a puff of air in between (enough to blow out a match held close to the lips when a word such as *pin* is pronounced). French has no such delay, and when a French speaker tries to say our *pin* we may mistake it for *bin*—we notice the non-aspiration of the [p] more than the lack of voicing.

Table 2–1 classifies the English consonants by place and manner. To accommodate other languages, more categories would have to be added: a *uvular* column for French and German to take care of the *r*-like sound described above, an extra row for the *suction* (tsk-tsking) stops, and so on. But many non-English sounds can be fitted into the empty

TABLE 2–1
The English Consonants

	Bilabial	Labiodental	Dental	Alveolar	Palatal	Velar	Glottal
STOPS	p b			t d		k g	
FRICATIVES		f v	θ ð	s z	š ž		h*
AFFRICATES					č ǰ		
NASALS	m			n		ŋ	
LATERAL				l			
SEMIVOWELS	w†			r	y		

* Classed as a fricative on the basis of acoustic effect. It sounds more or less like [f θ s], even though it is like a vowel without voice.

† [w] is velar as well as bilabial, since the back of the tongue is raised as it is for [u].

slots in the English chart. The velar fricative [x] (Scottish *loch,* German *Achtung,* Spanish *caja*) goes directly below [k]. The palatal nasal [ɲ] (French *guignol* 'puppet show,' Italian *bagno* 'bath') goes to the right of [n].

Vowel sounds are made by *shaping* the column of air rather than by obstructing it. The tongue can move forward or backward and up or down as the jaw is raised or lowered. The lips may be spread or rounded. These movements change the size and shape of the resonating cavities, and this in turn filters out certain harmonic frequencies and reinforces others. Vowels are *high, mid,* or *low,* depending on the height of the tongue (nearness to the palate); *front, central,* or *back,* according to the position of the highest part of the tongue on the horizontal axis; and most of them are *rounded* or *spread.* Examples:

high front (spread)	[i] as in *beat*
lower high front (spread)	[ɪ] as in *bit*
mid front (spread)	[e] as in *bait*
lower mid front (spread)	[ɛ] as in *bet*
low front	[æ] as in *bat*
central	[ʌ] as in *butt*
low back	[a] as in *pot*
lower mid back (rounded)	[ɔ] as in *bought*
mid back (rounded)	[o] as in *boat*
lower high back (rounded)	[ʊ] as in *put*
high back (rounded)	[u] as in *boot*

Spread and *rounded* are in parentheses because in English, and in many other languages, the higher front vowels are automatically spread and the higher back are rounded. French is an exception to this, with its front rounded vowels: in the pairs *fée–feu* ('fairy' and 'fire') and *père–peur* ('father,' 'fear') the first member has a front spread vowel and the second a front rounded one.

Diphthongs combine two vowel or vowel-like sounds in a single syllable. In English they contain a regular vowel plus one of the semivowels [y w r]. The tongue glides either toward or away from the position of [y w r], and for that reason the semivowels are often called *glides*. Examples:

[ay] as in *tie*	[ya] as in *yacht*
[ɔy] as in *Roy*	[yɔ] as in *yore*
[aw] as in *now*	[wa] as in *wan*
[ar] as in *car*	[ra] as in *rock*

All three semivowels may occur before any vowel (for example, *yeast, Yiddish, Yale, yet, yam, young, yacht, yawl, yoke, your, youth*); but *after* a vowel, [y w] are mostly restricted to [ay ɔy aw] and [r] is mostly restricted to [ɪr ɛr ar ɔr ʊr] as in *beer, bear, bar, bore, boor*. The semivowels are sometimes called *semiconsonants* when they are the first members of a diphthong, but the sounds are the same: a recording of *yacht, yore, wan,* and *rock* played backward will yield *tie, Roy, now,* and *car,* as in the chart above.

The vowels treated thus far are the *full vowels*. Diphthongs also count as full. Characteristic to English and important to the *rhythm* of the language are three *reduced* vowels, as heard in the last syllables of **Willie, Willa, willow:** [i ə ə]. (The [ə] of *willow, motto, thorough* contrasts with the full vowel [o] of *combo, alto, bingo.*) The sound [ə] is called *shwa* and is the most frequent vowel in the language (for speakers who stress the first syllable of *formidableness,* all the remaining vowels are shwa: [fɔrmədəbəlnəs]). Rhythmic effects appear in strings of syllables. A string of nothing but full vowels is unusual in English prose: **Irene Carstairs' pet chimpanzee Nimrod dotes on fresh horehound drops.** The syllables here are spaced out on a fairly even beat—typical of French, Spanish, or Italian, but not of English. When syllables with reduced vowels intervene—the usual thing in English—the reduced vowels borrow time from the preceding full vowels, producing an uneven beat. Compare **Gets out dirt plain soap can't reach** (all full vowels) with **Takes away the dirt that common soap can never reach** (every other vowel reduced[2]). In Figure 2–1, the reduced vowels appear as a triangle within the larger frame of the full vowels.

---

[2] See Bolinger 1963 and Lehiste 1972.

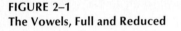

FIGURE 2–1
The Vowels, Full and Reduced

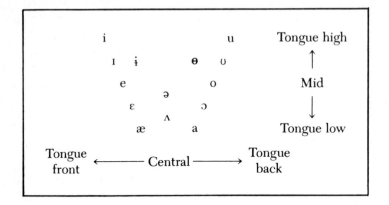

The vowels show more clearly than the consonants how readily one may find differences within a single language. The tongue moves freely and can take not only all the up-down, back-front positions shown in Figure 2–1 but other positions between. Most consonants offer easier targets—the teeth are in a precise location, and the tongue can aim true; but the continuum of the mouth cavity provides nothing definite to aim at. So we find speakers whose vowels will disagree here and there with those on the chart, in their position, and sometimes even in how many there are. Some dialects make the reduced vowel [ɨ] in the last syllable of *hairy, many,* or *courtesy* as high as the full vowel [i]. More and more American speakers are eliminating the vowel [ɔ] altogether, substituting [a]: pairs like ***taught–tot, caught–cot, caller–collar, auto–Otto, pauper–popper*** come to sound the same. Such confusion is apt to occur in a language with a large number of vowels because the space gets over-crowded. In a language with few vowels—say Tagalog, with just three [i a u], or Spanish with five [i e a o u]—there is less interference.

Many languages multiply the number of their vowels by adding one or more of the following *secondary articulations:*

Rounding, as in French *vie* ('life') and *vu* ('seen'). Rounding occurs in English but does not count (see above).

Nasalization, as in French ***beauté-bonté*** ('beauty,' 'goodness'), ***seauson*** ('pail,' 'sound'). Again, nasalization is often heard in English vowels, but it does not count.

Length, as in Latin ***mēto*** versus ***meto*** ('I measure,' 'I reap'). Consonants are sometimes lengthened too, as in Estonian. It may be hard to decide whether to treat a lengthened sound as a single sound with extra length or two identical sounds side by side. The latter interpretation is best for English expressions like ***cattail, ripe pear, sack coat.***

Breathiness, as in Gujarati (a language of India), which also allows nasalization for a further increase.[3]

Tone, a higher or lower pitch on a vowel. In Ticuna, a *tone language* of the upper Amazon, there are five steps of pitch. The form *čanamu* is actually four different words according to the combination of tones: numbering 1 for highest and 5 for lowest, we have *ča₃na₃mu₃* ('I weave it), *ča₃na₃mu₄* ('I send it') *ča₃na₃mu₅* ('I eat it') and *ča₃na₃mu₃₋₅* ('I spear it).[4] In the West Indies, even English has some tonal distinctions, inherited from African languages: **brother** with high-low pitch refers to one's kin, but with low-high it means a member of a religious or fraternal order—similarly with **sister, mother,** and **father. Worker** with high-low is 'laborer,' with low-high 'seamstress.'[5]

The use of tone is complex. It is not always easy to say that it is added just to make the vowels go farther. It sometimes functions more like an affix or "little word": a negative statement may have a different tone from an affirmative one, or an active sentence from a passive.

There are other secondary articulations, and some are used to multiply consonants. Aspiration, for example—automatic under certain conditions in English (see above) but absent in French—was used to supply extra consonants in Classical Greek and is used in North Chinese today. *Voicing* is the secondary articulation that gives extra consonants in English, French, German, and so forth (we think of it as primary because these are "our" languages).

PROSODY

Prosody is a kind of musical accompaniment to speech, as gesture is a kind of histrionic accompaniment, and gesture and prosody are sometimes hard to distinguish. Part of prosody is *rate,* which is as important in speech as in music. Someone in a hurry tends to speak fast, but rate can be controlled deliberately: **Take your time** may be said slowly, to suggest 'Do it carefully,' even if the speaker is impatient. Rate is the great distorter of articulations. To save time, we create a vocabulary of hurried expressions. In answer to **Why didn't you bring the pliers?** one may say

[aynno]   where they
                          ar
                            ＼
                          e.

---

[3] Fischer-Jørgensen 1967.

[4] Anderson 1959.

[5] Personal communication from S. R. R. Allsopp.

Even though [aynno] sounds more like *I know* than *I don't know,* the
lengthened [n] helps to signal the latter meaning. *Whatcha, gotta, gazinta,*
and so forth, are familiar spellings for such contractions. Speeding up and
slowing down are freely manipulated for various effects.

Accent is an element of prosody combining length, loudness, and pitch,
with pitch the leading element. It emphasizes important words and
phrases and gives a typical melodic shape to sentences. In

$$\text{You must }^{\text{au}}\text{tograph another }^{\text{pic}}$$
$$\text{ture for me.}$$

the important words are *autograph* and *picture,* which the dictionary
marks with stress on the first syllable ('*autograph,* '*picture*)—the accent,
signaled by an abrupt change in pitch, falls on that syllable.[6] At the same
time, the presence of two striking pitch changes, one early and one late,
is typical in English sentences. Speakers usually get the important words
in the right position to produce that shape. But the importance of the
word comes first—we could almost as easily have

$$\text{You must }^{\text{au}}\text{tograph an }^{\text{oth}}$$
$$\text{er picture for me.}$$

with *picture* deemphasized (the speakers have already been talking about
pictures, and the word does not need to be "pointed up") and the main
emphasis placed on the stressed syllable of *another* (*an'other*). It is possible for only one accent to appear, as in

$$\text{You must autograph another picture for }^{\text{me}}$$

This would come after some remark to the effect that a picture had already been autographed for someone else.

Intonation is the overall sweep of the pitch curve. It carries the accents, but it has additional features—range, direction, and relative height:

Range conveys emotion. Excitement spreads it, depression narrows it.

---

[6] Many authorities use the term *stress* instead of *accent.* In this book, *stressed* refers
to the syllable that is marked in a dictionary. It is the one that receives the accent
if an accent falls there, but has no pitch prominence otherwise.

Direction cooperates with *pause* to punctuate speech. At the end of a statement, the pitch tends to drift down; this, plus the following pause or silence, is a kind of period. The opposite direction is a kind of comma, occurring at a nonfinal break, as on **ready** in the following:

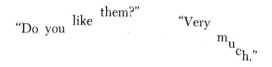

In questions answered by yes or no, the direction is often up all the way. Such a question, with its answer, resembles the example just given:

In both cases what is incomplete goes up and the completion comes down. The speaker decides. If a yes-no question is felt to complete something (perhaps it is the last in a series of questions) the pitch drops at the end.

Relative height accompanies degree of importance. A more important accent has a wider jump than a less important one. Similarly with a more important punctuation: if, in an example like the **If you're ready** one above, there happen to be two separations instead of one, a higher pitch occurs at the major break:

The first says 'If you're ready when I get there'—the higher rise puts the major break after **there**. The second says 'when I get there we'll go'—the major break is after **ready**. Both sentences cover the same range, but the relative high point occurs on different words to show a difference in meaning.

All languages share the main up-down uses of intonation, but tend to stereotype them into more or less arbitrary patterns. In English one can usually recognize a command regardless of the syntactic form of the sentence:

On your f_e_e_{t.}

makes a good command, but would be an abrupt answer to a question (commands are characteristically abrupt—we are assuming the right to control someone's actions). A good answer to a question would be

On your fe e_{t.}

coming after *How am I supposed to get there?* It would not be a good command (except perhaps to repeat a command).

Stereotyping is most noticeable with set expressions that always or almost always have a particular intonation, such as ***Don't look at me!*** ('I don't have the answer') or ***All right!*** (expressing grudging consent):

Don't look at me!   All right!

Here we might say that the words control the intonation. There are also cases where the intonation controls the words. For example, *kerplunk, kerboom, kersplash, kerwhack* add a syllable to give a running start to the accent, making it stand out more sharply. Sometimes we add an otherwise useless word just to pick up an extra accent for emphasis, as with *living* in the following threat:

I'll knock the living day lights out of you.

Though the differences are considerable, intonation patterns are widely shared. More languages associate a high pitch with questions than do the opposite. Almost all languages have some form of falling pitch to express finality.

SOUNDS IN COMBINATION: THE SYLLABLE

We analyze and talk about vowels and consonants as if they were individual things, but in speech a consonant can be heard properly only with a vowel next to it. Perhaps the "real" units of speech are not vowels and consonants separately but some larger unit, most likely the syllable. Syllables have been counted as long as there has been poetry. Children play with them in their jeering chants: *Fred-die-is-a-fraid-y-cat.* Early forms of writing were syllabic (see page 288), with separate signs for syllables, not for vowels and consonants. The syllable is a kind of natural minimum unit of speech—it is easier to say [bi] (as we do when we recite the alphabet—*a, b, c, d*) than [b] alone.

The syllable's chief place is in rhythm—each syllable is timed to an average beat of about one-sixth of a second,[7] and this pulsation is tied to other rhythmic activities of the body.[8] The syllable is the unit that pulls together all the phonic events that we sense to occur "at the same time," even though instruments may show some of them in sequence. When we make intentional changes in our speech, the syllable is the unit we attach them to. To make a word emphatic, we put an accent on its stressed syllable:

Beau$^{\text{tiful!}}$ De^{light}ful!

And if an insertion is made for humor or emphasis, it is fitted between existing syllables: *absoposilutely, fan-damn-tastic.*

Syllables have a typical internal structure: a *nucleus,* which is a vowel or a vowel-like consonant ([r] or [l], for example), with or without one or more *satellites* in the form of consonants before or after the nucleus. (Which way to shift a consonant that lies between two nuclei is sometimes easy to tell, sometimes not. *Ben Tover* has an aspirated [t], *bent over* does not, so we know the divisions are [bɛn tovər] and [bɛnt ovər]; but *one's own* sounds the same as *one zone.*) Probably the most striking impression a language makes on listeners who do not understand it and who notice sounds rather than meanings is the way its syllables are built. If the language has many satellites, especially voiceless ones, it sounds noisy; if few, it sounds musical. English stands about midway: *Willow Lane* is musical; *splashed* and *sprints* are noisy.

---

[7] Lenneberg 1967, pp. 113–15.

[8] Bullowa 1972, p. 2.

Some arrangements are excluded. Combinations such as [tl], [nw], [sb], and [sfl] cannot begin a syllable in English. A good test is to start with a nucleus, say [o] as in *oh,* and build to the left: *row, crow, scrow;* or [e]: *lay, play, splay.* It turns out that English can begin a syllable with any single consonant except [ɲ]; with certain clusters of two elements, especially stops and voiceless fricatives plus [l] or [r], or [s] plus certain other consonants (*truce, pry, plea, sly, free, snail, skill*); or with certain clusters of three when the first is [s] (*splurge, stray*). A similar buildup shows what clusters can end a syllable: *oh–own–owned, bur–Bearse–burst–bursts.*

Units of sound that—like the syllable—can be described without reference to meaning are hard to find at higher levels. There is the *breath group,* a series of syllables spoken with one expiration of breath, which generally coincides with a particular intonation shape. If the end of a sentence slows down and falls in pitch, the end of a paragraph will be still slower and deeper, and the end of a story will be slowest and deepest of all. But sentences, paragraphs, and stories are units of sense, and even breath groups usually correspond to meaningful phrasing. The syllable is probably the largest of the arbitrary units of speech—the *cat-* of *catapult* has nothing to do with cats.

PHONEMES AND ALLOPHONES

Thus far we have been concerned with sounds as sounds—their production, transmission, and reception. Now we must look at them as points in a system. While the actual production of a speech sound may vary slightly, its contrast to other sounds within a system must be distinct enough to differentiate meaning. These systematic units of distinct sound are called *phonemes.*

Since a phoneme is a kind of idealization, a way must be found to relate it to real acts of speech in the real world. This is done by setting up two entities, the *phone* and the *allophone.* The *phone* is a phoneme-token, a single instance of the utterance of a phoneme on a particular occasion by a particular speaker. It will differ in unimportant ways from every other phone of that phoneme ever produced. No two can be identical because the combination of head position, air pressure in the lungs, objects interfering between speaker and hearer, and other such disturbances at that moment in history is unique. The *allophone* is a phoneme-subtype, a particular *way* a phoneme is normally uttered in a given phonological environment, such as aspirated and unaspirated [t]. Since they differ as sounds, we might use two symbols: [tʰ] and [t⁻]. From here on, to show "the same phoneme," the symbol will appear between slant lines: /t/. The phoneme /t/ in English thus has the allophones [tʰ] and [t⁻].

Each allophone is described in relation to what causes the phoneme to be pronounced that way. In the words *intake, retain,* and *team,* the /t/ is aspirated. But in *catnip, enter,* and *stem* it is not. The common factors in the first three words are that the /t/ is unclustered (not combined with any other consonant in the same syllable) and followed by a full vowel. In the others it is either followed by a reduced vowel (*enter*) or by none (*catnip*), or is clustered with /s/ (*stem*). All three English voiceless stops [p t k] behave similarly: aspirated when unclustered before full vowels, which give sufficient time for the delay in voicing that causes the aspiration, and unaspirated otherwise. The /p/ of *pain* and *compost* is aspirated [pʰ]; that of *Spain, sip, apt* is unaspirated [p⁻]. The /k/ of *decay* is aspirated; that of *skill, decorate, act* is not.

Other environments produce other effects. In saying *hip* before a pause we have a choice of keeping our lips closed and not "releasing" the /p/, or opening them and letting the air out—the latter produces a mild aspiration. There are ways of symbolizing many more finespun distinctions, but they are not important here.

A still unanswered question is how we know we have a phoneme if all we ever hear is phones, described in phonetic terms as allophones. What right do we have to speak of allophones "of" /p/?

The proof lies in comparing utterances that are partly alike and finding the least things that make them different. Every native speaker of a language has a feel for this: a pun such as *The undertaker said he was going to buy his little boy a rocking hearse* exploits the small contrast between *hearse* and *horse.* Such *minimal pairs* reveal the phonemes when enough of them are accumulated.[9] A riming set like *bay–day–Fay–gay–hay–jay–Kay–lay–may–nay–pay–ray–say–shay–way* gives a hint of distinctive consonants /b d f g h ǰ k l m n p r s š w/, which is confirmed by other sets like *robe–rode–rogue–roam–roan–rope–roar.*

Even for a native there are uncertainties. Some phonemes are like arpeggios in music—they spread out in time and we are unsure whether to regard them as a single "chord" or as a succession of notes. *A gray chip* sounds so much like *a great ship* that we are tempted to say that they contain the same succession of phonemes, and to analyze the first sound of *chip* not as a single phoneme /č/ but as the succession /tš/. The

---

[9] English has 36 phonemes, give or take a few depending on whose dialect is being analyzed and who the analyst is. It has been calculated that 10 phonemes is probably the smallest number to be found in any language and 80 the upper limit, with 95 percent of the world's languages having between 14 and 43. See Sigurd 1963, pp. 96–97.

decision then turns on other evidence, such as the mistakes a speaker makes: **Crack some ice** can be fumbled as **Cack some rice**—we readily split the cluster /kr/; but **Chuck the Ape** would never be fumbled as **Tuck the Shape**[10]—the failure to split /č/ suggests that it is a unit. Other evidence is in the whole system of sounds. If /č/ and /ǰ/ in Table 2–1, page 22, were moved into the "stop" row, not only would that row be filled out better but the entire affricate row would become unnecessary. This amounts to ignoring the fricative half of the cluster and assuming that the affricates are merely palatal stops with automatic affrication—a neater pattern all around.

Neatness and economy lead some linguists to analyze the vowels differently too, identifying the vowel portion of the word **bay** not as /e/ but as /ey/, reserving the symbol /e/ for the vowel in **bet** and not using /ɛ/ at all. There are good phonetic reasons for this, since **bay** does have a pronounced glide, though some of it disappears in **bait** and most of it in **baiter.**[11] Such a scheme reduces the number of vowel phonemes and matches with the other diphthongs—/ay/ for example—that are needed anyway.

Such patterning is also the test for whether phonetically different sounds should be classified as allophones of one phoneme or as separate phonemes. In Table 2–1, /n/ is in the alveolar column. That is correct for the word **ten,** but in **tenth** the nasal is not alveolar but dental. Should it be called a separate phoneme? That would put two different nasal phonemes in **ten** and the **ten-** part of **tenth,** though they mean the same. Instead, we can regard the two nasals as allophones of the same phoneme /n/, explaining the difference by its patterning with neighboring sounds. The culprit here is the /θ/ in **tenth.** It is dental, and the /n/ *assimilates* to it. (Compare the way a handwritten *i* assimilates to a preceding *b* by beginning its stroke where the *b* leaves off rather than at the bottom of the line: *bi*, not *bi*.) It is less work for the tongue to anticipate the dental position of /θ/ than to take two positions, alveolar and dental, and the sound is the same to our English-trained ear.

Assimilation accounts for most allophonic variation. English /r/ is normally fully voiced, but in a cluster after a voiceless /t/, as in **tree,** it is partially devoiced. A radio ad for **Monk's Bread** may sound as if it were plugging **Monk Spread**—the /b/ of **bread** is partially devoiced after the voiceless /s/ and the /p/ of **spread** loses its aspiration after /s/, so

---

[10] See Fromkin 1973, pp. 112–13.

[11] The same reasoning leads to an /ow/ rather than an /o/ in **tow** (but compare **tote** and **toter**), an /iy/ instead of an /i/ in **bee,** and an /uw/ instead of an /u/ in **boo,** with /o/ then used instead of /ɔ/, /i/ instead of /ɪ/, and /u/ instead of /ʊ/.

that the /b/ and the /p/ have neither voice nor aspiration to distinguish them. We class them separately because the similarity can be attributed to conditioning by the environment: this is *conditioned variation.*

There is also *free variation,* not caused by the phonological environment. We are free to say **Stop!** with a released or an unreleased /p/. The two dialectal varieties of /s/ have already been noted.

Whatever the variation, two principles guide the identification of phonemes: *phonetic similarity* and *complementary distribution.* The first says that the dental /n/ of **tenth,** the alveolar /n/ of **ten,** and the palatal /n/ of **inch** are enough alike to be classed together. The second is a way of disposing of the features that differ. The distributions (places of occurrence relative to other sounds) of dental /n/ and palatal /n/ are not the same as that of alveolar /n/; instead, they *complement* each other: each occurs where the two others do not—they do not contrast with one another in the same environment, as /n ŋ m/ do in **ran-rang-ram.** So they are "the same /n/," with different allophones. Similarly the dialectal /ɨ/'s are "the same /ɨ/"—the complementing environments here are the two different dialects.

Languages are not so neatly organized that all observers will reach the same conclusions. Take the American English /t/ in words like **butter–totter–matter–pewter–bitter–atom–motto–pity–duty.** Most speakers reduce it to a bare tap (a *flap,* mentioned earlier) which picks up voicing from the surrounding sounds and becomes virtually indistinguishable from /d/: **bitter** sounds like **bidder, latter** like **ladder, He hit 'er** like **He hid 'er, let 'em** like **led 'em,** and so on. Shall we call it /t/ or /d/? Most dictionaries choose /t/, reasoning that in some dialects /t/ and /d/ are still quite distinct and some trace of that difference must remain even for those who make them sound alike. If we pronounce a clear /t/ in **atomic** we are not apt to be "thinking of" a /d/ when we say **atom** even if we do make it sound like **Adam.** Besides, when we slow down and say **atom** emphatically, we make a clear /t/. "A word is a word," and **atom** should be the same in **atom** as in **atomic.** On the other hand, the Merriam-Webster *Third New International Dictionary* prefers /d/ whenever [d] is heard—"a sound is a sound."

In such situations, no solution is perfectly satisfactory. These are uncertainties to be tolerated, areas of vagueness in the language itself. But the noteworthy and comforting fact is that vagueness in phonemes is the exception rather than the rule. Languages are remarkably efficient in keeping their signaling units clear and distinct.

Key terms and concepts

phonology
phonetics
  articulatory phonetics
  acoustic phonetics

consonant articulations
  stop
  fricative
  bilabial
  labiodental
  dental
  alveolar
  palatal
  velar
  uvular
  affricate
  lateral

voicing
  voiced
  voiceless

vowel articulations
  high, mid, low
  front, central, back
  rounded, spread
  full, reduced

semivowel
diphthong
shwa
tone language

prosody
  rate
  accent
  intonation

syllable
  nucleus
  satellites

breath group

phoneme
  phone
  allophone

minimal pair
variation

Additional remarks and applications

1. Tongue twisters are phrases that are difficult to articulate: the phrase *six sick sheiks* is a dictionary example; the phrase *precious brass paper fastener* was stumbled over by a speaker. Try saying them fast. What makes them difficult?

2. The syllable of a word to which an accent is applied when the word is accented is the *stressed syllable*. It seldom varies—knowing where the stress is, is part of knowing the word. Mark the stressed syllables in the following words: *amiableness, intentionally, conversationalist, interconversion, contravene.*

3. When written, a sentence like *Was she more or less courteous* is ambiguous. Is it ambiguous in speech? If not, why not?

4. There is a construction in English that smacks of archaism yet survives in certain forms. An example is ***I don't want to go but go I must.*** Could its survival be due to its intonational effectiveness? Explain.

5. Compare the following two sentences:

What do you have in the clothes line?
What do you have on the clothesline?

Do you hear a difference between ***clothes line*** and ***clothesline?*** If so, is it one that is likely to be heard all the time?

6. The most complex consonant clusters in English occur at the ends of words—for example, /ksθs/ in ***sixths,*** /lkts/ in ***mulcts.*** Find two or three more examples of at least three consonant sounds together. Why does this happen only at the ends of words? (Consider how often /s z t d/ are found at the ends of words, and why.)

7. The words ***azure, pleasure, measure, Asian, fusion,*** and a good many more have the phoneme /ž/ in the middle of a word. Can you think of any English word in which it occurs at the beginning? The end? Look up the origin of the words ***rouge*** and ***beige*** and note how loanwords from a foreign language can extend the range of native phonemes.

8. Make a phonemic transcription of the following:

    a. Tell us who did.
    b. Find Chuck Connors.
    c. Get George here now.
    d. Avoid the no-passing zone.
    e. It was quite easy bicycling.

For further reading

Abercrombie, David. 1967. *Elements of General Phonetics* (Chicago: Aldine Publishing).

Bolinger, Dwight (ed.). 1972. *Intonation* (Harmondsworth, England: Penguin Books).

Denes, Peter B., and Elliot N. Pinson. 1973. *The Speech Chain: The Physics and Biology of Spoken Language* (1963) (Garden City: Anchor Books).

Householder, Fred W., Jr. 1971. "Sounds," Ch. 4 of *Linguistic Speculations* (Cambridge, England: Cambridge University Press).

Hyman, Larry M. 1975. *Phonology: Theory and Analysis* (New York: Holt, Rinehart & Winston).

Lyons, John. 1970. *New Horizons in Linguistics* (Harmondsworth, England: Penguin Books).

SOUNDS
AND WORDS 3

The *picture* stage—where out-and-out contrast is the only function of distinctive sounds—begins to be modified as soon as the child picks up the first rules of inflection, the plural of nouns and the past tense of verbs. This grammar lesson includes learning to attach /s/ to *cat* to make *cats,* /z/ to *dog* to make *dogs,* and /əz/ to *witch* to make *witches.* All three have the same function, so the child has no more reason to think of them as different than he has for assuming that a released /p/ in *stop* means something different from an unreleased one in the same position. The child would even find it difficult to *say* something like /kætz/ or /dɔgs/ or /wɪčz/. So the contrast between /s/ and /z/, which has been making an absolute distinction between *fuss* and *fuzz* in the child's vocabulary, makes no difference at all in this new context. The same happens with the past tense: to make *worked,* the rules call for adding /t/, to make *buzzed,* /d/, and to make *skidded,* /əd/. The distinction that still contrasts *bat* with *bad* is of no use in processing verb endings. The story is repeated with possessive endings: *Jack's, John's,* and *Louise's* duplicate the /s z əz/ of the plural. Thus for certain purposes /s/ and /z/ are felt to be automatic variants of the same underlying sound, as are /t/ and /d/.

SYSTEMATIC PHONEMES AND DISTINCTIVE FEATURES

The real complications develop later as the child stops saying /pæθs/ and /wayfs/ and begins to say /pæðz/ and /wayvz/, and even more as she begins to learn the many words that English has taken from foreign languages, especially Greek and Latin. More and more the sounds that previously served only to make words as different as possible are seen to group themselves in pairs or sets that attach to words that are related. As a rule, the members of each pair are phonetically similar. The sound of *f* resembles that of *v*—position and manner are the same, only voicing is different—and though they make an absolute distinction between *half* and *have,* they are clearly related in *half* and *halve.* As more and more sophisticated words are picked up, the [č] of *picture* is entangled with the /t/ of *pictorial,* and similar connections are established between *fact* and *factual, rite* and *ritual,* and *rapt* and *rapture,* always guided by meaning (no such connection is made between *mute* and *mutual*). *Finish* is associated with *final, vineyard* with *vine,* and *linear* with *line,* creating a connection between /ɪ/ and /ay/. Schooling accelerates the process. Many people will eventually connect *strive* with *strife* and add this to *wife–wives, life–lives, knife–knives,* and other pairs in which /f/ and /v/ are associated, and some will make the same connection with *bereave–bereft* and *cleave–cleft.* These two pairs illustrate the bond between /i/ and /ɛ/ that is also to be found in *receive–reception, succeed–success, redeem–redemption.*

The process of interrelating sounds is never finished, for we go on learning new words all our lives. But by early adolescence, the English-speaking child has two systems of sounds: the earlier scheme of simple oppositions and the ever-growing network of interconnected pairs and groups. We have been calling the units of the first system *phonemes* and will continue to do so, though the term *autonomous phonemes* is sometimes used, alluding to the fact that they are described independently of any particular word-forms. The units of the second system are most often called *systematic phonemes.*

The list of systematic phonemes turns out to be almost identical to that of autonomous phonemes, but it is described differently. Instead of looking merely for contrasts that can be assigned to one distinctive unit or another, with the result that /m/ and /n/ are no more like each other than either is like /ǰ/ or /w/ (since *met* and *net* as words are just as different from each other as either is from *jet* or *wet*), the analyst looks for both resemblances and differences. Take for example the following pairs:

Noun	*Verb*	*Noun*	*Verb*
life	to live	breath	to breathe
half	to halve	wreath	to wreathe
grief	to grieve	bath	to bathe
staff	to stave		
calf	to calve		

Here one sees that there is some kind of verb-forming process involving a relationship between /f/ and /v/, and a similar process involving /θ/ and /ð/. In both cases it is not a whole phoneme that changes in converting from noun to verb, but only the feature of voice. Instead of having separate entries for these pairs in our dictionary, it is possible to enter them just once with an *underlying* /f/ or /θ/ respectively, and some such notation as "verb [+ voice]" to derive the *surface* forms with /v/ and /ð/.

As we have already seen, processes of this kind—pluralization, verb suffixation, formation of possessives, and now verb formation—involve natural classes of sounds. The pairs /s z   t d   f v/ differ only in that the first member is voiceless and the second is voiced. The pair /t č/ that distinguished *rite–ritual, pictorial–picture, fact–factual* differ essentially only in the addition of palatalization to the second sound. Rules for systematic phonemes can be set up to show a change of just one feature at a time. If /f/ is assigned the articulatory features of labiodental, fricative, and voiceless, and /v/ the features labiodental, fricative, and voiced, the rule for *half–halve* can be written as voiceless ⟶ voiced.

In practice, the strictly articulatory features are not the ones that are used in describing systematic phonemes. They are not quite general enough. As we saw in the last chapter, it was possible to simplify the consonant chart by moving certain items from one slot to another. For example, the [f v] pair, being labiodental, occupied a different column from that of [p b], which are bilabial. By calling both simply "labial" we can save a whole category of sounds. The same principle guides the selection of distinctive features, but it is carried to an extreme of generality that enables it to be used for many languages. (For a time it was thought that just a small set—say a dozen or so—of distinctive features would be enough to characterize all the phonemes of all languages, but that hope has receded as our inventory of sounds from around the world has grown. Distinctive features are language-specific.)[1] In Table 3–1 we see the distinctive features of English and how they are represented in each systematic consonant phoneme. A plus signifies that the feature is present, a minus that it is absent.

To get the largest coverage possible out of the categories, they are defined somewhat more precisely and arbitrarily than the traditional sense allows:

Consonantal and *vocalic* are used rather than *consonant* and *vowel* to suggest that the distinction between vowels and consonants is not as rigid as was previously supposed—there are sounds that share both the traits of consonants (typically, complete or partial blocking of the air stream and, acoustically, abrupt movements of the clusters of overtones)

---

[1] Tae-Yong Pak 1971.

TABLE 3–1
Feature Specifications for English Systematic Consonant Phonemes

	p	b	t	d	č	j	k	g	f	v	θ	ð	s	z	š	ž	h	m	n	r	l	y	w
CONSONANTAL	+	+	+	+	+	+	+	+	+	+	+	+	+	+	+	+	+	+	+	+	+	−	−
VOCALIC	−	−	−	−	−	−	−	−	−	−	−	−	−	−	−	−	−	−	−	+	+	−	−
HIGH	−	−	−	−	+	+	+	+	−	−	−	−	−	−	+	+	−	−	−	−	−	+	+
LOW	−	−	−	−	−	−	−	−	−	−	−	−	−	−	−	−	+	−	−	−	−	−	−
BACK	−	−	−	−	−	−	+	+	−	−	−	−	−	−	−	−	−	−	−	−	−	−	+
ANTERIOR	+	+	+	+	−	−	−	−	+	+	+	+	+	+	−	−	−	+	+	−	+	−	−
CORONAL	−	−	+	+	+	+	−	−	−	−	+	+	+	+	+	+	−	−	+	+	+	−	−
CONTINUANT	−	−	−	−	−	−	−	−	+	+	+	+	+	+	+	+	+	−	−	+	+	+	+
VOICED	−	+	−	+	−	+	−	+	−	+	−	+	−	+	−	+	−	+	+	+	+	+	+
NASAL	−	−	−	−	−	−	−	−	−	−	−	−	−	−	−	−	−	+	+	−	−	−	−
STRIDENT	−	−	−	−	+	+	−	−	+	+	−	−	+	+	+	+	−	−	−	−	−	−	−
SONORANT	−	−	−	−	−	−	−	−	−	−	−	−	−	−	−	−	−	+	+	+	+	+	+

and the traits of vowels (typically, free flow of air through the mouth and steady or slow-moving overtone clusters). The differences between the categories are relative. So /r/ and /l/ are viewed as being rather like both consonants and vowels and are accordingly given pluses in both the consonantal and vocalic rows, whereas /y/ and /w/ are viewed as being rather unlike both consonants and vowels and are given minuses.[2]

The features *high, low, back,* and *coronal* relate to distinct positions of the tongue during articulation. "High" means that either the front part or the back part is raised. "Low" means that the tongue is kept down, to interfere as little as possible with the flow of air (true of /h/ in English, which has no constriction). "Back" means that the part of the tongue

---

[2] Besides the fact that it simplifies the classification, there are certain justifications for this in the way the corresponding sounds are made. Thus /r l/ are more vowel-like than /y w/ because, like vowels, they can be prolonged indefinitely as steady-state sounds, whereas /y w/ cannot; this makes it possible for /r l/ to be used as the "nucleus"—the central and most prominent part—of a syllable, as in the second syllable of the words *copper* and *maple.* (Typically the syllable nucleus is a vowel.) At the same time they are more consonant-like than /y w/ because they obstruct the air passage more.

involved in the articulation is the back part. "Coronal" means the opposite—the part of the tongue involved is the tip or blade. The sound of /r/ is coronal because it is made by curling the tip back (it is also neither high nor low, since the tongue hangs about midway in the mouth). An articulation that does not involve the tongue at all will of course get a minus on both counts—/p/, for example, is neither back nor coronal.

Anterior refers to a general *front* position in the mouth, whether of the tongue or the lips.

Continuant indicates whether during articulation the air stream continues to flow through the mouth without being interrupted (though not necessarily without being interfered with); it is simply the reverse of stop ("stop" is what "minus continuant" in the table means).

Nasal has the obvious meaning, namely that the air stream passes freely through the nose, whether or not it is checked in the mouth.

Sonorant refers to absence of any interference with the flow of glottal sound (voicedness); thus /m/ and /n/ are sonorants because the vibrating air passes unimpeded through the nose, but they are minus continuant because the air is checked in the mouth: they are "oral stops."

Strident refers to a high degree of turbulence leading to a noisy sound. The distinction here is rather arbitrary, because /θ ð/ are just about as noisy as /f v/. (The distinctive feature scheme has been criticized because of its arbitrariness and also because it mixes criteria from both articulation and acoustics—"high" is physiological, but "strident" refers to a quality of sound. Still, if the system works in practice, its hybrid origins should not be held against it.)

Systematic phonology has been both hailed and decried as a way of showing how a language carries its past along with it. The rules that derive surface forms from underlying forms bear a more than coincidental resemblance to changes that have taken place in the past, and when we set up a rule such as /f/ ⟶ /v/ we are stating something that is both a historical fact and a present reality. It is the latter because we cannot avoid associating /f/ and /v/ given all the word pairs that tie them together. Furthermore, the living kinship between /ay/ and /ɪ/ (pairs like **divide–divisible, divine–divinity, vice–vicious, deride–derision**) reflects a change that occurred in English in the tenth century. Both sounds stem from an original /i/, and if we set up an underlying form with that vowel we get a rule that is both historical and descriptive.

An example of a historical rule showing the economy that results from this kind of notation is the one that spells out the actual change that created such pairs as **breath–breathe** and **half–halve.** It reads as follows: [+ continuant] ⟶ [+ voiced] / [+ sonorant] _____ [+ sonorant] "Continuants became voiced when they were both preceded and followed by a segment that was sonorant."

The diagonal line / means 'in the environment of,' and the blank line is where the segment in question went. As all English vowels are sonorant, the formula includes vowels as well as /m n r l y w/. Besides the forms already mentioned, this takes care of *wolf–wolves, scurf–scurvy, teeth–teethe, use–use* (noun and verb), and similar pairs.

Such a rule may even be general enough to eliminate a phoneme. It is no accident that the phoneme /ŋ/ is absent from the chart of systematic phonemes. If we study the behavior of this phoneme in English, we soon realize that it is something of an oddity. The other nasals, /m n/, occur freely in initial position, but /ŋ/ never does: *mine, nine,* but no *°/ŋayn/*. When /ŋ/ occurs anywhere except before /g/ or /k/ it is almost always at a separation of some kind, either between one word and another, as in *hangman,* or just before a suffix, as in *ringing, hanger, singable.* But what makes /ŋ/ seem most suspicious is the fact that we often change an /n/ to an /ŋ/ in rapid speech when a /k/ or a /g/ follows, as in *uncooperative, incapable, ingratitude,* and *on guard,* especially in expressions that are used a great deal (it is more apt to happen with *conquest* than with *inquest,* and always with *handkerchief* but not always with *handcuff*). This makes /ŋ/ look like a mere variant of /n/. To account for it in *ring, sing,* and so forth, we posit underlying forms with /g/. In Standard English there is no [g] sound in *ringing, singing,* and the like, so an additional rule will have to delete the /g/ after the [ŋ] variant is accounted for. But the advantage is that there are dialects of English in which a [g] is heard—for example, urban New York; and there are also forms that in some environments actually have the /g/ even in Standard English—for example, *stronger, longer,* and *younger.* Assuming an underlying /g/ and then deleting it accounts for the rather uncertain status of /ŋ/ as a phoneme and also describes the process that took place in the history of English: there were real /g/'s that were dropped.

One of the advantages of distinctive features is that they explain what combinations of sounds a language permits. English allows clusters of three consonants at the beginning of a word only if the third consonant is /l/ or /r/, as in *splash, scratch, sclerose, stripe,* and so forth—no *°stf-, °stm-, °sks-.*[3] This would be odd if no underlying relationship could be found between the two sounds. When their distinctive features are compared, however, they are seen to differ only in the fact that /l/ is anterior and /r/ is not.[4] Similarly, if we look at the consonants that can immediately precede /l/ and/or /r/ we find that they are /p t k b d g s f/, of

---

[3] Throughout, an asterisk is used before an item, term, or sentence that is unacceptable in English.

[4] If the tongue is positioned for [l] and drawn back gradually, the next distinguishable sound will be [r] (the tongue tip must keep contact with the roof of the mouth).

which the first six are the only English sounds sharing the features [+consonantal −continuant −nasal −strident], while the last two share everything except the coronal feature.

Whatever value linguists eventually assign to underlying forms, splitting the atom of the phoneme into distinctive features was a necessary step in the analysis of language.

WORD SHAPES

In Chapter 2, page 30, the buildup of sound-units was stopped at the syllable, the farthest one can go without a deeper knowledge of the structure of the language. A man from Mars, given the well-known Martian technology, could devise a machine to tell something about the syllabic structure of English or Inibaloi without knowing a word of either language. But as for the words themselves, to know anything about their structure one has to be able to discriminate them, and that can only be done if one has some notion of their meanings, for otherwise it is usually impossible to tell where one stops and the next one begins.

But knowing that much, as we have seen in this chapter, there is a good deal that can be said about word structure. It is enough to know what the units are—without necessarily being able to define each one semantically—to be able to describe words and some of their relations in phonological terms.

For example, knowing the way words are shaped in English, we could predict that it might well have the words *spout, rout, tout, bout, dou(b)t, shout, grout, knout, lout, pout, trout, scout, snout, gout, flout, kraut, sprout,* and *clout,* which in fact it has. And we could also predict that it might have the words *°shrout, °slout,* and *°frout,* which it does not have. At the same time we could exclude *°tsout, °bnout, °shprout,* and *°vrout,* not because such words are necessarily hard to pronounce, since we manage the [vr] easily enough with a foreign name such as *De Vries,* and we actually say *tsout* [tsawt] as a condensed form of *it's out.* The accuracy of our predictions merely reflects the fact that the words of any language have *canonical forms*—normal combinations of sounds—that can be described independently of their meaning.

There are, besides, the associations among words that we have been examining in this chapter. Knowing the structure of English, we can see that *one knife* and *two knives, one bath* and *two baths,* and similar correlations put words in relationships that can be described by positing underlying forms along with rules to generate the actually occurring forms. It would be unreasonable not to conclude that *knife* and *knive-* are in some sense "the same," despite their difference in sound, which is as great as that between *duff* and *dove* or between *shuffle* and *shovel.*

As a preliminary to relating the two, we say that *knife* and *knive-* are *morphs*—that is, they are actual spoken forms, minimal carriers of meaning. The technique of relating morphs calls for setting up another unit, the *morpheme*, which is to the morph what a phoneme is to a phone. Just as we class phones together as *allophones* of a single phoneme, so we class morphs together as *allomorphs* of a single morpheme.

If all meaning-bearing units were as big as words, the morpheme would be unnecessary as a unit. But *knive-* is something less than a word, and the same is true of other elements, such as *trans-, contra-, pre-, de-, -dom, -ize,* and *-ing.* The smaller unit is therefore necessary, and we say that *knife* and *knive-* are allomorphs of a single underlying morpheme of the shape /nayf/,[5] which requires no change in deriving *knife* but adds voice to make *knive-*.

But how do we know that such morphemes as *trans-, contra-, de-,* and the like are not words in their own right? That one morpheme can also be one word is plain enough in forms such as *proud, fashion,* and *camera.* They cannot be broken into smaller meaningful parts. And we do say such things as *pro and con* as if *pro* and *con* were independent words.

It is usually easy for a native speaker to *sense* what a word is, but not so easy to *define* it. How can we be sure that *roadblock* is one word and *road machinery* is two? If a morpheme is 'a minimal unit of meaning,' that definition will not serve for *word* as well. Or perhaps a word is the smallest unit of language that can be used by itself. Yet there are forms that we would like to regard as words that never occur alone, such as *the* or *from* or *am.* The best definition—at least for languages like English[6]—is probably in terms of separability. Words are the least elements between which other elements can be inserted with relative freedom. So in the sequence *the man* we can insert *young* to get *the young man,* but there is no way to insert something *within the* or *man.* And though we can insert *-est* between *young* and *man* to get *the youngest man,* we cannot insert anything between *young* and *-est. Youngest* therefore is a word but *-est* is not. And one can sense an insertion point because there is a pause point. A speaker may be heard to say *The—uh—what do you call it?—rappelling they do is pretty dangerous. The* is separately coded in the brain as a sign of 'definiteness' and can be uttered separately, even though it requires something to follow. But it would be unusual for someone to say *The work—uh—force was late on the job that day. Workforce* is a compound word; one will not normally start to say it until it is possible

---

[5] /nayf/ is shorthand for four columns of distinctive features, one for each systematic phoneme.

[6] The "word" problem is ably discussed for a language much unlike English in Thomas 1962.

to say all of it. As with all categories in language, that of the word has vague borders; more will be seen of them in the next chapter.

Returning to the question of morphemes and allomorphs, something of their variety can be seen in a sentence like *Every*/*one* / *admire*/*s* / *Bill*/'*s* / *man*/*li*/*ness. Everyone* is a compound containing the morphemes *every* and *one* (which also happen to be words when used separately); *admires* is a verb containing the stem morpheme *admire-* and the suffix morpheme *-s,* meaning 'third person singular'; *Bill's* is a possessive containing the proper noun *Bill* and the possessive morpheme *-'s;* and *manliness* is a noun containing the base noun morpheme *man-* plus the adjective-forming suffix morpheme *-ly* plus the abstract-noun–forming suffix morpheme *-ness.* As for allomorphs, *every-* normally has only one, /ɛvrɨ/, but *-one* may appear as /wʌn/ or as /wən/, depending on speed and emphasis. The *-s* of *admires* has the same three allomorphs as the possessive in *Bill's* and the plural in *dogs:* /z/ in *admires,* /s/ in *takes,* and /əz/ in *catches. Bill* has only one, but *man* has at least two: /mæn/ in the form here and when used as a independent word, and /mən/ in many compounds, such as *workman, fireman.* The suffixes *-li-* and *-ness* have one each, /lɨ/ and /nəs/. The only puzzle is *admire.* Is it two morphemes or one? The *ad-* looks suspiciously like the *ad-* of *address, adjoin,* and *adhere,* which is perhaps vaguely sensed as having something to do with the meaning 'to,' even for a person who is unaware of the Latin source. And the meaning of the word as a whole may seem enough like that of *miraculous* and *miracle* to suggest that *-mir-* is entitled to be considered as a morpheme. If so, there are three allomorphs in these three words: /mayr/, /mər/, and /mɪr/. The difficulty in deciding whether to split *admire* up or leave it intact will be looked at more closely in the next chapter. It is a difficulty that afflicts the majority of English words taken from Greek and Latin.

PHONOLOGICAL AND MORPHOLOGICAL CONDITIONING

Two different approaches are needed to describe allomorphs. One approach relates to elements that are actually there, in the spoken chain. The other relates to elements that are not there. An example of the first is the phrase *ten percent* contrasted with *ten to six.* In *ten percent* the /n/ may accommodate itself to the following /p/, so that *ten* comes out *tem.* There are thus two allomorphs for *ten,* /ten/ and /tɛm/. Nothing needs to be known beyond the sounds themselves to predict that this will or may happen. Since the /n/ is "conditioned" by a neighboring sound, the type of change involved is called *phonological conditioning.*

The second approach—required for allomorphs that do not depend on actually spoken neighboring events—is exemplified in the word *dear.* There is nothing in the spoken chain to account for the difference between *dear* with its /dɪr/ allomorph and *darling* with its /dar/ allomorph. If there were, the same thing would have to happen to **year,** creating **year–yarling** rather than **year–yearling.** If we posit an underlying morpheme which generates now /dɪr/ and now /dar/, it is not to take care of what happens in the course of an utterance but of what we know about the catalog of words. The term used for this type of difference between allomorphs is *morphological conditioning*.

The allomorph /dar/ for *dear* is one of many etymological relics in English, and these, plus oddments of borrowings from foreign languages, make up most of the cases of morphological conditioning. The noun plurals in *ox–oxen, goose–geese,* and *sheep–sheep* are relics. Those in *insigne–insignia, umbo–umbones,* and *jinnee–jinn* (to pick examples as outlandish as possible) are borrowings. Together they compel us to recognize some rather peculiar allomorphs of the plural morpheme: in *geese* it is the change of an internal vowel (*foot–feet* is another example); in *sheep* it is zero (as also in *deer–deer*); and in *jinn* it is the *loss* of the final vowel. The three other words use exceptional suffixes, which is also the case with more familiar borrowings such as *stigma–stigmata* (from Greek), *datum–data* (from Latin), and *cherub–cherubim* (from Hebrew).

The changes that verbs undergo show a great variety of morphological conditioning. *Sing–sang–sung* is like *goose–geese:* both have internal changes. The form *does,* based on *do* /du/, has one internal change (/u/ ⟶ /ʌ/); *don't* has another /u/ ⟶ /o/), even though it is the same tense as *does;* and *did* has a third (/u/ ⟶ /ɪ/), which reflects the past tense. In the forms *mean–meant, feel–felt,* and *deal–dealt* there is morphological conditioning in both the verb itself (/i/ ⟶ /ɛ/) and the past tense morpheme. The regular allomorph of the latter would be /d/, not /t/: compare *lean–leaned, seal–sealed* and *sell–sold.*

Since all morphologically conditioned allomorphs pertain to the catalog of words, they have to be listed in the dictionary with the individual words or word sets that they belong to. It is not necessary for a dictionary to record the plural of *safe* or *birth.* A general rule covers them. But the plurals of *half* and *bath* have to be listed, or at least cross referenced to some special rule for their formation; they are unpredictable.[7]

General rules are in the domain of phonological conditioning, not morphological conditioning. The rule for /tɛm/ in **ten percent** is an *op-*

---

[7] This is not to say that there is no *historical* predictability. The change was brought about by phonological conditioning in the past. But now it depends on our knowledge of the word itself and of other words rather than on the environment.

tional general rule. There are also *obligatory* general rules, typically involving inflections and such words as articles, pronouns, prepositions, and the like, termed *function words.* An example is the rule that covers the plural morpheme, the possessive morpheme, and the verb form *is,* as in

the bills	Bill's	Bill's here.
the roses	Rose's	Rose's here.
the pats	Pat's	Pat's here.

The allomorphs in each row are the same: /z/ in the first, /əz/ in the second, and /s/ in the third. The phonological conditioning is as follows:

1. The allomorph is /z/ after a vowel or after a consonant that is $\begin{bmatrix} +\text{voiced} \\ \begin{cases} -\text{coronal} \\ -\text{strident} \end{cases} \end{bmatrix}$.[8]

2. The allomorph is /əz/ after a consonant that is $\begin{bmatrix} +\text{strident} \\ +\text{coronal} \end{bmatrix}$.

3. The allomorph is /s/ the rest of the time.

Another example is the indefinite article in English, which is phonologically conditioned in two ways. First, the choice between *a* and *an* is determined by whether the following word begins with a consonant or a vowel: *a pear, an apple.* Second, many speakers shift to a full vowel when the article is emphasized: *He lives in a* /ə/ *big house; Give me an* /ən/ *orange; I don't want just á* /e/ *lawyer, I want the bést lawyer; I don't want just án* /æn/ *editor, I want the bést editor.* So we have four allomorphs: /ə ən e æn/.

The rule for vowel reduction is fairly general among function words. The normal thing is for the vowel—whatever it is—in the accented form to become a shwa /ə/ in the unaccented form: *He works só-o-o* /so/ *hard* versus *Don't work so* /sə/ *hard; It's all right, bút . . . !* /bʌt/ versus *Nobody went but* /bət/ *me; I don't know the place he went to* /tu/[9] versus *He went to* /tə/ *Chicago; What's he asking for?* /fɔr/ versus *He's asking for* /fər/ *money; That's it!* /ɪt/ versus *Throw it* /ət/ *off.* But reduction sometimes also brings in morphological conditioning: a few func-

---

[8] This bracketing means a consonant that is voiced and either not coronal or not strident.

[9] Most function words at the end of a sentence take their full, non-shwa form whether accented or not. Thus *to* in *I don't want to* has the form /tu/ as a rule—though sometimes shwa appears, and then some writers give us the benefit of the spelling *I do' wanna.*

tion words have somewhat more drastically altered allomorphs. The negative word *not* often loses its vowel completely and becomes a consonant cluster attached to an auxiliary verb; the accented *I have nót* thus pairs with *I haven't* /nt/. Similar instances of "contraction" are *I am, I'm; she is, she's; you are, you're.* The shwa sound /ə/ is one step down from the full vowel, which is why it is called reduced; the complete loss of the vowel is the ultimate in reduction. Even *was* can be reduced by these two steps: first to /wəz/ and then to just a prelabialized *z*-sound, /wz/. *Not* skips the shwa step: there is no */nət/ in such forms as *isn't* and *hadn't,* only /nt/. (Though some speakers do say /kænət/ for *cannot.*)

Returning once more to morphological conditioning, we occasionally find an extreme case in which two forms have no physical resemblance whatever. (Certain of the allomorphs of the plural morpheme are of this type; the *-a* of *data* is totally unlike the *-s* of *cats.*) The past tense of *go* is *went,* actually borrowed from a different verb, *to wend.* But since *go* and *went* pattern the same as *do–did, write–wrote, talk–talked,* and all other verbs, they have to be regarded as "different forms of the same word," and must therefore contain the same morpheme with two very different allomorphs. The same is true of *bad* and *worse.* This kind of relationship is called *suppletion.*

There is one further kind of conditioning besides phonological and morphological: *stylistic conditioning.* An informal way of saying *What's cooking?* is *What's cookin'?* with the style allomorph /ən/ standing in for the *-ing* morpheme. Similarly *I s'pose* passes for *I suppose.* Probably the majority of such variants are at least to some extent phonological. *S'pose* is the result of informally rapid speech. Even those variants that were not originally phonological may eventually be considered so.

Table 3–2 summarizes the different kinds of conditioning in English.

THE COMPLEXITY OF ENGLISH MORPHOLOGY

English has an extremely complex morphology because of the vast importation of words from everywhere, particularly from other Western European languages. If only a relatively small number had been borrowed, they would have come in as indivisible units—few persons have the knowledge of Hindi, for example, to see smaller elements in the word *swastika.* But when dozens of Latin words having the negative prefix *in-* with its variants (*insufficient, illogical, irreverent, impossible*) are borrowed, not only the words themselves but the prefix too becomes part of the morphology of English. Borrowings from other Western languages are fitted in more or less as Latin words are, accommodating themselves to what is already there. So when Italian *imbroglio* was adopted in the

TABLE 3–2
Types of Conditioning

Phonological conditioning	ten cents /tɛn/	
	ten percent /tɛm/	
	pots /s/	*(the plural*
	mugs /z/	*morpheme)*
	só /so/	
	so /sə/	
Morphological conditioning	dear /dɪr/	
	darling /dar/	
	half /hæf/	
	halves /hæv/	
Suppletion	goose–geese /u/ → /i/	*(the plural*
	sheep–sheep /ø/*	*morpheme)*
	datum–data /əm/ → /ə/	
	go	
	went	
Stylistic conditioning	cooking /ɪŋ/	
	cookin' /ən/	

* The symbol ø stands for 'zero.'

eighteenth century it attached itself to *embroil,* which had come in from French more than a century earlier. *Imbroglio* now shares the semantic range of *embroil* with the more clearly related *embroilment;* the latter means the act or process of embroiling, the former the condition or result of embroiling. (With the verb *to produce,* on the other hand, the noun *production* embodies both senses.) The problem that a child faces in learning the morphological relationships between adjectives and verbs in English can be seen in the following list. The verb means 'to cause to be' whatever it is that the adjective means:

full   to fill
strong   to strengthen

old	to age
legal	to legalize
shiny	to shine
white	to whiten
angry	to anger
liquid	to liquefy
pregnant	to impregnate
uncomfortable	to discomfort
lively	to enliven
perfect	to perfect
wise	to wise up (in one sense)
open	to open
wicked	(nothing)

In addition, the child must constantly be on guard against drawing lunatic analogies:

If outlaws are people who disobey the laws, then in-laws should be law-abiding people.

In short, there is a point beyond which trying to dig up underlying forms is a desecration. They are tired etymological bones that have earned their rest.

Key terms and concepts

systematic phoneme

distinctive features
   consonantal, vocalic
   high, low, back
   anterior, coronal
   continuant
   voiced
   nasal
   strident, sonorant

morpheme
   morph
   allomorph

conditioning
   phonological
   morphological
   stylistic

suppletion

Additional remarks and applications

1. What phonemic contrasts do the following pairs point to?—*gristly–grisly, confusion–Confucian, spite–spied, crutch–crush, rode–roan,*

mutt–much, lean–dean. Are the two members of each pair widely different from each other? If you could measure the difference in terms of the number of distinctive features that separate one phoneme from another, how many points of difference would you say there are in /f/–/v/? In /m/–/p/?

2. Some speakers pronounce the noun *rise* as [rays] rather than [rayz]. What rule does this illustrate? Is *house* a similar case?

3. Does the pair *prolong–prolongation* support the idea that no systematic phoneme /ŋ/ is needed in English? What is unusual about the word *gingham* in regard to the /ŋ/?

4. Is /sf/ common as an initial cluster in English? Think of some examples. What kind of word does it occur in?

5. What is unusual about the following English words: *Tsar, tsetse, tsamba?* Would you judge them to be words of long standing in the language? Why?

6. Describe the allomorphs of the plural morpheme in *alumnus, octopus, antenna.* In *antenna* does the form of the plural morpheme depend in any way on the meaning?

7. British English tends to favor *knelt* and *dreamt* where American English favors *kneeled* and *dreamed.* What are the differences in terms of allomorphs? The British also favor *spilt* and *smelt* (*spilled* and *smelled*) more than Americans do. Is the situation here identical with that in *knelt* and *dreamt?*

8. Discuss the allomorphs in *child–children* and *write–wrote–written.*

9. In Spanish the stops /b d g/ all have fricative allophones (for example, /d/ between vowels sounds like [ð]). What kind of conditioning is this?

10. The two possessive forms *my* and *mine* were formerly selected according to a rule that required *my* before a consonant and *mine* the rest of the time (*Mine eyes have seen the glory, mother mine, It's mine*). Now the rule is to use *my* before any noun. What change has occurred in the type of conditioning? Has the same change occurred in *thy–thine?*

For further reading

Anderson, Stephen R. 1974. *The Organization of Phonology* (New York: Academic Press).

Falk, Julia S. 1973. "Phonetic Features" and "Phonemics," Chs. 8 and 9 of *Linguistics and Language* (Lexington, Mass.: Xerox).

Gimson, A. C. 1962. *An Introduction to the Pronunciation of English* (London: Edward Arnold).

Juilland, Alphonse, and Alexandra Roceric. 1972. *The Linguistic Concept of Word: Analytic Bibliography* (The Hague: Mouton).

Schane, S. A. 1973. *Generative Phonology* (Englewood Cliffs, N.J.: Prentice-Hall).

WORDS AND THEIR MAKE-UP 4

When the language is supplied with subatomic particles (distinctive features), atoms (phonemes), and molecules (syllables), the next step is to go from physics to biology, to find the cells and their assemblies that make up the living matter of language. Life needs more than form; it must have meaning. The question is how to relate units of meaning to units of form.

Meaning seems to emerge as the units of sound in the language are structured into ever larger units:

| distinctive features | → phonemes → syllables → morphemes → words → | collocations and idioms |

Distinctive features—at the smallest end of the scale—are meaningless. At the stage of phonemes, some non-arbitrary meaning may occur; but meaning really begins to emerge only as phonemes are grouped into syllables that take the form of morphemes. With words we are on familiar ground: they are 'the smallest elements that are independently coded' (p. 43), the common pieces of the language that are constantly regrouped to form messages.

This relationship between words and meanings is understood by every speaker. It is the one thing about the practical use of language that we know children can be effectively taught.[1] People struggling with an idea will say *I can't think of the right word,* but they are never heard to say **I can't think of the right prefix* or **I can't think of the right sound* (though they may say *I cant think of the right way to put it,* which has to do with something higher up on scale than words).

COLLOCATIONS AND IDIOMS

Words as we understand them are not the only elements that have a more or less fixed correlation with meaning. In fact they are not the first units that a child learns to imbue with this association. In the beginning a child apprehends *holistically:* the situation is not broken down, and neither is the verbal expression that accompanies it. That is why the first learning stage is *holophrastic:* word and utterance are one, an undivided word representing a total context. Only later are words differentiated out of this larger whole. A child asked to say the first thing that comes to mind on hearing the word *throw* will say *ball* rather than *toss,* and if asked to define *a hole* will say *a hole in the ground.*[2] The associations are "horizontal" (that is, are expressed in the syntax) and are made with external reality. Such habitual association of words, the characteristic company they keep, is known as *collocation.*

These whole chunks that we learn persist as coded units even after analysis into words has partially split them up. An extreme example is *How do you do?* That it is functionally a single piece is proved by its condensation to *Howdy.* Such expressions are termed *idioms,* defined as groups of words with set meanings that cannot be calculated by adding up the separate meanings of the parts. Some idioms are virtually unchangeable, like *Hold your horses,* meaning 'Don't be so impetuous'; neither subject nor verb can normally be changed to yield, say, **They hold their horses* or **He was holding his horses,* nor can the object be changed to yield **Hold your stallions.* Others allow a limited amount of manipulation; for example, *He's dead to the world,* meaning 'He's fast asleep,' can be changed for person and time: *She's dead to the world, They were dead to the world* (but not **He was dead to the universe*). Some idioms allow certain transformations but not others. *He found fault with them* can be made passive—*Fault was found with them*—but unlike *He sought help from them,* the noun cannot be turned into a pronoun.

---

[1] Cazden 1972, p. 129.

[2] Ibid., p. 72. For more detailed discussion of the stages of language acquisition by the child, see Chapter 8.

Based on *He sought help from them* we can have *He didn't seek it from me,* but based on *He found fault with them* we cannot have *°He didn't find it with me.* There are families of idioms. One, using the expression (*to be*) *worth,* has its most compactly idiomatic form in *to be worth while,* but also appears with several other nouns accompanied by an article: *to be worth the bother, to be worth the trouble,* and so forth. Other nouns can be fitted in, of course, but the result is not sensed as a stereotype in the same unitary way. *It is not worth the bother* functions as a unit. It does not raise the question "What bother?" To say *?It is not worth the bother involved*[3] would be a rather unusual expansion, whereas *It is not worth the struggle (the strain) involved* is normal, since *to be worth the struggle (strain)* is a constructed phrase, not a stereotype. *To be worth the effort* seems to lie about midway between idiom and non-idiom. The most complex member of the group is the most idiomatic one, *to be worth while.* Though *worth while* retains the stress of two words, the combination is generally written *worthwhile,* and is often put in front of a noun: *a worthwhile effort.* But it can also be separated by certain possessives, as in a radio ad: *It's worth your while to visit our showroom.* At the same time, for many if not most American speakers, the possessives that can be inserted are only those corresponding to the personal pronouns, never nouns (*°It's worth John's while*) or indefinites (*°It isn't worth anybody's while*). The interrogative is impossible (*°Whose while is it worth?*).

We might describe these differences as degrees of tightness. The three idioms *to take fright, to take courage,* and *to take heart* stand in order of increasing tightness, as can be seen when the normal word order is reversed:

> The fright that he took was indicative of his timidity.
> ?The courage that he took was indicative of his inner resources.
> °The heart that he took was indicative of his optimism.

If idioms can vary so widely in tightness, the question arises whether everything we say may be in some degree idiomatic—that is, whether there are affinities among words that continue to reflect the attachments the words had when we learned them, within larger groups. This is not a welcome view to most American linguists, who like to analyze things down to the smallest bits. British linguists, however, work in a different tradition. They use the term *collocations* for those looser groupings about which something can be said over and above what is apparent from looking at the individual parts. Knowing the parts, one can deduce the

---

[3] Throughout, a question mark preceding an expression indicates questionable acceptability.

meaning, so that a collocation is not quite an idiom; but it is in some way specialized. (This would make *to be worth the bother* and *worth the trouble* collocations, but leave *to be worth while* an idiom.) The British linguist T. F. Mitchell illustrates collocation as follows: "Men—specifically cement workers—work *in* cement works; others of different occupation work *on* works of art; others again, or both, *perform* good works. Not only are good works *performed* but cement works are *built* and works of art *produced*."[4] Why do builders not *produce* a building or authors not *invent* a novel, since they do invent stories and plots? No reason, as far as dictionary definitions of words are concerned. We don't say it because we don't say it. There is evidence that idioms and collocations—"automatic speech"—are processed in special ways by the brain.[5]

The range and variety of collocations is enormous. Some examples follow. Not all persons will agree with every judgment of acceptability that is marked here with an asterisk, question mark, or no symbol at all; but the important thing is that such judgments can be made. Since it is our experience of expressions that are repeated over and over in given circumstances that makes for collocations, it would be remarkable if that experience were uniform all over the English-speaking world. Consider:

1. Stereotyping of the definite article

    I heard it on the radio.   ?I saw it on the TV.
    ?I heard it on radio.   I saw it on TV.

2. Set coordinations

    There was plenty of food and drink.
    There was plenty of food.
    *There was plenty of drink.

3. Linked function words

    I thought he would help me. But no, he was busy, he said.
    I thought he would help me. *And yes, he was willing to.

4. Nouns stereotyped with particular adjectives

    good likelihood   strong likelihood   *high likelihood
    *good probability   strong probability   high probability
    good possibility   strong possibility   *high possibility
    good chance   *strong chance   *high chance

---

[4] Mitchell 1971, p. 50; see also Greenbaum 1970 for a study of how certain verbs and certain intensifiers tend to group together into collocations.

[5] Van Lancker 1979.

5. Item-to-category stereotype

(Instead of being tied to a particular word or words, the word is tied to a grammatical category. This example is of a verb that must always be used with an adverb of manner.)

I regarded them with curiosity.
*I regarded them.

He regarded me strangely.
*He regarded me for ten minutes.

6. Adjective and noun

She was there the livelong day.
*She was there the livelong morning (week, year).

They slept till broad daylight.
*They slept till daylight was broad.

7. Preposition and noun

His methods are above reproach.
*His methods are below (beneath, far from, near) reproach.
His methods are beneath contempt.

By the time children begin to think about language, the analyzing process has gone far enough to make words the entities of which they are most aware. Words become more and more sharply defined for us as we grow older. When, for example, we finally notice that the word *else* has a peculiar distribution, one that permits it to be used right after indefinites (*somebody else*) but not after nouns (*some person else*), and not even after all indefinites (*someplace else, where else, *sometime else*), we tend to suppose that we always had it as a free combinatory unit but some mysterious process has entangled it with a particular set of words. Actually, it has never *dis*entangled itself. We go on using it exactly as we have heard it used. *Sometime else* is impossible for the same reason that *to uncomfort* is impossible: neither *else* nor *un-* has fully emancipated itself from the original context. This is why in language it is so hard to be sure whether we are dealing with something freely and freshly constructed from its least elements or something assembled from rather large chunks consigned to us whole. It seems that the brain stores both the parts and the wholes, and we retrieve them when we need them.

But when the analyzing process pushes into the parts of the words themselves, morphemes that are less than words are singled out. *Sandwich* has been disintegrated to form *fishwich*, using *-wich* as something less than a word. From *psychotherapy, psycho* has been analyzed out as a separate word. We can just as easily find words that are close to the status of affixes. *Ago* is an example. It follows words referring to periods of time, just as its synonym *back* does, but unlike *back, ago* is normally unstressed, which is characteristic of suffixes:

$$\text{It}\ ^{\text{happened}}\ ^{\text{ye}}_{\ \ \ \text{a}}\ ^{\text{ba}^{\text{c}}_{\ \ \text{r}}}\text{k.}\qquad\text{It}\ ^{\text{happened}}\ ^{\text{year}}_{\ \ \text{a}}\ _{\text{ago.}}[6]$$

A diagram of the three elements that are kept in storage—collocations (including idioms), words, and morphemes—can be made using the phrase *indelible ink.* This phrase is chosen because it is not exactly an idiom—the meaning responds nicely to the separate meanings of *indelible* and *ink*—and yet association tests show how tight the connection is between *indelible* and some writing material (ink, pencil).

The broken vertical line in Figure 4–1 signifies that morphemes as morphemes may or may not be stored: much depends on the perceptions of individuals. Few if any speakers in a lifetime will be responsible for making some new combination using the negative prefix *in-* (say *inobdurate*), and some will not even give it passive recognition—hence the description "low yield" as against "high yield" in putting words together to make phrases. In learning our language we read the diagram down. Linguists tend to read it up, which has caused a great many misconceptions when they have tried to fit their descriptions to psychological reality.

LEXICON, SYNTAX, AND MORPHOLOGY

The units of lexicon—words, idioms, and collocations—are the prefabs of language. We may alter them in certain ways, as when we pluralize *raisin* to *raisins* or passivize *Put a stop to it* to *A stop was put to it,* but the parts retain certain preset relationships with one another. How they are *analyzed*—and now and then created—is the province of lexicon. What we *do* with them is the province of syntax. A visitor to a zoo is surprised to see two animals in adjoining cages and exclaims *A coatimundi and a polar bear!* Only this situation would be likely to bring together those two animal names. Their association is purely syntactic. The

---

[6] If *ago* is accented, as it may be in *a long time ago,* it is for emphasis on the phrase as a whole, not on *ago.*

FIGURE 4–1
Collocations, Words, and Morphemes

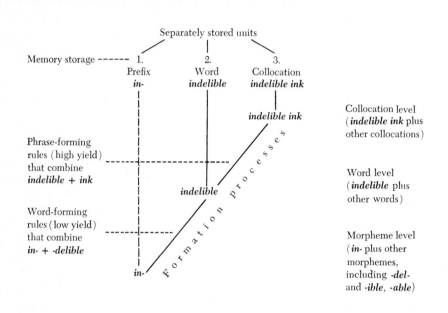

utterance may never have occurred before, and even if it has there is no connection between the present saying and any former one, as there always is between any instance of lexicon and its repetition. *Polar* plus *bear* is such an instance: the combination has been repeated again and again.

The unpredictability of syntax is often hailed as a sign of creativity. "Not to repeat" is seen as synonymous with "to invent." Perhaps the two are the same, at least sometimes. Still, the joining of the coatimundi and the polar bear in a sentence was not an invention of the speaker but a response to a situation, which also included the element of not-previously-identified (hence *a* and not *the*) and the element of togetherness (hence *and* and not *or*). Whether our syntax is a response to images—directly from experience, or prompted by another speaker, or envisioned from memory, or imagined in some act of psychological creation—or is part of the creative process itself is a question that cannot be answered with our present knowledge. The important fact is simply that in syntax we analyze the rules of communication, but in lexicon we analyze static form. This is the separation that must be made in principle, though it is sometimes hard to maintain in practice.

One part of the joint domain of syntax and lexicon that linguists treat separately is morphology, a sampling of which we have already had in connection with underlying forms. It is usually treated as part of lexicon because the elements most affected are words. So whether we are concerned with a syntactic modification, as when *friend* is equipped with a plural ending to comply with a communicative event ('we are talking about more than one') or whether we are concerned only with the make-up of some complex lexical form, as when *friend* is seen to be joined with *-ship* in *friendship,* we treat both *friends* and *friendship* as instances of morphological togetherness: *friend* + *-s* and *friend* + *-ship.* But the behavior of the two—*grammatical* morphemes such as *-s* and *lexical* morphemes such as *-ship*—is quite different and is treated separately.

Lexical morphemes: the fabrication of prefabs

Hearing our exclamation *A coatimundi and a polar bear!* no native speaker would think to himself, "There is something new here; I'll bet she made that sentence up." But hearing *I appreciate her inobduracy* a crossword-puzzle fan might well say, "Where did she get that word? I'll bet she made it up." We can analyze words, but once in a while the process is set in reverse and we create one, whether by accident or by design. The raw material generally conforms to the morphemes that can be discovered by analyzing words that already exist—practically all words that are not imported bodily from some other language are made up of old words or modifications using standard affixes like *-ness* or *un-.* The less accidental the coinage the more respect it shows toward existing formative elements. This is especially true of scientific terms: *decompression, polystyrene, perosis, cacogenesis*—old morphemes are re-used in systematic ways. But no etymological pedigree is required. The coiner may mix elements of diverse origins—as in *monolingual,* half Greek and half Latin, or in *atonement,* with its two English words *at* and *one* tagged with a Latin suffix—or even carry over a whole phrase or sentence as in *touch-me-not, what-you-may-call-it,* or *IOU.* And a speaker may ignore the official roster and patch something up with splinters, as with *bumber,* altered from *umbr-* in *umbrella,* and *-shoot,* based on the *-chute* of *parachute,* that form the word *bumbershoot.* In between are fragments of all degrees of standardized efficiency and junkyard irregularity. *Hamburger* yields *-burger,* which is reattached in *nutburger, Gainesburger,* and *cheeseburger. Cafeteria* yields *-teria,* which is reattached in *carpeteria, groceteria,* and *washateria.* Trade names make easy use of almost any fragment, like the *-roni* of *macaroni* that is reattached in *Rice-a-Roni* and *Noodle-Roni.* Recently *alcoholic* has given part of itself to the creation of *workaholic.* The fabrication may re-use elements that have been re-used many times, or it may be a one-shot affair such as the punning reference to being a member of the *lowerarchy,* with *-archy* extracted from *hier-*

archy. The principle is the same. The only thing a morpheme is good for is to be melted down and recast in a word.

The elements that are re-used most freely are called *productive,* the others *unproductive,* though both terms are relative. The suffix *-ate* is a Latinism that can hardly be used to make new words—but then some wag thinks up **discombobulate** and people accept it. At the other extreme the suffix *-er* looks as if we ought to be able to attach it to any verb and make a noun meaning 'one who performs the action': **worker, player, murderer, digger, eater.** Yet a glance at anomalies such as the following shows that we are less free than we think:

> They accused him–they were his accusers.
> *They blamed him–they were his blamers.
> They admire him–they are his admirers.
> *They loathe him–they are his loathers.
> She robs banks–she is a robber.
> ?She steals things–she is a stealer.[7]

These examples suggest why *-er* varies so in productivity. It is not that the language cannot *form* the noun *loather* but simply that we have no use for it. What retinue of people would it designate? Similarly we already have **thief** and do not need **stealer.** The absence of a word need not be due to some mysterious restriction on its formation, but to certain connections, or the lack of them, with the real world and with the stock of words already in existence. Words are not coined in order to extract the meanings of their elements and compile a new meaning from them. The new meaning is there *first,* and the coiner is looking for the best way to express it without going to too much trouble.

By the same token—this connection with the flux of events—the meanings of morphemes can vary as widely as their forms. When an old dress is cut down to a skirt, its former function may be partly remembered, but when a remnant of it becomes a dustcloth the old function is forgotten. So while **builders** build and **talkers** talk, **undertakers** no longer undertake —the general sense that the word once had has been restricted to a narrow kind of undertaking, and *-er* is no more recognizable than the low-yield *-ian* of **mortician.** The speaker who first put together the word **escapee** was not bothered by the fact that the proper form was **escaper,** since *-ee* is etymologically for persons acted upon, not for persons acting. It was enough that **escapee** suggested the same 'set category of persons' idea that is carried by words like **employee** and **draftee.**

The high informality of word making in English reflects the vast expan-

---

[7] *Syntactically,* that is, in construction with a noun object, all these are possible: **Who are the blamers of the innocent, the loathers of all that is good, the stealers of sense and virtue?** But it calls for rather stilted discourse.

sion of our culture. A supermarket that once stocked eight thousand items and today carries some fifteen thousand is one ripple in a tide of growth that carries our vocabulary along with it. We have to have names for those new items. All cultures exhibit this growth to some extent: the list of content-carrying words—nouns, verbs, adjectives, and most adverbs —is the one list in the catalog that has no limit. Phonemes, syllable types, rules of syntax, and certain little "function words" that will be discussed later are "closed classes"—they are almost never added to; but the major lexicon is open-ended. The relationship of morphemes to words is therefore the hardest thing in language to analyze. Asking what morphemes a word contains and what they mean is asking what the coiner of the word had in mind when he coined it and possibly what unforeseen associations it may have built up since.[8] It is less an analytical question than a question about history.

Still, in spite of the difficulties, looking for morphemes is a necessary part of linguistic analysis. This is true partly because not all languages are quite so unsystematic (or so rich in conflicting systems) as English; some of them have more regular habits of word formation. By its very irregularity English illustrates the variety of these habits.

The make-up of words

There are two fairly well defined ways to make words. One uses words themselves as raw material for new words. It is called *compounding* or *composition*. The other attaches a lesser morpheme—an *affix*, the general term that includes *prefixes* and *suffixes*—to a major element—a base, frequently a word, which may already have one or more affixes incorporated in it. It is called *derivation*. **Roadblock** and **warning light** are compounds; so is **slide rule**: the separation or lack of it in writing is a fair indication of how deep the heat of fusion has penetrated, how much the individual component has kept of its own identity. There is no clear dividing line between compounds and idioms, but there are two main criteria: the productivity of the processes through which the expressions are formed and the "one-wordness" of the result. The expression **black sheep** meaning 'ne'er-do-well' could qualify as an idiom semantically; its meaning is not predictable from the combined meanings of **black** and **sheep**. But in addition it is constructed the same as **scarlet fever, short circuit, dumb show** ('pantomime'), and, with backshifted stress, **hót seat,**

---

[8] How we analyze a word into morphemes can change in the course of the word's history. A *wiseacre* is generally thought to be someone who acts wise but is not entitled to—*wise* is morphemicized by the speaker in spite of the fact that *wiseacre* originally meant 'soothsayer' and the *wise-* part is related to *witch.* More examples of such "folk etymology" will be given on pages **248-49.**

fát lady, shárpshooter, whítefish, páleface, mádman—that is, with *adjective plus noun*. The process is one that is repeated over and over in the creation of expressions whose parts are themselves words but which have been given (or have taken on in the course of time—see pages 255-56) an unpredictable meaning.

The "one-wordness" of compounds can be seen in the way the expressions are handled morphologically. They tend to fill a single grammatical slot in a sentence (for example, that of a verb, a noun, or an adjective) and to be inflected as single words are—on the end. *Fát lady* (in a circus) is a compound; *fátter lady* is not. The idiom *to put a stop to* is just as unitary in meaning as *to check, to stymie,* or *to inhibit.* But we do not think of it as "a word" because it is inflected internally, with *put* behaving independently: we say *He's putting a stop to that,* not °*He's put a stop to-ing that.* The occasional compound-like structure that does allow an internal inflection tends to be regularized by the ordinary speaker: the *attorneys general* type is becoming as rare as °*jacks-in-the-box* or °*wills-o'-the-wisp.*

Unlike *to put a stop to,* the expression *to bad-mouth* results from two highly productive processes of formation—first a compound noun made with adjective plus noun, as in *He has a bad mouth;* then a conversion of the noun to a verb—and it shows its one-wordness in the normal inflection: *He bad-mouthed me.* So we put *to bad-mouth* down as a compound and *to put a stop to* as an idiom.

A feature that is often used to define noun compounds is shift of stress. Instead of *raw híde* we say *ráwhide,* and so for *hárdwood, wísecrack,* and *retáining wall.* But it is an uncertain criterion. Older generations (and Scots of all generations) prefer *Salvation Army, paper dólls, right ángle,* and *two-by-fóur,* where many younger Americans say *Salvátion Ármy, páper dolls, right angle,* and *twó-by-four.* Some speakers vacillate, preferring to stress the second element in *chocolate cáke* and the first in *spíce cake.* No one criterion will suffice to define any of the types of word grouping that one finds in English; all are gradient.

The productivity of compounding is limitless. Words are the loosest elements and combine most freely, though according to rules that linguists are only beginning to detect.[9] For example, the student who wrote that a textbook must have *easy-to-understand instructions* sensed that she was free to make a compound of this kind by using the words *easy* and *hard,* but not necessarily other adjectives—she would probably not have written °*a nice-to-read book* or °*a comfortable-to-wear jacket.* All the same, one cannot be sure of restrictions: a real estate flier reads *The at-no-cost-to-you gift is just our way of pointing out a good thing.*

Derivation is less productive. There are comparatively few affixes in

---

9 Marchand 1969 and Adams 1973 are recommended.

English which the average speaker would feel free to attach in order to make a new word—which is another way of saying that there are few of which the average speaker is fully aware. And awareness stems from a fairly high degree of stability of meaning. As we have seen, even the agentive *-er* is rather unpredictable. But *de-*, with the sense 'remove' or 'extract,' is easily attached, as in to *de-scent* a skunk, to *de-bug* an office, to *desensitize* a nerve. A writer or speaker is free to make a word to order using it, as in ***The vice president, manager and secretary were de-hired.***[10] Other readily usable affixes are *-an* 'inhabitant or national of,' *anti-* 'against,' *astro-* 'pertaining to the stars or to astronomy,' *electro-* 'pertaining to electricity,' *-esque* 'in the style of,' *extra-* 'exceeding the usual limit,' *-ful* 'amount as measured by' (*cupful, jugful*), *inter-* 'between,' *-ish* 'approximately,' *-ism* 'doctrine,' *-itis* 'irritation of,' *-ize* 'act or make according to the norm of,' *micro-* 'very small,' *neo-* 'new,' *non-* (negation), *-ocracy* 'rule of,' *omni-* 'all,' *out-* 'surpass' (in some respect, as in *outbid, outrun*), *pan-* 'universal,' *pre-* 'before,' *post-* 'after,' *pro-* 'for,' *pseudo-* 'pretended, false,' *re-* 'again' (with the same shading off into the unrecognizable as with *de-*: for example, *to resent*), *semi-* 'half,' *super-* 'surpassingly,' *trans-* 'across,' *ultra-* 'extremely,' *-ward* 'in the direction of,' *-wise* 'as far as X is concerned.' In the last decade, *mini-* and *maxi-* have gained popularity in such coinages as *miniskirt, minireview,* and *maxi-coat.* Specialists in various fields employ technical affixes, of which those in chemistry are among the most elaborate. At times the affixed element is so much like a word that it is hard to tell a derivative from a compound. 'Teaching oneself' is called *auto-instruction* or *self-instruction;* the formations are similar but *self* exists as a separate word in the relevant sense. Other such morphemes are *-like, off-,* and *-most* (*doglike* devotion, *offset* screwdriver, *foremost* contender).

The make-up of derivatives can be highly complex. In *irrevocable* there are four morphemes, of which three are affixes—the two prefixes *ir-* and *-re-* and the suffix *-able*—and one is the base, *-voc-*. All are *bound*, which is to say that they are never used alone. The base *-voc-* appears in *vocation, provoke, vociferous,* and *vocabulary,* but not as an independent word (though *voice,* from the same historical source, is a word). In *ungetatable* there are also four morphemes, but now the *bound* morphemes *un-* and *-able* are matched by the *free* morphemes *-get-* and *-at-*.[11]

---

[10] *Reader's Digest* (April 1974), p. 162.

[11] A practical approach to analyzing morphemes is to cut affixes from the front and the end of the word repeatedly until only the smallest meaningful unit remains; for example,

$$\text{cut 1} \Big/ \quad \Big/ \text{ cut 2}$$
$$\textit{un} \Big/ \textit{guess} \Big/ \textit{able,}$$

revealing two bound and one free morpheme. Each unit so cut should occur, with essentially the same meaning, in at least one other word.

From another standpoint *irrevocable* can be analyzed as *ir-revocable* and *ungetatable* as *un-getatable,* and then of course both *revocable* and *getatable* are free, since they are also words. This expresses the inner structure better than the mere chopping up into morphemes, because it shows the order in which the elements are attached.

Returning to compounds, the variety is as great as the productivity. All the major categories of words are represented. There are compound prepositions, such as *alongside of* and *notwithstanding;* compound conjunctions, such as *whenever* and *whereas;* compound adverbs, such as *indeed* and *moreover;* compound pronouns, such as *you-all* and *myself;* compound numerals, such as *twenty-five* and *nine-tenths.* There is even a compound indefinite, *another.* As for nouns, verbs, and adjectives, the array of forms is too rich to be more than sampled. Some types with nouns:

1. Noun plus noun: *handbook, skylab, shoehorn*

2. Adjective plus noun: *greenhouse, fát lady* (at a circus), *redneck*

3. Noun plus adjective: *attorney general, notary public, cousin german* (first cousin)

4. Verb plus noun: *killjoy, breakwater, cutthroat*

5. Noun plus verb: *windbreak, toothpick, barkeep*

6. Noun plus verb plus *-er: man-eater, party-pooper, purse-snatcher*

7. Verb plus verb: *make-believe*

8. Verb plus adverb: *holdout, runoff, takeover*

9. Adverb plus verb: *downpour, outlay, afterblast*

Not all these arrangements are equally productive. Probably 1, 6, and 8 are responsible for more new nouns than any of the rest. The almost day-to-day striking of new coins with the verb-and-adverb stamp can be seen in formations with *-in,* and incidentally lets us see the meaning veering away from 'in' toward something like 'happening related to': *sit-in, love-in, wade-in, teach-in.* In the Nixon era people were organizing *impeach-ins.*

Adjectives may have such varied components as those in *garden-fresh, red-hot, easygoing, half-witted, man-eating, store-bought,* and *bowlegged.* Also verbs: *to deep-fry, to bad-mouth, to hand-paint, to underestimate,* and *to write up.*

There are other ways of classifying compounds than according to the parts of speech that their elements belong to. Certain nouns, for example, can be classed together as epithets for persons: *muttonhead* (noun plus

noun) and *redneck* (adjective plus noun) are functionally similar, and
clubfoot, sorehead, fishface, droopy drawers, and *peg leg* belong to the
same class. Another scheme is to classify them according to the syntactic
relations of the elements. Thus *haircut, neck-shave,* and *back rub* have a
nominalized verb as the second element and the object of that same verb
as the first; while *cockfight, horserace,* and *rainfall* have the nominalized
verb plus its subject: the cocks fight, the horses race, and the rain falls.

Compounding and derivation are not the only ways of making new
words. Some, especially trade names, may be pure inventions—as pure,
at least, as such creations ever are, given the fact that some analogy with
what we already know invariably influences our "free" choice of sounds.
Dreft, the name of a soap powder, was coined with a hint of *soft, drift,
lift, sift, deft. Kodak* was attention-getting because of its innovative use
of the *k-* spelling, which has been imitated since in many other trade
names. A rich source of terms relating to social and political organization
is the combined pronunciation of the initial letters of composite names,
sometimes pronounced letter by letter, as in *FBI, TVA, SPCA;* sometimes
merged, as in *UNESCO, SEATO, NATO, UNICEF.* Such words are
called *acronyms.* Of late, the composite name has tended to be chosen
on the basis of some already existing word that is felt to express the aim
or style of the organization—for example, *PANIC* for *People Against
National Identity Cards, PUSH* for *People United to Save Humanity,
DOOM* for *Drugs Out Of Meat.* Naturally this leads to a drying up of
acronyms as a source for anything new.[12] A third device is *reduplication.*
The same morpheme is repeated, with or without modification: *hush-
hush, mishmash, helter-skelter, fiddle-faddle.*

Finally, new words that are new only in a grammatical sense are made
by a process called *conversion:* a word belonging to one part of speech
is converted to another part of speech, as when English turns nouns into
verbs. Some of the examples of compound verbs just cited are actually
converted nouns: *sandpaper, spotlight, blacklist.* The majority of one-
syllable nouns in English also exist as one-syllable verbs: *hunt, to hunt;
walk, to walk; sight, to sight; play, to play.* Another name for conversion
is *zero-derivation*—'nothing is added,' contrasting with ordinary derivation, which does add something. *Beauty* is made into a verb by adding
-fy: beautify. Lovely becomes a noun through the addition of *-ness: loveliness. Equate* takes *-ion* to become the noun *equation.* No matter how
it is done, the essential meaning of the root word remains unchanged.
Much of the business of derivation is simply getting the parts of speech
to match up. We have a noun *queen* and need an adjective to mean 'like
a queen'; hence *queenly.* We have an adjective *scarce* and need a noun

---

to mean 'condition of being scarce'; hence *scarcity*. But derivation en-
larges the lexicon in other ways too—for sex in *princess*, for endearment
or contempt in *princeling*, for abstraction in *kingship*, and so on.

   Word-building formulas can be expressed as transformations, more
commonly used in sentence building, as will be seen in the next chapter.
For example, the conversion of adjectives to adverbs by adding *-ly* is
regular enough to write with the rule

$$[+\text{Adj}] \longrightarrow [+\text{Adv}] / \underline{\qquad} \text{ -}ly$$

—'a form that carries the feature "adjective" becomes a form that carries
the feature "adverb" in the environment of an added *-ly*.' Thus from *nice*
we get *nicely*, from *vain* we get *vainly*, and from *dreary* we get *drearily*.
Likewise, one kind of zero-derivation may be shown as

$$[+\text{Adj}] \longrightarrow [+\text{Adv}] / \underline{\qquad} \text{ø}.$$

as in *fast runner, run fast.*

   Table 4–1 summarizes the principal ways of forming words discussed
in this section.

Grammatical morphemes: inflections and function words

Most morphemes are like the ones already described: bits of form and
meaning that provide the stuff for an expanding lexicon. At the first moment one of them is pressed into service, we say that a new word has
been created. As with other creative acts, we cannot be sure which way
it is going to go. The person who first invented the expression *stir-crazy*
might have said *jail-happy, cell-silly, pen-potty,* or anything else that
came handy and was colorful. But once *stir-crazy* had made its bow, anyone wishing to compare two individuals in terms of this affliction was
almost certain to do it in just one way: "Abe is *more stir-crazy* than Leo."
The use of *more*, or of the suffix *-er* in *crazier*, is seen not as a way of
making new words but as a way of doing something to the words we
already have. It is manipulative, not creative. In the early part of the
Second World War, someone might have said *The news is that Hitler
threatens to blitz London,* and someone else might have replied *I don't
know what "blitz" means but if he ever blitzed that place he'd get blitzed
right back.* The second speaker added *-ed* automatically to something he
had never heard before. He did not create a "new word" but used the
"same word" in a "different form."

   Morphemes such as *more*, *-er*, and *-ed* belong to the grammar of a
language and are accordingly called *grammatical morphemes*. By and

TABLE 4–1
Ways of Forming Words

	Noun	Adjective	Verb	Adverb	Preposition
COMPOUNDING	short-circuit face-lift shoot-out	near-black high-rise childlike	overwork waterlog playact	crosswise heavenward nevertheless	notwithstanding
DERIVATION	microorganism cupful dedication	foolish trans-Pacific eatable	bedevil glamorize outbid	neatly	despite
INVENTION	Kodak				
ACRONYMY	NATO	AWOL			
REDUPLICATION	jimjams chitchat	lovey-dovey namby-pamby	crisscross flim-flam	(to go) hippity hoppity	
CONVERSION (zero-derivation)	ripoff	fun ("a fun game")	to brunch	easy ("take it easy")	adjacent ("adja- cent the build- ing")

large they do two things: they signal relationships within language, and they signal certain meanings that are so vital in communication that they have to be expressed over and over. An example of the first function is the morpheme *than* (which also happens to be a word), which simply relates the terms of a comparison: *John is older than Mary.* An example of the second function is the morpheme that pluralizes nouns. We can say, without committing ourselves as to how many dogs there were, *John suffered several dog bites.* But if we mention *dog* in the usual way we are forced to reveal whether there was one or more than one: *John was bitten by his neighbor's dog(s).* English speakers feel that "number" is important enough to be automatically tagged to the word. They also demand grammatical consistency: a singular must go with a singular and a plural with a plural; that is why we reject *°this men, °they has,* and *°she like.* Languages do not always agree on the particular kinds of meanings that are given this sort of preferential treatment but certain ones are typical: number, tense, definiteness, animateness, possession—even, in certain languages, such things as size and shape.

The two uses of grammatical morphemes just mentioned—to signal relationships within language and to signal certain favored meanings—are usually separated by linguists but are really impossible to keep apart. *Jill's book* uses the possessive morpheme *-'s* to describe ownership, a fact of the real world. *Jill's smoking* does not use it to say that *Jill* owns smoking but to show that *Jill* is the grammatical subject of the verb *smoke.* The word *that* in *That's the woman!* combined with a pointing gesture singles out an object in the real world. In *I didn't mean that* it refers to something just said, something in language.

The last example with *that* and the earlier one with *than* reveal that grammatical morphemes, like lexical morphemes, may be whole words as well as parts of words. Both the suffix *-ed* and the word *that* are grammatical morphemes. When we attach them, grammatical morphemes are called *inflections.* When we leave them by themselves they are called *function words.* The suffixes *-s, -ed, -'s,* and *-ing* are inflections. (English likes to inflect by using suffixes, but other languages may incorporate their inflections at the beginning or in the middle of words.) *That, the, my, us, he, and, when, than,* and numerous similar forms are function words.

The difference between inflections and function words is not in what they do with meanings and relationships. They are so similar in this respect that one occasionally finds an inflection and a function word both playing the same role or even alternating with each other, like *-er* and *more* in *quicker* and *more rapidly.* The difference between them lies in their behavior as physical entities. Function words share the freedom of words. Other words may be inserted between them and the items to which they belong. Thus *the man* can be split to give *the big man, the great big man, the wonderful great big man,* and so on; *more beautiful* can have additional *more's* inserted, giving *more and more beautiful* (we cannot say °*prettier and -er*); and *who* can be separated fore and aft by pauses: *the man—uh—who—uh—had to leave.*

Grammatical morphemes are relatively more stable in meaning than lexical morphemes. The contrast is especially marked when we compare the two kinds of suffixes. A grammatical suffix—that is, an inflection— tends to be simply additive: we can pretty safely predict that if the plural *-s* is added to a new noun, it will mean 'more than one.' There are exceptions—*scissors, trousers, pliers*—but they cannot approach the variety of even a relatively stable lexical morpheme.

Despite its usefulness, the line between grammatical and lexical morphemes is an arbitrary one. This can be seen in the behavior of the comparative suffix (inflection?) *-er.* We feel that when we say *redder* we are using a "different form of the same word *red,*" not a different word, as would be the case with *curvaceous,* based on *curve.* So *-er* seems to qualify on this score as a grammatical morpheme. It also qualifies on the score of its relationship to *more,* which is suppletive, like that of *go* and *went: -er* is used with one-syllable adjectives (*hotter, scarcer*) and two-syllable ones ending in a reduced vowel (*lovelier, narrower*), *more* with the rest (*more beautiful, more sullen*). But when we look closely at the adjectives that take one or the other form of comparison, we find things more characteristic of lexical morphemes. For one, the lower in frequency—that is, the less familiar—the adjective is, the less it is apt to be used with *-er*, even given the right phonological conditions. Sentences such as *?Problems were rifer than ever, ?Mary was chaster than Elizabeth,* and *?You look wanner than you did last night* are distinctly odd; and **He is apter to go than to stay* is impossible. On the other hand, a longer adjective that is widely used more readily takes *-er.* Compare the much-used *handsome* with the little-used *winsome: Jerry is handsomer than Jim; ?Olivia is winsomer than Charlotte.* A bad-sounding combination is avoided even when the adjective is a common one: **sourer.* This does not happen with grammatical morphemes; *casts* takes its inflection *-s* despite the resulting sequence of alveolars. All in all, we are simply unable to make a neat determination of whether to call *-er* and *more* grammatical or lexical.

The same is true of many full words. We would like to distinguish between function words and "content" words, as lexical words are often called because they seem to "contain" more meaning than function words. But the distinction is hard to draw. Ordinarily *man* is a content word; certainly it is one in *Do you see that man over there?* But if in answer to *Why is he on trial?* someone says *Because he killed a man,* de-accenting *man,* then *man* is little more than 'somebody'; it is a function word filling an otherwise empty grammatical slot.

Given the haziness of the line, we can only make certain *relative* statements about function words. They are used relatively more often than lexical words to point to elements in language or to the roles of speakers and hearers, and less often to point to things and events in the real world. They are relatively fewer than lexical words. They belong to classes that are relatively closed—new nouns are added every day, but new prepositions very rarely. And they can be *listed* with relative assurance. Grammar books recognize the following:

1. The verb *to be* when it merely links: *Flowers are pretty.*

2. The prepositions: *to, at, for, by,* etc.

3. The identifying words, or determiners, such as the articles, possessives, and demonstratives, which relate things to their environments: *the house, that man, my daughter, some idiot, another candidate, the same problem, which piece*

4. The quantifiers: *many, few, more, less, any, none,* etc., and the numerals

5. The coordinating conjunctions: *and, or, nor, but, also, so, yet*

6. The relatives, which attach adjective clauses to their antecedents: *the man who, the place where, the time when, the dog which;* also the ones that "include their antecedent"—*He gave me what* (= *that which*) *I wanted.*

7. The adverbial conjunctions, which bring adverb clauses into certain logical relationships (time, condition, concession, cause, etc.) with the sentence as a whole: *because, when, before, while, although, if, providing, unless,* etc.

8. The conjunctive adverbs, which relate a following sentence to a preceding one in certain logical ways: *besides, instead, nevertheless, still, accordingly, thereupon, hence, later,* etc.

9. The intensifiers: *too, very, quite, somewhat, a little, pretty,* etc.

10. The auxiliary verbs: *can, may, have, do, be* (in certain functions), etc.

11. The pronouns, pro-adverbs, and other pro-words, which stand in for lexical words or phrases: *it, she, he, I, them, hers, his, so* (as in *So he did*), *there, here, then,* etc.

The English inflections can be listed more easily than the function words, though still not with complete confidence, as we have seen with the comparative *-er.* They are the following:

1. Noun, plural: *cat, cats*

2. Noun, possessive: *cat, cat's*

3. Verb, present: *to earn, earns*

4. Verb, past: *to earn, earned*

5. Verb, present participle: *to earn, earning*

6. Verb, past (or passive) participle: *to earn, earned; to fall, fallen* (*they have earned, they have fallen*)

7. Adjective, comparative: *sweet, sweeter*
8. Adjective, superlative: *sweet, sweetest*

The shortness of this list compared with the length of the list of function words puts English into the class of *analytic* languages (see page 13): it is one of those languages that tend to analyze out the grammatical functions and put them in separate words rather than incorporating them as affixes within lexical words. Latin is an example of the opposite type.

Table 4–2 summarizes the distinctions among the various kinds of morphemes discussed in this chapter.

TABLE 4–2
Types of English Morphemes

Kinds of Morphemes	Degrees of Independence	
	Words	**Affixes**
Lexical morphemes	Words incorporatable in new words by COMPOUNDING (*clam* + *bake* → *clambake*) Words incorporatable in new words by DERIVATION (*push* + *-y* → *pushy*) (*mis-* + *fire* → *misfire*)	More or less productive prefixes (*un-* in *un*denatured) Unproductive prefixes (*di-* in *di*gest) More or less productive suffixes (*-able* in orbit*able*) Unproductive suffixes (*-ose* in verb*ose*) Word fragments (*-burger* in cheese*burger*)
Grammatical morphemes	Function words (*the, of, which, my, when, and, if* . . .)	Inflectional suffixes (*-s, -ed, -ing* . . .)

Key terms and concepts

idiom
collocation
stereotyping
lexicon
morpheme
  lexical morpheme
  bound vs. free morpheme
  productive vs. unproductive
    morpheme
  grammatical morpheme
    inflection
    function word

word coining
compounding
derivation
acronym
reduplication
conversion (zero-derivation)
affix
  prefix
  suffix

Additional remarks and applications

1. List some scientific terms and divide them into morphemes.

2. See if you can find some words using informal morphemes, such as **bumber-, -teria, -nik** (as in *peacenik*). Magazine and newspaper ads may prove a good source.

3. *To overpower* and *to subdue* are synonyms, and have approximately the same frequency of use. Is it as easy to attach the *-er* suffix to one as to the other? If not, what is the trouble? Would there be the same trouble as a rule in attaching an inflectional suffix?

4. Read the following sentences aloud and decide whether there is evidence for regarding any expressions that they contain as compounds (hyphens have been omitted):

   a. She's a seven year old.
   b. She's seven years old.
   c. Do you like graham crackers?
   d. I won't accept that, not by a damn sight.
   e. Looking out I saw a lone shark cutting through the water.
   f. Larry Livermore is a loan shark.
   g. Who invented the talking machine?
   h. She's crazy about oyster stew and ice cream.
   i. Who are the members of the grand jury?
   j. He's a combination smart Aleck, nosey Parker, and gloomy Gus.
   k. She tripped because she's near sighted.
   l. She's admired because she's so far sighted.
   m. You're a pain in the neck.
   n. Only from Harger-Haldeman can you buy with such a small down payment.
   o. He calls it a gunny sack but I call it a burlap bag.

5. Note the different stress patterns in the two columns below and see if you can attribute the difference to a difference in function. (Some of the combinations are normally written solid.)

a stone fence	a book shelf
a brick wall	an ink eraser
a screen door	a table top
a paper doll	a garbage collector
an aluminum ladder	a stone mason
a cotton dress	a paper hanger

6. Three typical noun-forming suffixes in English are *-dom* (as in **kingdom, officialdom**), *-ion* (*relation, confusion*), and *-ness* (*gladness,*

oneness). List some more nouns having these suffixes. Find other noun-forming suffixes and give examples. Do the same for adjective-forming suffixes (such as *-less, -ish,* and *-ous*), and verb-forming suffixes (such as *-fy, -ize,* and *-en*). Which of these suffixes are still productive?

7. Collect from advertisements some trade names and acronyms, and discuss their formation.

For further reading

Adams, Valerie, 1973. *An Introduction to Modern English Word Formation* (London: Longmans).

Aronoff, Mark. 1976. *Word Formation in Generative Grammar,* Linguistic Inquiry, Monograph 1 (Cambridge, Mass.: M.I.T. Press).

Bolinger, Dwight. 1971. *The Phrasal Verb in English* (Cambridge, Mass.: Harvard University Press).

Greenbaum, Sidney. 1970. *Verb-Intensifier Collocations in English* (The Hague: Mouton).

Makkai, Adam. 1972. *Idiom Structure in English* (The Hague: Mouton).

Marchand, Hans. 1969. *The Categories and Types of Present-Day English Word-Formation,* 2nd ed. (Munich: C. H. Beck).

Matthews, P. H. 1974. *Morphology: An Introduction to the Theory of Word-Structure* (Cambridge, England: Cambridge University Press).

Sears, Donald A. 1972. "The System of Compounding in English," *Linguistics* 91, 31–88.

Sheard, J. A. 1966. *The Words of English* (New York: Norton).

THE STRUCTURE
OF SENTENCES 5

To make a sentence, one must (1) relate the parts that make it up, (2) indicate the functions of the parts, through notions such as *agent, action,* and *recipient of action,* and (3) mark the sentence as a discrete unit of language. Various syntactic devices are used to accomplish these ends. In English they fall roughly into three systems:

1. The inflectional system: the *-s* plural, the *-s* possessive, the *-d* past, and the objective form of the personal pronouns (*he–him, she–her,* etc.).

2. The phrasal system: here the order of words becomes grammatically significant. The sentence can be defined as a noun phrase plus a verb phrase, and there are smaller units, such as prepositional phrases and adverb phrases.

3. The compositional system: this includes both compounding (*folk + lore → folklore, reading + readiness → reading readiness*) and the joining of bound morphemes (*carni- + -vore → carnivore*), especially affixation (*counter- + revolution → counterrevolution*). The latter may be called *bound-morpheme derivation.* Composition is coming to be relied on more and more.

The three systems cooperate in that all are in operation at all times; but they also compete, when a speaker or writer chooses a construction that emphasizes one at the expense of the others. Suppose we want to express the notion of 'what enables the car to roll.' We can say (1) *the car's wheels,* (2) *the wheels of the car,* or (3) *the car wheels*—respectively (1) an inflection (possessive *-s*), (2) a phrase, and (3) a compound. *The car's wheels* gives a little more attention to the wheels than to the car; *the wheels of the car* does the opposite. *The car wheels* makes 'car' nonspecific—the wheels could be unattached.

English has a wide range of choice: the compound *book-lover* competes with the bound-morpheme derivative *bibliophile,* and the compound *viewpoint* competes with the phrase *point of view.* (But often we use these devices for a more radical difference in meaning—*daytime* is not the same as *time of day,* nor *outrun* the same as *run out.*)

The three systems differ in how freely they can be manipulated. The inflectional system has strict rules: a plural subject, for example, requires a plural verb. The compositional system is fairly open, but we cannot invent compounds or derivatives entirely at will: we can say *They saw their friend off* but not *°They gave their friends a see-off,* though *send-off* is normal. Compounds are coinages, tied to a time and a place: *send-off* is a stock compound. The phrasal system is the most open of all. None of the following contain a precise term for an astronautical landing, but any one of them is suitable for referring to it:

> The astronauts touched down in the vicinity of Barbados.
> The astronauts came down at 6 P.M.
> The astronauts let themselves down from their capsule.
> They plunged down (got down, splashed down).

The fact that other things or persons have been said to touch or slip or flop down does not bar these phrases from use with astronauts. But on the compositional side there is no such freedom. The astronauts may come down, but this is not a *comedown* nor a *letdown.* These are terms already preempted for other uses. To name the astronauts' landing it was necessary to look elsewhere. The splash was only incidental, but *splashdown* was chosen. (A term like this may or may not survive. *Hitdown*—used by newscasters to refer to the Space Lab—may be quickly forgotten.)

Though relatively free, the phrasal system too has its problems with restrictions of various kinds. First, there are collocations: *I like it better* but not *°I enjoy it better; last night* and *yesterday evening* but not *°last afternoon* and *°yesterday night.* Second, besides the rules that seem to make sense because they guide us in interpreting a sentence (adjectives before their nouns, interrogative words at the beginning of a question), we find minor rules that exclude what appear to be perfectly sensible forms of expression. Why is it we can say *Music's charm is that it is so* *soothing* but not **Italian's charm is that it is so melodious* nor **German's verbs are hard to learn?* Only because there is an insignificant rule or part of a rule that forbids us to use the possessive with the name of a language. When forming a sentence we are free to ad-lib, but only up to a point.

TOGETHERNESS

The first rule of syntax, which means etymologically 'a putting together,' is that things belonging together will be together. It transcends all other rules; it is applied by very young speakers and very young deaf users of sign language alike, who will say *beautiful flowers* and *flowers beautiful, my mother* and *mother my, he came* and *came he*, indiscriminately.[1] The words are embraced by their proximity—a nearness in time if a message is spoken, a nearness in space if it is written, or a grouping under a single rhythm or intonation curve.

Two kinds of examples illustrate how pervasive the principle of togetherness is in language. One is our resistance to putting something between two things that are more closely related to each other than they are to what is inserted. Teachers find it hard to enforce the rule of interior plurals in forms like *mothers-in-law* and *postmasters general*—speakers want to put the *-s* at the end. They are even more reluctant to say *hardest-working person,* inserting the *-est* between the members of the compound *hard-working.* Compare the earlier remarks on compounds (page 62).

The second kind of example appears when two things that formerly did not belong together come to be viewed as if they did, because they occur side by side. Certain prepositions which once were felt (as is customary) to be more closely bound to the following noun, have acquired a closer attachment to what precedes, as spelling sometimes indicates: *lotsa* for *lots of, kinda* for *kind of, sorta* for *sort of.* And the last two have taken the further step of being used as unit adverbs: *kinda nice.*

Given mere togetherness, and ignoring the traffic rules of syntax, one can interpret a series like *Sick John mad me* if the words are known. It could mean 'When John is sick I'm mad,' or perhaps 'John is sick and mad at me.' But the interpretation depends on the principle of the reasonable guess. We depend on it not only to fill in the blanks but to interpret many sentences that remain ambiguous even when the traffic signs are operating. The speaker who said *I went to check on the dry*

---

[1] Tervoort 1968, pp. 457–58. The speaking child at this stage will be using language more appropriate to the crib, but the principle is the same.

clothes ran no risk of misunderstanding. Within the situation it could only mean 'I went to check to see whether the clothes that are drying are dry.' Getting clothes dry was the objective and *dry* and *clothes* gravitated together.

This example illustrates another kind of relatedness, which is more fundamental than anything within syntax. It is the relation between what is said and what it is said about. If one adolescent calls *Chicken!* to another adolescent, no syntax is needed to make the connection. Such connections are what language is mainly for. We call them *meaning*.

Operators

Nevertheless, without something more than mere togetherness, sentences would be intolerably ambiguous much of the time even with the help of the situation. As few as three words side by side can be baffling unless they are ranked and grouped; as a rule we join more than three words, so that ranks over ranks and groups within groups become a necessity.

The traffic signals that provide this information are the grammatical morphemes—function words and inflections—plus such other devices as characteristic types of emphasis or pause or pitch and characteristic arrangements. Together they can be called *operators*. They tell the hearer what goes with what, how close the connection is, what is subordinate to what, where an utterance begins and ends.

As we noted earlier with the possessive *'s*, not all grammatical morphemes are pure traffic signals. Some refer to facts in the real world. The same is true of other operators. Take intonation. A level span by itself at a low pitch in the middle of an utterance is an operator that marks the accompanying words as 'not belonging'—for instance, the parenthetical *I wouldn't put it past him* in the sentence

If he ^{does} $^{it—}$

$\qquad$ and I ^{would}n't ^{put} it ^{past} $_{hi}$m—he's ^{in} for ^{trou}

$\qquad\qquad\qquad\qquad\qquad\qquad\qquad\qquad\qquad\qquad$ ble.

But this is impure, because parentheses suggest 'unimportance' as well as grammatical 'incidentalness.' Similarly with word order: in *red brick* versus *brick red* the arrangement tells us which word is the modifier and which is the head. But in *A hundred dollars that mistake cost me!* the word order conveys an emotion; the matter-of-fact statement is *That mistake cost me a hundred dollars.*

Two examples will show how different operators play on different aspects of a sentence. In *I saw Mary and John together; the former was talking to the latter* the function words *former* and *latter* direct the hearer to select the first and second items just mentioned, in that order. In *I saw Mary and John together; she was talking to him* the function words *she* and *him* direct the hearer to select personal nouns with the semantic feature "female" and "male" respectively. The means are different but the gross meaning of both sentences is the same.

The more complex a sentence is, the more we depend on the operators for meaning. If they are omitted or garbled, the connections are lost no matter how clear the content words may be. But if the operators are preserved and nonsense words substituted for the content words, one's feeling of disorientation is less acute. John Algeo illustrates both situations with the following sentences:

> Oll considerork meanork, ho mollop tharp fo concernesh bix shude largel philosophigar aspectem ith language phanse vulve increasorkrow de recent yearm engagesh sho attentuge ith scholarm.
>
> In prefarbing torming, we cannot here be pretolled with those murler dichytomical optophs of flemack which have demuggingly in arsell wems exbined the obburtion of maxans.[2]

Though we recognize *consider, mean, concern,* and several other familiar words in the first sentence, we have no idea what to do with them. We might think of a foreign language that happened to share a number of cognates with English. But with the second sentence we are back home. Perhaps it is just from some scientific treatise in an unfamiliar field; if we met the writer on the street we could exchange a greeting.

Constructions and constituents

Even if his statement were factually true, one might doubt the sanity of a person who said something like *George was walking down the street with Mary's elbow.* The absurdity is that it ignores the rankings of what it brings together. George has to accompany something at the same hierarchic level as himself: *George was walking down the street with Mary,* including her elbow.

The same is true with sentences and parts of sentences: togetherness has to be sorted level by level. We saw this even in the internal organiza-

---

[2] Algeo 1972, p. 278.

tion of words, with *indelible ink* (page 58). The two words *ungraceful* and *disgraceful* show two different patterns of hierarchic organization:

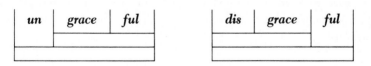

In *ungraceful, -grace-* is "together with" *-ful*, and *un-* is "together with" *-graceful*. *Disgraceful* reverses these connections.

Any such self-contained stretch of speech is called a *construction*, and its parts are its *constituents*. What the diagrams show is a difference between *ultimate constituents* and *immediate constituents*. The ultimate constituents are all the morphemes, one by one. The immediate constituents are just what-goes-with-what. Thus *dis-* in *disgraceful* is an immediate constituent of *-grace-* (and vice versa), while *disgrace-* as a whole is an immediate constituent of *-ful.*

Analysis by immediate constituents is the most effective way of showing the inner layering of sentences. For example, *He said he wanted to marry her* is analyzed as follows:

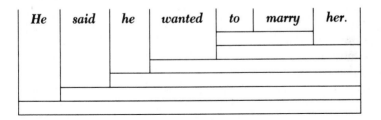

By itself, immediate-constituent analysis tells us how a stretch of speech is layered, but it tells us nothing about the nature of the elements nor the manner in which they are related. For example, *behind the house* and *only a few* have the same constituent diagram,

but the first is actually more closely related to *in back of the old stone house on the hill,* with a diagram that looks at first glance to be quite different:

in	*back*	*of*	*the*	*old*	*stone*	*house*	*on*	*the*	*hill*

What is needed to complete the analysis is something about parts of speech, or word classes, and about subjects, predicates, modifiers, and so on, or the functions of the classes; so we label the spaces:

It	*grows*	*in*	*back*	*of*	*the*	*old*	*stone*	*house*	*on*	*the*	*hill.*
							Compound noun				
						Noun modified by adjective			Inner noun phrase		
						Inner noun phrase			Prepositional phrase		
			Compound preposition		Outer noun phrase, object of preposition						
	Main verb		Prepositional phrase, complement of main verb								
Subject	Predicate										
Sentence											

The labeled diagram reveals both the layering and the unlimited possibilities of embedding constructions within constructions: *in back of the old stone house on the hill* is a prepositional phrase that contains a prepositional phrase, *on the hill.* And *on the hill* could be lengthened to contain two more prepositional phrases, *on the hill up the river from here,* in which *up the river from here* modifies *hill* and *from here* modifies *up the river* as a unit.

WORD CLASSES

Labeling a sentence diagram requires agreement about the names used. They can be names of *classes* or names of *functions*. Those of the diagram on page 80 are not consistent. *It* is called a *subject*. That is a functional term—it does not name a class of words but the role played by a word in a sentence. *Grows* is called a *verb*, which is a class of words. Instead of calling *it* a subject we could have called it a *pronoun*, applying the name of its class. And instead of calling *grows* a verb we could have called it a *predicate*, applying the name of its function in the sentence. Classes and functions determine each other, but not in any one-to-one fashion. Since we have to start somewhere, we start with the classes, pretending that we know them independently of their functions. This is simpler because classes are exemplified by the words that are their members, and words are easy to lay hold of.

The obvious place to start is with the function words, first because the classes are small, and second because, true to their name, they have functional relationships with nouns, adjectives, and verbs that help to identify the latter, much larger, classes of words.

The classes of function words have already been enumerated (pages 69–70), but a closer look at one of them is necessary as an example of what most distinguishes classes of function words from classes of lexical words: the fact that function-word classes are closed rather than open. We can readily add a new noun or verb (open classes), and sometimes do so deliberately; but a new pronoun or preposition or other function word always finds its way in through some subtle readjustment—an example is the word *plus*, which has become a new conjunctive adverb: *She's the best candidate, plus everybody likes her.* There is less difference, from language to language, in the open classes—nouns and verbs are universal and adjectives are nearly so, and their make-up is not so radically different that a noun cannot be borrowed from one language into another. But the grammatical morphemes, item for item, are where differences are greatest, and function words of course share in this peculiarity.

Classes of function words have a strong tendency to form paradigms, reflecting their tightly structured area of meaning. Taking personal pronouns as our example, we see them distributed across a matrix of features, which include *person* (first, second, third), *number* (singular and plural), *case* (subjective, objective, possessive), *modification* (adjectival, nominal), and *gender:*[3]

	Subjective	*Objective*	*Possessive*	
Singular			*Adjectival*	*Nominal*
First person	I	me	my	mine
Second person	you	you	your	yours
Third person	he (*masculine*) she (*feminine*) it (*neuter*)	him her it	his her its	his hers its
Plural				
First person	we	us	our	ours
Second person	you	you	your	yours
Third person	they	them	their	theirs

A paradigm of this sort becomes its own justification. That is, if it were not for the tight organization there would be no reason for including everything that is there. If a pronoun is defined as a substitute for some other word, then in the first three columns only the third-person forms really belong. The rest have primary uses—they are not substitutes for anything. In *I did it* the word *I* is not a substitute for a noun but a word with its own referent, 'the speaker.' Except for the paradigm the word *you* would not appear four times; but since *I-we-me-us* have to be distinguished along these parameters, so does *you*. And the paradigm is further justified by the matching paradigm of verb forms: *I am, you are, he is.*

An example of a different scheme, taken from Weri, a language of New Guinea, is shown in Table 5–1. Two sections are needed in the table because the case suffixes can only go in a certain order. Several of them may be attached to a single base, but they are always attached in the sequence shown: the agentive can only come after the first emphatic, the additive after accompaniment, and so on. Differences from the English system are striking. To begin with, there is a distinction, found in many languages of the world, between *inclusive* and *exclusive* first person: 'we' meaning 'you and I' is distinct from 'we' meaning 'he (she, they) and I.' Then the scheme of number has the peculiarity that the first person inclusive patterns as if the 'I' were not present: 'you and I' is singular, 'you two and I' is *dual*, and 'you three (or more) and I' is plural. The dual number is another difference from Modern English, though up to the

---

[3] Certain forms have been left out for simplicity: the reflexives (*myself, themselves,* etc.) and the interrogatives (*who, whom, whose,* etc.).

TABLE 5–1
Weri Personal Pronouns

Bases			
	Singular	*Non-singular*	
		dual	*plural*
First inclusive	tepir	tëarip	tëar
First exclusive	ne	tenip	ten
Second	në	arip	ar
Third	pë	pëarip	pët, pëar

Suffixes				
Order 1	*Order 2*	*Order 3*	*Order 4*	*Order 5*
emphatic -ëmint	*accompaniment* -rëng *referent* -in *benefactive* -ëmiin	*agentive* -uk	*emphatic* -iir	*additive* -ta

SOURCE: Adapted from Boxwell 1967.

thirteenth century English too had a dual: *wit* 'we two.' The case endings differ from anything in English.[4] While the *agentive* is akin to the English subjective ("subject-like") in that it indicates the actor, the *emphatic* may mean, for instance, 'just he' as well as 'he himself.' *Accompaniment* is like English *along:* 'I you-along go-we-two' is 'I go with you.' The *benefactive* is similar to the English indirect object, which has no separate form in the English pronoun system but does turn up in the word order: *He planted us a row of sweet potatoes* indicates who benefits by the action. The *referent* includes direct objects. And so on. In addition, there is a scheme of final affixes that express 'and,' 'or,' 'question,' and 'question-location.' An example of a base combined with three suffixes is *pë-mint-ok-iir* 'he-emphatic-agent-emphatic,' as in *pë-mint-ok-iir ëër-a* 'He alone washed himself' (*-ok* is an allomorph of *-uk*).

---

[4] But we might recognize a nominalizing suffix *-s* in the forms *yours, hers, ours,* and *theirs,* based on *your, her, our, their.* In *I have your copy, your* is a modifier. In *I have yours, yours* is like a noun.

Turning to the major classes in English, we find that nouns and verbs can be identified by their association with grammatical morphemes. Proper nouns take the possessive suffix (*Mary, Mary's*) and common nouns take both that[5] and one or both of the articles (*a, an; the*). Verbs can be identified as follows:

1. Verbs may carry one of four inflectional morphemes: *past* (*study, studied; fly, flew*), *perfective* (usually *-ed* or *-en*, as in *had studied, have flown*), *third-person-singular present* (*study, studies*), and *-ing* (*study, studying; fly, flying*).

2. Verbs accept *to* and the auxiliaries *can, may, will*, etc. *(to study, can study).*

3. Verbs combine with *do* and *did (He does like it; Did you like it? I don't like it).*[6]

The classes of noun and verb are confirmed by comparing them—they must agree with each other in number when they are together in a sentence (as subject and predicate—functions again!): *The tree grows, Trees grow.* Adjectives can only be partially identified by the inflections that they take *(pretty, prettier, prettiest,* but not *beautiful, °beautifuler, °beautifulest);* they are more easily identified by the ones they do not take (*°the beautifuls, °she beautifuled*). But their association with nouns is what determines them as a class. While there are many ifs in these tests, the scheme interlocks so tightly that most classes can be identified in a variety of ways, which leaves no doubt that they exist in the language and in the minds of speakers. A further proof of their reality is the fact that languages have ways of converting words from one class to another: *danger,* noun; *dangerous,* adjective; *dangerously,* adverb; *to endanger,* verb. English does this recognizably though rather heterogeneously.

Nouns, verbs, and adjectives are three of the *parts of speech,* the traditional name for the major classes of function words and lexical words, which also include adverbs, pronouns, prepositions, interjections, and conjunctions. Three of the latter are comparatively clear-cut: pronouns (*he, she,* etc.), prepositions (*from, at, by,* etc.), and conjunctions (*and, or, but, if,* etc.) are closed sets. But the class of adverbs is a dumping ground. It includes words that modify only other modifiers, such as *very*

---

[5] Not a fully reliable test, in view of the "group possessive" in such expressions as *Mac here's wife don't like it.* (Example from Gordon T. Fish, personal communication.)

[6] Does the "verb" *to be* pass this last test? There is some question as to whether *be* should be called a verb, at least in some of its uses. It was included among the function words in Chapter 4.

(*very good, very quickly,* but not **He eats very*); words that modify
only verbs, such as *aside* (*They turned aside,* but not **an aside tasty
food*); words that modify only sentences, such as *necessarily* (*I don't
necessarily believe that,* 'It is not of necessity true that I believe that,'
but not **Behave necessarily!*); and words that combine two or more of
these functions, such as *happily (He worked happily, They are happily
married, Happily we had no more trouble).*

The traditional parts of speech are deficient not only in making the
adverb too inclusive, but in failing to recognize a number of other grammatical classes—some included within the traditional ones, others overlapping or intersecting them. Common nouns, for example, divide into
count (*jewel, leaf, flare-up*) and *mass* (*jewelry, foilage, anger*). We can
tell which class the noun belongs to by the way it combines with certain
grammatical morphemes. Mass nouns combine in the singular with *much,
enough,* and *some* (pronounced [sm]); count nouns combine with *many,*
the indefinite article (*a, an*), the cardinal numerals, and with *enough* and
some only in the plural. Examples: *enough foliage,* **enough leaf, enough
leaves;* **two foliages, two leaves.* The membership of the two classes is
not fixed. Mass nouns can be converted to count (usually in the sense
'kind of': *gasoline, various gasolines*) and count to mass (mostly as a
joke: *Get more car for your money!*). And there are many nouns that are
freely used either way: *There's a lot of caramel in this candy bar; Give
me a caramel.*

Mass and *count* do more than cut the noun class in half—they do the
same with verbs, in a very special way. Any verb can be either mass or
count according to its form. In *too much talking,* the verb is mass. In *He
talked for a moment* it is count, in the sense that there can be many such
moments of talking. Grammarians refer to this distinction in verbs as
aspect. If a noun or verb refers to one instance of something *(a flash, he
jumped),* the instances are countable; if not, the sense is mass *(light,
jumping).* (See page 198 for aspect in Black English.)

Verbs are also subclassified—into *transitive* and *intransitive.* A transitive verb "takes a direct object"; an intransitive verb does not require one.
Thus *John needs* is not a sentence, but *John needs sympathy* is. On the
other hand, **John knelt his body* is incorrect—*to kneel* is intransitive:
John knelt. As with mass-count, most verbs can be shifted either way:
I flew in a plane, I flew a kite. A broader way of viewing transitivity is in
terms of completeness. Does a verb in a given sense require a complement
—no matter whether direct, indirect, or prepositional? From this standpoint *to depend* in its usual sense is transitive because we have to add
on something. Similarly *to be fond: Jane is fond of him,* not just **Jane is
fond.* The incomplete **They told* can be completed with either a direct
object *(told the story)* or an indirect one *(told me). To be sure* is transitive just like *to know: I'm sure it's OK.*

Classes are basically semantic: nouns are thing-like, verbs are event-like, adjectives are quality-like. The tie that holds each major class together goes back to some unifying experience of our childhood, which the language dramatizes by making it in some way grammatically distinctive. The child's awareness of a common bond—says the psychologist with the longest record of looking at meaning—is derived "from actual behavior toward things signified."[7] Our earliest experiences are grouped around actions and things, and the corresponding classes of verbs and nouns are found in all the languages of the world. We get a sense of detachable qualities as soon as we can see differences playing on samenesses—at least as early as our games of marking and coloring. This is a physiological peg for adjectives. A class may rest on any pervasive sense experience. Some languages dramatize the child's experiences with things in space through sensations of size, shape, and quantity. In the Senufo languages of Africa, nouns designating large objects are formally distinct from nouns designating small ones.[8] In Tarascan, a Mexican language, things are stick-like, tortilla-like, and ball-like. The human body likewise provides some useful metaphors. Luo, a language of Africa, as well as Tarascan, has an affix signifying 'mouth-shaped.'[9]

Since meanings can cluster in infinite ways, it should not be surprising that many smaller groups of words embrace some common feature that reflects itself in a freedom, or lack of it, to combine with other items or classes. A great deal of the current work in syntax has to do with discovering and defining these lesser classes and their syntactic effects in hopes of finding which ones are widespread and perhaps universal.

One such class is that of sensory verbs. They are obviously related in meaning: *to see, to hear, to smell, to feel, to observe, to notice.* And they function alike, taking other verbs as complements without *to: I heard him shout, I saw her turn, I felt the table move.* This is not true, however, of the verbs *expect, want, ask, promise* and many others, which require the *to: I want you to wait, She promised to be ready.* Here is a grammatical class to which not all synonyms have yet been attracted: the less frequent a verb of perception is, the less likely it is to be used this way. We are unlikely to say *°I discerned him come* or *°I descried the light flash* (OK *flashing*), though *I perceived it happen* is marginally possible.

Finally there are what might be termed *empty classes,* with no specific words or morphemes as members but detectable, like an invisible star, by their gravitational effect on syntax. They may actually catch our attention by the fact that other languages do embody them directly in words or

---

[7] Osgood 1971, p. 18.

[8] Welmers 1950, p. 131.

[9] Friedrich 1972.

grammatical morphemes. An example is the paired opposites *essence* and *accident* that are overtly manifested in certain languages—for example, Spanish, Portuguese, and Gaelic. *Essence* refers to *what* something is, its inner nature; *accident* refers to the *way* something is, the superficial appearances or positions it assumes. In Spanish the function words **ser** and **estar** make the distinction systematically. One says **Es lista** 'She is ready' in the sense 'ready-witted'—she is clever by nature. But for 'She is ready' in the sense of 'all set' to do something, the expression is **Está lista. Es bonita** means 'She is pretty' in the sense that she is a pretty girl; **Está bonita** means 'She is pretty' in her new dress, with her new hairdo, etc.— that is, she *looks* pretty. English has only indirect manifestations of the contrast. We say *I thought her (to be) clever* but not *°I thought her (to be) ready.* We say *I thought her to be pretty—a really pretty girl,* but not *°I thought her to be pretty in her new dress. To think X (to be) Y* is an expression of essence. On the other hand, the use of *all* as an intensifier can only be in expressions of accident: *My hands are all dirty* but not *°That joke is all dirty.* A little soap and water will clean up the hands, but a dirty joke is dirty by nature.

Table 5–2 summarizes the main intersections between major and minor categories that have been discussed.

Classes and functions

A noun may be "used as" a subject, a predicate nominative, an indirect object, a direct object, or a prepositional object, and a few other things besides:

Mr. Whitmore is a **peach** because he gave **Sally** an **A** on the **exam.**

subject	predicate nominative		indirect object	direct object	prepositional object

The same class thus fulfills five functions, and other classes similarly may have more than one. A verb may function as subject, as in *To run would be cowardly.* Such is the confusion between classes and functions that we are prone to say of this last case that "the verb is used as a noun"—meaning that it shares certain of the functions that are typically fulfilled by nouns.[10] It is better to use the term *nominal* for 'used as a noun,' *adjectival* for 'used as an adjective,' and so on. Thus *to run* is a nominal, and so would be *to run fast* in *To run fast can be dangerous.* The noun **mud**

---

[10] Certain of the functions, not all of them. This particular verb form—the infinitive— cannot be an indirect object nor the object of a preposition.

TABLE 5–2
Major Categories and Their Intersections with Some Minor Ones

Major Category	Example	Characteristic Associated Elements	Example of Shared Form	Mass and Count Categories (respectively)	Transitive and Intransitive Categories (respectively)
NOUN	teacher	teacher's the teacher	danger	more danger °more teacher	°He is an inhabitant He is a native.
VERB	to study	studied did study	to endanger	jumping he jumped	°They revealed. They lied.
ADJECTIVE	pretty	prettier	dangerous	much sugar °numerous sugar °much dog numerous dogs	°She is fond. She is nice.
ADVERB	now intentionally	to work now to act intentionally	dangerously		°He works very. He works hard.

is adjectival in **mud fence,** as is the prepositional phrase in **the woman in the green dress** and the **who** clause in the phrase **the woman who is wearing the green dress.** Much of the power of language comes from our ability to bring constructions down to the level of individual words. A whole sentence, with a full array of internal functions of its own, may serve a single function in a larger sentence. The process is called *embedding* and the productivity it yields is called *recursiveness* or *recursive power.* In **I know you don't intend to use that advantage,** everything from **you** on is an embedded nominal, the object of **know.**

Some examples of nominals:

Noun phrase: **Your early arrival** would be no surprise to me.

Infinitive phrase: **For you to arrive early** would be no surprise to me.

-ing phrase: **Your arriving early** would be no surprise to me.

Clause: **That you should arrive early** would be no surprise to me.

—and of adjectivals:

Adjective: The only river **navigable** is to the north.

Infinitive phrase: The only river **to be trusted for navigation** is to the north.

-ing phrase: The only river **permitting navigation** is to the north.

Prepositional phrase: The only river **for navigating** is to the north.

Clause: The only river **that is navigable** is to the north.

—and of successive embeddings:

I went {yesterday}

I went {after [somebody] telephoned me}

I went {after [somebody (special)] telephoned me}

I went {after [somebody (that I really wanted to see)] telephoned me}

I went {after [somebody (that I really wanted to see/right then/)] telephoned me}

I went {after [somebody (that I really wanted to see/as soon as I could/)] telephoned me}

Grammatical and psychological functions

Subjects, objects, modifiers, and the like are not always meaningful functions; sometimes they are no more than grammatical habits. In the sentence **It's raining,** the word *it* is the grammatical subject, but to claim that *is raining* "tells what 'it' is doing" is true only in a vague sense. English requires that a sentence have a subject even when there is no subject to talk about. And it is just as apt to announce a subject and then talk about something else: here we see the difference between grammatical functions and psychological ones. Separate terms are needed, and at least two are in fairly common use to refer to psychological functions: *topic* (sometimes called *psychological subject*) and *comment.* The topic is what is talked about, the comment is what is said about the topic. In **Jane is admired by all of us** and **Jane we all admire,** a comment is made about the topic **Jane,** even though **Jane** is subject in the first and object in the second. While the grammatical subject of a sentence is usually also the topic, the roles often change. In answer to **What color is your house?** one may say **My house is red,** where the subject, **my house,** is also the topic, and the predicate, **is red,** is also the comment. But one may also answer with **I live in a réd house,** where **I** is subject but not topic. The topic is **I live in a . . . house** (which means the same as **my house** for the purpose of answering that question) and the comment is *red*. There is a tendency to put topics first in a sentence, with the result that when something other than the subject becomes the topic, it is often fronted: ***Every cent she had her husband squandered.*** But the opposite may happen too: ***Réd is the color of my house***, with everything deemphasized except *red*. (The comment normally carries the main sentence accent.)

Classes as features

There is another way of viewing classes besides the one adopted in this chapter. Instead of saying that the class of Canadians includes Marie Robichaud plus other individuals, and the class of Catholics includes her and others, and so on, we start with her and say that she *is* Canadian and Catholic. The classes she belongs to become a way of describing her, using the "features" [+Human −Male +Adult +Canadian +Catholic] and so on. The minus sign is a way of economizing on the total number of terms where two classes complement each other. Since "human" divides into "male" and "female," we may use only one term with a + or a − sign. Somewhat chauvinistically, " − Male is used for "Female," although "Male" could as logically be noted as " − Female."

So with language. The noun *furniture* is a mass noun: this means, if we take count nouns as basic, that it is [−Count]. It is also [−Animate], since it refers to a thing rather than a living creature. Dictionaries use these labels up to a point, but only for the most obvious class memberships: *furniture* is [+Noun]. (No minus sign will serve here because there are more than two parts of speech.) The noun *cloth* is [±Count], for we can say either ***She wrapped it in a cloth*** (count) or ***She wrapped it in cloth*** (mass). The verb *to damage* is [+Verb +Transitive +Intensifiable −Animate], the last feature referring to the kind of object it can take: we do not say *The accident damaged John*—rather, ***The accident injured John.***

SENTENCES

The fundamental unit of syntax is the sentence, which is as hard to define as the word. Yet we feel as secure in talking about sentences as in talking about words, so they must be psychologically real and not just a linguistic construct. The traditional definition is that the sentence is the minimum part of language that expresses a complete thought, and certainly some sense of completeness is essential to it. Just as the divisions between words are "insertion points," so the divisions between sentences are "stop points." The stops may be skipped three-fourths of the time (though seldom in the didactic speech of elders to very young children), yet they occur often enough for us to build up a repertory of types of constructions and varieties of intonation that come to be recognized as complete units. The linguist accepts as "sentences" the ones that he can use to the best advantage to predict others. For example, if someone asks *Like a slice?* and receives the reply *Yes, I would,* conversationally both the question and the answer are sentences, but together they suggest that underlying them are the complete versions *Would you like a slice?* and *Yes, I would like a slice.* Only the complete versions are suitable for describing syntactic relations. The abbreviated sentences are not ignored, but are described as "transformations" of the full forms.

There are many ways of classifying sentences. One is according to their social purpose: questions, answers, comments, commands, presentations, and the like. Grammatical functions probably started as social functions thousands of years ago. The same terms are often used for both. There are conversational, or real, questions, which are used only when the speaker seeks an answer, and grammatical questions, which have a certain form in English (inversion of the subject and auxiliary verb: *Can you wait?* rather than *You can wait*) and are most frequently used to ask real questions but often have other purposes (*Do you think I'm an idiot?* does not expect an answer). As societies grew more complex, the simpler social functions became diversified and the old forms had to be adapted to new purposes. So we have questions that do not really ask, statements that do not really assert, imperatives that do not really command. For syntax, it is the grammatical functions that count.

Following are the major sentence types in English that do not have the added complexity of embeddings or other transformations:

1. *Mother fell.* (Nominal plus intransitive verbal.)

2. *Mother is young.* (Nominal plus copula plus complement.)

3. *Mother loves Dad.* (Nominal plus transitive verbal plus nominal.)

4. *Mother gave Dad breakfast.* (Nominal plus ditransitive verbal plus nominal plus nominal.)

5. *There is time.* (*There* plus existential plus nominal.)

The verb *to be* is a chameleon. The "complement" in the second sentence may be an adjective, a noun (*Mother is boss*), or an adverb (*here, early*). All that *is* does is to associate the complement with the subject. Many languages express no verb here at all, and English often omits it too: *A nice fellow, George = George is a nice fellow.* In sentence 5, *is* expresses something akin to existence and could, in fact, be replaced with *exists.* The term *ditransitive* in 4 refers to a subclass of verbs that may take two objects, one direct and one indirect.

These simple sentences can be expanded without enlarging their basic structure. In 1, we could have *the woman* or *all ten trees,* which qualify as nominals as much as *mother* does; in place of merely *fell* we could have *fell down* or *fell down abruptly.* In 2, *young* could be replaced by *like her father.* In 4, *gave* could be replaced with *taught* and *breakfast* with *a lesson.* In 5, *is* could be replaced with *might be* and *time* with *some other reason.* Substitutions of this kind are minor structures which are parts of sentences and cannot be defined as disguised sentences that have worked their way into the larger structure. The distinction can be seen by comparing *the wood* and *heavy wood.* Both *the* and *heavy* are traditionally called adjectives, since they seem to be attached in the same way to nouns. But there is an important difference. *Heavy wood* can be paraphrased as *wood that is heavy* but *the wood* cannot be paraphrased as **wood that is the.* Since *that is heavy* contains all the elements of a sentence (*that,* subject; *is,* copula; *heavy,* complement), *heavy wood* can be viewed as a transformational reduction: *wood (the wood is heavy)* ⟶ *heavy wood.* The accepted practice among most American grammarians has accordingly been to view *the wood* as a "phrase structure" in its own right but *heavy wood* as something else. Such phrase structures include, besides all the simple sentences, the nominals that are made up of a noun with its determiners *(all the other people, half an apple, the same guy, my two friends, that first time),* the verb and its auxiliaries *(might leave, would have taken, had to be studying),* the verb and its complements *(give John the letter, tell a story to them, go to Westlake),* and various lesser structures such as an adjective or an adverb with an intensifier *(very hot, too near)* and a determiner with an intensifier *(almost all, fully six hundred).*

Transformations

The simple sentences listed in the last section by no means cover the variety that one finds in English or in any other language (whose simple sentences may or may not be like those of English). Here are some other kinds of sentences:

1a. *Came the dawn.*

2a. I told him to be ready and *ready he was.*

3a. *Him I dislike.*

4a. **Them I gave nothing.**

5a. If there is to be war, **war there must be.**

Comparing these with the five simple sentences on page 91 we see that each clause in heavy type represents simply an inversion. **Came the dawn** is the same as **The dawn came** (the same structure as **Mother fell**) except for the shift of **came** to front position; the same happens in 5a, with **there must be war** changed to **war there must be.** This illustrates the most rudimentary kind of transformation, the one that merely moves words around. Besides this re-ordering, transformations can be used to relate sentences through *replacement, deletion,* and *addition.* Examples of replacement:

1b. "Did the dawn come?"—Yes, *it* did."

2b. If I have to be a failure I'll be *one* in my own way.

3b. "Does Miss Hedda Hopper play Miss Hedda Hopper in the film?"—"Yes, Miss Hedda Hopper plays *herself.*"

4b. "Did Mother give Dad oatmeal?"—"No, *she* gave *him that* yesterday."

5b. "Will there be time tomorrow?"—"Yes, there will be time *then.*"

6b. I don't think the Rams can win this game; for them to *do so,* they'll have to score twice in thirty seconds.

Replacement is a way of avoiding repetition and cutting down on excessive bulk. A short "pro" word such as a pronoun or a pro-adverb (*it* for *dawn* in 1b, *then* for *tomorrow* in 5b) takes the place of a longer segment. In 2b, the indefinite pronoun *one* replaces the indefinite *a failure.* In 3b, the reflexive pronoun *herself* avoids repeating the same nominal. In 4b, the demonstrative ("pointing") pronoun *that* replaces *oatmeal,* and in 6b, *do so* replaces the whole predicate.

Deletion may affect anything from a single word up to a full sentence. If the statement **She graduated with highest honors** is responded to with **Yes, I know,** an entire sentence, which otherwise would be embedded after *know,* has been deleted. Obviously this can occur only in an environment where the hearer can tell immediately what has been left out. Other examples:

1. "Why did you do it?"—"Because I wanted to *(do it).*"

2. "I hope he'll be there!"—"I'm sure he will *(be there).*"

3. They got sore at me, but I don't know why *(they got sore at me)*.

4. "He's heading off tomorrow."—"Oh? Where *(is he heading off)?*"

5. I thought she would be at home, and she was *(at home)*.

These show the commonest deletions: after the *to* of the infinitive, after auxiliary verbs (*will, may, can,* and so forth), after interrogatives (*why, where, who, when,* and so forth), and after *to be.* Imperatives usually delete their subjects: *(You) stand here.* Almost equally common is the deletion of both subject and auxiliary verb at the beginning of a question. This is especially frequent when the subject—just as in the imperative—is *you: (Do you) want a bite?* Deletion is also frequent when two sentences are conjoined: *June wanted to leave last night but (June) couldn't (leave last night).* In this example one can also think of *but couldn't* as a reduction from a replacement, *but she couldn't.*

Addition usually comes about when sentences grow so complex that function words have to be inserted to keep the relationships clear. The passive sentence *This truck is powered by a diesel engine* contains a form of the verb *to be* and a preposition *by* which do not appear in the active *A diesel engine powers this truck.* Most embeddings involve an addition of some sort—for example, the addition of *that* when one sentence is put in apposition to a noun in another sentence: *I heard the report + The market had advanced ⟶ I heard the report that the market had advanced.* The same happens when direct discourse is changed to indirect: *John explained, "Those measures were necessary"* becomes *John explained that those measures were necessary.* If the quotation is a command, *to* is added; if a yes–no question, *if* or *whether: John said, "Leave right now" ⟶ John said to leave right now; Jennifer asked, "Were they gone?" ⟶ Jennifer asked if (whether) they were gone.*

The grammatical morphemes that are added in this way have sometimes been called "transformationally introduced particles," suggesting that they add nothing to the meaning. In fact, the main reason for using the term *transformation* is that the sentences seemed to be paraphrases of each other, just different ways of saying the same thing. But their sameness is generally not identity in the fullest sense but just a mutual truth value. *Came the dawn* and *The dawn came* are logical equivalents —if one is true the other has to be true, and if one is false so is the other. But language is more than logic and meaning is more than truth, and to exclude other values is to insist that language is nothing but a transmission belt for factual knowledge. The sentence *Came the dawn,* with its initial verb and its postposed subject, is intended to set a scene and *present* something on it. The word order signals that presentational intent, which is absent in **The dawn came** but is found in other sentences using the same device of order: **Up stood the witness, There rang out a strange sound.** Predictably, **Came the dawn** and **Up stood the witness** have verbs that are suitable for bringing-onto-the-scene. Other verbs are not acceptable in this construction: ***Up gave the enemy,** ***There will help another attempt.** With careful probing, other similarly elusive meanings can probably be found in every transformational change.

Transformations then are a way of *relating* structures that have features in common. If they share all but one, the transformation helps to focus on that one. We are then in a better position to hypothesize a meaning for it.

Deep structure

Possible answers to **Will you go?** include *I will not go, I won't go, I will not,* and *I won't.* They are all appropriate under the circumstances, they share the same elements, and they have the same truth value. Accordingly they are good candidates for derivation from the same source. But what source? *I will not go* gives everything that is needed to derive the three others, but then we find that a mere *No* is just as good an answer and has no obvious representation in *I will not go.* Still another kind of answer that it would be nice to account for is **Not this time.**

The appropriateness of a simple *No* suggests that the meaning of negation is somehow logically outside the rest of the sentence—that the two main constituents are *no* and *I will go,* where *no* denies everything else. The fact that it is physically *inside* the sentence *I will not go* thus appears to be the result of some transformation. If so, none of the four sentences can be regarded as basic. The underlying sentence from which all are derived must be represented by a more abstract form, that is, by the *deep structure* of those sentences. (This can be thought of as the syntactic analog of the underlying forms discussed in Chapter 3.) In transformational grammar, every sentence has an underlying deep structure that is acted upon by transformations to produce a *surface structure,* which is the syntactic form of what is actually said. *No* is a surface structure from which a transformation has deleted everything except 'negation.' *I won't* is a surface structure in which the negation has been moved in and attached to the auxiliary, and *go* has been deleted.

The completeness of a surface structure such as *I will not go* often makes it look as if it ought to be the transformational source of the others. But if deep structures are necessary for some cases they are best assumed for all. A seemingly more basic surface sentence *(The dawn came)* has merely been acted on by fewer transformations than its counterpart *(Came the dawn).*

A deep structure can be shown with a tree diagram. A crude representation of our negative answers would be

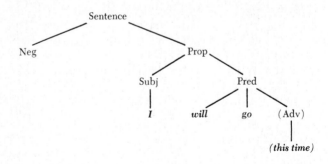

Prop is the proposition: what it is that the sentence negates. Providing the slot Adv—in parentheses to show that it is optional—makes it possible to derive *Not this time, Not yet,* and other such answers from the same deep structure.

We have already seen some of the transformations that are needed to produce the example sentences from this one deep structure. Most of them require that *not* be moved in next to the auxiliary, and two require an additional morphological transformation that reduces *not* to *-n't.* But what about Neg? This is an abstract element that is "realized" as *no* when everything else is deleted, but as *not* otherwise. The generating of either *no* or *not* under Neg must then be "sensitive" to the other transformations; otherwise we might get **I no go* or simply **Not,* and would be unable to generate *never* from *not ever.* Not only must Neg be sensitive to the other transformations; they in turn must be sensitive to Neg. Suppose instead of *Will you go?* our original question had been *Did you go?* The answers would have had *did* for every instance of *will,* but the plain *No* answer seems to be a denial of *I went,* where no *did* appears. But since with plain *No* everything else is deleted anyway, we can assume that whenever Neg appears, a form of *do* will automatically appear with any verb that does not already have some other auxiliary. The verb form is thus sensitive to the presence of Neg. We see this whenever someone denies a proposition: "You say he *went.* I say he *didn't go.*"

An analysis proves its value if it helps to solve other puzzles besides the one for which it was designed. Consider the following examples:

How I did yearn for them!

I do so want you to be happy!

"Do you deny that you were there?"—"I do indeed deny that I was there."

"I wish he had been more considerate."—"He did apologize, you know."

Here we have forms of *do* again, and now they are keyed to affirmation. There are of course various ways of showing affirmation—a nod of the head, an assertion with emphatic intonation, as in "Why didn't you go?" —"*I went,* you idiot!" But when affirmation (or negation) is made *verbally* explicit, the effect is to introduce a form of *do* if no other auxiliary is already present. And since questions of the **Did you go?** type also call for an explicit **Yes** or **No,** they too introduce a *do.* So our diagram can be revised slightly:

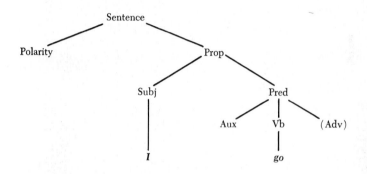

Polarity is realized as Neg, Aff (affirmative), or Q (question), and Q may be combined with Neg or with Aff:

$$\text{Polarity} \longrightarrow \quad (Q) \quad \left(\left\{ \begin{array}{c} \text{Neg} \\ \text{Aff} \end{array} \right\} \right)$$

Comment: Choose at least one.

The parentheses indicate an optional choice, "either Q or Neg-Aff or both"; the braces indicate a forced choice, "Neg or Aff but not both." From this deep structure we can derive *I did go* (with Aff), *I didn't go* (with Neg), **Did I go?** (with Aff + Q), and **Didn't I go?** (with Neg + Q), and of course the other possibilities by deleting one or more elements. The form *I went* would not have this deep structure; it fails to make Polarity explicit. As already mentioned, the effect of Polarity if there is nothing already under Aux is to put a *do* there. But suppose the auxiliary *can* is already there. Then the effect with either Aff or Neg is to produce the full form of *can* rather than the reduced form *c'n.* Thus *I can* /kæn/ *go* is explicitly affirmative, *I can* /kən/ *go* is merely affirmative, with no focusing or emphasis on affirmation. A good deal more would have to be added to develop all the implications, but the main advantage is apparent: this kind of representation enables us to bring together all the types involving explicit affirmation and explicit negation, which obviously belong together because of certain equal effects that they have.

In the example with Polarity we traced a number of surface structures back to a single deep structure. The same technique can be used to illuminate a relationship in which a single surface sentence corresponds to two or more deep structures. When this happens we call the surface sentence "structurally ambiguous" (not quite the same as "ambiguous" applied to two different homonyms, like *sale–sail, beer–bier*). The sentence *I cooked the meat dry* may mean that I used a dry-cooking process, adding no liquid ('I cooked the meat when the meat was dry'), or it may mean that I cooked the meat till it was dry. (Our being able to paraphrase in this way when ambiguity causes trouble proves our awareness of the underlying difference.) The deep structures are not the same, as can be seen in the following:

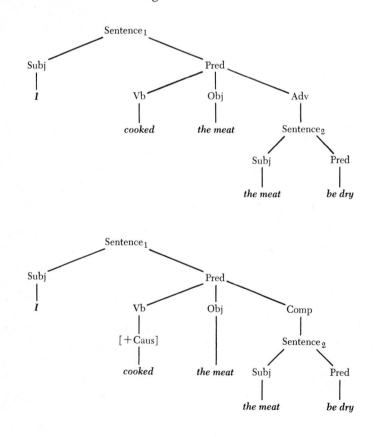

For the meaning 'cooked till it was dry' the deep structure adds a feature to the verb, [+Caus] or causative: the cooking caused the meat to be dry. The causing has *be dry* as its complement (Comp). This feature is needed for a variety of verbs, some of which are always causative in particular senses: *to convert, to make, to turn.* It is even combined with the resultant condition in one group of verbs, which typically has the causative suffix *-en: to whiten, to lighten, to soften, to madden, to sicken, to sharpen.* Noting this and other similar phenomena, one group of linguists has undertaken to fit the meanings of individual words into the same structural scheme used for phrases and sentences. Thus the deep structure of *John sharpened the knife* would be something like

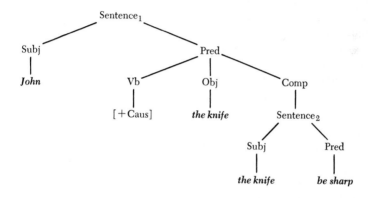

If we were to put the verb *to whet* under [+Caus], the result would be *John whetted the knife sharp.* (A transformation erases Sentence₂ and "moves up" the constituents *knife* and *sharp* into the higher sentence; the second *knife* is then deleted by another transformation.) But with no verb specified under [+Caus], the causative suffix *-en* is generated and attached by a transformation to *sharp,* which has already been moved up by another transformation. The correctness of using the same deep structure for both *John sharpened the knife* and *John whetted the knife sharp* can be seen in another transformation that often takes place when the objects of verbs are extremely long. Instead of *John whetted every knife that he could lay his hands on sharp* we may say *John whetted sharp every knife that he could lay his hands on.* We could almost hyphenate the verb and the adjective: *Whetted-sharp. Sharp* belongs to the verb as much as to the noun: *whet-sharp = sharp-en by whetting.*

 Thus a number of things dovetail when a model of this kind is used, which confirms its correctness: (1) causatives are needed elsewhere as much as they are needed here; (2) apparently different but actually synonymous sentences are reconciled; (3) a peculiarity of sentence order is shown to result from the same kind of re-ordering transformation that creates a single word form. Deep-structure analysis does not answer all the questions of syntax, but it does well enough with some of the most important ones.

These examples also show how the richest syntactic resource of a language is built into its structure: the recursive adding of sentences to sentences. The Comp(lement) is itself a sentence. The knife *was* sharp, the meat *was* dry, at the end of the process.

Hidden sentences, higher and lower

Contained sentences may lose more than most of their bulk. Some virtually lose their identity, and only with the opening of the door to deep structure, which seems to lead to more and more subterranean galleries waiting to be explored, are some of these mummified remains coming to light. Take the so-called *performatives*, as in the sentence *I tell you he did say it! Tell* here is a performative verb because the saying of it performs the act that it refers to: if I say *I tell you* then I'm telling you, not like saying *I smoke cigars*, where the saying is not the same as the smoking. The expression *hereby* often marks a performative verb: *I hereby pronounce you man and wife.* The performatives of most interest to linguists are the ones that use expressions of saying: *declare, ask, command,* and their synonyms. When instead of speaking performatively we *report* someone else's assertion, request, or order it is necessary to use one of these expressions explicitly: *He declared (said, asserted, remarked, observed, told me, announced, claimed) that he didn't care how the election turned out.* So it is fair to ask whether the same expressions are present in direct discourse. When I say *I don't care how the election turns out,* perhaps I am really saying *I declare that I don't care how the election turns out.*

It has been argued that this is indeed the case,[11] and certain remains of performatives in larger sentences seem to confirm it. *John incidentally was one of those rejected* does not mean that John's rejection was incidental but that the speaker is making an incidental remark: *I incidentally tell you that John was one of those rejected.* Other adverbs that are often used this way are *frankly, definitely, positively, truthfully, emphatically, honestly.* They are among the ones often called *sentence adverbs,* which modify whole sentences and not smaller parts. (For another kind of sentence adverb, compare *The play ended happily* and *The play ended, happily;* the first *happily* is a descriptive adverb, and the second is a

---

[11] See Ross 1970.

sentence adverb meaning 'it is a happy fact that.') They are *outside* the sentence proper, and so can be analyzed as higher sentences, sentences which have others subordinate to them. The deep structure of *It honestly didn't work* would then be:

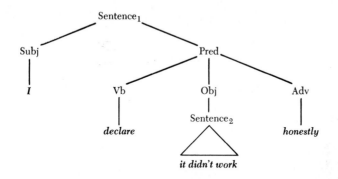

Lower sentences too get lost in the shuffle. This is especially true of *existence predicates.* Speakers often bring something in by merely assuming that it is there, without according it a proper introduction. In the sentence *Snow is possible tonight* we have an adjective, *possible,* apparently describing *snow.* The forecaster can even say *Possible snow tonight,* putting the adjective directly in front of the noun. But while a suitable description for *snow* may be *white, crystalline,* or *stark and beautiful, possible* hardly qualifies. So the sentence must be represented in deep structure by something like *(That there be snow tonight) is possible.* Similarly in *The blighting is caused by insufficient water* we seem to be saying, rather incoherently, that some kind of water is causing the blight. What we intend of course is *The blighting is caused by (there is insufficient water).* There are many such *there be*'s lying around, and no doubt countless other syntactic orphans, if we could recognize them.

SYNTAX BEYOND THE SENTENCE

Sentences containing reduced higher sentences are already one step beyond the tightest definition of a single sentence, because they shade off into explicit combinations of sentences tied together by conjunctions, plus their verbal and nonverbal indicators of intent. Also, much of what is found in such complex sentences can be found in combinations of simple ones, where relationships are not specified by grammatical operators but left to be inferred. The relationship between these separate sentences is called *paratactic*—a "side-by-side" *(para-)* arrangement rather than a "with" *(syn-)* arrangement. Instead of *It's raining, so I'm coming in,* one can say *It's raining. I'm coming in.* The specific function word *so,* show-ing 'consequence,' is omitted. In *I wanted to help him. Unfortunately it was too late.* There is an "adversative" relationship which can be ex-pressed by joining the two sentences with *but: I wanted to help him, but unfortunately it was too late.* The three sentences *He came in. He looked around. He sat down.* imply a coordination that can be made explicit, in a single sentence, with *and: He came in, (and) (he) looked around, and (he) sat down.*

Paratactic relationships are not the only ones that tie sentences together. Another is *coreference*—an element in one sentence refers to an element in another. Pronouns are the most familiar examples:

"Why don't you use your credit card?"—"I don't have *one.*"

He couldn't open the door. *It* was locked tight.

They didn't just fine him. *That* would have been too easy.

There are other pro-words too:

"Weren't they the right size?"—"I thought *so,* but they turned out to be too big."

"Are you going back to Gray's Lake?"—"I hate *the place.*"

"Shall we invite Swerdloff?"—"I can't stand *the man.*"

And since deletions are done usually "under identity," omitting some-thing from a construction is generally a guarantee that the missing ele-ment is somewhere in the context. So, for comparatives:

"Did she get there at six?"—"No, (she got there) earlier (than six)."

"Why don't you take this one?"—"It isn't as nice (as that one [re-ferred to still earlier])."

Other deletions:

"He's tall."—"(He's tall) And handsome."

"I don't want to take that stuff."—"You don't have to (take that stuff)."

This is evidence for intersentence links. It is also evidence for a type of organization that might be called conversational ping-pong. Most spoken language consists of *dialog,* that may take the form of simple pairs where an answer closes off a question but just as often stretches out in chains of responses and responses to responses. Generally no one speaker holds the floor long enough for there to be any hint of a still higher level of organization, of something more than a succession of gives and takes.

But an eloquent speaker does sometimes launch into a monolog—more often in a story-telling culture than in a TV-watching one—and writers do compose paragraphs which are sometimes read aloud. Are there markers of *closure* for paragraphs, similar to the ones we found for sentences—pause, intonation, and typical structures?

Unquestionably, paragraphs are marked by pause and intonation, just as sentences are (see page 30). A statement normally has a terminal fall; this is "finality" in both a logical and an affective sense: the speaker has "finished" that much of his subject and stops momentarily for breath. Each connected sentence tends to drop a little lower, and the lowest pitch of all is attained at the end of the series. Occasionally a word such as *finally* will identify the last sentence.

But our awareness of paragraphs in English is due more to their semantic content than to any formal indicators. The most readable prose is the kind that provides for some kind of logical transition at the beginning. The commonest device is the topic sentence. There are hackneyed ways of introducing it—*Next I want to speak of . . . ; We turn now to . . . ; Leaving that for the moment, what can we say of . . .* —but as a rule, nothing in syntax to label either the beginning or the end.

Not all languages leave paragraph divisions so much to chance. In Yagua, a language of Peru, narrative paragraphs tend to begin with a statement of action that carries a particular emphatic suffix.[12] An even tighter scheme is found in certain "chaining" languages of New Guinea— for example Fore, which has distinctive suffixes for "final verbs" and "medial verbs," the former occurring at the end of a unit which, for length and content, is best regarded as a paragraph.[13]

As for still more inclusive units of organization—entire themes or discourses or stories—it is doubtful that any grammatical signs of closure can be found.[14] Such units are at the highest level of awareness and are most apt to be announced and concluded with verbal formulas: *. . . and now my story's begun; . . . and now my story's done.* But whole texts do have their system, and the system is being investigated. We must have light on it to understand the relationship between linguistics and literature.[15]

---

[12] Powlinson 1965, p. 109.

[13] Longacre 1970.

[14] Except perhaps in the tightly knit poem. See Smith 1968 for identification of poetic closure.

[15] See van Dijk 1972 and Pavel 1973.

Key terms and concepts

syntactical devices
  inflectional system
  phrasal system
  compositional system
syntax ("togetherness")
operator
constituent
  ultimate
  immediate
word classes
  open (lexical words)
  closed (function words)
word function
part of speech
noun
  mass vs. count
  animate vs. inanimate
verb
  transitive vs. intransitive
subject and predicate
  topic (psychological subject)
    and comment
nominal

adjectival
embedding
feature
sentence
transformation
  reordering
  replacement
  deletion
  addition
pro-word
surface structure
deep structure
structural ambiguity
performative
closure

Additional remarks and applications

1. Deduce as much as you can about the words and structure of the following nonsense:

> Degressably, the slem that Quisian had arvingly craduced thrammed a ranglin through both markles of wismy cluff so hort that umbody flasped. Thereupon, the dramp nording the wendorous plorin stambored its tilfored cormel aside hypaxically till all the bohams could prentiously desorm.

If you had to decide between calling it English and calling it a foreign language, which would you choose? Why?

2. The radio comedian Fibber McGee once said *to waste a guy like me's time,*[16] fumbling over the phrase intentionally. What was the point of

---

[16] "Fibber McGee and Molly," 2 March 1948.

the joke? Express this as a restriction on the formation of the possessive, which also excludes *all of them's money, *both of us's friends. Could the latter be expressed as *both of our friends?* What do you make of the following, from a literary magazine?—*They* [two veteran Hollywood chaps] *are William Demarest and Raymond Walburn, both of whose talents have long been recognized.*[17]

3. Classify the following as mass or count: *evidence, clue; quarrel, strife; client, clientele; vocabulary, verbiage; ectoplasm, ghost.*

4. *Abstract* and *concrete* are sometimes recognized as two opposing classes, like mass and count. Study the following, decide which sentences are acceptable to you, and see if the abstract-concrete distinction has anything to do with it. (Imagine the sentences as answers to some such question as *Why didn't you do so-and-so?* or *Are you going to do so-and-so?*)

   a. I didn't have the money to.
   b. I didn't have the dollars to.
   c. I didn't have the mental equipment to.
   d. I didn't have the electrical equipment to.
   e. I don't have the willpower to.
   f. I don't have the horsepower to.
   g. I don't have the power to.
   h. I don't have the gasoline to.
   i. I don't have the right preparation to.
   j. I don't have the right tools to.

   Think up other examples.

5. Even though you understand the sentence *He threw me a cheerful greet as I came in,* what is nevertheless wrong with it? State your answer in terms of word classes. Do the same with *How many centuries ancient is it?* (Suggestion: Consider a class of words including *old, heavy, deep, long, wide,* and so forth, which have a property that is lacking in *ancient, weighty, profound, lengthy, spacious,* and so on. Do the antonyms *young, light, shallow, short,* and *narrow* have this same property? Can you say *How many feet narrow is it?*)

---

[17] *Saturday Review of Literature* (30 June 1951), p. 22.

6. What is there about the interpersonal situation in which sentences such as *Want a bite?* and *Sit down!* are used that makes it easy to omit *you?* Can you think of similar situations where *I* is left out? Relate your observations to the general concept of *redundancy* (the amount of explicitness needed to avoid ambiguity).

7. Compare the following sentences:

> If it's going to rain, I wish it would rain.
> If it's going to rain, I wish it would.

In the second, *rain* is transformationally deleted because it is the same as the preceding *rain* ("deletion under identity"). Do the two sentences mean the same? See if the following implications are equally applicable to both sentences:

> desire for the rain
> impatience at the rain's inability to make up its mind

In the following two sentences, decide whether the implications of (a) acceptance or determination and (b) resignation are equally applicable to both:

> If I have to drive it in, I'll drive it in.
> If I have to drive it in, I will.

Does it appear that even with as simple a transformation as deletion we cannot be sure that there will not be some change in meaning?

8. Some transformations are held to be obligatory. An example is the reflexive transformation, whereby a deep structure such as *Beatrice loves Beatrice* has to be transformed to *Beatrice loves herself.* Following are three violations of that rule. See what if anything justifies them, and consider whether they suggest a need to keep meaning in mind at all times:

> a. *We* call upon *us* all to act without violence.[18]
> b. I don't see how *you* can resist *you.* (Wife to hero in a movie, who has just spilled perfume on his clothes.)[19]
> c. (An item from the Boston *Globe*):[20]

"Rusty, if you were sitting at your trial, would *you* find *yourself* guilty?" Bailey recalled asking Calley as he spoke last night before several hundred

---

[18] War Resisters League circular, March 1970.
[19] *Rally Round the Flag, Boys,* 1959.
[20] 4 October 1971, p. 10.

Yale University students. Calley, whom Bailey described as "a pretty honest fellow," replied, "*I* would find *me* guilty of manslaughter," Bailey said.

9. Given a question–answer pair such as *"Why do you insist he did it?"* —*"Because I'm stubborn,"* decide whether something is wrong with this one: *"Why do you suppose he came?"*—*"Because I'm well-informed."*

10. What has happened in the following, and what does it illustrate about a transformational relationship between statements and questions?

> "Did they suffer?"—"Terribly."
> "Did it work?"—"Perfectly."
> "Is he tall?"—"Incredibly."

11. Discuss sentence a, after comparing it with b and c:

> a. I never thought that it made any difference.
> b. I thought that it never made any difference.
> c. I didn't think that it ever made any difference.

12. How is it possible to answer the question *Are you sure you wouldn't like to see that program?* with either *Yes* or *No* (in both cases with a "firm" falling intonation) and mean the same thing?

For further reading

Givón, Talmy. 1979. *Understanding Grammar* (New York: Academic Press).

Herndon, Jeanne H. *A Survey of Modern Grammars,* 2nd ed. (New York: Holt, Rinehart & Winston).

Jacobs, Roderick A., and Peter S. Rosenbaum, (eds.). 1968. *Readings in English Transformational Grammar* (Waltham, Mass.: Blaisdell).

Lyons, John. 1969. *Introduction to Theoretical Linguistics* (Cambridge, England: Cambridge University Press).

———. 1978. *Noam Chomsky,* rev. ed. (Harmondsworth, England: Penguin Books).

Palmer, Frank. 1971. *Grammar* (Harmondsworth, England: Penguin Books).

Thomas, Owen, and Eugene R. Kintgen. 1974. *Transformational Grammar and the Teacher of English, Theory and Practice,* 2nd ed. (New York: Holt, Rinehart & Winston).

Weaver, Constance. 1979. *Grammar for Teachers* (Urbana: National Council of Teachers of English).

MEANING 6

At what point does language break free from its own system? Distinctive features make phonemes, phonemes make morphemes, morphemes words, words sentences, sentences discourses, discourses monologs or dialogs or stories, and these may develop into novels, trilogies, encyclopedias. Looking up and down the stairway it seems as if there is no escape. Yet at some point—and not necessarily from the last and highest step of its tower—language must make contact with the outside world. This contact is what we call *meaning*.

The term *meaning* is used in many ways, not all of them equally relevant to language. Saying *I didn't mean to hurt him* or exclaiming indignantly *What is the meaning of this!* refers to an intention. *Another child means an extra mouth to feed* or *Smoke means fire* signifies an inference. *The German hund means 'dog'* is a translation. And so on. The meaning of "meaning" that, while not itself linguistic, is closest to language is that of flashing a red light to get someone to stop. It is not quite the same as *Smoke means fire.* We do not make smoke in order to mean fire. Traffic lights, like words, are part of a communicative system with arbitrary values. We infer the meanings because we put them there ourselves. It is the same with language: *A red light means 'Stop'* and *X linguistic form has 'Y' meaning* are equivalent statements—they express the value of the code, the price tag or label that we have attached.

Traffic signals are to linguistic signs what counting on two fingers is to calculating with a computer. Traffic signals are ordinarily one for one: red for stop, yellow for caution, green for go. Only rarely do two or more together have a special meaning, as in Massachusetts, where red plus yellow means 'walk.' But this is the usual thing with language: linguistic signs are built of units that are built of units of lower rank. Not all levels are penetrated equally by meaning.

It is pointless to look for meaning in distinctive features, phonemes, and syllables, for these are members of the phonological hierarchy and are meaningless by definition (pages 10, 18, 30, 38), though we did observe a curious relationship between vowels and the notion of size (Chapter 1, pages 10, 11). With morphemes we begin to find units to which meanings are attached, and this carries on through words and sentences. So the question comes down to which of these levels—from morpheme upward—is the real tie with the outside world.

The answer must depend on how we picture the outside world. If we see it as a kind of idealized collection of entities that keep their shapes no matter what kaleidoscopic patterns they take whenever they are shaken up, our choice will fall on morphemes or words. If we see it as the patterns themselves, it will fall on sentences. This is because a sentence—a particular sentence, not a sentence type—does not mean in the same way that a word means. The meaning of a sentence is something in the outside world at a given time and in relationship to given persons, qualities, and objects. The meaning of a word is potential, like that of a dollar bill before it is involved in a transaction. The statement **X** *word means* 'Y' carries a prediction of how a speaker will use **X** word. To make it refer to a real event we must turn it into a sentence—an exclamation like *John!* when we unexpectedly see a friend or *Run!* when danger threatens. The same is true of sentence forms, though not of sentences themselves: the sentences **Boy meets girl** and **Girl meets boy** involve the same forms, including that of X-as-subject, which suggests something about who takes the initiative. A speaker will use this or any other form in an actual sentence to match some real event, but the arrangement is only a linguistic potential, a bit of linguistic substance with a meaning that tends to remain constant.

The problem of meaning, then, is one of fitting together the partially fixed semantic entities that we carry in our heads, tied to the words and forms of sentences, to approximate the way reality is fitted together as it comes to us from moment to moment. The entities are the world reduced to its parts and secured in our minds; they are a purse of coins in our pocket with values to match whatever bargain or bill is likely to come our way. The problem of meaning is how the linguistic potential is brought in line with non-linguistic reality whenever a speaker creates an utterance, or even—since we manipulate our environment almost as readily as our language—how the real is brought in line with the potential.

THE SEGMENTATION OF REALITY

The expression *outside world* does not mean what is "outside us" but what is "outside language." It may well be inside us. If I say I have a headache, or that I saw you with a red hat in my dream last night, I am relating something that no one else can observe, yet I put it into words as readily as I refer to the weather or to the latest baseball scores.

This is the sense in which we must take the term *reality,* for it includes both what is viewable only from within and what can be seen by anyone. In fact, the inner view is more important for most of the things adults talk about. Utterances about what is going on at the moment, like *Now I get up, now I walk to the window, now I look out,* are exceptional; more usual are *Last night I got up because I couldn't sleep* or *If you'll hand me that wire I'll attach this hook,* where we look inward on our memories or our plans. Whatever it is that represents these past and future or imagined events in our minds is the main part, if not the whole, of reality as we grasp it. The link to meaning is there—beyond the reach of any instruments we now have. As one team of psychologists sees it, meaning is the part of language that is least understood "because in all probability it reflects the principles of neural organization in the cerebral hemisphere."[1]

What conditions need to be met for the signs of language, limited in number, to designate reality, which is infinite? The first condition is that reality must be *segmented.* Whenever we manipulate an object we separate it from its environment. Part of the act of separating it is the act of naming it: a cloud, a wall, a stick, a laugh. Language gives us a map of reality in which everything is covered but much detail is left out. The second condition, necessary for the first, is that the segments must be *repeatable* and that we must have some mechanism to recognize similarity between one appearance and the next so as to call the two by the same name. A wall in the dark must still be a wall in the daylight. The third condition is built-in *vagueness;* absolute identity of segments cannot be required, for dealing with the continuum of experience would then be impossible; explicitly or implicitly we have to be able to say **X is Y** and mean 'X is a kind of Y,' 'X is like Y.' Otherwise we might learn to apply the name *dog* to Fido but could never extend it to other dogs. A fourth condition is simply *memory,* which is not specific to language; there must be provision for storing the linguistic units to make them available for future use.

How is the connection between linguistic unit and segment of reality made, so that when the segment presents itself the speaker will respond

---

[1] Locke, Caplan, and Kellar 1973, p. 10.

with the unit—or, in the role of hearer, so that when the unit is presented the segment will be invoked? The basis for this is the permeation we noted on page viii. As we grow expert in the use of language, "outside world" is taken in a less and less material sense; but in the beginning it is concrete—the child learns to make verbal responses to things in a way that embodies those responses as part of the complex manifestations of the things themselves. For a dog to become a recognizable and repeatable segment of reality, the child needs to make enveloping contacts with it—feel the hair, see the tail wag, listen to the bark—and hear, from older children and adults, utterances replete with the pattern of sounds, /dɔg/. The attributes of a particular dog are not only a texture of hair and a certain size and shape and color of eyes; they include also the name *dog.* It is true that the color of eyes and texture of hair are "always there" and the name *dog* is intermittent, but the dog's bark is intermittent too and yet is characteristic. Continuity is not a requirement; all that is necessary is a predictable relationship.

Given permeation, we need one more psychological mechanism: an instinct for taking the part for the whole. This is characteristic of all human behavior. A mother is identified by a voice or the touch of a hand; a glimpse of a face is enough to identify the person behind it. If through permeation the name of a thing becomes part of the complex that to our minds is the thing, the name can then be abstracted to stand for it. Sentence patterns as well as words are names in this respect. Linguistic units differ from other identifying features in two ways: the linguistic units are put there in order to be abstracted later, and human beings vocalize them.

The child's first experiences, with assistance from parents and playmates, make it possible for the first abstracting to be done from objects that can be seen, touched, heard, tasted, and smelled. But not much of the vast complex of language, least of all the parts that direct its own functioning, can be learned in this way. Very soon it is the verbal object that has to be manipulated and abstracted not from the flow of events but from the flow of words. If this had to be done completely out of touch with solid objects, the child could not build on the foundation he already has; fortunately most early talk is about visible and tangible things and about the here and now. When words that signify relations are first slipped in, what they relate is part of the world of direct experience, and the relationship can be sensed.

As time goes on, more and more segmentation takes place inside language, with new meanings feeding on old ones. The raw material is now the unending string of sentences that the child hears, and instead of recurring events with their more or less stable aspects, there are recurring words with their more or less stable contexts, all tending to focus on particular characteristics of the concepts behind the words.

The word *boy* makes a good example of how a meaning is abstracted. The first step is from concrete reference—the child hears the word applied to an individual, perhaps to himself. For all he can tell, *boy* could be a proper name. A later concrete application to another individual does not necessarily dispel this impression—more than one man is called *Jack,* more than one boy can be called *boy.* But two Jacks together are seldom referred to by an adult speaker in any such terms as *°Look at those two Jacks,* nor one as *°He is a Jack,* though children will try to generalize *Jack* as soon as they learn to generalize *boy.*[2] The context of numerals and articles plus one appropriate situation after another establishes a distinction between a name that can apply to any individual with the necessary traits and a name that applies arbitrarily to just one or a very few. The child now perhaps formulates a theory: "Boy means 'male' (like me, or like Jack) and 'young' (like me, or like Jane)." This leaves out 'human,' which is apt to be taken for granted, and for the time being no conflict arises when a parent says *Come here, boy* to a dog. But this will be discarded as it comes clear once again that *Bowser is a boy* is never heard; *boy* in this case is relegated to the category of nicknames. Meanwhile other contexts are building up, establishing a category of 'human' within which *boy* is consistently applied, and the crude theory is refined till it fits within a matrix of features of meaning, as in Figure 6–1. Nearly all utterances in which *boy* occurs will be consistent with this scheme. But a few will not—for example, *The boys are out for a good time tonight,* where *boys* refers to men. The unusual nature of such utterances will show not only in their low frequency but in the special circumstances of their use: always playful, seldom or never in a context like *°The boys are at work today.* A kind of vague association is set up whereby 'play' of any kind partly neutralizes 'non-adult.' The other features stay fairly clear; nature makes sharp distinctions between human and non-human, male and female. But adult and non-adult may give some contrary readings: that is, no speaker will be heard to say *Look at that boy over there!* referring to a three-month-old infant. Here it will always be qualified: *Look at that baby boy over there!* So the child comes to a kind of relative concept of boyness in which 'male' and 'human' are set but 'non-adult' is elastic at both ends. At age ten a boy is more a boy than at age three months or age nineteen.

No one term is abstracted in a vacuum. *Boy, girl, man, woman, child, baby,* and later *youth, adolescent, young man, young woman,* all abut or overlap in a self-limiting scheme of shared features that does more to define the meaning of each member than any experience of one term alone.

---

[2] One child at two years and six months: *That's a Fifi here.* (Weir 1962, p. 111.)

FIGURE 6–1
Features of the Meaning of <u>Boy</u>

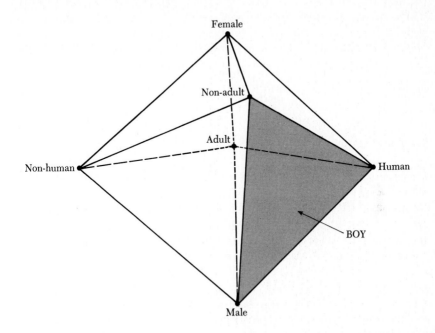

The more abstracting we do, the more general our vocabulary becomes, and the better adapted to coping with unforeseen circumstances. But we cling to the more concrete and specific meanings too—our memories do not give up one hold on reality to acquire another. It is hard to prove sometimes whether there is a single very abstract meaning or a set of relatively more concrete ones tied together in a bundle.

An example to show such a bundle of relatively disconnected fibers might be an ordinary noun or verb. Take the verb *to kick*. A bicyclist is heard to say *I find that the easiest way to shift gears is just to kick the trigger,* accompanying the statement with a gesture of the hand simulating the fingers holding on to the handlebar with the wrist twisting up to the left. Why *kick,* which ordinarily refers to a blow with the foot?

We have to imagine the possible choices. *To hit* suggests a motion in which hand and arm swing free. *To push* suggests a steady pressure. *To punch* is a motion outward from the body. *To whack* is delivered with a flat surface. *Kick* avoids these inappropriate meanings, suggests 'sudden motion after which the moving organ returns to rest,' carries a hint of an upward motion like that of a kick with the foot, and already has certain mechanical associations, such as the kick of a gun or of a motor. **To kick with the hand* is not a use of the verb within a well-defined semantic area, but is an extrapolation from various different relatively concrete uses, tied together by a literal or metaphorical association with the physical sensations of kicking. A new use of *kick* is arrived at by taking a new position relative to a number of old ones, within a field hedged in by all the verb's synonyms. There is some abstracting with *kick,* of course: we operate both abstractly and concretely. One is as much a part of our stored capacities as the other.

THE ANALYSIS OF MEANING

Semantic features

Our words come so naturally and unconsciously that they seem rather simple tokens of reality. This is partly because on the few occasions when we do think about the relationship between words and things we almost always pick the simplest examples from the category: *dog, toy, sun, page, house.* Yet the truth is that literally any combination of things, traits, or ideas can be segmented, whether or not a single word exists for what we wish to carve out of the jumble of our world. If we should ever need to talk regularly and frequently about independently operated sawmills from which striking workers are locked out on Thursday when the temperature is between 50° and 60°F, we would find a concise way to do it. Of course, it is no small accomplishment for our language to be able to perform that segmentation in the way just illustrated—by accumulating segments already named, which intersect at the desired point. Sometimes the accumulation—if it is not too long—becomes a set unit, and we forget or only dimly remember its former associations. This is true of compounds (see pages 61–62).

But it is not necessary that a linguistic unit be morphologically complex —like a compound—in order to be semantically complex. Some of the simplest words harbor an amazingly explicit set of wayward traits. Digging them out, classifying them, and showing their relationships is termed *componential analysis* or *feature analysis,* and the traits themselves are *semantic features,* which supposedly do the same for meaning that distinctive features do for phonology.

The diagram for *boy* is a sample of how the semantic atoms of a word can be spelled out. The abstract features [+Human +Young +Male] have to be used to analyze a great many words and accordingly have a claim to being the kind of irreducible component that one hopes to find. Other words incorporating [+Young] are *child, cub, litter, calf, sapling.* Others with [+Male] are *boar, gander, stamen, testosterone, tenor.* And others with [+Human] are *corpse* (as against *carcass*), *tresses* (as against *mane*), *tell, talk* (as against *bray, cackle, trumpet*).

In the last chapter we saw that grammatical classes themselves can be treated as features of meaning (see Chapter 5, page 90). If we note that **Smith is a bigger quack than Jones** can mean that Smith is more of a quack, while **Smith is a bigger headshrinker than Jones** can refer only to Smith's size or importance, we can say that *quack* "belongs to the class of intensifiable words," or "has the feature [+Intensifiable]" (and *headshrinker* has the feature [−Intensifiable]). It is a common practice to adopt these grammatical features as the ones that are stated first and then add the rest. So *dog* might have the display

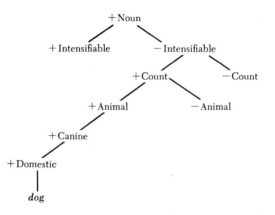

Feature analysis got its most recent impetus from anthropologists, who have used it to describe kinship. Family relationships are sharply defined, but cultures differ in what degrees and directions of kinship are to have separate names. In English we have two words for 'sibling,' **brother** and **sister,** where sex is the distinguishing feature. Among the Black Tai of Vietnam and Laos the prime separation is by age: 'older than self' and 'younger than self.' In Greek the same word is used for both 'brother' and 'sister' with an inflection for gender. English has something similar with **cousin,** where the same word is used for both sexes (though **boy-cousin** and **girl-cousin** are virtual compounds, since we are unlikely to say *man-cousin* or *woman-cousin,* regardless of age). **Aunts** and **uncles** are distinguished for sex, but in Italian the same word is used, with a gender ending: **zio, zia.** In Latin they are differentiated by side of the family:

patruus	father's brother
avunculus	mother's brother
amita	father's sister
matertera	mother's sister

Likewise, the offspring of uncles and aunts in Latin are distinguished as *patruelis* (paternal cousin) and *sobrinus* (maternal cousin).

Most human institutions and artifacts can be spread out semantically in this fashion. A manufactured object is made up of predetermined parts and has predetermined functions. With the features [Keyboard Percussion String Reed Wind Bellows Manual] one can define musical instruments, as for example *flute* [–Keyboard –Percussion –String –Reed +Wind –Bellows –Manual]. Some examples will show the great variety of features that we build into the words that segment nature in all its variety:[3]

1. Some such feature as 'entity in its own right' is needed to distinguish *disease* from *illness* and *ailment.* Diseases are classified and labeled, and a disease can be "caught"; we do not ordinarily say *°catch an illness* or *°catch an ailment.*

2. A feature of 'belongingness' distinguishes *to return,* when it takes an object, from *to take back.* *We took Junior back to the zoo* might refer to letting him visit the place again, but *We returned Junior to the zoo* calls him an inmate.

3. A feature 'enemy' distinguished *U-boat* from the neutral *submarine* in the First World War.[4]

4. The verbs *to warp* and *to bend, to kneel* and to *genuflect* show a contrast in which the first member of each pair emphasizes the retaining of a condition or a position. Something that is warped stays that way till it is repaired; one who kneels stays in that position till the purpose of kneeling (to pray, to receive the crown) is fulfilled. But bending a spring can be followed by automatic springing back, and genuflecting normally includes straightening up again. Some such feature as 'goal' or 'completion' is involved in *warp* and *kneel.*

Features are useful for analysis only if they are shared—the more widely the better. At least some of the ones just cited do appear in other words. 'Goal,' for instance, is what distinguishes *arrive* and *reach* from *leave* and *depart.* It also distinguishes *I went home* from *I headed home* and *I contributed it* from *I offered it.* 'Belongingness' is necessary for *steal, borrow, property, bequeath,* and *trespass.*

'Space' and 'time' are needed to separate certain prepositions: *until* refers only to time, *underneath* only to space, while *before* and *after* are

---

[3] Since linguists would not necessarily agree on whether to regard these meanings as formal features, the bracketed plus and minus signs will not be used for them.

[4] Barber 1964, p. 100.

indifferent; and the same two features distinguish *long* and *far* as adverbs *(How long did you stay? How far did you go?), now* and *here, when* and *where,* and many other pairs.

Given the huge size of the lexicon in any language it might actually be hard to find many features that are unique to particular words. Perhaps the question ought to be turned around. Is the proportion of features that are really widespread and stable high enough to justify the notion that with a comparatively small number (say a few hundred, contrasted with words in the thousands) the whole lexicon can be accounted for?

On the question of how stable a feature is, take the close synonyms *lonely* and *lonesome.* Both **One lonely person stood up and protested* and **One lonesome person stood up and protested* strike us as inappropriate for the meaning 'one lone person,' though *lonesome* is worse than *lonely.* But if on leaving someone a woman were to say *Don't be lonely,* we would probably take her to mean 'Go out and get some company,' whereas *Don't be lonesome* could only be a command to suppress our feelings. A feature of 'aloneness' attaches tightly to *lone* and loosely to *lonely,* but is only inferred with *lonesome.*

It may be that these apparently over-specific features are not so in reality, but are cases of something more general. Perhaps it is what the *culture* packs in a word that really counts, not the features that already happen to be floating around in the language and gravitating together. In that case all the language does is name the cultural totality, not by any regular analytic-synthetic procedure, but by throwing together whatever resources it has in a way that tends to be more regular than irregular.

In spite of such uncertainties, it is still possible to use a feature approach to teach a great deal, in a simplified way, about a large part of the lexicon. This is especially true in foreign language study. Contrastive feature analysis helps the student avoid the more flagrant errors of usage: French *une jeune fille* may be translated as *girl* or *young lady,* but *une fille* is not necessarily either a girl or a lady.

Field relationships

Feature analysis makes a fundamental assumption about meaning that is highly debatable: that features are *contained* in words. Yet to decide what a given feature is, it is necessary to move "outside" the word, contrasting it with one or more other words. So perhaps, as some linguists have argued, the way to treat meaning is not with features but with relationships of "oppositions" in a field, a segment of reality symbolized by a number of words. A given word would then have meanings according to the whole semantic range of its field and how its functions are shared with all the other words in the same field. Circumstances could then account for a good deal of trading back and forth, which would take care of apparent instability, and also for the development of meanings that are more the property of the field than of any word in it. This sort of relativity is familiar enough with words that signify opposites. *Hot* and *cold* as primary sensations are more or less absolute; we learn them in association with two kinds of discomfort. But in their field relationships they crowd each other now toward one extreme and now toward the other. A *cold meal* may actually be at room temperature; it is simply one that is [− Hot].

The words for dimensions provide a more complicated example. *Length* always has to represent the maximum dimension. We would not say *The rectangle is 2 feet long and 10 feet wide.* Likewise, inside a house we would not say *That wall is 4 feet long and 7 feet high*—we would replace *long* with *wide.* But speaking of the façade of a building we probably would prefer *It is 40 feet long and 90 feet high* to *It is 40 feet wide and 90 feet high.* Width is not apt to be selected because buildings create a special set of relationships in which the maximum *horizontal* dimension gets called 'long.' A low building could be described as *100 feet wide, 50 feet deep, and 40 feet high,* or as *100 feet long, 50 feet wide, and 40 feet high,* though with *long* preferred because it is *along* the base. The field relationships give options to suit our point of view.

A fair example of a feature within a field that can come and go for a word in the middle of the field is found among the words *coax, persuade,* and *convince.* It is our old friend 'goal,' which is clinched with *convince: I was convincing him to go* would not be used except to imply success— he eventually did go. But with *persuade* it depends on the context: *I persuaded him to go* implies that he went, but *I was persuading him to go* leaves some doubt. We cannot say *I convinced him and convinced him but he wouldn't do it,* but *I persuaded him and persuaded him but he wouldn't do it* is possible. At the other extreme, *coax* tells us nothing about whether he went, even in *I coaxed him to go. I coaxed him to go but he wouldn't* is a normal sentence.

In the set *fall, topple, collapse,* we have what appears to be 'unintentionality.' Lacking any indication to the contrary, we would assume that *Jane fell* meant that it happened without her intending it. Yet this feature is not permanently stuck to *fall,* though it is to the two other verbs: we can say *She fell on purpose* but not *She toppled on purpose. Topple* is completely unintentional, *fall* is just mostly so.

Field relationships are not confined to sets of synonyms. They may extend to a feature of the landscape that is required to be present for a certain word to be used, even though it would seem strange to think of a matching feature in the word itself. For example, words like *budge* and *far,* though not explicitly negative, are always or almost always used when a negative (or an interrogative or a conditional) is somewhere in the environment. The verb *to afford* establishes exactly the same kind of connection with 'possibility' that *budge, much, far,* and so forth establish with 'negation.' In its usual sense, 'to have the (economic) means for,' or 'not to lose by,' there is generally a *can, be able,* or *be possible* in the context. But all that is necessary is that such a meaning be implied. Though we do not say **I afford a house like that* or **I afford to offend him,* we can readily say *I afford a house like that?!! Is there a chance of your affording it?* or *When it comes to affording something like that . . .* (with a shake of our head).

Except for their comparatively narrow range, these restrictions that cause words to cluster in sets—'negation,' 'possibility,' 'intentionality,' and the like—are the same as others that operate on a grander scale. The grammatical classes are only the most obvious cases—noun, verb, and so on. Other restrictions—just as comprehensive, though not as visible—are linked to the social code in which we happen to be functioning at the moment of speaking (more will be said on this subject in Chapter 9). An example is the expressions *at this time* and *right now.* The first is aloof and formal, the second informal and relaxed: *The doctor can't see you at this time (right now).* One of the most pervasive features is emotional loading: the speaker betrays an attitude of approval or disapproval. The adverbs *soundly* and *roundly* are synonymous, but in *He soundly berated them,* the speaker indicates approval of the action, while *He roundly berated them* is neutral. Some more obvious pairs, with the neutral term first and the loaded one second, are *big–overgrown, sweet–cloying, uninformed–ignorant, odor–fragrance.* Otherwise innocent-looking words may be classed for occupation, geographical area, age of speaker—any basis that is part of the reality of our lives.

Dynamic relationships

If the interconnections of meanings are partly determined by field relationships, they are no less so by the dynamic relationships in a sentence. The first tells us what features are potential, the second what features are actual. Such interplay is to be expected, considering that potential features were abstracted from actual sentences in the first place, and that whole chunks up to sentence size persist in memory. Take the meaning of the verb *to wear.* It is in a field relationship with *to have* and *to carry* in the following:

John has long hair.

John wears a sweater.

John carries a gun.

These are ranged according to intimacy. What is inalienably John's, his hair, is normally expressed with *have* (though *have* is used with other kinds of possession too); clothing goes with *wear,* and accouterments such as canes, umbrellas, and guns most often go with *carry.* Depending on the point of view (closeness to the body) one may refer to wearing a gun or a sword; but *wear* is not apt to invade the territory of *have.*

The dynamics of a sentence may sometimes reverse the direction of certain measure words, turning them around. Thus *young* normally opposes *old,* but *a young girl* usually refers to a girl in her teens—there is a field relationship between *young* and *little (a little girl of four).* One dictionary defines grain as 'a small, hard particle.' Why *small,* if particles are normally small? Because if *grain* were defined just as 'hard particle,' one might infer a *minute* particle. *Small* makes it larger, given the field relationship between *small* and *minute.*

Other factors

There is more to the interpretation of a sentence than the dynamic inter-relationships of its words and their field relationships with other words. The crudest outside factor is the physical setting. If someone says of a child running along the beach *She likes the sun and air,* the utterance is not apt to be interpreted as *She likes the son and heir.* This elimination of irrelevant meanings has been given the unprepossessing name of *dis-ambiguation.* Here the setting has cleared up the ambiguity. If we saw the sentence written, the spelling would clear it up. When Groucho Marx heard someone remark sympathetically *It must be tough to lose a wife,* he chimed in with *Yes, it's practically impossible,* disambiguating the ambiguity by using a word (*impossible*) whose features are compatible with only one sense of *tough.*

Why should disambiguation be necessary? Why not simply have one word for one meaning, one meaning for one word? Two things make it impossible. First, speakers' brains do not interlock like electrical power grids, and what goes on in one brain never quite matches what goes on in another. Second, there is simply too much to verbalize. The situation is the same as with phonemes. By re-using words in patterns of repetition and combination it is possible to get along with a number much smaller than the totality of meanings that we have to come up with in a lifetime. Most words embody meanings that radiate from a central core, so that a bit of context is enough to determine which branch to follow. Take the word *cell.* In the phrase *cells of the body* we are off on one track; with *cells of the honeycomb* we take another; and with *cells of a battery* we take a third. As one of our earlier discussions indicated (see pages 53–57), these contexts are probably part of collocations: hearers do not have to make a fresh start interpreting *cell of the body* every time they hear it. On the other hand, even if the senses of a word are unrelated to one another, having them all bundled together makes storing them easier. Not every filing system is totally logical; memory works in strange ways.

The number and variety of factors that finally yield an interpretation of a sentence show how the lexicon has to be stretched to cover everything; holes in the fabric must be closed by the inferences that we intend our hearers to draw when we speak. The holes have been called "inferential gaps."[5] In the process of filling a gap we often read new features into words, which may become permanent—part of the *reference* of the word rather than an inference based on its relationships. This accounts for differences among speakers, some of whom may already view a feature as referential—that is, as *in* the word—while others take it still as inferential. An example of an inferential meaning that has now become referential for everyone is the sense 'desire' for *want.* At one time *to want* signified merely 'to lack' (as it still does in **They were tried and found wanting**). But **I want it** was used so often as a polite hint, just as today we might say **I don't have any butter** to imply 'I desire some butter,' that the inferred meaning became the central one. An example of a meaning that is still not settled for all speakers is that of *convince,* cited earlier in this chapter as having the feature 'goal.' We understand **I convinced him to go** as meaning that he went. But for those who accept **I convinced him to go but at the last minute he was unable to,** the 'goal' meaning of the shorter sentence is an inference. The referential meaning is that I gained his will; once that is gained, it is assumed that his compliance is gained as well.

Inferences take the shape of "if he says *that,* he must mean *this,*" and *that* and *this* must be related, somehow, in our experience. It may be through connections in the real world. Someone ordered to **Turn the oatmeal off** understands it to mean "Turn the gas (or electricity) off at the burner under the oatmeal.' When a lawyer advises a client that he need not pay because **the statute of limitations has expired on that bill,** he does not mean that the statute is no longer in force but that the period of time during which according to the statute of limitations the bill was legally collectable has expired. In both these examples the meaning intended is several steps away from the meaning expressed. If we could not take such metaphorical shortcuts, communication would bog down in legalistic formulas. The metaphorical gap may be wide or narrow. It is narrow in **Don't eat with your knife.** Since people eat with knives, forks, and spoons, this injunction makes no sense unless we interpret *to eat* in part-for-whole terms as 'to put food in the mouth.' Similarly with

---

[5] Kirsner and Thompson 1976.

What time is it in the kitchen? where *What time is it?* stands for the related question *What does the clock say?* The gap is wide in *I cut all the flagstones,* where the speaker intended *cut* as 'cleared by cutting' and *flagstones* as 'grass around the flagstones.'[6]

The analytical strategies of inference and disambiguation may not always be called for. If an utterance, or part of one, matches closely enough with some remembered formula, it may be captured directly—collocations again. Our minds are probably equipped to handle both processes at the same time. It would be hard to decide which is uppermost in our understanding of a sentence like *They set the clocks and put out the lights before going to bed.* If our minds are already calculating by the time we hit the verb *set,* then the process is one of keeping two alternatives before us—*did set* or *do set?*—not committing ourselves until a decisive word comes along. But if we automatically jump to conclusions, then we will not wait until all the parts are arrayed in front of us but will simply take the verbs *set* and *put* one way or the other, past or present, and hope for the best. The analytical process will not be invoked unless we strike a snag—we might, for instance, have taken the sentence to mean that they always do those things before going to bed, and then the speaker goes on to add *but forgot to lock the doors,* which forces us to reassess the verb and pick a different meaning. This would seem to be more efficient and is probably the way things happen, especially as ambiguity is rarely so complete as in the example just quoted and our guess is more likely to be right than wrong. It may well be based on the statistical probabilities that we learn to sense through long experience with the language. Someone hearing *Did you see that gull?* would guess the highly frequent meaning 'bird' rather than the infrequent 'gullible person.'

Meanings that are inside and central, meanings that are inside but peripheral, meanings that hover on the outside like hungry flies—a word is anything but the tight package of form and meaning that it is usually thought to be. Yet meanings are stable—just stable enough to make inference possible, not so stable as to make it unnecessary. Given nature's size, language otherwise could not reach around it.

MAPS OF SEMANTIC SPACE

Pity the poor analysts who have to do the best they can with meanings that are as elusive as a piece of wet soap in a bathtub. They would like

---

[6] Context supplies much of what we need to interpret speech; therefore, much can be suppressed. As Jespersen noted, ". . . an impression is often produced not only by what is said expressly, but also by what is suppressed. Only bores want to express everything." (Jespersen 1924, p. 309).

to take a definite feature, say [+Human], and tie it to definite verbs, say *study, think, murder,* or *invent (Bell invented the telephone, *The cow invented the milking machine).* But it slips out of their grasp. *The girls left, *The fog left, The fog went away*—so far so good; but what about *The train left*—or *the mail, the bus, the cargo, the ship?* 'Human' is too specific for *leave,* which requires instead something like 'routinely moving under human control.'[7] Plucking a word out of a sentence is like plucking a morpheme out of a word. Words are environmentally conditioned just as morphemes are, though less drastically. If we fail to detect a loss or specialization of meaning, it may be due to the bluntness of our tools.

But if we shut our eyes to the indeterminacy that we know is there, semantic space can be sketched or modeled in fairly obvious ways. This is especially true if the area chosen is well defined, as it is with kinship terms, and if the features are chosen to fit the case without worrying if they are so general as to fit everything else in the world.

If the field is restricted to the meanings of a particular word, the simplest diagram is the branching tree, like the one used on page 115 in abbreviated form to analyze *dog.* Different senses are shown by separate branchings.

Figure 6–2 shows two diagrams for the senses of *bachelor,* a tree diagram and a circle diagram. The circle diagram makes it possible to show low-level features that are shared between meanings (for example, 'young' does not have to be repeated as it does in the tree diagram). It also does not make the apparent assumption that 'human' versus 'animal' is more basic than 'male' versus 'female.'

Only a tremendously complicated multidimensional model—possibly nothing less than a map of the neural connections in the brain—will do full justice to the network of meaning. Till that is attainable we have to be content with partial and rather trivial samples of this or that small patch of the fabric.

Words with shared features: synonyms and antonyms

For practical purposes we say that *to peel* and *to skin* are *synonyms.* This means that they are close enough to allow the speaker a choice between them in a significant number of contexts. The measure of synonymy is replaceability. Two terms may share all but some small part of a field, but they are not synonyms unless one can be used instead of the other. Thus *man* and *boy* share practically an entire field except for the feature of 'age,' but are still kept well apart unless the speaker him-

---

[7] *Routinely* because while we might say *The rig that was moving the house left early,* we would not say **The house that was being moved by the rig left early.*

FIGURE 6–2
The Tree Diagram Versus the Circle Diagram*

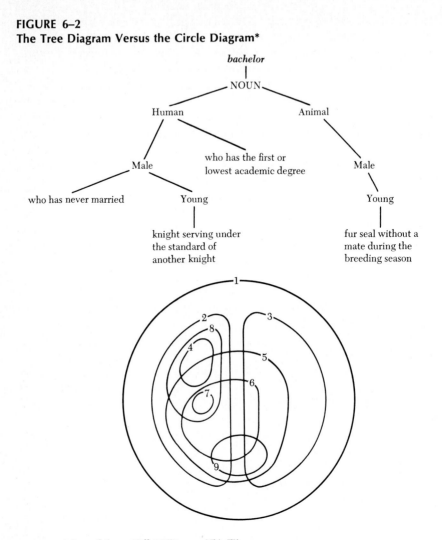

SOURCE: Adapted from Hill 1973, pp. 274–75.

* In the circle diagram, the first circle represents *noun*, which includes all senses of the word. The second circle represents all uses which apply to human beings, and the third represents the only sense which is animal. Circle 4 represents 'holder of the lowest academic degree,' and circle 5 gives all senses of the word which designate males. Circle 6 gives the senses which designate young adults, whether human or animal. Circle 7 represents 'knight serving under the standard of another knight,' and circle 8, which encircles both 4 and 7, is a circle designating the meaning 'apprentice,' or lowest in a hierarchy. Finally, circle 9 encloses the two instances of unmated males, one human, the other 'unmated fur seal.'

self is unsure of his meaning. The reason is that it is precisely the age difference that we want to emphasize.

The companion term for synonym is *antonym,* and the same measure of replaceability applies, except that now it is between *A* and not-*A*. In answer to *Is it wet?* one has a choice between *No, it isn't wet* and *No, it's dry.* There are of course other kinds of not-*A*; for example, *pernicious* is not-*A* with respect to *wet*—but it is also irrelevant because *wet* and *pernicious* are not even in the same field. For one term to replace another, with or without *not,* it is obvious that they must be in a close field relationship to each other. The contrary opposition between *wet* and *dry,* within a field of 'presence of moisture,' can be shown diagrammatically:

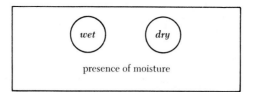

The effect of adding *not* is to make the areas cross. In the diagram below we see the antonymic pair *wet–dry* included within the overlapping ovals *not-dry* and *not-wet.* Along with *wet* is shown its synonym *moist,* and a synonym of the synonym, *dampish.* The reason *not-wet* and *not-dry* overlap is that it is possible for something to be both things at the same time, as in sentence d of the following set (the meanings of a through d are located on the diagram):

    a. It is quite moist—in fact, it is rather wet.
    b. It's not wet, just moist.
    c. It is somewhere around moist or dampish.
    d. It is neither wet nor dry, just dampish.

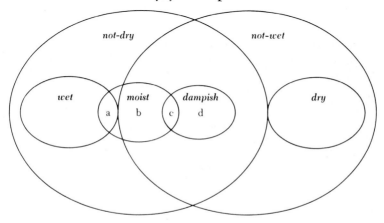

Overlapping is characteristic of contraries—there is usually a middle ground. With some antonyms it is spaced out quite neatly: *large–medium–small, right–center–left, open–ajar–shut.* There may even be inner and outer antonymic terms: in *always–often–seldom–never, never* equals *not-ever* (the older sense of *ever* is *always: forever = for always*) and *seldom* equals *not-often.* Similarly with *hot–warm–cool–cold* and *good–fair–poor–bad.* Even in some such semantic field as 'having control over something,' with its antonyms *to keep* and *to dispose of,* it is possible to squeeze in a fence-sitter: *He neither kept it nor disposed of it; it was stolen.* It may be that there is always a middle ground except in some artificially designed human activity where doubts are settled by definition. Between *fair weather* and *foul weather* there is the possibility of *middling weather,* but between *fair ball* and *foul ball* there is no **middling ball,* no matter how ardently an umpire might desire it. Between them, *fair ball* and *foul ball* make a clean sweep of the field of 'batted ball':

fair ball	*foul ball*
'batted ball'	

There is no restriction on the other semantic ingredients nor on the grammatical features that can be shared by an antonymic set. *To hurry* and *to go at a leisurely pace* are antonyms differing in grammatical form, though of course both are verb phrases. Some pairs of antonyms are opposed in terms of more than one set of features: *to work* and *to rest* are antonyms on the basis of 'presence or absence of productive activity'; *to work* and *to loaf* are opposed on the same basis plus the basis of 'concern versus indifference.' The basis of antonymy between *noise* and *silence* is not the same as that between *noise* and *music.* Words from all major categories can form pairs: nouns such as *good* and *evil;* adjectives such as *good* and *bad;* adverbs such as *fast* and *slow;* prepositions such as *out* and *in;* pronouns such as *his* and *hers.*

Since both antonyms and synonyms occupy the same field, it is possible for the same pair of words to be both synonymous and antonymous. This should not be surprising, because we have already seen many instances where a given meaning can be foregrounded at the expense of other meanings. As was noted earlier, *peel* and *skin* are synonyms in *to peel (to skin) a banana.* They are antonyms in *You have to peel a raw potato but you can skin a boiled one.* There is still a third relationship that has already been mentioned: the meaning of *to skin* in some situations is included within that of *to peel.* This is a special kind of synonymy called *hyponymy:*

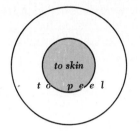

If we say *You can peel off bark and you can peel off a rind, and you can also skin off bark, but you can't skin off a rind,* we are saying in effect that in terms of 'amount of force needed,' *to skin* is enclosed in the range of *to peel.* Hyponymy is more typical of scientific terminology than of everyday language. The term *vertebrate* is *defined* so as to include *fish, reptile, mammal,* and other categories of the same phylum.

And the truth is that synonymy and antonymy in general are less scientific than stylistic. "Speaker's choice" has to do with meeting communicative emergencies as they come up. Sometimes it is a matter of precision. A writer or speaker is about to say *He delivered a lengthy apology* and realizes that *apology* may be taken to mean an excuse and not a justification, which was what was intended; so the speaker uses *justification* instead. At other times it is a matter of contrast, of finding something that sounds different. This is often necessary to keep from attracting our hearer's attention to the words we use instead of their meaning. Every language has some words (*homophones*) that sound so much alike that if we use them together we are liable to be misunderstood or thought to be making a pun: *That was a fine fine you had to pay!; That weakness is one that he does not to my knowledge acknowledge.* If we replace the second *fine* with *penalty* and the *acknowledge* with *admit to,* the problem is avoided. Or again it may be a matter of *connotations,* the associated and emotional meanings of a word. Some words are up-beat and others are a put-down, as in the old saying "Horses *sweat,* men *perspire,* women *glow.*"[8]

These cases—and the ambiguity of *apology* as well (the fact that the "one word" *apology* has two senses creates the same problem as do "two words" such as *fair* and *fare*)—are just a mild example of a kind of conflict that sometimes causes words to disappear (see pages 263-64). Instead of being virtually driven out of the language, as *niggardly* has been, *fine* and *acknowledge* are simply driven out of the immediate context where they cause trouble. This choice of a near synonym for the pur-

---

[8] A word game that illustrates the connotative differences of synonyms asks players to create triplets on the pattern of "She's *skinny,* you're *thin,* but I'm *slender.*"

poses of a given context is largely a matter of style. A good writer neither avoids repeating the same word when it fits the context nor blurs meaning by repeating a word in shifting contexts. The first is the flaw of "elegant variation," the latter is the mark of a writer either poor in words or word-deaf.

Other word sets

Synonyms and antonyms are not the only sets of words that are joined through shared or opposed semantic features. There is probably no limit to the groupings that would make sense for one purpose or another. Examples of these types of semantic fields:

1. Converses: *come–go, buy–sell, read–write, give–receive*. These are close enough to each other to be expressed sometimes by the same word: *The landlord rents the house to me, I rent the house from the landlord.*

2. Characteristic object: *eat–food, drink–beverage, hear–sound, spell–word, harvest–crop*

3. Cognate object: *wrap–package, ask–question, run–race, live–life, bequeath–bequest.* Literally a cognate object must have the same historical derivation as its verb *(live a life, sing a song),* but more freely it is used for any object that is the necessary result of the action of the verb; the existence of the object implies in turn that the action took place.

4. Characteristic action: *heart–beat, mind–think, fire–burn, wind–blow, rain–fall*

5. Cognate subject, action, object: *employer–employ–employee; donor–donate–donation; inventor–invent–invention; thief–steal–loot; preacher–preach–sermon;* and with an indirect object added, *payer–pay–payment–payee; giver–give–gift–receiver.* As is evident from these examples, the semantic sharing is often matched by a sharing of morphemes.

6. Characteristic quality: *water–wet, summer–warm, feather–light, prairie–flat*

7. Symptom and state: *smile–happiness, smoke–fire, groan–pain*

8. Co-hyponyms: *matter* includes its hyponym *solid,* but also includes *liquid* and *gas;* the included terms are *co-hyponyms.* Other examples: H_2O includes *ice, water, vapor; color* includes *red,*

yellow, orange, and so on; *organ* includes *stomach, heart, liver; school larnin'* includes *readin', writin', 'rithmetic.* Here belong all the groupings not only of nature but also of our daily associations: *curriculum* includes *mathematics, history, chemistry; baseball scores* include *hits, runs, errors; church service* includes *prelude, offertory, sermon, doxology.*

ARBITRARINESS: ICONS AND SYMBOLS

Meanings in which form imitates nature are called *iconic,* and the forms are *icons.* Meanings that are arbitrary and conventional are called *symbolic,* and their forms are *symbols.* Everything points to icons as more primitive than symbols. Children invent them. Two speakers without a common language resort to them for communication. But however vivid the beginnings, the color has long since faded to a uniform gray. As we saw earlier (pages 9–10), even in our common onomatopoetic words the imitation must give way to the system of sounds that the language imposes. The result is almost always an imperfect copy. If we listen to the note of the whippoorwill we observe an appreciable pause between *whip* and *poor: whip-poorwill, whip-poorwill.* But English has the habit of reducing interior syllables and clicking them off at a faster rate; the result is that we say something like *whipperwill.*

But if through the centuries our art has declined, our apparent sophistication has grown. We are not bothered by imperfect copies. Until someone—perhaps a poet foregrounding sound and sense—calls them to our attention we do not even notice them. This is the effect of permeation. Language has become an almost purely conventional code, with a few exceptions listed as curiosities. Certainly there is no essential relationship between the sound of any phoneme, or the combined sounds within any word, and any event beyond language, barring the frayed remnants of some occasional onomatopoeia.

Though the system in all its smaller parts may be more symbolic than iconic, we sense it as iconic, and treat it so in daily small acts of creation and readjustment. More of this will come in the chapters on variation, where it will be seen that most change in language that is not due to accident arises from the underlying iconic drive to make sound conform to sense. When a child says *gooder* instead of *better,* it is only because *good* has been learned as the proper symbol for 'good' and any deviation from it adds to the arbitrariness—makes it less iconic. Whenever a speaker uses a metaphor—speaks of *following suit, playing into someone's hand, trumping the other fellow's ace,* or *getting a raw deal*—he makes or repeats an icon.

Even the symbols themselves turn out to be somewhat less arbitrary than they appear at first sight if we look beyond just the primary association of word and thing. Given a particular word for a particular thing, if other words for similar things come to resemble that word in sound, then no matter how arbitrary the relationship between sound and sense was to begin with, the sense is now obviously tied to the sound. The relationship between sound and sense is still arbitrary as far as the outside world is concerned (and would appear that way absolutely to a foreigner), but within the system it is no longer so.

Something of this nature must have happened with those two past-tense endings, -/d/ and -/t/, that have begun to cluster around opposite meanings: -/d/ for 'relatively gradual,' -/t/ for 'relatively abrupt.' Even speakers who use only one of them—Britishers favor -/t/, Americans -/d/—still sense the difference. *Spilled* seems more natural than *spilt* in *The water spilled drop by drop over the rim; spilt* more natural than *spilt* in *The milk spilt all over the floor when she dropped the pitcher.*[9] Of course it helps when there is a suggestion of sound-symbolism. The voiced sound of /d/ is less abrupt than the voiceless sound of /t/ (compare *jolt, volt, bolt, halt, dealt* [a blow]). But associations of this kind do not depend on sound-symbolism alone. *Demoniacal* is a more menacing word than *demoniac,* probably because it echoes *maniacal.* To call an accusation *baseless* is more telling than to call it *groundless,* probably because it echoes *base* with its meaning of 'low, contemptible' (and also because the initial [b] makes a lip gesture possible).

Often we find words clustering in groups with a vague resemblance in sound—too hazy to carve out as a definite morpheme—to which has been given the name *phonestheme.* Most of the words ending in *-ump* suggest heaviness and bluntness: *rump, dump, hump, mump, lump, stump, chump, thump, bump.* Children sense these associative possibilities and coin words with them: *If the house is as old as that it's raggy, shaggy, and daggy,* remarked one seven-year-old. The markers of multiple-choice tests find phonesthemes useful as distractors for their questions; if *twisted* is offered as an equivalent for *knurled,* as was done in one test, it is on the assumption that persons not fully acquainted with *knurl* will assume that it is related to *twirl, whirl, birl, tirl, furl,* and *gnarl.* Shifts of meaning often go in the direction of a family of words having phonesthematic ties. The word *bolster* no longer suggests a padded and comparatively soft support but rather a stiff and rigid one, because of the attraction of *brace, bolt, buttress.* (Of seventeen persons tested on this point, thirteen voted for 'rigid.') Phonesthemes are often a principal ingredient of new words: *hassle* probably follows from *tussle,*

---

[9] See Quirk 1970.

bustle, wrestle. Some loan words may have been adopted less because of cultural need than because their sound was in some way suggestive: Hindi *jungle* has associations with *jumble* and *tangle*.[10] One anthropological linguist holds that connections of this kind may be part of our innate equipment for learning our native language—an indispensable aid to memory.[11]

If words become parts of things to our minds, as they must if language is to do its job efficiently, at least a partial association of sound and sense can hardly be avoided. When other aspects of things hit our eyes we do not hesitate to infer a kinship in the things if we detect a similarity in the aspects, and it is only natural for us to do the same with words: no two peacocks ever spread their fans in the same way, but one's doing it should mean somewhat the same as another's; two words such as *flout* and *flaunt* are not identical, but they are similar enough so that they *ought* to be related in meaning. And who nowadays feels comfortable with *disinterested* as a synonym of *impartial?*

Key terms and concepts

semantics	the "something like" principle
segmentation of reality	synonym
feature (or componential) analysis	antonym
semantic feature	hyponym
field relationship	arbitrariness
dynamic relationship	icon
disambiguation	symbol
reference and inference	phonestheme

Additional remarks and applications

1. Comment on the meaning of *meaning* in the following:
   Seven o'clock *means* breakfast in our household.
   Keep out. This *means* you.
   Do you *mean* to wait?
   Without love, life would have no *meaning.*

2. Do traffic and other such signs have, in addition to their one-to-one relationship to what they mean, a tendency to be suggestive or

---

[10] Jespersen 1921, p. 409.
[11] Durbin 1973.

pictorial? Would green for 'Stop' and red for 'Go' be just as good as the reverse? What is the sign used in many communities that means 'Watch out, children playing'? Check the international road signs; to what extent are they iconic? symbolic?

3. Seeing similarities is sometimes linked to being able to abstract, supposedly a higher intellectual faculty. Consider a child who has had only cats as pets and on seeing a dog calls it a cat. Or a child who on seeing a strange man calls him Daddy. Is this a kind of abstraction, or is it a lack of ability to discriminate? How is it necessary for language?

4. Might it be said that the meanings of words like *unique, perfect, unparalleled, full, empty, complete,* and *unsaturated* have an 'absolute' feature? What happens to them when intensifiers are added—*very unique, highly unsaturated, most perfect?*

5. There are several number paradigms:
    a. one, two, three, four . . .
    b. first, second, third, fourth . . .
    c. all, half, a third, a fourth . . . a twenty-first . . .
    d. single, double (dual), treble (triple), quadruple, quintuple . . .
    e. once, twice, thrice, four times . . .

    What are the semantic features of each set?

6. A feature that is assumed to be present unless otherwise specified is called *unmarked;* if it needs to be specified it is *marked.* (The "unmarked value" is the *usual* value of a term.) Decide which of the two features 'dead' and 'living' is unmarked in *coral* and in *tree.*

7. What is there about the meaning of prepositions that makes *the tree beside the lake* and *the money inside the box* more usual than *the lake beside the tree* and *the box around the money?*

8. The following verbs have a 'causative' feature (see pages 98–99): *to blush, to redden, to flush.* A separate feature in each is the nature of the cause. Identify it. (Try adding such phrases as *with anger, with running, with embarrassment, with pleasure, with alcohol.*)

9. A medicine advertises that it *helps your pain while you sleep.* Most people would rather have their pain hindered than helped; explain the apparent anomaly. Is there something similar in the following question-and-answer pair? *"How's your headache?"*—*"It's better now."*

10. See if in your speech the following can be arranged in an age sequence from youngest to oldest, and discuss the relationship of this
arrangement to the meanings of the individual words:

baby boy	young boy
man	little boy
boy	young man

(You may need to try each in some such context as *I saw a* _____
sitting there.) Is there a difference when the expressions are used
to refer to someone within his hearing? (For example, *This* _____
would like a ticket to the show.)

11. Does English have formal ways of building antonyms? Name the
antonyms of the following words: *decent, likely, pro-French, to trust,
clockwise.* Compare the use of *not* in the following pairs of sentences: *He is trustworthy, He is not trustworthy; He is American,
He is not American.* See if you can replace the *not* with *un-*.

12. Do we generally try to avoid rimes and alliteration in making phrases?
Consider whether the following are normal; if any are not, what do
we usually do about it? *mighty mild, mighty miffed, pretty prim,
awful lawful, very various, very varied, really reedy, quite quiet.*

For further reading

Bierwisch, Manfred. 1970. "Semantics," in John Lyons (ed.) *New Horizons in Linguistics* (Harmondsworth, England: Penguin Books).

Hayakawa, S. I. 1978. *Language in Thought and Action,* 4th ed. (New York: Harcourt Brace Jovanovich).

Leech, Geoffrey. 1974. *Semantics* (Harmondsworth, England: Penguin Books).

Lyons, John. 1977. *Semantics* (Cambridge, England: Cambridge University Press).

Steinberg, D., and L. Jacobovitz (eds.). 1971. *Semantics: An Interdisciplinary Reader in Philosophy, Linguistics, and Psychology* (Cambridge, England: Cambridge University Press).

Ullmann, Stephen. 1962. *Semantics: An Introduction to the Science of Meaning* (New York: Harper & Row).

MIND AND LANGUAGE 7

$\mathbf{A}$ little girl asks, "What does the wind do when it doesn't blow?" or "Where did I live before I was born?" and we smile at her naiveté. But if she asks, "Where will I live after I die?" most people in our culture will take her seriously.

The idea embodied in these questions has weighed on linguists and on philosophers and psychologists working at the borders of linguistics for a long time: How is our thinking influenced by the language we use? Is thinking even possible without language? The second question is broadly psychological and philosophical; the first has sociological overtones as well, for it involves not only such passive things as our world view and our attitudes toward others as their language affects us, but the active arts of persuasion: if a government can change economic behavior by tampering with the monetary system, it can also implant thoughts and influence actions by tampering with language—and this invokes the great questions of truth, reform, and propaganda. As with governments so with individuals: every argument is in some measure an attempt to influence thinking through language.

LANGUAGE AND THOUGHT

No one denies that language and thought are related. But how and how closely? The ultimate in closeness was claimed by a now outmoded school of psychology which held that thinking is merely talking to oneself, in an implicit sub-vocal way.[1] The opposite view was expressed by W. D. Whitney a century ago: "Language is the spoken means whereby thought is communicated, and it is only that"[2]—thoughts are generated in their own sphere and then formulated in language. A more comfortable position lies somewhere between the two extremes: language is a tool in the way an arm with its hand is a tool, something to work with like any other tool and at the same time *part of* the mechanism that drives tools, part of *us*. Language is not only necessary for the formulation of thought but is part of the thinking process itself. Two famous metaphors describe the relationship: "Talking about language is building a fire in a wooden stove"; "Talking about knowledge or science is rebuilding a boat plank by plank while staying afloat in it."[3] We cannot get outside language to reach thought, nor outside thought to reach language.

Thinking is not done in a vacuum, but is always about something. What is the nature of an object of thought? It is rarely the image of a material thing standing before us; most often it is recalled from past experience or transmitted from the experience of others. In the latter case it almost inevitably comes via language. Memory of our own past experience too is largely possible because we have put that experience into words. Any writer knows the anguish of searching for a word to pin down an idea which refuses to materialize until the word for it "comes to mind."

The most primitive act of thought is that of focusing on an object and distinguishing it from the blur that surrounds it. A child accomplishes this literally by feel—picking up and handling, reinforced by sight, sound, smell, and taste. Handling is a self-directed gesture language. The same movements will be gone through another time when the object is handled again, and by provoking this reaction the movements become part of the representation of the object. Even adults feel at a loss to describe a physical object like a spiral staircase without using their hands. In Chapter 8 we will see how an earlier gesture language was probably transferred to a spoken one. Words are not the first associations we have of things, but they are substituted for things so early and implanted so deeply that it is almost impossible to think of a cow without thinking the word *cow*. And even if we manage to, it is usually with the aid of a verbal crutch such as **milk-giver, bovine animal,** or **moo-moo.** We may

---

[1] See Watson 1919, Ch. 9.

[2] Silverstein 1971, p. 100. Whitney was not denying all forms of interdependence. He later went on to say (p. 101) that "there are grades of thought, spheres of ratiocination, where our minds could hardly work at all without the direct aid of language." But these aids are in the nature of cue cards or promptings, to help us arrange our thoughts and keep track of where we are.

[3] Attributed by Quine 1960 to Otto Neurath.

imagine we have captured a wordless thought but may only be fooling ourselves—the words perhaps are hovering in the background.[4]

As for any kind of thinking that is more complicated than simple identification and naming, a well-known linguistic philosopher has flatly stated, "Conceptualization on any considerable scale is inseparable from language."[5]

LANGUAGE AND LOGIC

Linguistics is a science, and sciences are by definition logical systems. A language may be treated as data for descriptions that can be tested for truth or falsity. But is a language in itself a logical system? This one question is two in disguise: does a language contain devices that are like the ones used in formal logic, and is it the purpose of language to be logical?

Aristotle assigned to language a position superior to logic, that of *meaningful expression* in general. Logic is the restricted language of affirmation and negation, of propositions which are true or false. A modern logician would include more than this—for example, what is probable. But language still includes not only propositions but fantasy (in poetry and fable) and expressions of desire: we do not say *I want a beer* to acquaint the hearer with the logical truth of our existence and our desire, but to get the desired object. Language, linked to a modicum of direct experience, is what gives us our knowledge of the world; what we do with it—grasp a part of the world through it, reweave it in imagination, or express its truths in propositions—answers to our intentions. Language is the uncommitted means for everything.[6]

Obviously if language is to serve logic as well as poetics and pragmatics, the devices used by the logician must already inhere in it. The fact is that the processes of most importance to logicians are also very general linguistic processes: for example, affirmation and negation, conjunction and disjunction, definiteness and indefiniteness, condition and concession, which are loosely embodied in the words *yes* and *no, and*

---

[4] The imagining of *individual* persons and things—for which we have proper rather than common nouns—is probably a different matter. Suppose you see the face of a young actress who reminds you of an old-time actress whose face, as you think of her, is clear in your mind—you may be able to say, "She has larger eyes than this actress has." Later perhaps you recapture the name; but the image came first. What words—loosely, common nouns—help us to do is to abstract and generalize; and that kind of thinking is, at least to a much higher degree, word-dependent.

[5] Quine 1960, p. 3.

[6] See Coseriu 1958.

and *or, the* and *a,* and *if* and **although.** (We have to say *loosely* because logic must always define its terms more exactly than they are used in natural language.) An example of how the meaning of such a linguistic form can be explained by a logical proposition is the word **unless,** for which *if not* is sometimes given as the equivalent, although the two are not quite the same: **Professor Arid will pass you in Linguistics 123 if you don't fail the final exam and if you don't make less than a C on your term paper** is an acceptable sentence, but ***Professor Arid will pass you in Linguistics 123 unless you fail the final exam and unless you make less than a C on your term paper** is not—*unless* implies a unique circumstance whereas *if not* includes the possibility of two or more.[7]

Another specialized language is mathematics. It points outward to the external world rather than inward. Its specialty is making precise the way we deal with things in space—amorphous space, where we group things together by addition and multiplication, separate them by subtraction and division, and compare them for equality and inequality; and structured space, where we locate them in geometrical ways. Mathematics is less language-dependent than logic is; in fact, it is an alternate route to a *special* part of the real world. What logic and mathematics share is a precise notation, which is a reflection of precise definition, and is to be found to some degree in all sciences.

It is possible, using the special languages of logic and mathematics and adding some specific content, to engineer a robot that will perform in ways strikingly like a human being in accepting instructions and solving problems. Simulating "a network form for the representation of knowledge in the mind" is one of many ways in which computers have been applied to the study of language.[8] What gave *computational linguistics* its start was the hope of creating a translation machine that would make scientific work published in one language easily and quickly available in others. That proves more difficult than was expected (largely because, as we saw, words are not fully detachable units, see pages 52–57), and though work continues in some quarters, most computational linguists are now engaged in other tasks. An instance of the kind of robot just mentioned is one that would learn how to drive a car. It is given a basic vocabulary, or "primitives," such as **turn, push, brake, accelerator, left, right, front, behind.** It analyzes commands and translates them into its control program. Some commands can be obeyed directly, such as **Push accelerator.** Others depend on having "condition" built into the program: **If speedometer high, push brake.** Furthermore, comparisons may reveal conflicts which will require internally generated commands that must be

---

[7] Proposition and examples are from Geis 1973.

[8] For a brief survey of other applications, especially to dictionaries, see Kučera 1969.

analyzed and effected in their turn—a kind of "thinking" that will change the robot's memory structure.[9] Characteristically the situations in which such a device can be successful have a limited and highly predictable range of objects and events. It may turn out that the chasm between the human brain and mechanical simulations of it is that between finiteness and virtual infinity: the network in the brain and the intricacy of its interconnections are astronomical. Nevertheless, computer models are about the only way of experimentally testing theories of how the brain operates. One computational linguist sees a two-way relationship, with linguistics contributing as much to computer theory as computation contributes to linguistics.[10] Computers have been engaged in tasks as various as testing grammar theories, reconstructing prehistoric languages, editing bilingual dictionaries, studying the perception of sounds, simulating the memorization of meanings, making Braille translations for the blind, and translating non-literary texts from one language to another.

CONTROL BY LANGUAGE

The general question of the interdependence of thought and language yields to the particular one of fluidity and rigidity. In our culture mind (or spirit) has always been conceived as a kind of ectoplasm, formless in itself but freely shaped by the act of thinking. Nothing is impervious to it; it penetrates all walls and envelops all concepts. Language has never had this reputation. It is a structure, warping whatever filters through it. The problem of rigidity was first popularized in the 1930s by a school of philosophy, still active, known as *general semantics*, which saw in our use of *words* a kind of surrender of the flexibility and refinement of thought for the sake of traffic in verbal *things*. Much was made of the uncritical use of generalizations, of the difficulty of pinning a statement like the following down to a set of precise referents: "It is the ability of a community to achieve consensus on the great issues and compromise on the lesser issues which lies at the heart of the democratic process. . . ."[11] The critical reader must ask: Can communities as a whole have abilities? Can the difference between great and small issues be recognized? Is there ever consensus without compromise? Is democracy a process? And so on.[12]

---

[9] Furugori 1974. See Minsky 1967, Chapter 3, for a key concept that human neural functions parallel machine functions.

[10] Hays 1973.

[11] Speech by W. W. Rostow of the Department of State, 26 January 1964.

[12] For a more recent statement of the general semanticist's position see Hayakawa 1978.

The Whorf hypothesis

It remained for a linguist, Benjamin Lee Whorf, to turn the question away from individual words and toward the framework of whole languages. He was not the first to take this step—Fritz Mauthner in 1902 declared that "if Aristotle had spoken Chinese or Dakota, his logic and his categories would have been different."[13] Others, including Wilhelm von Humboldt and Whorf's own teacher, Edward Sapir, earlier held similar opinions. But Whorf was the most successful in dramatizing it. Since every language has a form and no two forms are the same, it follows that no two cultures having different languages can have identical views of the world. Instead of a perfectly flexible rubber mask that shapes itself to reality, each language is a Greek mask, with its own built-in scowl or grin. Whorf's perception of language as a pair of glasses with more or less warped lenses through which we view our surroundings was sharpened by his work with Hopi, a language about as different from English as any language can be. Whorf maintained that French or German or Russian fails to give us perspective, since in fundamental structure these languages—in common with others of Indo-European stock—are the same.

One of the chief things that English and its sister languages impose upon the experience of all their speakers is a prior categorization of the reality outside us into nouns and verbs. The noun pictures things as detached from the processes that surround them, making it possible to say *The wind blows* or *The light flashes,* though wind cannot exist apart from blowing nor flashing apart from light. Indeed, it *forces* us to: by itself, *snowing,* as our English teacher said, "is not a sentence"; where no subject is handy, we must plug in one: *It is snowing.* Whorf writes:

> English terms, like *sky, hill, swamp,* persuade us to regard some elusive aspect of nature's endless variety as a distinct *thing,* almost like a table or chair. . . . The real question is: What do different languages do, not with . . . artificially isolated objects but with the flowing face of nature in its motion, color, and changing form; with clouds, beaches, and yonder flight of birds? For as goes our segmentation in the face of nature, so goes our physics of the cosmos.[14]

Two examples will show the arbitrariness of this segmentation, its dependence upon the local interests and transitory needs of the culture that attempts it. The word *vitamin,* coined in 1912, covers such a strange agglomeration of chemicals that *Webster's Third New International Dic-*

---

[13] Cited in Coseriu 1958, p. 7.
[14] Whorf 1941.

tionary requires fourteen lines to define it, in spite of its having only one sense. Yet to the average user of the term it seems to name something as definite as the house next door. 'A thing in nature' becomes 'a thing in commerce,' and the pill-taker is not concerned with what it "really is" Similarly, the term *complex* was applied around 1910 to a combination of psychological factors that, as the name implies, were difficult to separate and simplify; but the existence of the term and the identification of some particular ailment as a "complex" gave all that was needed for a new entry among our realities.

Coupled with a categorization of "thingness" in nouns is a categorization of "substance" in the subgrouping of mass nouns. English and related languages have a technique of combining these with certain formalized "counters" in order to carve out segments: *a piece of meat, a glass of water, a blade of grass, a grain (bushel) of wheat.* A device of language pictures the universe as filled with taffy-like aggregations that can be clipped into pieces: *earth, air, stone, iron, light, shade, fire, disease,* even—and especially—abstractions like *love, honor, courage, dictatorship,* and *accuracy.*

Out of this substance-operated-on-by-numbers, this notion of *jewels* as "contained in" *jewelry* and *guns* as "contained in" *artillery,* our language has evolved an elaborate vocabulary having to do with an all-containing *space*—the term *space* itself is a mass noun that subsumes in an abstract way all other mass nouns. And here is where the world view of our language departs most radically from that of the Hopi: our concepts of space are so pervasive that we are able to transfer them almost totally to *time.* We treat time as a mass—*I spent a lot of time*—and carve time into units and count them—*five hours.* Time and space use many of the same prepositions, adjectives, and nouns: *before, after, in, at; long, short, same, different, right, wrong, hard, nice, more, less; stretch, segment, amount.* And, of course, we capture events in our space-like nouns —the word *event* itself, plus *rain, dance, movement, riot, courtship.* This, Whorf points out, is almost never done in Hopi. Whereas time, for us, is a quantity, as in *Ten days is greater than nine days,* in Hopi it is *duration: The tenth day is later than the ninth.*[15] Events of brief duration cannot be captured as nouns in Hopi: "lightning, wave, flame, meteor, puff of smoke, pulsation, are verbs."[16]

So when Western philosophers—from Plato and Aristotle with their concepts of matter and form to Kant with his *a priori* space and time— have imagined that they were intuiting general laws that applied to all of nature or at least to all of humanity, what they actually were doing

---

[15] Whorf 1949, pp. 37 and 24.
[16] Whorf 1957, p. 215.

was exteriorizing a way of looking at things that they inherited from their language. Much that is difficult in recent physics as well as in philosophy and logic has been the struggle to climb out of this rut, all the harder to escape because we are in it, unconsciously, from the moment we begin to speak. Whorf surmised that a world view such as that of the Hopi might be more congenial to the concepts of modern physics than the languages of Western Europe.

Partial escape from the trap

Linguists now feel that Whorf's position was exaggerated. Western philosophers and physicists *did* evolve their analyses in spite of their language; Whorf *does* explain his position in English, implying that a reader of English can grasp the concepts that English presumably fails to embody in its structure; and in some ways language answers to nature rather than the other way around.[17] It must be, then, that languages are more pluralistic than a catalog of their bulkier categories seems to suggest. English escapes from its hidebound subject-predicate, noun-verb formulas in the construction **There's singing at the church,** using an *-ing* form whose *raison d'être* is precisely that it does blur the line between noun and verb, and omits the subject. Another example is inceptiveness, the "get-going" phase of a continuing action, which many languages categorize sharply (Latin, for example, with the suffix *-escere*); to the casual outsider it might appear that English lacks suitable means for expressing this. But the lack is handily made up by liberal use of the verb **start: He came in and started calling me names.** These and other examples suggest that the differences between languages are not so much in kind as in explicitness and degree. What one language builds into the broadest layers of its structure another expresses informally and sporadically; but both have it.

All the same, some very common category in our language will magnify our way of seeing certain things and will diminish others. Better examples than those in comparisons of structure can be found in comparisons of lexical equivalence; for we do unquestionably "structure" our universe when we apply words to it, sometimes quite arbitrarily—especially when the phenomena are continuous and do not exhibit natural seams and sutures.

The example most frequently cited is that of colors. The visual spectrum is a continuum which English parcels out into six segments: **purple,**

---

[17] Bull 1960 argues that this is even true of time, all languages being constrained by the nature of time (or man's view of it) to express certain relationships in similar ways.

blue, green, yellow, orange, and *red.* Of course painters, interior decorators, and others concerned with finer shades and saturations employ a more elaborate vocabulary; but the additional words are generally defined with those six as reference points: *turquoise* is 'between blue and green'; *reseda* is 'between green and yellow'; *saffron* is 'between yellow and orange'. In Zuni, orange and yellow are combined into a single range named *łupzʔinna.* In Navaho, the two colors *łičiiʔ* and *łico* divide somewhere between red and orange-yellow. How these different habits of naming can affect our "thinking"—symptomized by the efficiency with which we communicate—can be shown through recognition tests: the monolingual Zuni, presented with a small set of different colors and then asked after a brief period to pick out the ones he saw from a much larger collection, will have trouble recognizing the ones for which his language does not have convenient names.[18] Young Wolof children can more easily discriminate colors for which their language has names, though adult Wolof monolinguals are not limited in this way.[19] It seems that whatever initial advantage a concentration on one part of the color spectrum may produce is reduced later as more possibilities of naming and categorizing are opened up. Other continuums present the same problem across languages—temperature, for example, where English *hot–warm–cool–cold* do not coincide lexically or grammatically with the corresponding terms in other languages.[20] Even with continuums, however, linguistic relativism is not absolute. A study of color categories in numerous languages has revealed that they fall into a rather definite evolutionary sequence. *Black* and *white* are basic and always to be found. Next is *red,* followed by *green* and *yellow,* singly or together; after that *blue,* then *brown,* and finally any combination of *pink, purple, orange,* and *gray.*[21]

According to the authors of the Wolof study, more important than mere naming to the influence of language on thinking is how deeply a language organizes concepts into hierarchies:

> In a way quite different from that envisaged by Whorf, we seem to have found an important correspondence between linguistic and conceptual structure. But it relates not to words in isolation but to their depth of hierarchical imbedding *both in language and in thought.* This correspondence has to do with the presence or absence of higher-order words that can be used to integrate different domains of words and objects into structures (emphasis added).[22]

---

[18] See Landar, Ervin, and Horowitz 1960.
[19] Greenfield and Bruner 1971.
[20] See Prator 1963.
[21] Berlin and Kay 1969. See review by George A. Collier in *Language* 49 (1973), 245–48.
[22] Greenfield and Bruner 1971, p. 77.

Schooling supplies some of this hierarchical organization through dis-placement (talking about things not present) and writing (which frees words from things), thus providing words that elicit other words and concepts that elicit other concepts. This in turn will "push a certain form of cognitive growth better, earlier and longer than others. . . . Less tech-nical societies do not produce so much symbolic imbedding nor so many ways of looking and thinking."[23] By insisting overmuch on *grammatical* relativism and picking only superficial examples of *lexical* relativism, linguists and anthropologists have perhaps missed the most important cognitive manifestation of all, the intricacy of lexical organization. It is an area that is only beginning to be studied.

The "semantic differential"

If the lenses of our language that stand between us and reality are slightly warped, they are also tinted. It is one thing to see a certain kind of fish narrowed down to *eel;* it is something slightly different to see eels as repulsive creatures. Yet our language—plus other associations that we *act out* in connection with eels under the tutelage of fellow members of our culture—decrees both things; the focus and the affect. Every term we use apparently has the power to sway us in one direction or another. Experi-ments on this semantic differential, as it is called by the psychologist Charles E. Osgood and his co-workers, show that persons presented with pairs of antonyms such as *wise–foolish, good–bad, deep–shallow,* and *light–heavy* will relate other terms in rather consistent ways to each of these extremes, even when there seems to be no logical connection. The technique is to draw a seven-point scale with the antonyms at either end, for example

light ____ ____ ____ ____ ____ ____ ____ *heavy*

and to give subjects a term such as *skittish* with instructions to locate it at one of the points. While it would not be surprising, in view of associa-tions with other terms such as *lightheaded,* if everyone agreed that *skit-tish* ought to go well over to the "light" end, what is surprising is that subjects will even agree on where to locate something as apparently out-landish as *wood* on a scale between *severe* and *lenient.*[24]

Osgood has found a number of affective dimensions to which concepts can be related in this way, but the most consistent ones in the more than

[23] Ibid., p. 79.
[24] See Osgood, Suci, and Tannenbaum 1957, and Weinreich 1958.

twenty languages tested are three, which he has labeled "evaluation," "potency," and "activity." Evaluation is by all odds the most predictable: virtually every term and its associated concept seems to attract or repel, however slightly.[25] English even formalizes this to some extent in its system of lexical intensifiers, where *well* and *badly* figure as synonyms of *very (well thought out, well out of danger, well sufficient; badly bungled, badly needed, badly upset).*

Does this mean that, in addition to making us see reality in certain shapes and sizes, our language is also one of the most powerful factors in forcing us to take sides? If all the speakers of a given language share a prejudice, language will transmit it. Take for example the associations of insanity. Most of them are "funny": *crazy, nutty, loony, daffy, half-witted, harebrained, loopy,* and so on. They reflect a culture in which psycho-pathological states are not diseases to be treated but deviations to be laughed at. It has required a vigorous reorientation of our attitudes to put mental disease on a footing other than ridicule or shame so that it *could* be treated. We can excuse language by saying that people use words, words don't use people. But this is like saying that people use guns, guns don't use people—the *availability* of guns is one factor in their use.

The evils of word availability have been impressed on us ever since the women's liberation movement first drew attention to them at the beginning of the 1970s. Language consecrates the subordinate role of women in the loss of surnames at marriage, in the labeling of wed or unwed status by *Mrs.* and *Miss* (marital-status labeling is not required of men), in the greater caution expected of women in speech (women are more "polite" than men), in the many opprobrious names for women[26] (*slut, gossip, crone, hoyden, slattern*—the list is endless), in the con-tempt attached to *spinster* but not to *bachelor,* and in hosts of other ways. Even an epithet for males is an indirect slap at a female: *son of a bitch.* The network of associations among these verbal habits traps us in a set of attitudes from which we can extricate ourselves only by earnest atten-tion to both the attitudes and the words.

We have learned the dangers of acquiescing in defamation in the past decade or two from the upward struggle of minority groups. This has bred an awareness—and conscious avoidance—of the *unintentional* use of the most obvious slurs, such as the noun *nigger* and the verb *to Jew down.* The taboo extends even to unrelated homophonous terms—for example, *niggardly.* But this is a superficial awareness, and we are only beginning to examine other usages that betray—and at the same time help to transmit—uncritical prior judgments. The white (honky?) who

---

[25] Osgood 1971.
[26] See Stanley 1972 (2).

would never think of using the word *nigger* may give himself away by venturing opinions on *the black problem.* The presupposition here of course is that problems are to be identified and defined in white terms— the speaker who uses this phrase is shocked if someone retorts that it is rather *a white problem.* At the same time there are growing signs of a deeper understanding. The very existence of such an expression as *If you're not part of the solution you're part of the problem* shows an awareness of the impertinence of assuming that one has the right to stand outside the process and judge it or manipulate it.

If the consensus within a society is such that its institutions and the terms associated with them are never questioned, the two will perpetuate each other and language will help to mold the attitudes of its users. On the other hand, a competitive society results in competing values, and some measure of neutrality is thereby achieved. Language is used by all parties to every controversy, Republicans and Communists, atheists and religionists, militarists and pacifists; by being pulled in all directions it is forced to remain more or less impartial.

A better term would be *potentially* impartial. If people use language to get the cooperation of their fellows, then little if anything that is ever said is entirely neutral; communication is more often to influence than to inform. From the orators or advertisers who calculatingly choose expressions that will sway their audience to the scientists who in their enthusiasm call their discoveries *proof* or *an important departure,* all speakers are guilty of decorating their information. And since everyone does it, the devices for doing it inhere in the language and are hard to avoid.

CONTROL THROUGH LANGUAGE

Naming

As we inherit our nouns—and the categorizations of reality that they represent—we also inherit the right to *make* nouns, which is one of the few truly inventive privileges that our language affords us: anyone can make up a name for something and many people do, while inventing a new suffix or a new syntactic pattern is practically impossible.

The act of naming, with all it implies in the way of solidifying and objectifying experience, becomes one of our most powerful suasive tools, enabling us to create entities practically out of nothing. The speaker who says *We want no undesirables around here* projects his inner dislikes onto the outer world. Turning *undesirable* into a noun makes it possible to avoid a clearly tautological *We don't want the people we don't want.* As long as people were left to their own resources to find things to do, 'being without work' was generally a matter of choice or ability; when large numbers of people became dependent upon industry, the condition was objectified as **unemployment.** We are used to having *things* about us; naming reassures us that the elusive threat has been cornered. A noun tells us, "It is there; it is something that can or ought to be dealt with."

The importance of the name, rather than the real virtues, of a commercial product is proved by the long record of litigation over trade names like **aspirin** and **cola.** One of the great triumphs of modern advertising has been to condition the public to accept the fabricated name-entities of commerce—to ask for Clorox rather than sodium hypochlorite, for Snarol instead of metaldehyde. Consumer advocates have tried with some success to battle the advertisers in the drug industry by persuading doctors to use generic names in their prescriptions. All such efforts are handicapped by the unpronounceability of scientific terms. Advertising performs a service by cutting through the naming habits of scientists— at a price.

Favorable and unfavorable naming: epithets

Over and above the mere fact of naming—which already to some extent prejudices the case—is the clearly prejudicial application of epithets, terms that are crudely and frankly favorable or unfavorable. We find them in all four of the "content" parts of speech—nouns, adjectives, verbs, and adverbs—and they operate at all levels of awareness; but in general the adjective and adverb are more aboveboard than the noun or the verb. If someone says **That wretched picture bored me to death,** the hearer can deal with the detachable adjective and, if he likes, replace it: **I didn't think it was wretched; I thought it was interesting.** Similarly with **He deliberately insulted me**—the hearer is free to substitute **But perhaps he did it unintentionally.** Adjective and adverb overtly attach one idea to another. The noun and verb are sneakier: the comparison is smuggled in, the person or thing or act is not *like* something good or bad but *is* that something. For many epithets we can actually recover metaphors of fairly recent origin: **He is a bum, He is a prince, She is a tramp, She is an angel, He brayed, She cackled.**

Epithets form a special part of the lexicon not only because of their function—to insinuate a comparison without the hearer's being aware of it—but also because of their grammar. The sentence **The comedy displeased me** is normal because **comedy** designates something. The sentence ***The folly displeased me** is not normal because **folly** does not designate, it only describes. **His folly displeased me** is normal because it contains a hidden sentence in which **folly** is the predicate: **his folly** = 'he did something that was folly (foolish).' The subjectiveness of epithets shows up in constructions with infinitives. We can say *He is a shyster to treat his friends that way,* since *shyster* embodies a subjective judgment. We do not say *°He is a lawyer to treat his friends that way,* since that kind of statement is felt to be objective; but it becomes normal if something is added to show that it is an opinion, a subjective judgment, such as *must be, I would say he is,* or a very emphatic intonation: *He must be a lawyer to treat his friends that way.*[27]

The hidden temptations that the lexicon offers the average user of the language are practically irresistible. The most insidious are not antonyms like *clumsy–graceful, easy–difficult,* or *democratic–fascistic* but terms that are synonyms in that they name the same objective fact, yet antonyms in the attitude that they solicit toward the fact:

Favorable	*Quasi-neutral*	*Unfavorable*
upright, righteous, virtuous		goody-goody, puritanical, sissy
conciliation		appeasement
patriotism		chauvinism, jingoism
defense		militarization
farsighted, man of vision		visionary, starry-eyed idealist
smile		leer
indoctrination		brainwashing
man Friday	assistant	lackey
loyalty	adherence	partisanship
intercede	intervene	interfere, butt in
bachelor girl	single (woman)	old maid, spinster
the good things of life	luxuries	extravagances
venerable	old	old-fashioned, antiquated, superannuated
innovative	new	newfangled
gaze upon	look at	stare at

The hidden temptations are embraced openly in commerce and politics. The following excerpt from a sales publication advises how to put a customer's suspicions at rest:

> An alert real estate salesman should learn how to express himself and use psychology. . . . Don't say *down payment;* say *initial investment.* Don't ask for a listing; ask for an *authorization to sell.* Don't say *second mortgage;* say *perhaps we can find additional financing.* Don't use the term *contract;* have them sign a *proposal* or *offer.* . . . Don't use the word *lot;* call it a *home-*

---

[27] See Bolinger 1972 and 1973.

site. Don't say *sign here;* say *write your name as you want it to appear on your deed.*[28]

As for politics, a study of some twenty thousand lines of Soviet newspaper text showed the highest frequency of concepts relating to the Soviet bloc to be, in this order: *solidarity* (with various synonyms, such as *unity* and *brotherhood*), *building the future, peace, growth (development,* etc.), *greatness, struggle,* and *tasks (obligations, historic mission);* and the highest relating to the West to be *aggression (war-mongering), colonization, imperialist, oppression, encroachment on freedom, international tension,* and *reactionary.*[29]

Not all the self-serving uses of words are quite so Augean as these examples, and of course politics is only one of the stables. A school administration that prefers not to pay the going rate for Ph.D.'s may persuade itself that Ph.D.'s are *overqualified,* and the motive then is business. And when the ordinary citizen excuses himself from nobility by saying that someone who gives up his life for an ideal must have a *martyr complex,* the motive is personal. We are good at believing our own rationalizations.

Elevation and degradation

Since the epithet is language aimed at the heart of social action, it is bound to receive from the culture as well as give to it. While we are not concerned here with semantic change, but rather with the existence at any one time of linguistic forms that influence us, it is pertinent to note how the stock of terms with favorable or unfavorable connotations is maintained against the social realities that undermine it. Two processes are at work, or rather two directions of a single process, which are generally called *elevation* and *degradation.* If for reasons that have little to do with language a thing that has carried an unfavorable name begins to move up in the world, the name moves up with it. A word, like a person, gets a reputation from the company it keeps. In religion, many once-opprobrious names have faded. Probably the majority of religious eponyms—names imitating the personal name of the founder—were unfavorable to begin with. But many were in time adopted by the followers of the religion (*Christian, Lutheran, Calvinist*); others have become milder (*Campbellite*); and few but the most recent might still be resented (*Russellite, Buchmanite*).

---

[28] *The Sonoma County Realtor,* Santa Rosa, California. Quoted in *Consumer Reports* (October 1972), p. 626.

[29] Oppenheimer 1961–62.

The opposite effect is observed in the negative associations of a term attached to something that moves down. The most prolific source of negative *connotation* (the emotional meaning that adheres to the denotative meaning) and of the constant replacement of terms that are downgraded is social *taboo*. The taboo against strong language results in minced oaths: *darn* for *damn, gee* for *Jesus.* The taboo against referring to certain bodily functions results in a succession of replacements, each term being discarded as it too vividly comes to suggest its referent: H. L. Mencken listed two pages of synonyms for *latrine,*[30] itself borrowed as a polite word from French. What was a denatured term for one generation ceases to be for the next one, as the direct association with the buried taboo reasserts itself.

The denaturing process is called *euphemism.* The most common and familiar examples are the political euphemisms, some of which have already been listed. When *taking out* a city is used for *destroying* it, an innocent term is substituted for a wicked one. Ordinary noncommercial and nonpolitical euphemisms are often merely humorous: the plea is not to elevation but to tolerance. *Belly* becomes, besides the elevated *abdomen,* the facetious *paunch* and *bay window.* A *libertine* is a *wolf.* The synonyms of *drunk* have proliferated to the point where a nonsense word inserted in the blank of *He was just a little bit* _____ will suggest it.

Euphemism is not restricted to the lexicon. There are grammatical ways of toning something down without actually changing the content of the message. Take the two sentences *He has been known to take a bribe now and then* and *He is known to have taken a bribe now and then.* Both report the same events; yet the first sentence, by suggesting less immediacy, is milder.

Code switching

A larger device for changing the emotional tone of discourse is used when a speaker changes styles to put himself closer to his hearer. He may "switch codes"[31] to get obstacles out of the path of his message. If I am an English-speaking Canadian who knows some French and live in a bilingual part of Canada I may use French even with French speakers who know English, if that will facilitate our communication. But not all instances of code switching are aimed at clearing the channel. Some may actually obstruct it, though they serve other purposes—solidarity, social distance, prestige, concealment, and so on. A speaker or writer may switch codes with deliberate intent to deceive. An instance—referred to

---

[30] Mencken 1945, pp. 640–41.
[31] See pages 201–02 for discussion.

at the time as a masterpiece of public-relations technique—occurred in the Second World War when General George Patton was criticized by his commander-in-chief, Dwight Eisenhower. A spokesman for Allied Headquarters in Algiers covered this up by announcing that "General Patton had never at any time been reprimanded by General Eisenhower." In the Army code, *to reprimand* is to administer an official rebuke as a punishment, and it follows strict rules of disciplinary procedure. Naturally the public took the word in its more general sense.

A more commonplace variety of code switching is designed not only to disguise but to impress. Sometimes what is disguised is mere empty-headedness. But often it is the unpalatability of the message, which is glossed over with high-sounding phrases, a kind of euphemism on a large scale. *Officialese* is the name usually given to this code as used by bureaucrats and writers of official reports, whose strivings yield such things as *It is imperative that the present directive be effectuated expeditiously,* where the meaning is *Do it now.*

Theodore Roszak has this to say about officialese applied to unpalatable messages:

> When knowledgeable men talk, they no longer talk of substances and accidents, of being and spirit, of virtue and vice, of sin and salvation, of deities and demons. Instead, we have a vocabulary filled with nebulous quantities of things that have every appearance of precise calibration, and decorated with vaguely mechanistic-mathematical terms like *parameters, structures, variables, inputs* and *outputs, correlations, inventories, maximizations,* and *optimizations.* . . . The more such language and numerology one packs into a document, the more 'objective' the document becomes—which normally means the less morally abrasive to the sources that have subsidized the research.[32]

Americans have perhaps been more severely bitten by aspirations of grandeur than other speakers of English. At least, its symptoms have been with us for a long time and its condemnation likewise. James Fenimore Cooper remarked that the man of true breeding "does not say, in speaking of a dance, that 'the attire of the ladies was exceedingly elegant and peculiarly becoming at the late assembly,' but 'the women were well dressed at the last ball'; nor is he apt to remark, that 'the Rev. Mr. G____ gave us an elegant and searching discourse the past sabbath,' but, that 'the parson preached a good sermon last Sunday.' "[33] Cooper himself,

---

[32] *The Making of a Counter Culture* (Garden City, N.Y.: Doubleday, Anchor Books, 1968), pp. 142–143.

[33] Quoted by Mathews 1961, p. 127. See also James Thurber, "The Psychosemanticist Will See You Now, Mr. Thurber," *New Yorker* (28 May 1955), pp. 28–31; and Ethel Strainchamps, "Caveat Scriptor," *Harper's Magazine* (August 1960), pp. 24–27.

however, was no angel of clarity. In *The Last of the Mohicans* he wrote, "Without any aid from the science of cookery, he was immediately employed, in common with his fellows, in gorging himself with this digestible sustenance." Mark Twain translated this to "He and the others ate the meat raw."[34]

Officialese has its stereotypes, which are designed to impress. But its success is also due to another quirk of human nature, our willingness to accept complication for profundity. Where profound thoughts make for hard words, hard words pass for profound thoughts.

Non-neutrality in grammar

Words are plentiful enough to supply all needs, suasive and other. We are not surprised when many turn out to have suasion as the main reason for their existence.

Grammar has too much else to do, and cannot be specialized for any non-neutral purpose. Nevertheless, certain grammatical devices lend themselves better than others to suasive language, mostly because of what they leave unsaid. This is especially true of what one linguist has termed *syntactic exploitation*.[35] Here are two examples:

1. The deleted agent of the passive. A well-known nature program on television has the slogan *Man protects threatened animals.* It does not say by what or by whom the animals are threatened, but the content of the program makes it clear that man himself is the threatener. The slogan gives credit while concealing blame. One English verb is even stereotyped in this way, without an agent: *to be supposed to,* as in *John was supposed to be here at ten o'clock.* By whom was he supposed? Newspaper headlines take advantage of the absence of the agent to slant a piece of news: instead of *Board Member Accuses Principal of Misconduct,* the item is made to sound more sinister by being worded *Principal Accused of Misconduct*—the reader infers that the principal is being accused by more than just one person.

2. "Experiencer deletion."[36] Certain impersonal verbs carry with them a reference to a personal standpoint, that of the one who undergoes the experience. Typical verbs are *seem, appear,* and *strike*—for example, *It strikes me that he is asking too much. Strike* requires that the experiencer be named: we cannot say **It strikes that he is asking too much.* But *seem* and *appear* offer a choice: *It seems (to me) that he is asking too much.*

---

[34] *Letters from the Earth* (New York: Harper & Row, 1962), p. 140.
[35] See Stanley 1972 (1).
[36] Smith 1975.

Not mentioning the experiencer may make it appear that indefinite numbers of experiencers are involved. And by the device of "subject raising" a human subject may be promoted in place of *it* and the responsibility placed on him rather than on the experiencer: *It seems to me that John is lying* becomes *John seems to be lying,* and *It is certain* (in my view) *that John is lying* becomes *John is certain to be lying.* Other examples: *It is obvious* (to whom?) *that . . . , It is a known fact* (known to whom?) *that, Clearly she . . .*

Suasive syntax exploits many other forms, innocent and necessary in themselves but deceptive when misapplied. The subject of a sentence is the *actor* often enough to create an expectation, and this enables speakers to excuse themselves from responsibility by getting out of the actor slot and putting something or someone else there. *This thing won't work* (*fit,* etc.) is a common way of referring to one's own ineptitude with a physical or mechanical object. In describing an automobile accident a speaker may say *I was driving down the street when all of a sudden that other guy drove right across my path;* that way the speaker puts the responsibility on the other fellow. In some places the lexicon dovetails with the grammar in letting us off the hook. There are pairs like *fall–drop* and *escape–forget:* instead of *I dropped it* and *I forgot it* we can say *It fell* (out of my hands) and *It escaped me* (slipped my mind). Many verbs give a choice between transitive and intransitive, making it possible to say *It broke* (on me) and *It tripped me* instead of *I broke it* and *I tripped over it.* The *get* passive is often used in this way: *The dishes got broken* rather than *I broke the dishes.*

Hidden sentences are another complex of devices necessary to economy in language but open to deceptive use. In a sentence such as *Did you see that pornographic movie?* the modifier *pornographic* says something about *movie* which is left implicit: that the movie *is* pornographic. When we do not have to be explicit about our propositions we may be too relaxed, and may attach a modifier at the most obvious grammatical juncture and trust that the hearer will understand where it belongs: *She's lost her first tooth* for 'She's had her first loss of a tooth,' or *There is a definite shortage* for 'There is definitely a shortage.' This linguistic shorthand makes it possible to refer to a *careless mistake* and spare the feelings of a *careless person* who makes the mistake.

Grammatical ambiguity can be of many kinds, and is heavily relied upon in dishonest advertising. In a sentence such as *Athletes have found chewing a natural aid to high-speed effort* the indefinite subject can be taken to mean either 'some athletes' or 'all athletes'; the advertiser is legally protected by the first meaning and lets us infer the second. Lexical ambiguities lend themselves to the same kind of abuse. Sugar refiners take advantage of the fact that there is no legal definition of brown sugar, only a general belief that it is "natural," to market a refined sugar with refined brown syrups added and call it *brown sugar.*

Elements smaller than words make their contribution to the lexicon of epithets. Certain affixes, used mainly in coining words that are epithetical, have graduated to the status of words themselves: the *pros,* the *antis,* and *isms,* alongside the properly affixal use in such words as *pro-Arab, anti-religion, McCarthyism.* One suffix much used in epithets, especially in connection with a certain type of compound, is *-er* (alternative *-or*). The epithetical use trades on a fraudulent association. Most often this suffix means 'a professional, habitual agent':[37] a *singer* is one who sings professionally, an *actor* one who acts, a *bookseller* one who sells books. The epithet adopts this for things that are not occupations, implying that the person stigmatized is fully employed in the activity: *woman-chaser, hymn-singer, troublemaker, Bible-banger, mudslinger.*

Finally, if we look beyond words and propositions to the nonverbal parts of communication we find much in gesture that is suasive and even more in intonation. Questions and commands solicit actions on the part of others, and are the utterances most clearly demarcated by intonation; but statements too may insist or wheedle.

Truth

Suasion makes us realize that probably the most important ingredient of communication is the attitude of the communicators toward each other: an intention on the part of the speaker not to misinform, and good will on the part of the hearer in trying to interpret as the speaker intends. Literal truth is not enough, if for no other reason than that so much about language is always present but only vaguely inferred and scarcely subject to definition. Take, for example, the simple matter of coordination in a sentence and the matter of the sequence of the items coordinated, and what we infer from them. Coordination implies 'These items are on the same level' and are equally important: we do not say *°He is an embezzler and a lover of horses,* even though each part may be separately true. As for sequence, if there is a possibility of inferring one item from another we normally place first the one on which the inference can be based: *The clock is accurate and dependable* is more likely than *The clock is dependable and accurate; The house is broken down and* (therefore) *uninhabitable* is more likely than the reverse. So when a certain brand of meal advertises itself as *Enriched and degerminated,* it is falsifying on both counts. Enrichment and degermination do not belong on the same level, and nothing about degermination can be inferred from en-

---

[37] Marchand 1966, p. 138.

richment. The readers are tricked into regarding degermination, which they may only vaguely grasp anyway, as a virtue. A truthful statement would read, "In order to keep the stuff from spoiling we had to remove the germ, but we *did* add some synthetic vitamins to compensate for the loss."

Not long ago a noted linguist could declare, "The grammatical rules of a language are independent of any scale of values, logical, esthetic, or ethical."[38] That was before students of language became interested in what lies beyond the sentence; we now realize that understanding language includes understanding the circumstances of its use. The question of appropriateness to external facts is as relevant as that of appropriateness to classes of speakers or appropriateness to the occasion of speaking. If one were to state rules defining an appropriate conversational situation, two of them would have to be that a speaker assumes that his hearer will believe what he says, and the corollary that the hearer expects what is being communicated to be true.[39] Thus the best definition of truth is that which is intended not to deceive (and is not simply erroneous). This brings truth down from the stratosphere and makes it a product of our efforts.

Not that our instincts are always a help to our better selves. A language that would enable us to report things as they are and that would be used by speakers without the infusion of their own personalities and prejudices is the ideal of every science; and every science has to some extent developed a denatured language to make this possible. But whether our human condition will permit it to be realized generally is doubtful. It would seem that language is bound to be suasive as long as it is human, that the effort to be neutral cannot be carried out in the language as a whole but must represent a will and a purpose in each small act of speech.

Key terms and concepts

logic
computational linguistics
general semantics
Whorf hypothesis
semantic differential
naming
epithet
elevation and degradation

connotation
euphemism and taboo
code switching
officialese
non-neutrality
syntactic exploitation
grammatical ambiguity
truth

---

[38] Hjelmslev 1961, p. 110.
[39] Lakoff 1972, p. 916.

Additional remarks and applications

1. How important is naming something to knowledge of it? Imagine yourself tramping through the woods and coming across a flower that you admire but can't name. You feel frustrated and reproach yourself for "ignorance of" the flower. You are free to examine it closely and perhaps to describe it more fully than any layman ever has before, yet you still feel that something vital is missing. Describe your predicament in terms of names as part of an organized system.

2. How might language be one basis for animistic religion? What would be the missing sentence in the following proportion?

   > *The man moves* : *The sun moves*
   > *The man sleeps* :   ?

3. Even where a category thoroughly permeates a language structure, it may have little or no semantic value. In the Romance languages, for example, *gender* affects nouns and adjectives and has a certain semantic basis in words that actually discriminate according to sex (*mother,* feminine; *soldier,* masculine). For speakers of these languages would words like *table, house, vision,* which are feminine, or *foot, tree, danger,* which are masculine, carry a sexual connotation? The Italian word for woman's handbag is *borsetta* (feminine). When some men began carrying handbags, the stores soon advertised a *borsetto* (masculine). What does this tell of submerged meaning in gender?

4. Take a paragraph from a newspaper and pick out words and expressions that only someone familiar with your culture (town, state, region, country) could grasp in their entirety.[40]

5. How do you feel about the frequent replacement of **Mrs.** and **Miss** with **Ms.**? How does the repetition of *he or she* or *he/she* instead of the "common gender" *he* strike you, as in *Everybody is entitled to do as he or she thinks right?* Instead of admiring someone's **horsemanship** should we admire his or her **horsepersonship**—or is this a snide question? Even before women's liberation, what had already happened to such terms as **authoress** and **aviatrix**? Why do you suppose the same thing had not happened to *actress*—or would you perhaps even here say *She is a good actor?* (Or would you say both *She is a*

---

[40] See Lakoff 1975.

good actor and *She is a good actress,* with a difference—has the taboo caused a split in the meaning?)

6. Comment on the following names given to nonindustrialized societies or nations: *savage, uncivilized, backward, underdeveloped, developing, emerging.* What does each reveal of attitudes?

7. Translate the following sentences into ordinary English:

    a. The major limitation on the exchange programs of the Department of State appears to be their chronic fiscal starvation.

    b. The principal use of federal funds today is to accelerate the development of particular university resources when university priorities in on-going programs do not accord with national needs.[41]

8. Following are two of the general rules observed by the editors of *United Nations World* magazine. Relate them to syntactic exploitation:

    a. There is no place in the world *distant* or *far.*

    b. No place, culture, custom, or people is *strange, exotic, queer,* or *bizarre.*

9. Discuss the word *unwelcome* in *I rejected his unwelcome suggestion* as a hidden sentence. Find other examples of how we exploit syntactic disguises for ulterior purposes.

10. Discuss the nature of the ambiguities in the following sentences and why it was possible to exploit them:

    a. The oil utilities, in an area where they had to compete with natural gas, promoted the slogan *No heat costs less than oil heat.*

    b. The milk industry, caught in a dangerous misstatement when it promoted the slogan *Milk is good for every body* (some people are allergic to cow's milk), switched to *Milk has something for every body.*[42]

---

[41] These two passages are from Harold Boeschenstein et al., *The University and World Affairs* (New York: Ford Foundation, 1960).

[42] Example from William Bright, private communication.

For further reading

Adams, Robert M. 1977. *Bad Mouth: Fugitive Papers on the Dark Side* (Berkeley and Los Angeles: University of California Press).

Berlin, Brent, and Paul Kay. 1969. *Basic Color Terms: Their Universality and Evolution* (Berkeley and Los Angeles: University of California Press).

Bolinger, Dwight. 1972. *Degree Words* (The Hague: Mouton).

Carroll, John B. (ed.). 1956. *Language, Thought and Reality: Selected Writings of Benjamin Lee Whorf* (Cambridge, Mass.: M.I.T. Press).

Eschholz, Paul, Alfred Rosa, and Virginia Clark (eds.). 1978. *Language Awareness,* 2nd ed. (New York: St. Martin's Press).

Greene, Judith. 1972. *Psycholinguistics: Chomsky and Psychology* (Harmondsworth, England: Penguin Books).

Newman, Edwin H. 1974. *Strictly Speaking: Will America Be the Death of English?* (Indianapolis and New York: Bobbs Merrill).

Osgood, Charles R., George J. Suci, and Percy H. Tannenbaum. 1957. *The Measurement of Meaning* (Urbana: University of Illinois Press).

Montagu, Ashley. 1967. *The Anatomy of Swearing* (New York: Collier Books).

Rank, Hugh (ed.). 1974. *Language and Public Policy* (Urbana: National Council of Teachers of English).

Slobin, D. I. 1971. *Psycholinguistics* (Glenview, Ill.: Scott, Foresman).

GROWTH: THE CHILD AND THE RACE 8

How does a baby learn a language?" and "How did language begin?"—these two questions come readily to mind when we think about human development. But till recently not only were the answers unsatisfactory but one of the questions was not even supposed to be asked in respectable scientific circles: for example, the Linguistic Society of Paris in 1911 reaffirmed its policy of rejecting any paper dealing with the origin of language.[1] Today partial answers, coming from the fields of psychology, anatomy, and anthropology, confirm one another and recall how "ontogeny recapitulates phylogeny"—how the history of the individual repeats in some ways the history of the race. Here we look first at how language is acquired by children, and then at how human beings may have acquired it in the first place.

The development of the interdisciplinary field of psycholinguistics has renewed interest in an old idea: that the human infant is born with an instinctive predisposition for language. For a long time language had been thought to be part of external culture and nothing more. Even the physiology of speech was seen as more or less accidental: our speech organs were really organs of digestion which happened to be utilized to

---

[1] Brown 1973, p. 63, echoes the position: "Speculation about the prehistoric beginnings of language is not a respectable activity."

satisfy a social need. Speech was an "overlaid function." A child in a languageless society, deprived of speech but permitted to chew and swallow, would not have the feeling of missing anything. But now we feel that the organs of speech in their present form were shaped as much for sound production as for nourishment. The human tongue is far more agile than it needs to be for eating and touching. More than that, everyone has experienced the discomfort and sometimes real danger of getting food caught in the windpipe; by adapting itself to speech the human pharynx created a hazard that did not exist before. On the receiving end, the sensitivity of the human ear has been sharpened to the point that it can detect a movement of the eardrum that does not exceed one tenth of the diameter of a hydrogen molecule. We can conclude from all this— as one scientist does—that the notion of speech as a purely overlaid function is "unquestionably false."[2]

Instead, the infant has an "instinct for language"—not for any particular language or grammatical category so much as an inborn set of general-purpose capacities used in language but also available for other skilled activities.

So acquiring a language calls for three things:

1. *predispositions*, as well as physical *capacities*, developed through countless centuries of natural selection;

2. a preexisting language *system*, any one of the many produced by the cultures of the world;

3. a *competence* that comes from applying the predispositions and capacities to the system through the relatively long period during which the child learns both to manipulate the physical elements of the system, such as sounds and words and grammatical rules, and to permeate them with meaning.

The development of so finely graded a specialization of our organs of speech and hearing and of the nervous system to which they are attached is not surprising if we assume that society cannot survive without language and that individual human beings cannot survive without society. Natural selection takes care of it.[3] Language is species-specific. It is a uniquely human trait, shared by cultures so diverse and by individuals physically and mentally so unlike one another—from Watusi tribesmen to nanocephalic dwarfs—that the notion of its being purely a socially transmitted skill is not to be credited.[4]

---

[2] Lamendella 1975, Ch. 2, p. 36.
[3] See Hockett and Ascher 1964.
[4] Lenneberg 1966.

A predisposition for language implies that a child does more than echo what he or she hears. The notion of mere plasticity has been abandoned. The first months are a preparation for language in which babbling, a completely self-directed exercise, is the main activity. Imitation begins to play a part, of course, but it too is experimental and hence creative. We see how this must be if we imagine a child already motivated to imitate and being told by his mother to say *Papa*. This sounds simple to us because we already know which features to heed and which to ignore, but the child must learn to tell them apart. Shall he imitate his mother's look, her gesture, the way she shapes her lips, the breathiness of the first consonant, the voice melody, the moving of the tongue? Even assuming that he can focus on certain things to the exclusion of others, he has no way of knowing which ones to select. He cannot then purely imitate. He must experiment and wait for approval. Imitation is an activity that is shaped creatively.

Also it is guided by meaning, at least part of the time. Imitating just for the fun of imitating does not necessarily precede imitating with some connection to reality. In one case a child adopted his own babbling sound *gigl*, which he had originally produced spontaneously but his father imitated deliberately when they were together, as a sign for 'Daddy's here,' or something of the sort: he reverted to it whenever his father appeared on the scene. Only later did the child get around to producing an imitation just for the fun of it.[5]

IS LANGUAGE LEARNED OR INHERITED?

As early as 1887 the ethnologist Horatio Hale declared that young children have an instinct for language.[6] But he went too far: he theorized that the instinct is not just one for quickly grasping and internalizing whatever existing language a child is exposed to, but one that would enable two children to invent a language out of nothing. We know there is some equipment at birth, or we could never learn to speak. But how explicit is it?

Part of the answer can be inferred from those resemblances—we call them universals in this context—that are so widespread among cultures everywhere as to make it unthinkable that they arose by accident. Two striking examples are intonation and sound-symbolism.

We know two things about intonation. It is the first part of language

---

[5] Engel 1970, p. 29.
[6] Cited in Langer 1948, p. 86.

that a child learns. A child of twelve to eighteen months who speaks no sentences will be heard using sentence intonation on separate words in a perfectly normal way: *Doggie?* with rising pitch, meaning 'Is that a doggie?' or *Doggie,* with falling pitch, to comment on the dog's presence. Secondly, intonation patterns in similar ways in languages all over the world. The similarities are so prevalent that when they are not found one looks for something that interferes with their realization, such as happens in certain tone languages.[7]

Resemblances in sound-symbolism of the type mentioned on page 10 are equally widespread. In one study of 136 languages, 38 were found to have clear evidence of the representation of smallness by means of particular sounds, most often by front and high vowels, and in some tone languages by high tone. The number is greater if one includes the languages that have distance symbolism ("nearness" resembles "small-ness").[8]

Striking as the specific language-to-language resemblances in intonation and sound-symbolism are, they do not prove very much about any supposed linguistic inheritance, for both are a kind of gesture. The mouth shape for high-front vowels shows a narrow opening between tongue and palate; the analogy with both smallness and nearness is obvious. Intonation is even more deeply entrenched. It is gestural in some respects, as when a downward dip of pitch accompanies a submissive or placating bow of the head. But it is also connected with the physiology of speech and with the nervous system in general. The universal lowering of pitch toward the end of unexcited discourse results automatically from running out of lung power: subglottal pressure raises and lowers pitch, other things being equal. The equally universal raising of pitch for questions and other keyed-up utterances is probably the result of higher nervous tension in the body as a whole, which has the local effect of tensing the vocal cords. Given such beginnings, it was only natural for these audible effects to be simulated. If lowered pitch is the normal thing when one is "through," one can adopt it as a gesture to symbolize finality and fake it when necessary. This "innate referential breath group," as the terminal falling pattern has been called, is adopted by children as the phonetic marker of complete sentences.[9] As for nervous tension, it is raw material with a communicative potential so obvious that it was bound to be used in identical ways again and again in the languages of the world, which could occur without any specific inheritance of intonational patterns. Of course this does not rule out some specific capacity of children to hear

---

[7] See Chang 1972, pp. 408–09.
[8] See Ultan 1978; Tanz 1971; and Nichols 1971 (especially pp. 826, 828, and 833).
[9] Lieberman 1967, p. 47.

and develop intonational patterns sooner than phonemic ones. It simply fails to prove the linguistic independence of any such capacity. It is probably musical as much as linguistic.[10]

Nevertheless it is clear that human beings in some sense are programmed for language. The proofs are indirect, but there are too many to be ignored. The psychologist Eric Lenneberg sums them up:[11]

1. Speech, which requires relatively precise and swift movements of the tongue and lips, all well coordinated with laryngeal and respiratory motor systems, is all but fully developed when most other mechanical skills are far below their levels of future accomplishment.

2. Certain diseases, such as muscular atrophy, affect other motor skills but do not necessarily delay language.

3. The stages of development are relatively clear-cut and are found in children everywhere in the world.

4. Children of deaf parents go through the same stages of pre-language vocalization as other children, even though their parents are unable to respond.

5. Deaf children vocalize in the early stages of childhood as much as hearing children do.

6. At least in the early stages, progress from one stage to the next does not require practice. Children who have been prevented from babbling (for example, by surgery) will babble spontaneously, as other children do, once the physical damage is repaired.

The most convincing evidence for an inborn *capacity* for language is Lenneberg's third point, the developmental schedule in children.[12] All children pass through the same stages (not necessarily at the same rate), of which there are three if we start counting after one-word utterances have begun to be used. The first stage is that of basic semantic and grammatical relations. Verbs are there, though uninflected; so are descriptive adjectives; and nouns are discriminated for such functions as agent, direct object, and indirect object. This is basically a stage of two-word sentences, though some longer combinations are found (see Table 8–1 for examples). The second stage brings in the elements most con-

---

10 Van Lancker 1975 reviews the literature on this.
11 Lenneberg 1967, pp. 131–40.
12 Most of what follows in this section is based on Brown 1973.

TABLE 8–1
Sentence Types at the Stage of Prevailing Two-Word Sentences

Ordered Constituents Present	Constituents Omitted	Example
Agent-action-dative-object-locative	None	*Mother gave John lunch in the kitchen.* (non-occurring)*
Agent-action	Object	*Mommy fix.*
Agent-object	Action	*Mommy pumpkin. (is cutting a)*
Agent-locative	Action	*Baby table. (is eating at a)*
Action-dative	Agent, object	*Give doggie. (you give it to)*
Action-object	Agent	*Hit ball. (I)*
	Agent, locative	*Put light. (I, there)*
Action-locative	Agent-object	*Put floor. (I, it, on)*
Agent-action-object	None	*I ride horsie.*
Agent-action-locative	None	*Tractor go floor.*
Action-dative-object	Agent	*Give doggie paper.*
Action-object-locative	Agent	*Put truck window.*
Agent-action-object-locative	None	*Adam put it box.*

SOURCE: Adapted from p. 205 of *A First Language: The Early Stages,* by Roger Brown. © 1973 by the President and Fellows of Harvard College.

* No actual examples of this occurred in the study from which the other examples were taken. In the other examples the words in parentheses are needed to complete the child's meaning as the experimenter observed it.

spicuously lacking in the first, those essential grammatical morphemes with which meaning is modulated: inflections of the verb and noun, articles, prepositions, and auxiliary verbs. See Table 8–2 for the order in which they are acquired. In the third stage the child advances to a complex grammatical interplay of which the best illustration is the ability to use tag questions correctly. At Stage 2 a child can express a tag question but only with some such stereotype as *hunh*—for example, *You like it, hunh?*—but at the third stage the proper selection is made: *You like it, don't you? He ate them, didn't he? She's here, isn't she?* What determines the three-stage order is relative complexity of meaning and grammar. It cannot be the frequency of individual forms in the adult speech heard by the child—if that were the case, *the, a, and,* and such things as inflectional endings would appear first, whereas in fact certain of these forms, such as *and, but,* and *because,* are not fully understood

TABLE 8–2
Mean Order in Which Three Children Acquired
Fourteen Grammatical Morphemes

Morpheme	Example	Average Rank
1. Present progressive	*-ing* (as in **Mama talking**)	2.33
2–3. *in, on*	*on table*	2.50
4. Plural	*-s (shoes)*	3.00
5. Past irregular	*went, broke*	6.00
6. Possessive	*-'s (Pat's hair)*	6.33
7. Uncontractable copula	*is*	6.50
8. Articles	*the, a, an*	7.00
9. Past regular	*-ed (played)*	9.00
10. Third-person regular	*-s (plays)*	9.66
11. Third-person irregular	*-s (does, has)*	10.83
12. Uncontractable auxiliary	*is (is working)*	11.66
13. Contractable copula	*'s (Pat's funny)*	12.66
14. Contractable auxiliary	*'s (Pat's going)*	14.00

SOURCE: Adapted from p. 274 of *A First Language: The Early Stages,* by Roger Brown. © 1973 by the President and Fellows of Harvard College.

until early adolescence.

The scholar responsible for assembling the evidence for these regularities, the psycholinguist Roger Brown, agrees that they are impressive, but does not accept the arguments for innateness:

> Linguists and psycholinguists when they discover facts that are at all general have, nowadays, a tendency to predict that they will prove to be universal and must, "therefore," be considered innate. The Stage 1 meanings have proved to have some generality . . . and I do feel tempted to hypothesize universality. But not innateness . . . because . . . it is my impression that the first meanings are an extension of the kind of intelligence that Jean Piaget calls sensorimotor. And Piaget has shown that sensorimotor intelligence develops out of the infant's commerce with objects and persons during the first 18–24 months of life . . . an essentially practical intelligence that is acted out rather than thought. . . . Piaget's description of the time when each thing is conceived by the child in terms of the schemas into which it can enter—as "graspable," "suckable," "scratchable," and so on—is irresistibly suggestive of the development of lexical entries for nouns and verbs

which describe the combinations in which they can enter. Which is not to say that the sensorimotor process is linguistic but that the linguistic process does not start from nothing and can build on data that are not linguistic.[13]

This parallel development of motor skill and language skill is shown in Table 8–3. Grammatical relations, of course, are not the same thing as playing with objects, and clearly there is *something* about language that goes beyond sensorimotor intelligence. But there is no way at present to test whether it is innate or learned.

Yet there is no question that human infants come into the world with vastly more preformed capacity for language than used to be thought possible. There is evidence that even a four-week-old infant is especially tuned to react to speech sounds as against other sounds.[14] But whether or not the genetic design contains elements that are explicitly linguistic hinges on the overall question of explicitness. There is so much inter-dependence in the unfolding of our capacities that we cannot be sure that the linguistic ones do not start as nonlinguistic, only to be made linguistic by features of the environment. Suppose that language and tool using have the same basic mechanisms, as some anthropologists maintain (see pages 180–81). At a certain point the infant discovers that he has a right hand and a left hand, and he discovers objects. This is an event external to his brain, but at the same time it is inevitable, and along with other external events it molds capacities around the use of tools. At the same time or later the infant discovers words as objects. He is already equipped to use objects, and a simple transfer molds this capacity around a subject and a predicate—a thing and what you do to it. It is not neces-sary to have a predisposition to grammatical subjects and grammatical predicates; that can take shape from the objects that lie around the child as he matures, whether they are things of nature, cultural artifacts, or words.

ARE ADULTS INNATELY TEACHERS OF LANGUAGE?

We do not know the extent to which children are taught and the extent to which they learn on their own. If learning is instinctive, then children will learn whether or not adults appoint themselves to be their teachers. But if there is an instinct to learn, for all we know there may be an instinct to teach. It is probable that parents unconsciously adopt special

---

[13] Ibid., pp. 198–200.
[14] Mattingly 1973.

TABLE 8-3
Developmental Milestones in Motor and Language Development

At the Completion of:	Motor Development
12 weeks	Supports head when in prone position; weight is on elbows; hands mostly open; no grasp reflex
16 weeks	Plays with rattle placed in hands (by shaking it and staring at it); head self-supported; tonic neck reflex subsiding
20 weeks	Sits with props
6 months	Sitting: bends forward and uses hands for support; can bear weight when put into standing position, but cannot yet stand without holding on. Reaching: unilateral. Grasp: no thumb apposition yet; releases cube when given another
8 months	Stands holding on; grasps with thumb apposition; picks up pellet with thumb and finger tips
10 months	Creeps efficiently; takes side-steps, holding on; pulls to standing position
12 months	Walks when held by one hand; walks on feet and hands—knees in air; mouthing of objects almost stopped; seats self on floor
18 months	Grasp, prehension, and release fully developed; gait stiff, propulsive, and precipitated; sits on child's chair with only fair aim; creeps downstairs backward; has difficulty building tower of three cubes
24 months	Runs, but falls in sudden turns; can quickly alternate between sitting and stance; walks stairs up or down, one foot forward only
30 months	Jumps up into air with both feet; stands on one foot for about two seconds; takes a few steps on tiptoe; jumps from chair; good hand and finger coordination; can move digits independently; manipulation of objects much improved; builds tower of six cubes
3 years	Tiptoes 3 yards; runs smoothly with acceleration and deceleration; negotiates sharp and fast curves without difficulty; walks stairs by alternating feet; jumps 12 inches; can operate tricycle
4 years	Jumps over rope; hops on right foot; catches ball in arms; walks line

SOURCE: Adapted from Lenneberg 1967, pp. 128–30.

Vocalization and Language

Markedly less crying than at 8 weeks; when talked to and nodded at, smiles, followed by squealing-gurgling sounds usually called *cooing*, which is vowel-like in character and pitch-modulated; sustains cooing for 15–20 seconds

Responds to human sounds more definitely; turns head; eyes seem to search for speaker; occasionally some chuckling sounds

The vowel-like cooing sounds begin to be interspersed with more consonantal sounds: labial fricatives, spirants, and nasals are common; acoustically, all vocalizations are very different from the sounds of the mature language of the environment

Cooing changing into babbling resembling one-syllable utterances; neither vowels nor consonants have very fixed recurrences; most common utterances sound somewhat like *ma, mu, da,* or *di*

Reduplication (or more continuous repetitions) becomes frequent; intonation patterns become distinct; utterances can signal emphasis and emotions

Vocalizations are mixed with sound-play such as gurgling or bubble-blowing; appears to wish to imitate sounds, but the imitations are never quite successful; beginning to differentiate between words heard by making differential adjustment

Identical sound sequences are replicated with higher relative frequency of occurrence, and words *(mamma* or *dadda)* are emerging; definite signs of understanding some words and simple commands *(Show me your eyes)*

Has a definite repertoire of words—more than three, but less than fifty; still much babbling but now of several syllables, with intricate intonation pattern; no attempt at communicating information and no frustration at not being understood; words may include items such as *thank you* or *come here,* but there is little ability to join any of the lexical items into spontaneous two-item phrases; understanding progressing rapidly

Vocabulary of more than fifty items (some children seem to be able to name everything in environment); begins spontaneously to join vocabulary items into two-word phrases; all phrases appear to be own creations; definite increase in communicative behavior and interest in language

Fastest increase in vocabulary, with many new additions every day; no babbling at all; utterances have communicative intent; frustrated if not understood by adults; utterances consist of at least two words—many have three or even five words; sentences and phrases have characteristic child grammar—that is, are rarely verbatim repetitions of an adult utterance; intelligibility not very good yet, though there is great variation among children; seems to understand everything said within hearing and directed to self

Vocabulary of some one thousand words; about 80 percent of utterances intelligible even to strangers; grammatical complexity of utterances roughly that of colloquial adult language, although mistakes still occur

Language well established; deviations from the adult norm tend to be more in style than in grammar

modes of speaking to very young children, to help them learn the important things first—impelled by the desire not so much to teach as to communicate, with teaching a by-product.

One psychologist noted the following ways in which she simplified her own speech when talking to her child:

1. the use of a more striking variant of a speech sound when there was a choice—for example, using the *t* of *table* when saying the word *butter* in place of the more usual flapped sound (almost like *budder*);

2. exaggerated intonation, with greater ups and downs of pitch;

3. slower rate;

4. simple sentence structure—for example, avoidance of the passive voice;

5. avoidance of substitute words like *it*—for example, *Where's your milk? Show me your milk* instead of *Where's your milk? Show it to me*.[15]

Most parents would probably add *repetition* to this list.

The stages of acquisition

If language is adaptive, and if children as they grow have different needs, then one can argue that the grammar used at any one age is perhaps the "best" grammar for that age. It follows that the way a child of three speaks is not just a bad imitation of the way an adult speaks, but is the way a three-year-old ought to speak. As one authority puts it, "The child approaches the language-learning task not once but several times; not with just one set of innate structures, but rather a succession of them corresponding to the developmental stages of human cognitive equipment."[16]

The first stage of communication is the *doggie* stage, when parents feel that their children have really begun to speak. Individual words are being pronounced intelligibly and are being related to things and events. It is called the *holophrastic* stage: utterance and thing are related one to one. The single word *mama* globally includes not just a person but a presence; it is a name and a sentence at the same time: 'Mama's here', 'Take me,

---

15 Gleitman and Shipley 1963, p. 24.
16 Lamendella 1973, p. 31.

Mama,' or whatever. And if one equals two, two also equals one: the parental *all gone* is a single word, *awgone,* symbolizing the fascinating sensation of a disappearance.

Next is the *joining* stage, syntax in its simplest form. The child brings together two of his names for things or actions, perhaps wavering between them if both happen to be appropriate for a situation. This is the most mysterious and at the same time the greatest step of all: from a simple inward-outward connectedness to a connectedness within language. It was once thought to be a uniquely human accomplishment, but now we know that at least some animals are capable of it. The joining stage is fully in hand when putting words together becomes a form of play. There is much self-directed repetition; children's monologs sometimes sound like students doing pattern drills in a language lab. One study of the sleepytime monologs of a two-and-a-half-year-old revealed substitution drills, buildups, breakdowns, and variation drills with sound-play:

What color?	Bobo's not throwing.
What color blanket?	Bobo can throw.
What color mop?	Bobo can throw it.
What color glass?	Bobo can throw.
	Oh.
Block.	Oh.
Yellow block.	Go.
Look at all the yellow block.	Go.
Clock off.	Go.[17]
Clock.	
Off.	

But more than repetition, there is adventure. When a child of this age runs to her parents and says *House eat baby*—the sort of expression that unimaginative adults brush aside as preposterous or even punish as "untrue"—she is only exulting over the discovery that she can do the same with her words as with her building blocks: put them together in dazzling ways. And creativity goes further when a child says "I'm spoon-fulling it in," or refers to a "strokey cat."[18]

The third stage can be called the *connective* stage and is a solution to the complexity—and confusion—that would otherwise afflict most combinations of three or more words.[19] A two-word sentence has little

---

[17] Weir 1962, pp. 82, 109, 120.

[18] See Britton 1970, p. 43.

[19] That is, *content* words—all those words other than grammatical indicators such as *that, and, when, he, by,* etc. See pages 67–69.

need for connective tissue. The elements are of equal rank, and if one knows their meanings it is not even necessary to put them in any particular order—a child is as apt to say *awgone shoe* as to say *shoe awgone.* But the longer the sentence becomes, the more need there is for directing traffic, and the grammatical signs are posted one by one: verb endings, conjunctions, prepositions, articles, auxiliaries. At the same time the child is growing intellectually, and some of the connectives open up new depths of experience. Past and future tenses reach out from the moment of living and speaking—*I used to live in Denver; He's going to jump;* modes and conditions prefigure unreality as if it were real—*They won't leave me alone! He would cry if you did.*

This step-by-step increase in complexity is illustrated in the responses given by one child at various ages to the command *Ask your daddy what he did at work today.* At two years and five months it was *What he did at work today?,* which shows enough understanding to separate the inner question from the command as a whole (*Ask your daddy* is not repeated), but no more. At the age of three, the response was *What you did at work today?* with the right change of intonation and with *you* for *he.* The child is now really asking a question but has "optimized" its form—that is, he has fitted a newly acquired expression into the mold of an old one that resembles it and is familiar and easy, in this case making the word order of statements serve also for questions. Finally, at three years and five months, the child made the right transformation of the verb and produced *What did you do at work today?*[20]

Optimizing occurs at all stages. Whenever a child is mentally ready to progress to a new stage, she will try for a time to use just the means that she already knows. She may learn a new word but not be equipped to handle all the sounds in it, and say *woof* for *roof.* She may want to ask a question but still lack the grammar for it, and say *What you did at work today?*

The fourth and final stage in the development of communication is the *recursive* stage. It comes with an awareness of linguistic structures as such. Until children have some notion of how a sentence is put together, they are unable to manipulate it as a grammatical unit. Indeed, the furthest advance that human language has made is in the power to fold in on itself, to treat a complex structure as if it were a simple entity—a kind of abstracting like that of algebra. Building a complicated sentence like *I hear that you don't like it* involves saying something like "Let S (sentence) equal N (noun)," where S is represented by *You don't like it,* a sentence that is being treated as if it were a noun, the object of *I hear.* The same awareness that enables children to build complex sentences

---

[20] Gleitman and Shipley 1963, p. 14.

also enables them to talk about language and to make stylistic choices.

In real life there are no stages, only gradations. But to talk about gradations we have to clump them as if they were discontinuous, to pretend that there is a line instead of a shading between violet and red. The spectrum of language learning has been divided up for discussion as if the lines between the linguistic structures were absolute. A favorite generalization used to be that children have complete control of their language by the age of five or six. Without disparaging the truly phenomenal control of an enormously complex system that six-year-olds do achieve, we must realize that no limit can be set and that learning by the same old processes continues through life, though at a rate that diminishes so rapidly that well before adolescence it seems almost to have come to a stop. The rate might be described as a curve that starts by virtually touching infinity and ends by approaching zero.

The grammars of childhood

We have distinguished four stages in the development of language: holophrastic (or one-word), joining, connective, and recursive. These will serve as labels for the grammars to be talked about here.

The grammar of the holophrastic stage is the lack of grammar. With only single words, nothing can be related within language. The only relation is the most important relationship of all, the one between language and situation. Very young children probably resort to naming "as an almost reflexive concomitant of perceptual identification"—that is, to help recognize and contemplate what they perceive.[21] One team of psychologists suggests how the child arrives at a concept of nounness and verbness. To begin with there is a repeated connection between the mother's voicing of something and the appearance of an attention-getting object. Many neurons are excited when this happens, and different groupings are excited at different times; but since the mother's vocalization is a constant, one set of neurons is repeatedly excited. This creates a neural assembly, which viewed subjectively is "the abstract idea of a name." The child then perceives two things on any such occasion: the particular word that the mother uses, which is a lower-order cognition, and the interconnection with other acts of naming, which is a higher-order cognition, an abstract sense of nounness—there is a double perception, half on the surface and half in depth. "Verbness" is acquired in the same way, and once the two classes are established directly the child has an indirect means as well as the direct one of putting new items in the proper cate-

---

[21] Flavell, Friedrichs, and Hoyt 1970, p. 338.

gory: if the child knows the words *people, dog,* and **Bobby** and hears **People kivil, The dog kivils,** and **Bobby kivils,** the word *kivil* stands in the same relation to familiar nouns as do other verbs that are already known, and is properly categorized as a verb. Nounness and verbness become complementary abstractions.[22] At this stage there is nothing to suggest that the child differentiates between noun and verb. Things and activities are both merely named.

The grammar of the joining stage is the beginning of grammar proper, when two names are brought into relation with each other. How this happens has been described by tape-recording the utterances of two Hungarian-speaking children from the time they began to speak till they were ten years old and transcribing them phonetically. The joining of two elements is revealed not to be something that happens in a flash and then is secure forever, but something that comes about many times by chance; the union may be as quickly dissolved, but is eventually cemented. One such happy collision of names occurred for the boy, Pierre:

> During the months of April and May (age one year and eight to nine months) we had the rare opportunity of recording through several repetitions the *progressive formation* of the bipolar phrase. In one of those historic moments, Pierre was busy looking at one of his favorite pictures, of a rider jumping his horse over a hedge. His reaction during the previous month had been to waver between saying *ló* (horse) and **ugrik** (jump), the two elements of the parental sentence **Look, the horse is jumping over the hedge.** He used one or the other expression indifferently, as if either were capable of representing the situation as a whole. But the day of our recording, May 29, he seemed attracted by the picture to the point of fascination. The one-word utterances *ló* and **ugrik** were repeated at rhythmic intervals and the pauses between them became shorter. The pitch curves, which had been independently parallel at first, became complementary, as if to express an awareness of their mutual existence and rapport, and finally, with the fifth repetition, the two expressions were joined in a single bipolar phrase.[23]

After this inspired beginning Pierre went back to his single repetitions, and many other such relapses occurred till well past the age of two. We cannot read the child's mind and know when he means a succession of two words to be taken as more than just a succession, but we can observe how he joins them rhythmically and intonationally.

The second grammar is a good working grammar, and if only two things had to be dealt with at a time it could serve indefinitely. The shift to the third, or connective, grammar is a struggle for children, not only

---

[22] Hebb, Lambert, and Tucker 1971, pp. 220–21.
[23] Fónagy 1972, pp. 41–43.

because manipulating three or more things is much harder than manipulating two but because it marks the beginning of arbitrariness. The second grammar is the simplest and most logical: an invariant term is tied to a more or less stable concept. The learning of pure reference is the thread that the second grammar has in common with the first.[24] The only room for arbitrariness is in the order in which the elements occur, and in this respect children seem to imitate what they hear but without any strict necessity—they often reverse the sequence.

In the third grammar children would like to carry on with the one-to-one correspondence of form and meaning, but now they are forced to conform. As they learn the grammatical morphemes, which are the symptoms of the third grammar, they master forms from the standpoint of correctness as well as meaning. This goes hand-in-hand with juggling ever more complex utterances; in fact, the complexity is one motive for it, since an important use of the function words is to keep the interrelationships clear in a sentence containing several words. Children grasp the meanings of the grammatical morphemes before they are able to organize and produce them themselves—they will, for example, obey more readily a command expressed according to the adult model than one using childish syntax.[25] The third grammar forces them not only to have categories but to mark them—nouns for plurality, verbs for agreement, adjectives for comparison, if the language is English—and to do so at times in inconsistent ways, as when the past of *go* is not admitted as **goed* but has to be *went.* Mastering the third grammar extends well into middle childhood.

The fourth, or recursive, grammar might be termed the grammar grammar—the one in which grammar is not only used but used with some awareness of it as grammar. The foundations of course are laid in the preceding stage. Children are constantly being corrected—sometimes by others but mostly by their own observation—and when they are forced to substitute *deer* for **deers* and *fought* for **fighted* they set up some kind of proportion such as "*deer* is to *deer* as *dog* is to *dogs*" or "*fight* is to *fought* as *work* is to *worked.*" They may at first learn *fought* and the plural *deer* as isolated words, but eventually the abstract proportion has to be mastered because otherwise it is impossible to handle such things as tag questions and negations: *"He hit me!"—"No he didn't!"—"Yes he did!"* presupposes a category of pastness to which *hit* and *did hit* both belong. But the pattern does not come easily. Here as in the other stages we see the physical event often preceding the cognitive grasp of it —for example, sounds are babbled before they are learned as a system.[26]

---

[24] Scholes 1969.

[25] Shipley, Smith, and Gleitman 1969.

[26] Jakobson 1968. The reference is courtesy of Paul T. Hopper.

In his second grammar, Pierre put words together before he actually caught on to the interesting possibilities of what he was doing. Similarly children will often anticipate the third grammar by using a correct inflected form such as *fought* before they learn the rule for adding the past tense morpheme *-ed.* After they do learn the rule they may then shift to the incorrect °*fighted* for a time and not return to *fought* till the fourth grammar begins to set things right. The clearest sign of the fourth grammar emerges a little later: children's ability to talk about what they do. By the age of four to six most children can pass fairly sophisticated judgments on some errors of syntax. Children start to do this at about the same time as they begin to be able to perform other "meta-cognitive" functions, such as explaining their judgments of space and number or working out strategies for remembering. One can say of the child's new power that it consists in a detachment of language from the immediate situation, whereby it can be used not just for interaction with the present scene but for *control* of the environment, including control of itself.

To illustrate talking about language, here is an interview between a mother (M) and her seven-year-old daughter (D). (The girl had played such games before and was quite adept.)

M: We're going to talk about sentences this morning. And I want your opinion about these sentences.

D: Yes, I know.

M: Are they good sentences, are they bad sentences, do they mean something, are they silly, whatever your opinions are.
Okay: *John and Mary went home.*

D: That's okay.

M: That's an okay sentence?

D: Yes.

M: Does it mean the same thing as: *John went home and Mary went home?*

D: Yes, but it's sort of a little different because they might be going to the same home—well, it's okay, because they both might mean that, so it's the same.

M: Here's another one: *Two and two are four.*

D: I think it sounds better *is.*

M: *Two and two is four?*

D: Am I right?

M: Well, people say it both ways. How about this one: *Claire and Eleanor is a sister.*

D: (laugh) *Claire and Eleanor are sisters.*

M: Well then, how come it's all right to say *Two and two is four?*

D: You can say different sentences different ways! (annoyed)

M: I see, does this mean the same thing: *Two is four and two is four?*

D: No, because *two and two are two and two* and *two and two is four.*

M: Isn't that a little funny?

D: *Two and two more is four,* also you can say that.

M: How about this one: *Boy is at the door.*

D: If his name is *Boy.* You should—the kid is named *John,* see? *John is at the door* or *A boy is at the door* or *He's knocking at the door.*

. . . .

M: Why do you like to play a game like this? What's the difference how you say things as long as people understand you?

D: It's a difference because people would stare at you (titter). No, but I think it's fun. Because I don't want somebody coming around and saying —correcting me.

M: Oh, so that's why you want to learn how to speak properly?'

D: That's not the only reason.

M: Well, what is it?

D: Well, there's a lotta reasons, but I think this game is plain fun.[27]

Grammar that is conscious of itself is about as far as grammar can go. And the fullest potential of human language is realized when it becomes its own metalanguage: "All our discussion about language is carried on in that very medium. Can one talk about flatworm communication in the flatworm system? Can a chimpanzee . . . talk about talking?"[28]

The division into four grammars naturally makes things seem much tidier than they ever truly are. A later grammar does not supersede an earlier one; it incorporates it. And there are always tasks belonging to one stage that are never fully carried out till later. Even pronunciation problems drag on. A child of thirty months who can handle sentences of several words still has to struggle with certain difficult sounds such as [θ], [æ], and palatals other than [č] and may continue to substitute [b] for [v].[29] The conquest of speech advances on all fronts at the same time.

THE ORIGIN OF LANGUAGE

So far we have been rehearsing what we know of the way each *infant* (from the Latin meaning 'without speech') becomes a member of human society. With speech an infant becomes a child. By observing young children learning their native language we gain insights into how language itself may have started—insights that are confirmed from various other lines of investigation. These include measurement of prehistoric human skeletons to see whether they had the anatomical prerequisites for

---

[27] Gleitman, Gleitman, and Shipley 1973, pp. 148–51.

[28] Bender 1973, p. 11.

[29] Weir 1962, p. 142.

speaking; investigations of non-speech systems, such as the sign language of the deaf, to see how necessary actual speech is to the process; the study of natural animal communication; experiments in teaching apes to communicate, to ascertain whether language requires fully developed human intelligence; and of course the excavation of archeological remains, especially of tools, which have their own peculiar relationship to language.

What most older theories about origins had in common was a tacit belief in the existence of language as something separate from people. For the Bible it lies at the root of creation: *In the beginning was the Word.* For the eighteenth-century philosophers it was invented; man was there beforehand, accoutered with all the powers that he has today except for speech. For speculative linguists it was discovered, in a kind of how-to way: you can bark like a dog to represent 'dog,' go *ding-dong* to represent 'bell,' and say *ta-ta* on leaving a friend, "waving" good-bye to him with your tongue. The insights of the theory of evolution came a century later: it took that long to realize that language was simply part of the development of the human race, inseparable from other physical and mental powers, modifying and being modified by them. All life forms transmit. Some use sounds, others smell, touch, taste, movement, temperature changes, or electrical charges. Their messages maintain social unity, warn off predators, attract mates, point to sources of food, and otherwise help keep the species going.[30] As Darwin made clear a century ago, the facial expressions that back up much of human language are an extension of those used by all the primates.[31] There was probably no quantum break with this past; too much of it is still with us. But there must have emerged a succession of differences, important enough to select for survival only those human beings who possessed them to a higher and higher degree.

The first great barrier in animal communication that had to be surmounted was *fixity of reference.* Most animal messages are connected with just one thing in the real world: a growl is a warning to an enemy; a particular scent is an attraction to a mate; a cluck is a summons to a brood of chicks. A dog does not come to his master and growl to indicate that there is an enemy approaching; the growl is *at* what stimulates it. But transferred meanings are the rule in human language. Basically one steals a purse or a paycheck, but one may also steal a base or steal the limelight. Form and meaning are detached from each other and to some extent go their own ways. It would be unfair to other species to say that no such detachment is to be found in the non-human world. There are birds that appear to vary their song in ways that are not instinctively

---

[30] See Sebeok 1969.
[31] Darwin 1873.

predetermined, and neighboring species of fireflies do not all use the same courtship flashes.[32] But this degree of freedom is exceptional. It is also exceptional in the human young up to a certain age. But children soon learn that *orange* not only means a particular piece of fruit regardless of what position or condition of lighting it is seen in, but can also be used of an entire class of similar objects.

The second barrier that had to be surmounted was *holophrasis,* the emitting of just one independent signaling unit at a time. Animal communication appears to lack syntax. Without it, propositional language is impossible—one cannot say anything *about* anything, but is limited to command-like or exclamation-like utterances, and those in turn are limited to the here and now. Again, human infants lack syntax up to about the age of two, but eventually get the hang of putting words together.

There were further barriers, but these two had to be leveled first, and we must ask why all the life forms on earth had to wait millions of years for *Homo* to do it. Was it because a certain level of intelligence had to be developed first? But how could that be, when intelligence seems so dependent on language?

The answer seems to be that something a step lower than human intelligence is enough to surmount the first two barriers. Here we can learn from the experiments with two famous chimpanzees, Washoe and Sarah. Washoe learned the American Sign Language to the point of transmitting not only one-word messages but messages using combinations as well, and the signs that she used acquired the same flexibility that human words have. For example, she learned the sign for 'more' as a way to get her trainers to keep tickling her, but then transferred the sign to a game of being pushed in a laundry cart, and afterwards extended it spontaneously to swinging by the arms and eventually to ask for the continuation of any activity. Examples of two-word sign-sentences that she invented were 'Open food-drink' for 'Open the refrigerator' and 'Open flower' for a request to be led through a gate to a flower garden.[33] As for Sarah, she used visual signs also, but in place of movements of the hands and fingers she was given plastic tokens of various shapes and colors. These she learned to a point where she was able to interpret fairly complex commands, amounting, for example, to compound sentences. In one experiment, after being taught to respond correctly to 'Sarah insert apple pail,' 'Sarah insert banana pail,' 'Sarah insert apple dish,' and 'Sarah insert banana dish,' she was confronted with 'Sarah insert apple pail Sarah insert banana dish,' which she duly obeyed; and finally the re-

---

[32] Jakobson 1969.

[33] Gardner and Gardner 1969.

dundant words were omitted so that the command read 'Sarah insert apple pail banana dish,' and again she responded correctly. To do so she had to recognize that 'banana' went with 'dish' and not with 'pail,' despite the fact that it was between the names of the two receptacles.[34]

The chimps will probably go on to higher things. The trainers of Washoe, the psychologists Allen and Beatrice Gardner and their team, are working on a younger generation of chimpanzees and have some expectation of teaching them to read.[35] Of course, the fact that chimpanzees had the intelligence to create syntax does not prove that they did create it; perhaps only the determination and diligence of human trainers could bring it off. But the brain capacity is there, and Washoe has taught signs to her adopted baby Loulis, whose favorite is the sign for 'hug.'[36]

The third barrier in communication was *lack of metalanguage*. Until elements of language were introduced that referred to language, it was not possible to turn syntax inward and enable it to build on itself. Take as simple an element as a relative pronoun. In a sentence such as **Do you know the person who wrote this?** the word *who* facilitates the joining of two sentences of which one defines an element in the other.

Looking back at the three barriers we can see that the surmounting of each one was a further gain in recursiveness, in the power to limit the units at one level of language sufficiently to make them manageable and at the same time, at another level, to use them over and over in building larger units. The breakaway from fixed reference made words available not just for single referents but for classes of them. The attainment of syntax made words usable not just one at a time but in combination. The arrival of metalanguage redoubled syntax.

PREADAPTATION[37]

We cannot suppose that any (except perhaps the last) of the long series of evolutionary steps that led to language was actually *aimed* at what it eventually produced. Rather, like the swimming bladder that preceded the lung, it was a mechanism that was on hand and could be adapted to a new use. The ancestors of the apes that first took to the trees to escape predators had to have the forelimb structure that made tree-climbing possible. That in turn created a selective pressure for still more special-

---

[34] Premack and Premack 1972.

[35] Gardner and Gardner 1978.

[36] *Newsweek* (28 May 1979).

[37] The term is Darwin's, and is taken here from Lieberman 1974, on which the information in the first part of this section is based.

ized use of those limbs, and structures properly called "arms" were the result. With the descent from the trees, the specialization of arms from legs led in turn to the possibility of standing and walking erect. This made it useful to modify the position of the head, which had to be moved forward to direct the eyes properly. Some progress must already have been made in that direction during the tree-climbing years, since clinging to a vertical trunk to some extent forces an erect posture. As this posture became the normal one, the larynx was pushed down, changing the configuration of the vocal tract and providing for a wider range of vocal sounds. (See Figure 8–1 for a comparison of the adult human vocal tract with that of a newborn human infant, an adult chimpanzee, and Neanderthal man. The important difference is the right-angled bend in the human tract and the location of the long pharyngeal cavity *above* the voice box, or larynx, where the cavity can serve as a resonator.) The "origin" of language from these adaptive changes covers millions of years. But of course it is the later phases that interest us most, for it is only with the *use* of the apparatus to carry messages that language as we know it can be said to begin.

No other primate uses the vocal organs to communicate anything but rudimentary warnings and emotive cries. That is why earlier attempts to teach apes to communicate with human beings were failures, and why Washoe was taught a sign language. The normal channel with primates is the visual one. They cannot speak because their vocal mechanism does not permit it: they do not move their tongues during a cry, and the sounds that their larynx produces cannot be modulated for fine pitch contrasts.[38]

Earlier human forms undoubtedly could manage better than a modern chimpanzee, but they too lacked the physical equipment to match the range of modern man. Reconstruction of skulls and vocal musculature reveals that Neanderthal man could not utter the three most stable vowels, [a], [i], and [u]; it would have been harder for him than for us to create sharply differentiated vowel sounds. He could have produced dental and labial consonants ([d b s z v f]), but may not have been able to make a contrast between nasal and non-nasal. Of course even with just two audible contrasts, a phoneme-like code is possible, as any digital computer will tell you—apes could talk if they knew how. But the fewer the contrasts that can be made, the more laborious the coding becomes, so primates would have required greater intellectual powers, not weaker ones. We can conclude that while the lower range of sounds possible for Neanderthal would not have precluded his talking, they required too high a grade of intelligence for him to do much of it. The drive toward vocal expression had begun, but still had a long way to go.

---

[38] Lieberman 1972, p. 35.

FIGURE 8–1
Air Passages of the Adult Chimpanzee, the Newborn Human,
Neanderthal Man, and the Adult Human*

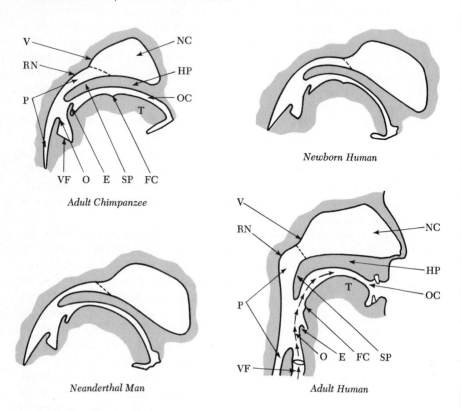

SOURCE: Adapted from Lieberman 1972, p. 109.

* The anatomical details are as follows: P = pharynx, RN = roof of nasopharynx, V = vomer bone, NC = nasal cavity, HP = hard palate, OC = oral cavity, T = tongue, FC = foramen cecum, SP = soft palate, E = epiglottis, O = opening of larynx into pharynx, and VF = level of vocal folds.

Meanwhile, as a basis for what was to become spoken language, a fairly elaborate system of gesture must have been in use.[39] Culture was already too far advanced at a time when *Homo* still did not have the power of speech for there not to have been some way of handing skills

---

[39] See especially Hewes 1971 and 1973. Most of the discussion here is based on Hewes.

down from one generation to the next—literally handing, for tool using was the most important skill and is best taught by demonstration, just as it is today. Washoe's trainers found that "a particularly effective and convenient method of shaping [the signs] consisted of holding Washoe's hands, forming them into a configuration, and putting them through the movements of a sign."[40] There is no great distance between signing how to use a tool and signing other meanings; manual shaping is the easiest way to do it. It would be easier to teach children to speak if we could reach into their mouths and mold their tongues. Even now it is the sounds that children can see that they learn most easily (such as the labials [b p m]).

Could a gesture language have become as expressive a medium of communication as spoken language? Today, among the congenitally deaf, it is very nearly so. The American Sign Language has its own scheme of arbitrary units, roughly corresponding to a syllabary in spoken language. And sign language is akin to speech in other ways. Though it was invented, it is now handed down by tradition and is undergoing the same kinds of changes as natural language. It is somewhat like a pidgin language, first imposed by necessity and then going native, becoming "creolized." An example of internal change is the word for 'sweetheart,' which half a century ago was formed by bringing the hands together at the edge of the little fingers and cupping the heart, but now is formed with all the fingers in contact except the thumb, more in keeping with other signs in the system. The word has been "leveled," as when a child alters **broke** to **breaked** to conform to other -ed words.[41] Furthermore, sign language has developed social distinctions and regional dialects.[42]

Whether sign language as elaborate as this could have been developed without being preceded by spoken language, or whether deaf people even today could survive if they were not sheltered by a society that mostly uses talk, are unanswered questions that may raise some doubts. But then it is not necessary to suppose that primitive sign languages were quite so advanced. It is enough to assume that there was gesture, that those skilled in using it had a better chance to survive, and therefore that any improvement in it would have been reinforced by natural selection. This set the intellectual stage for the transfer to speech, while the physiological stage was probably set by factors already mentioned—man's increasingly erect posture with its lowering of the larynx and the "bent tube" enlargement of the vocal tract. At the same time that the hands were no longer needed for locomotion and were free for tool using and

---

[40] Gardner and Gardner 1969, p. 672.

[41] Based on Bellugi and Klima 1973, especially pp. 12, 83, 87.

[42] Carl G. Croneberg, "Sign Language Dialects," in Stokoe, Casterline, and Croneberg 1965, pp. 313–15.

for gestures, the vocal mechanism was as if by accident being prepared to take over. And skill with tools was making it easier to lay up a supply of food so as to restrict the need to chew to a few relatively brief periods, which in turn freed the mouth and tongue for more verbal play.

These advances were reflected in a more complex social organization. If skill with tools is to be transmitted continuously it requires more than the tradition of a single family. As social interdependence increased, dependence on instincts was lessened, and this made for greater resilience in adapting to the environment. An ice age would not wipe out a race that could keep warm by clothing itself rather than having to pass through the tedious evolutionary stages that might develop more "natural" modes of protection such as body hair. Instinctive behavior receded farther and farther into the background, and what we call intelligence superseded it.

What makes it seem the more likely that the skills of tool using and language were tied together in human prehistory is that the brain itself houses them in the same general region. In its long development the human brain became lateralized, with functions calling for analysis—tool using, language, symbolic behavior in general—largely confined to one side (the left, for most people, which controls the *right* side of the body), and space perception, environmental sensitivities, and holistic appreciation confined to the other or more evenly distributed between the two.[43] One can see certain analogies in this kind of brain specialization between the special ways that tools are used and sentences are constructed. With tools, the left hand develops a holding grip while the right develops various precision grips—it "does something to" what is held in the left hand. A propositional sentence contains a topic (usually the grammatical subject) and a comment (usually the grammatical predicate), which does something to or tells something about the topic (see page 89). In a discourse, the topic is often "held over"—our imagery suggests the analogy with handedness.

Whereas language and tool using are related in the brain, language and primitive cries are not. In humans an electrical stimulus on the cortex —the region of highest organization—will cause vocalization; in animals the stimulus generally has to be applied below the cortex.[44] This makes it highly unlikely that there was any direct transition from emotional noises to propositional language; the old interjectional theory of the origin of language is largely disproved.

If tool using enabled gesture to become practical as well as emotional

---

[43] See Leakey and Lewin 1978, Chapter 10, for a report on the reconstruction of the cranium of 1470 (a *Homo habilis*, forerunner of *Homo sapiens*), which shows the speech area in the left hemisphere to be "probably more pronounced than that in apes" (p. 209).

[44] Van Lancker 1975, pp. 15, 16.

and provided the push for a systematic gestural language, it also helped to pave the way for the transfer to speech. One can explain the use of a tool through gesture only up to a point; beyond that, especially as tools themselves become more complex, using the hands for explanation interferes with using them for manipulation. Even an accidental sound might have been seized upon under those circumstances, but there were undoubtedly already many that were not accidental, such as vocal signs of approval or disapproval, warnings, persuasions—a great part, probably, of what still constitutes the emotive part of language—not to mention signals used in hunting, where concealment (and hence invisibility) would have inhibited the use of gesture. Besides, even now there remains a good deal of gesture in the use of sound, especially intonation—we can often predict a facial expression if we hear a speech melody. So sound and gesture were already overlapping, and the advantages of sound would have reinforced its use.

Here is how Morris Swadesh describes the possible origin of one vocalized meaning that must have overlapped most of the long period when gesture was the prevailing mode of communication:

> The use of nasal phonemes in the negative in so many languages of the world must in some way be related to the prevailing nasal character of the grunt. In English, the vocable of denial is almost always nasal; but it can vary from a nasalized vowel to any of the three nasal consonants: $\tilde{a}!\tilde{a}$, $\tilde{e}!\tilde{e}$, $\tilde{o}!\tilde{o}$, $m!m$, $n!n$, $\eta!\eta$. . . . Why is nasality so common? Surely because it results from the relaxation of the velum; . . . the most usual position of the velum is down, and the most relaxed form of grunt is nasal. The prevalence of nasals in the negative . . . may therefore be due to the fact that they are based on grunts.[45]
>
> . . .
>
> Simple nasality expressed relaxation and contentment. Joined with laryngeal constriction, it signified rather displeasure or frustration.[46]

Once the voice had assumed the major burden of communication, the subsequent refinement of language was largely a matter of cognitive growth which, like a liberated slave, demanded more and more of the freedom that an ever more finely tuned vocal apparatus made possible. The change to speech was not merely a recoding, vocally, of units already present in gesture. Vast new possibilities were engendered. The advantages of skilled sound-making redounded on the physical mechanism, which was steadily adapted to language and specialized away from digestion. Linguists of the extreme "language is but a cultural artifact"

---

[45] Swadesh 1971, p. 193. The exclamation point symbolizes a glottal stop: [?].
[46] Ibid., p. 200.

persuasion have argued that speech is merely an *overlaid* function, making an artificial use of organs that were designed by nature for the intake of food. But the human speech-and-digestive organs have developed traits in their later evolution that are not advantageous for eating. The shift of the larynx that made for better sound production "has the disadvantage of greatly increasing the chances of choking to death when a swallowed object gets caught in the pharynx. . . . The only function for which the adult human vocal tract is better suited is speech."[47] Human beings have *evolved* as speakers.

We can assume that the first vocal units were primarily consonantal—the instability of early vowels has already been noted (see page 179)—and independently meaningful.[48] While the idea of a language with words in which vowels have little or no function except as a transition from one consonant to the next or for affective connotations may seem strange, the fact is that such languages still exist—for example, Kabardian in the northern Caucasus and Bella Coola in coastal British Columbia. As the main burden was on single consonants, there were probably more consonantal contrasts than a language would show today. But as more and more meanings had to be expressed, it became increasingly difficult to add more consonants, and some other device was needed. That of doubling consonants (to express plurality or repetition) had probably already been in use, and could most readily be extended to other meanings; and the splitting off of transitional vowels would have occurred also, making vowels distinctive within syllables. Sentence-like combinations of consonant-words would also have provided the raw material for more complex words. In any case, there was probably a stage in which words were made up of two consonants with or without a vowel contrast. For the first time, distinctive units were on the way to becoming meaningless, but they were probably larger than the units that we regard as distinctive today—roughly, syllables rather than phonemes.[49]

The phonemic stage probably came as a result of the increasing number of syllabic units as vocabularies grew larger and larger. The problem would not have been with *recognizing* words; our memories are capable of storing vast quantities of images configurationally, and we recognize faces and voices with no difficulty, and probably process words the same way when we *hear* them. *Saying* them so that someone else can recognize them is a different matter. Word-speaking and syllable-speaking are

---

[47] Lieberman 1972, p. 94. See also LaBarre 1954, Chapter 10, where he builds his theory of the origin of speech on the "organic erotization of the mouth."

[48] What follows is based partly on Wescott 1967; Swadesh 1971; and Kuipers 1968.

[49] Wescott 1967, p. 72, dates the syllabic period from about 300,000 to about 50,000 B.C., and the phonemic period from then on, with phonemes becoming completely meaningless about 10,000 years ago.

like freehand drawing. When there are not too many pictures to draw, one can store the instructions in an informal way: "Put that curl a little over to the left and slant the eye down a bit but not too much." The difficulty of making even two hundred pictures in this way is obvious, and the number of words in all living languages runs to thousands. So it happened that formerly meaningful sounds were downgraded to a set of phonetic instructions. Instead of "put this curl a little to the left," children learn to "hit the /t/ phoneme in second position in this word"—like following a diagram numbered to guide the amateur's hand in drawing the picture of a face.

The beauty of this is that speakers can not only draw words as effectively as if they were real word-artists, but can exploit to the best advantage the limited range of their vocal apparatus. Only a comparatively small number of phonemes are needed; it is not necessary to crowd them; they can be made sharply distinct. Instead of five or six positions along the palatal ridge, two or three suffice, a good distance apart. Instead of a dozen tongue heights, three to five are enough. Even though you miss the target a bit, it is still easy to make each unit distinct from the rest. This brought language to the stage where all the components it has today were either realized or on the verge.

The preceding stages can be thought of as the evolution *toward* languages. Subsequent developments are the evolution *of* language. There is undoubtedly movement in some direction, as there always is; but we are too close to it, and seem rather to be drifting in circles. It is a commonplace among most linguists, for example, that "no twentieth-century language is any more advanced than ancient Greek." If we knew what the outcome of the next ten thousand years of evolution was to be, we could measure the factors existing now that are leading to it; but in our ignorance we are unable to mark the signals that are the signs of progress.

What we are conscious of is the apparent change-without-progress kind of evolution whereby a given language at one stage is converted into a different language at a later stage. What causes it? There are millions of little causes, but the cornerstone of the Tower of Babel was that "ultimate" achievement of an almost meaningless layer, first of syllables and then of phonemes. It increased the symbolizing power of language geometrically, but sacrificed nearly every remnant of mutual intelligibility between dialects from tribe to tribe. Concept and symbol were "freed from each other to the extent that change could modify either one without affecting the other."[50] Change can be fairly rapid, and when groups of speakers are separated for any length of time they end up by not understanding one another, especially if they come into steady contact with speakers of

---

[50] Chafe 1970, p. 31.

some other language and there is extensive cultural and linguistic inter-mixture. Such unintelligibility need not be intentional; it results from the fact that sounds can evolve on their own without destroying meaning, so long as meaning is free to marry itself to any sound. This freedom is not quite total, but it is nearly enough so to have created an enormous variety of languages. A later chapter will deal with some of the ways in which change operates.

LANGUAGE AND THE BRAIN

Evolutionary growth is intimately related to the development of the brain; humanity crossed what Sir Arthur Keith called a human Rubicon when the brain of *Homo erectus* reached a size of about 750 cubic centi-meters.[51] The more we learn about it—and our knowledge increases daily —the more we appreciate what a remarkable thinking machine the hu-man brain is, particularly those parts of it where language is centered.

Like the chemist who seeks to understand the physical structure of chemical elements, the linguist would be happiest if he could catch a specimen of talking man with a transparent skull and feed him tracers that would impart a glow to the speech centers of the brain and make each transmission from neuron to neuron visible to the eye. Short of this, a lot can be inferred from the effects of surgery, from experiments that do not involve mutilation, and from close attention to behavior.

History mentions a number of personages who at some point—usually past the age of forty—have been "struck dumb" and afterwards, often very soon afterwards (so that no physical cause was suspected), recov-ered their speech. Thus the prophet Daniel "set his face toward the ground and became dumb" (Dan. 10:15). Speechlessness is a common symptom of stroke or apoplexy, which in time was to give anatomists their first clue to the localization of language in the brain. Along with inability to speak, some form of paralysis on the right side of the body often occurs: hand, whole arm or side, or perhaps just the facial muscles. Postmortem examination made it possible to correlate these external ac-cidents with cerebral ones, and it was usually found that some trauma, such as a blood clot, had struck the left hemisphere of the brain. In 1861 the surgeon Paul Broca announced that speech was fixed in the left frontal region. Evidence has since accumulated showing that nearly all human beings have their language functions "lateralized" to the left,

---

[51] Quoted by Sagan 1977, p. 103.

though some left-handers have them to the right. Damage to the right side of the brain does not usually result in severe language impairment. Damage to the left side generally has serious consequences after early childhood. Lateralization is under way by the age of two and complete about the age of five, and from then on till puberty the left side of the brain continues to develop its language functions, but the right side is still "plastic" enough to take over if necessary. After puberty no one seems to be able to relearn a first language without some deficiency, usually very serious.[52]

Speech is not the only language function that can be tied with fair accuracy to a particular region of the brain. The person who is unable to speak as a result of a lesion in the left frontal region may still be able to understand, read, and write. If the damage is more to the side, there may be no loss of speech—the person may even become more voluble, but his speech tends to be dissociated from meaning: the words are there and can be understood, but they are strung together in strange ways. A small lesion at any point on the left side may result in some loss of relevance in what is said without affecting the fluency with which it is spoken.[53] So it is clear that the whole of the left side of the cortex (surface area) of the main part of the brain is somehow involved in language, though strict specialization is not a characteristic. A function may appear to be located in one part, but if that part is injured another part may take over. How the brain works is more a problem of fluid dynamics than one of ordinary mechanics. Some linguistic functions are more or less localized, particularly the ones that involve the perception of sounds and the muscular control of speech. But the cognitive functions —understanding, planning, and organizing—cannot be pinned down; locating them is "impossible by definition."[54]

Nevertheless, given approximate locations, it is possible to make some interesting correlations. One such is dynamic aphasia, resulting from an injury to the forward part of the left hemisphere. The victim is unable to answer questions, though he understands them perfectly well. He fumbles for words but cannot organize them. He can improvise a list of nouns fairly easily but has great difficulty with verbs. Experiments suggest that what he has lost is the power of "propositionizing," which is the stage between the idea of what is to be said and the production of the utterance; it is a kind of preliminary assembly around which the utterance is formed. All that is necessary to enable the victim to respond intelligibly is to give him some external references on which to hang the elements of

---

[52] Krashen 1973.
[53] Lenneberg 1973, pp. 119–21.
[54] Lamendella 1975, Ch. 2, pp. 17–18.

his sentence—some blank pieces of paper are enough, to which he can point one by one as he brings out what he wants to say.[55]

The losses that occur when the left hemisphere is hurt are not typically in *amount* but in *kind*. The victim does not lose, say, 50 percent of his total language ability, but may lose 90 percent of one special ability and only 10 percent of another. He may be able to read a word aloud but not be able to say it when shown a picture of what it names, or vice versa; he may be able to understand a word on hearing it but not on reading it, or vice versa.

It is probably no coincidence that "propositional" language and right-handedness are housed in the same half of the brain. Tool using and verbal problem-solving may well be the same at bottom. It is as if all human activity were roughly divided between "holding" functions and manipulative ones, lateralized in separate halves of the brain. Each of us is perhaps not one spirit but two: the clever, talkative, intellectual, maze-threading, problem-solving genie sits on the left hand, and the artistic, intuitive, whole-seeing, and wordless but passionate genie sits on the right. But since for lack of words he is unable to tell us about himself, the genie on the right remains largely a mystery. His rival may even suppress him. Gabby people get ahead in a gabby world.[56]

Key terms and concepts

origin of language
first language acquisition
  predisposition
  capacity
  competence
grammars of childhood
  holophrastic stage
  joining stage
  connective stage
  recursive stage

animal communication
preadaptation
American Sign Language
lateralized brain
  left hemisphere
  right hemisphere

Additional remarks and applications

1. What advantages do younger children learning their first language have over older children or adults learning a second language?

---

[55] Luria and Tsvetkova 1970.

[56] See Pines 1973, pp. 138–59. For left-handed persons the two genies may just switch places.

2. Observe a mother speaking to her child and see what modifications she makes in her speech. Does she say *Give Mommy the shoe* rather than *Give me the shoe,* thus helping to identify *Mommy?* Does she pronounce the important words in an especially distinct way—for example, the noun *shoe* in this same sentence? Explain how the need to do this for very young children might have a stabilizing effect on language.

3. Would you expect the holophrastic stage to be given up immediately once the child discovers that parts of the whole are separately meaningful, or would the two stages probably continue side by side? Consider the expression *It's good for you,* spoken by a parent every time a spoonful of medicine or a distasteful food is offered. Might the child interpret *good for you* as a unit and react negatively toward it? When you yourself say something like *I can't go out this evening—I'm tied up,* do you have a mental image of yourself bound with ropes, or is *tied up* just a colorless synonym for *busy?*

4. Otto Jespersen investigated the case of Danish twins, badly neglected and left in the care of a deaf woman, whom he first met when they were obviously able to converse with each other but in a way that was unintelligible to adults. It was clear, however, that their language was *based* on Danish. Does this suggest that all that is needed is the barest push from outside to set the language-learning process going? Do you think that without this push it would start spontaneously?

5. A child who substitutes [t] for [k], as in *tat* for *cat,* will also substitute [d] for [g], as in *doe* for *go.* Does this suggest that children develop the ability to discriminate between sounds before they develop the ability to reproduce them correctly?

6. Speculate on the possible connection between the lateralization of the brain and the persistent dualisms that have cropped up in human thinking over the centuries: body and mind, substance and form, constancy and change, argument and function (in logic), topic and comment (in language). Think of others.

7. Do the emotions conveyed by facial expressions in human beings still have "fixity of reference"? Or is this really two questions? (1. Does a smile, for example, indicate 'happiness'? 2. Is a person who smiles necessarily happy?) What has happened with all the expressions of emotion in human beings? How does this relate to the concept of *sincerity?*

8. A dog understands and obeys when his master says *Go get my hat.* Would you say that understanding the words involves segmenting

them into distinctive sounds, or reacting to some overall or particularly salient feature? Give reasons for your answer.

9. What do the act of speaking and the act of throwing a stone have in common in the demands that they make on physical and mental evolution? What value do you find in the teaching method of fifth-century Athens, in which budding orators learned to speak while doing exercises—casting the javelin and projecting the voice, for example?

For further reading

Aitchison, Jean. 1976. *The Articulate Mammal* (London: Hutchinson).

Curtiss, S. 1977. *Genie: A Psycholinguistic Study of a Modern "Wild Child"* (New York: Academic Press).

Dale, Philip S. 1972. *Language Development: Structure and Function* (Hinsdale, Ill.: Dryden Press).

Ferguson, Charles A., and Dan I. Slobin. 1973. *Studies in Child Language Development* (New York: Holt, Rinehart & Winston).

Hewes, Gordon W., William C. Stokoe, and Roger W. Wescott (eds.). 1975. *Language Origins* (Silver Springs, Md.: Linstok Press).

Krough, August. 1933. "The Language of the Bees," in *Scientific American Reader* (New York: Simon & Schuster).

LaBarre, Weston. 1954. *The Human Animal* (Chicago: University of Chicago Press).

Lane, Harland. 1976. *The Wild Boy of Aveyron* (Cambridge, Mass.: Harvard University Press).

Langer, Susanne K. 1948. *Philosophy in a New Key* (New York: New American Library).

Lilly, John C. 1969. *The Mind of the Dolphin* (New York: Avon Books).

Linden, Eugene. 1974. *Apes, Men, and Language* (Baltimore: Penguin Books).

Piaget, Jean. 1973. *The Child and Reality* (New York: Grossman Publishers).

Rumbaugh, D. M. 1977. *Acquisition of Linguistic Skills by a Chimpanzee* (New York: Academic Press).

Sagan, Carl. 1977. *The Dragons of Eden: Speculations on the Evolution of Human Intelligence* (New York: Random House).

Stam, James. 1976. *Inquiries in the Origin of Language: The Fate of a Question* (New York: Harper & Row).

Weir, Ruth. 1962. *Language in the Crib* (The Hague: Mouton).

VARIATION IN SPACE 9

A woman who was born in Vermont but has lived many years in England returns for a visit. She misses her way and asks a Vermonter, "Can you tell me where Church Street is?" He answers "Yup" and walks on.

The visitor is willing to accept *yup* for *yes* because she has lived there before, but not the literal answer which omits the information she needs. Is her annoyance due to a *linguistic* misinterpretation on his part—that is, has her question ceased to be a yes–no question? Not quite, for a simple *no* answer would be appropriate if one lacked the information—followed, of course, with an apology. The fault lies in the Vermonter's neglect of *compliance* in a social situation that clearly called for more than the laconic affirmative.

This incident, with its stereotype of the New Englander, illustrates three things about the relationship between language and the world around it. First, the same meanings are expressed in different ways from area to area: *yup* and *yes* are only two of the variants that also include the Scotsman's *aye* and the Connecticuter's *eeyuh*. Second, what is said has to be appropriate to the relationships between one speaker and another within a communicative situation; the rules of speaking involve more than a simple interpretation of grammatical correctness. The realities of place-to-place and person-to-person-to-situation can be pictured as two kinds of space, geographical and social. What these signify for *mean-*

ing is the third point: we learn the rules of space just as we learn those of grammar. "People not only know their language, they know how to use it."[1] Whether or not a given expression will be appropriate in a given situation, both of which we know from past experience, is part of our knowledge of the language and becomes one of the hovering meanings of the expression, like the inferential ones described in Chapter 6. In fact, the example used there (page 121) of the verb *want* in *I want something to eat* for 'I lack something to eat' shows just such a social meaning gravitating inward and becoming part of the lexical meaning of the word. In a broad sense, *all* of meaning responds to social space, since it is used in communicating with people and mostly about people. But a great deal of meaning responds directly to the interaction among speakers when they speak. Some of these keenly immediate meanings infuse the lexicon itself; others linger at the borders. *Want* is an extreme case of actual shift, but there are many others like it. The verbs *to come* and *to bring* retain their primary meanings of 'approach speaker' *(The train is coming)* and 'transport toward speaker' *(It is bringing my mother-in-law)*; but for reasons of courtesy, secondary meanings have been added whereby the speaker can take the point of view of his hearer: *I'm coming to your party and bringing you a nice present.* One who *comes* to a party expects to be there as a welcome guest; *I'm going to your party* would seem perfunctory if not rude. *I'm coming* violates the primary rule, since the approach is not toward where the speaker is; but a secondary rule supplants it within the social situation. It takes children quite a while to untangle these complications because they first have to grasp the role-playing involved.[2]

"Social space" and "geographical space" help to describe *synchronic* linguistics, referring to the way languages differ from languages and dialects from dialects at a given point in time. This is distinguished from *diachronic* linguistics, which deals with change that takes place over time in the course of evolution. But a slight redefinition is in order, to make it clear that geography in a literal sense has nothing to do with the matter. A tribe can strike its tents and move a thousand miles, but if its members stick together and avoid contact with speakers of any other language, the new location will be the same as the old as far as the language is concerned. The movement relative to mountain chains and rivers is irrelevant to the language (except that as new *things* are encountered new *names* will have to be provided—but that can happen to stay-at-homes too). So rather than geography we should think of membership within a speech community, which usually, though not necessarily, corresponds to some

---

[1] Teeter 1973, p. 95.
[2] Keller-Cohen 1973.

bounded area. It is easy to take geography too literally and miss the fact that ghetto speakers speak as they do just as much because of where they are in a linguistic sense as Southern States speakers do. The fact that one place is a kind of social prison while the boundaries of the other are open does not make one more or less of a speech community than the other.

The important distinction is between where one "belongs" and what one does. People can be seen as victims—willing or unwilling members of the communities where they were born or are confined—or as actors who are privileged to adopt more than one role. A careful student of social variation says, of the latter view, "As far as we can see, there are no single-style speakers."[3] At the very least we have one style of speaking at home and another style in the market place, both within a single speech community. As a rule there is no sharp line between informal and formal but a gradation that extends through several degrees of familiarity within the home (sister to sister, mother to daughter, daughter to mother), up a ladder with rungs for friend to friend, adult to child, boss to assistant, parishioner to priest, and ends in the frigid and rigid formality of envoy to monarch. The metaphor of "up" reveals the value that speakers place on these levels. Formal speech is esteemed either because it is associated with a dominant social class or because it is a mark of respect or both.

Each of the two ways of looking at variation in space has its specialists. Those who concentrate on where speakers belong follow the lead of classical sociology. They are interested in populations and statistics, in the assimilation of minorities and broad-scale language policy. The mapping of dialect areas is their oldest specialty—Southern States speech, North Midland speech, Tidewater Area speech, and so on. Those who concentrate on what speakers do follow the lead of social anthropology. Their concern is with the "ethnography of speaking,"[4] described as the "interrelations of speaker, addressee, audience, topic, channel, and setting."[5] The average speaker may be conscious of the difference between the two viewpoints when someone he talks to behaves in an unexpected way. If the other person is being served in our house and refers to the food as *grub,* we may object to his behavior or his attitude; the occasion (or our self-esteem) calls for more formality. But if he calls it *vittles* we are more apt to think of him as a hick or an old-timer: where is he from, what group does he belong to?

One particular kind of role-playing deserves to be elaborated on ahead of all the rest because the nature of language forces it on us: everyone behaves now as speaker, now as listener. Interest has focused excessively

---

[3] Labov 1970, p. 46.
[4] Hymes 1962.
[5] Labov 1970, p. 30. See also Hannerz 1970.

on the speaker's role, and the reasons are obvious. In phonetics speaking involves articulation, the only kind of processing that is open to easy observation. In grammar it covers what we hear people say, and can record or write down to analyze later. And it is limited in scope, being more compact than the larger ability to understand. But the speaker has to interact with others who are what they are, and whose idiosyncrasies he must somehow surmount. We saw on page 14 how within a fairly short while a listener can set up a series of correspondences to match what he hears with what he himself does. The more such adjustments he makes the larger his listening grammar becomes.

Since the speaker and hearer roles are the most fundamental of all, they have the profoundest effect on the grammars that correspond to them. In a sense, the speaking grammar (or *lect*) is a derivative of the listening one. If we understand speakers who use sounds, words, and rules that we do not use, and at the same time accept these lects as valid representatives of our language, it must be because we have an awareness of a larger grammar than the part that corresponds to our own way of expressing ourselves. This is to say that one who has had to interpret a representative variety of lects will formulate a general grammar of the language from which the special cases can be deduced—including his own.

If among roles those of speaker and hearer occupy a special place, among communities there is a community that is just as special: the Community of One. Every speaker has an *idiolect,* just as every collectivity of speakers has a *dialect*. We are most conscious of this in the pet words and expressions that individuals use. Theodore Roosevelt salted his speech with the word **strenuous.** Mark Twain enjoyed the sound of **mephitic.** Idiosyncrasies of speech can be used to caricature a person as effectively as the jut of a chin or the bulge of a nose. Idiolects differ from dialects just as dialects differ from languages: the range of variation in either case is narrower. That is why we can single out pet expressions—the narrow range favors a relatively higher frequency of the relatively fewer things that are said, by comparison with the larger group. This also makes it possible to do something with individuals that everybody enjoys doing with groups but that gets more and more dangerous the larger the group: to look for personality traits in the way language is used. There are undoubtedly characteristics of whole communities that are revealed through language. Many Spanish males accentuate their masculinity by glottalizing their speech, a trait that Latin Americans find extremely funny. With individuals, traits of speech are directly interpreted as indicators of personality. Both voice quality and choice of words are easy and spontaneous indicators. Syntax is less obvious, at least in speech. In written language it leads to questions of style, and that in turn to an art that may conceal as much as it reveals about the personality. It is a subject to itself.

SPEECH COMMUNITIES

Though *where* a community is does not necessarily determine the language used, it is traditional to distinguish between groupings in a society that are anchored to a location and groupings that are not. The study of dialectal variation got its start in countries with fairly stable populations where the most interesting differences were those associated with particular localities. The result has been an *areal linguistics* that has accumulated a great body of literature, and that can be separated, for convenience, from the study of other communities. But we will look at the latter first.

Non-areal communities

There is no limit to the ways in which human beings league themselves together for self-identification, security, gain, amusement, worship, or any of the other purposes that are held in common; consequently there is no limit to the number and variety of speech communities that are to be found in a society. The smallest of widening circles is the family, each with its own invented words, special meanings, and nursery terms.

Intersecting the family is a further grouping by sex and age; these represent, originally, not speech communities but biological facts. Males and females have a different linguistic birthright. Females are almost never dyslexic, which suggests that their genetic equipment for language is more stable: reading problems and speech problems affect the male half of the population. Females learn to talk earlier, learn foreign languages faster and better, and do more talking in their lifetime than males do, though social factors join biological ones in the later developments. The anthropologist Gordon Hewes states the evolutionary background for the differences:

> No one seriously supposes that the consistent precocity of girls in acquiring speech, and their lower incidence of speech defects, can be attributed to cultural learning differences. . . . The point is that [the observed differences between girls and boys] are compatible with our reconstructions of early hominid behavior, in which males would have been the principal hunters, trackers, and protectors of the group—with a survival premium on ability to analyze environmental noises, as well as spatial and constructional abilities—whereas females, as the main transmitters of speech to infants, as well as the sex with the greater need to detect the emo-

tional overtones of vocal messages, could be expected to be more pre-
cocious in language-learning and less prone to speech defects. . . .[6]

Age differences show biological factors even more clearly. We are not
born with language, and all the successive grammars sketched in Chapter
8 are correlated with biological growth. Adulthood also has its biological
trademark. The brain internalizes language at an ever slowing rate, with
the result that the elderly gradually lose the capacity to absorb new data
and end by speaking in ways that identify them as old, even if they stay
clear of the society of other old people.

With the biological foundation to build on, and social structures that
tend to throw women into the company of other women and children into
the company of playmates, it is not surprising that the communities of sex
and age come to rank among those with the most clearly marked linguistic
differences. After the first few months children learn more language from
other children than from adults. Even some of the traits of early childhood grammars that were noted in Chapter 8 may be transmitted from
child to child as much as they are re-formed with each generation: such
things as the past tense forms *throwed, fighted, runned.* We judge these
as "non-standard" because children are forced to *un*learn them; but there
are other things that make up the pool of childish expressions which children learn from children and then simply lay aside or forget later. *All
right for you* is a child's resentful dismissal of someone who has failed
him. *Get* with an infinitive complement, while used somewhat nowadays
by adults, is more usual with children: *He gets to go but I don't.* Rather
than a linguistic heritage this perhaps reflects a child's greater dependence on permission to do things. The most thoroughly documented case
for the transmission of language from children to children, very largely
bypassing the older generation, is that of Black English. In one study of
selected features of Black English, those who used the forms most consistently were children up to the age of five. Between five and eight the
children shift to predominantly standard forms, though around ten there
is a slight reversion, presumably an assertion of identity.[7] Later the standard comes to prevail more and more.[8]

Probably all societies institutionalize the differences between male
speech and female speech at least to some extent. Sex differences in
speech have been noted by writers in English since at least the sixteenth
century, and were recorded for Carib in Raymond Bréton's dictionary
published in 1664.[9] In Koasati, an Indian language spoken in Louisiana,

---

[6] Hewes 1973, p. 115.
[7] Hall and Freedle 1975.
[8] See especially the work of William Labov—for example, the age comparisons in Labov
    1972, p. 807.
[9] Data from Key 1972, p. 15. See also Key 1975.

there are morphological differences between words when used by men and when used by women. Roughly they involve the addition or substitution of an [s] in men's speech at the end of words that lack it in women's speech. The distinction is now fading, with women adopting men's forms. There apparently was no stigma attached to the women's forms, though, as male speakers were heard to admire it and to be annoyed by all the hissing in their own speech.[10] Sex differences have captured attention in recent years through the protests of women's liberation, which has campaigned for the abolition of differences that denigrate women. There are perhaps more of these in language *about* women than in language *of* women—some of them were mentioned in an earlier chapter (see page 144). But women's actual usage often reflects the same subordination. There is a great deal in women's speech in English that reflects extra politeness, one aspect of which is "leaving a decision open, not imposing your mind, or views, or claims, on anyone else." Two patterns reveal this decisively: the abundance of tag questions *(The price of gas is terrible, isn't it?)* and the high frequency of a rising intonation on utterances that are not syntactically questions, as when a woman responds to her husband's question **When will dinner be ready?** with

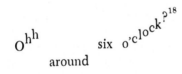

How much of women's speech is unjustly different and how much is simply different would be hard to decide and of course is irrelevant to the general question. In the role that they have traditionally played (whether the tradition is a just one or not—societies only sporadically get around to the question of justice), women have been the peacekeepers and socializers at home and elsewhere. This has caused them to avoid using "rough" language, and to be the first to say exaggeratedly nice things. The latter is one reason for the greater abundance of intensifiers. Women were probably the ones who turned **rather** and **quite** into pure expressions of degree. Their influence can be seen in the evolution of **such** and **so** from correlating determiners to plain intensifiers. Conservative male usage still requires that these words be followed by **that** or **as,** or have a **that** or **as** clearly implied by the context: **He is such a tall fellow (he is so tall) that**

---

[10] Haas 1964.
[11] The observation and the examples are from Lakoff 1973, pp. 54–57.

he practically tops the basket, but not *He is such a tall fellow!* nor *He is so tall!* Further, a man is free to use four-letter words, while women till recently were limited to such exclamations as *sugar* and *shoot.*[12] Unless it is continuously re-created, a distinct female speech is hard to maintain because with their traditional custody of children women transmit their speech characteristics to their male offspring.

If biology has some slight but genuine influence in setting apart the speech communities of young and old, male and female, its value where Black English is concerned is spurious. According to one theory, the historical basis for Black English is the African pidgin used in the slave trade, the only language available to blacks sometimes deliberately thrown together from different language backgrounds to keep them from communicating effectively with one another. As with all pidgins—which are discussed later in this chapter—the nuisance irregularities of morphology were discarded and syntax was simplified. The result was that as blacks gradually rebuilt a speech community in the lands to which they were transported, they had to reconstitute the grammar, which retained certain features of the pidgin even while it was being "relexified" with words taken in constantly from the standard (see Table 9–1). The result is that unlike the differences that set other non-standard dialects apart, a number of the ones that distinguish Black English are in the grammatical signals rather than in the lexicon.[13] Two of the most striking are the non-use of the copula *to be* under some conditions and the system of tenses. The fact that the copula is often a grammatical luxury has been brought out before (see page 91). Black English sensibly omits it when it is superfluous: *They sick.*[14] As for the tenses, they are elaborately systematized, as can be seen in Figure 9–1. *I singing* represents action in progress at the present moment. As for the tenses and aspects,

> *I do see him* is just anterior to the present and intrudes upon it, and is therefore the *past inceptive tense. I did see him* is slightly longer ago, or the *pre-present tense. I done seen him* is still further ago, or the *recent past. I been seen him* is even farther ago and is designated as the *pre-recent past.* Moving ahead from the present, if someone says *I'm a-do it,* he will do it in approximately 30 seconds, or in the *immediate future.* If someone says *I'm a-gonna do it,* he will do it soon, that is, in the *post-immediate future.* If he says *I gonna do it,* however, the execution may be indefinitely delayed.[15]

---

[12] Lakoff 1973, p. 49.
[13] Stewart 1968. For a full discussion see Dillard 1972.
[14] The example is from Dillard 1972, p. 53. The black speaker—aiming at the standard —may also say *Im is sick;* and there are other mixtures due to code switching.
[15] Fickett 1972, p. 19.

TABLE 9–1
Some Examples of Syntactic Differences Between Standard and Non-standard English

Variable	Standard English	Black Non-standard English
Linking verb (copula)	He *is* going.	He —— goin'.
Possessive marker	John*'s* cousin.	John —— cousin.
Plural marker	I have five cent*s*.	I got five cent ——.
Third-person singular (verb agreement)	He live*s* in New York.	He live —— in New York.
Past marker	Yesterday he walk*ed* home.	Yesterday he walk — home.
'If' construction	I asked *if he did it*.	I ask *did he do it*.
Negation	I *don't* have *any*.	I *don't* got *none*.
Use of 'be'	*Statement:* He is here all the time.	*Statement:* He *be* here.
Subject expression	John moved.	John, *he* move.
Verb form	I *drank* the milk.	I *drunk* the milk.
Future form	I *will go* home.	I*'ma go* home.
Indefinite article	I want *an* apple.	I want *a* apple.
Pronoun form	*We* have to do it.	*Us* got to do it.
Pronoun expressing possession	*His* book.	*He* book.
Preposition	He is over *at* John's house.	He over *to* John house.
	He teaches *at* Francis Pool.	He teach —— Francis Pool.
Use of 'do'	*Contradiction:* No, he *isn't*.	*Contradiction:* No, he *don't*.

SOURCE: From Hall and Freedle 1973, p. 445. By permission of S. Karger AG, Basel, Switzerland. Adapted from J. C. Baratz 1969, "A Bi-dialectal Task for Determining Language Proficiency in Economically Disadvantaged Negro Children," *Child Development* 40:99–100. While all the items in the third column are undoubtedly more frequent in black non-standard, not all are exclusive to it. *I ask did he do it* is cited for the *did he do it* part (the *ask* for *asked* is irrelevant here), but such questions are common in standard English and seem to be gaining ground. Similarly *John, he moved* and *I want a apple*, while not standard, are common among many speakers other than blacks.

The phonology of Black English is equally distinctive. We have already seen that one of the offshoots of African pidgin has a most un-English feature, phonemic tone (see page 25); the same importation of tonal contrasts from African languages influenced the intonation of the black dialect called Gullah, spoken on the Sea Islands of Georgia and South

FIGURE 9–1
Tense in Black English

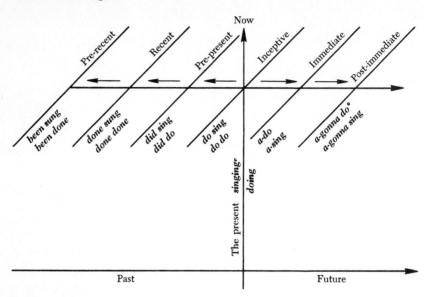

SOURCE: Adapted from Fickett 1972, p. 18. Reprinted by permission of the *Journal of English Linguistics*.

° The indefinite **gonna do, gonna sing** does not appear because it has no fixed relation to the other forms.

Carolina and the nearby mainland coast.[16] Black English in general seems to have been affected to the point of having sharper pitch variations than the standard, and this according to one theory may partly account for the fact that Black English has more pauses at wide intonation breaks and divides sentences into shorter clause groups.[17]

The African origin of Black English has been the focus of a controversy, some traditional dialectologists tending to regard it as little more than a special variety of Southern States English, others emphasizing the African heritage.[18] As with all encounters between speakers of different languages, exchanges have gone both ways. Probably much of what gives standard American Southern its flavor—at least in pronunciation—comes from Black English. "In Charleston and other Tidewater centers, educated white speakers employ a variety of English quite similar to their

---

[16] Turner 1949, chapter on Gullah intonation.

[17] Engel 1972.

[18] For the position of those emphasizing African language features of Black English (*Ebonics,* as they call it), see Williams 1975.

counterparts in Barbados, Trinidad, and elsewhere in the Caribbean,"[19] where the influence of the language spoken by the slaves is unmistakable. In the early years of the American colonies the English spoken was fairly uniform. But with black nurses in charge of white children in their formative years, and particularly with children of both races playing together rather freely up to a certain age, imitation of the phonological features was inevitable.

We turn now to communities that people can more or less voluntarily *join*. The language variety here can be properly called a *code*, though the term is loosely used of any variety (including the ones already described) that a speaker feels free to adopt for a particular purpose. Codes are often referred to as jargons, especially by outsiders who have difficulty understanding them. Private groups too easily insulate themselves from the correctives for their linguistic extremes, which need to be understood if they are to be laughed at or driven out of court. There is an enormous amount of sheer dead weight in the special vocabularies of certain professions or occupations—horses do not need to be measured in *hands*, distances at sea by *leagues*, depths by *fathoms;* a *two-syllable* word does not have to be called *disyllabic*. The most famous example of overextended specificity is the list of terms for 'group of birds or animals,' attributed to Joseph Strutt's *Sports and Pastimes of the People of England,* where the terms are explained as "a peculiar kind of language invented by the sportsmen of the middle ages, which it was necessary for every lover of the chase to be acquainted with."[20] Besides the fairly familiar **bevy of quails** and **brood of hens,** the nearly sixty group terms include **sege of herons, harras of horses,** and **shrewdness of apes.**

On the other hand, highly specialized activities in a technical field require special ways of talking. How this affects one part of the medical profession has been described as follows:

> It has taken hundreds of years and millions of dissections to build up the detailed and accurate picture of the structure of the human body that enables the surgeon to know where to cut. A highly specialized sublanguage has evolved for the sole purpose of describing this structure. The surgeon had to learn this jargon of anatomy before the anatomical facts could be effectively transmitted to him. Thus, underlying the "effective action" of the surgeon is an "effective language."[21]

---

[19] Bailey 1974, p. 15.
[20] From *Word Study* (February 1942), reprinted from *The Week-End Book* (Harmondsworth, England: Penguins, 1938).
[21] Bross 1973, p. 217.

Other occupational codes are similarly distinguished by their vocabulary. The carpenter, the physician, the mechanic, the farmer—each has particular objects and operations to name. But certain occupations—especially the ones whose operations are mostly verbal—develop other linguistic peculiarities as well. The intonation of sports announcers is marked by a half-high-pitched monotone. That of politicians is typical enough to caricature:

> I know that I speak for every
>   loyal A
>   merican. . . .

While we may fail to understand certain professional jargons by default, there are other jargons that by design we are not meant to understand. Their speakers use them for concealment, and they are typical of communities that want to shut the rest of the world out. They may be casual communities—no more, perhaps, than groups of children trying to fool other children by talking in pig Latin—but more usually they are communities that make fairly consistent use of their secret language to further private or antisocial activities. Among the Walbiri of Central Australia there is a kind of male-status secret language called tʸiliwiri, which boys start learning at thirteen. It consists in substituting words that are contrary in meaning in one semantic feature: 'hot' for 'cold,' 'flat ground' for 'hole,' 'older brother' for 'younger brother,' and so on (but not, for example, 'older brother' for 'younger sister,' which would differ by two features). Adult males can speak at normal rates and be understood.[22] The Hanunóo of the Philippines have an approved way of talking during courtship that calls for a high degree of skill in keeping messages from being understood by others, particularly by rivals and older adults.[23] The most furtive activity of all is that of criminals, and the most practical criminal jargon is that of pickpockets, who have to be able to transmit signals in full hearing of their victims without being detected. Here is one report:

> When the tool locates the victim's bankroll or wallet he may name that location to the stalls in argot. That is, he may say in an undertone *Left bridge* or **Right bridge,** or **Kiss the dog,** or whatever instructions may be necessary to inform the stalls, so that they can put the victim into position for the tool to work.[24]

---

[22] Cazden 1972, reporting Kenneth Hale.
[23] Conklin 1959.
[24] Maurer 1955, pp. 53–54.

One finds an element of concealment, or at least of exclusiveness, in any jargon, professional or popular, that makes for identity or cohesiveness within the community. Being able to talk the lingo of sociologists is a badge of membership in the guild. In fact, learning the professional jargon of any new subject—linguistics, art criticism, or whatever—is the major task of any student, who is "kept out" until able to speak it. Even college slang is to some extent a way of closing the doors on conventional speakers, while the educational establishment is supposedly trying to open doors a crack in the opposite direction: "There is reason to believe that this is exactly the success that education is after, for it serves to mark many people as unsuccessful and to let into the club only those who are willing to play the success games that the class in control asks them to play."[25] Language provides both its direct and its reverse snob appeal and snob identification.

There are secret languages that do not aim at concealment so much as at mystery, which come mainly in two kinds, incantations and glossolalia. Both have magical and religious ties. The spells of witchcraft and the esoteric speech of a medium at a seance are examples of the first. "Speaking in tongues" is another term for the second, which has long been associated with ecstatic religious experience. In Acts of the Apostles, 19:6, we read that "when Paul had laid his hands upon them, the Holy Spirit came on them; and they spake with tongues, and prophesied." The speaker is supposed not to be in control of what he is saying, and while the sounds generally conform to those of his language, his utterance is not intelligible unless the hearer can match it with a similar occult power of interpretation. Glossolalia was formerly restricted in the United States to minor Protestant groups but in recent years has spread to some of the larger denominations. Though social scientists have taken it to be a symptom of some form of mental disturbance, in one test the glossolalists turned out to be somewhat less neurotic than a control group from a conventional church.[26]

Areal communities

The largest areal communities are simply those that speak a distinct language—most often within a single geographical area but, as with Latin in the third century and English today, sometimes flung wide across the world and with discontinuities between. But what is a different language? And how large is large? Some mutually unintelligible languages are

---

[25] O'Neil 1970, p. 2.
[26] Wolfram 1973, p. 39.

spoken by only a few hundred people, and the distance to the next language may only be over the hill in either direction (see page 1). Intelligibility is as hard to pin down as difference and size: if we can make adjustments in our listener's grammar that expand it to include many speakers' grammars, we can do the same with a neighboring language if it is not too much unlike our own. There is no really satisfactory definition of *language* that will distinguish it from *dialect*.[27] Political boundaries force people on either side to turn their backs on each other most of the time, but even there one finds a gradation, albeit steeper than anything within the borders. What most distinguishes areal communities from non-areal ones is the relationship of inclusion: we speak of dialects *of* English and modern dialects *of* Latin, the latter referring to ways of speaking as diverse as French, Romanian, and Portuguese, each of which has dialects of its own and subdialects within dialects. A mechanic who belongs to the Methodist church and the Masonic lodge and coaches a Little League team on weekends belongs to four non-areal communities, not counting his other memberships—sex, age, politics, and so on. He is less apt to belong to two different areal communities, though even this overlap is common enough in parts of the world that still bear the marks of recent conquest, as happens throughout Latin America, where many speakers belong to the community of Spanish or Portuguese and to that of one or more native languages as well. A milder version of this is found in more homogeneous areas where a generalized variety of a language is used for official communication and a local variety for most other purposes. The official variety may or may not at the same time be the local variety for some fortunate segment of the population (the ruling class, as with Southern British, or the ruling area, as with Parisian French), but as it tends to be associated with literature and hence to preserve older forms, it is convenient to use as a point of reference in describing varieties. These can be studied as variants *of* the standard. This would ordinarily be done anyway, as the standard represents the seat of power. And such was the setting for the earliest work on dialects, which looked at local varieties not so much in terms of their own structure as in terms of the quaint differences from the standard. For many non-linguists the word *dialect* still carries the stigma of that association. Figure 9–2 shows, along the vertical or time dimension, the real histori-

---

[27] One has been proposed, which is that if two varieties have the same underlying forms, they are dialects of a single language; if not, they are different languages even though they may be mutually intelligible. The example given is the Spanish of Spain and that of Latin America, which together represent numerous dialects of one language, as against either of these when compared with the Spanish of the Sephardic Jews, a different language. See Agard 1971. The difficulty with this definition is that getting agreement on the underlying forms may be just the same problem under another name.

FIGURE 9–2
Diachronic and Synchronic "Derivation"

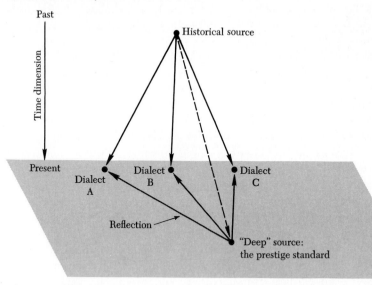

cal development over the centuries, and also shows the fictitious derivation, as a kind of reflection in the horizontal plane of the present, with the
standard masquerading as the source of the dialects. Ideally the historical
source and the standard would coincide, just as underlying forms ideally
converge with historically original forms (see pages 40–41).

Serious investigation of geographical dialects began in the latter part of
the nineteenth century. The first comprehensive study was made in North
and Central Germany by Georg Wenker. A smaller study followed in
Denmark, and between 1902 and 1908 Jules Gilliéron published his *Atlas
Linguistique de la France,* the most influential work of its kind. Since the
turn of the century materials have been collected for similar atlases all
over the world. In the United States the model has been the *Linguistic
Atlas of New England,* directed by Hans Kurath and published between
1939 and 1943. Other regional atlases have followed, the most recent
being the *Linguistic Atlas of the Upper Midwest,* by Harold B. Allen,
published between 1973 and 1976. Fieldworkers are now investigating the
English of the Deep South of the United States. The resulting *Linguistic
Atlas of the Gulf States* will show at least eleven regional dialects.[28]
Canada is the most important area in North America yet to be mapped
for English. The work has already begun under the direction of H. M.
Scargill (Scargill 1973). *The Linguistic Atlas of England* was published in
1978 (Orton et al.).

---

[28] Pederson 1971.

As the name implies, a linguistic atlas is a collection of maps showing the prevalence of particular speech forms in particular areas. What the dialect geographer most often selects to mark off a dialect area is simply its preference for certain words. Differences in pronunciation or syntax yield a more reliable measure, but words are easier to work with; information can even be gathered by mail through a questionnaire that asks what words a speaker uses for particular meanings: is a field enclosure made of stone called a *stone wall*, a *stone fence*, a *rock wall*, or a *rock fence?* Are drains that take rainwater off a roof called *eaves troughs, water spouting, gutters,* or *rain spouts?* For greater accuracy, detailed phonetic information is needed. Trained interviewers must be sent to the scene and may spend hours with a single informant. Does he pronounce *soot* to rime with *boot* or with *put?* Is his final consonant in *with* like that of *bath* or that of *bathe?* Does his pronunciation of *tomato* end with the same vowel sound as *panda,* or is it like *grotto?* The Swiss German atlas, published in 1962, was based on a questionnaire containing 2600 items, which took from four to eight days to administer. Its phonetic discriminations were exquisite—as many as twenty-one different tongue heights, for example, in front unrounded vowels.[29] Items chosen to test differences in vocabulary, pronunciation, and syntax are the ones most likely to reveal the peculiarities of everyday speech: names of household objects, foods, parts of the body, weather phenomena, numbers, and so on.

Unless he is combining his interest as a linguist with an extracurricular one as a folklorist or sociologist, the dialect geographer is less concerned with the items in a questionnaire for their own sake than as indicators of where to draw the boundary lines and how to trace the routes of speakers who have migrated from one area to another. The latter—the fanning out of dialects from their original centers and their crisscrossing and blending as the wave moves outward—is of special significance in a country like the United States, with its history of westward migrations, its ethnic mixes, and its extraordinarily mobile population.

Boundaries are set by mapping the farthest points to which a given form has penetrated. When a line—termed an *isogloss* if it has to do with words, an *isophone* if with sounds—is drawn connecting these points, it is usually found to lie close to the lines drawn for other forms—for instance, the same speakers who say *snake feeder* for 'dragonfly' are also apt to pronounce the word *greasy* as *greazy.* The interlocking lines form a bundle of isoglosses (or isophones) and represent the frontier of the dialect in question.

---

[29] Moulton 1963.

MAP 9–1
Word Geography of the Eastern States

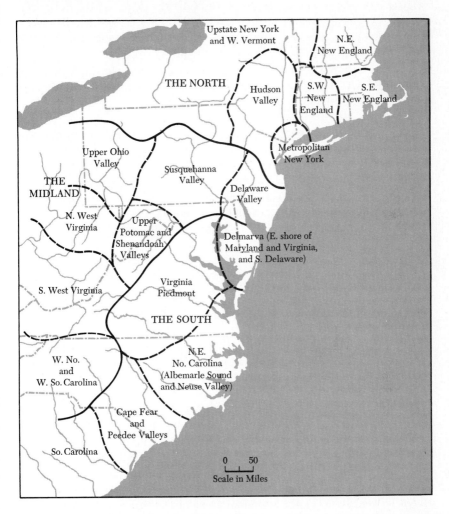

SOURCE: Adapted from Kurath 1949. Used by permission of The University of Michigan Press.

   In the eastern part of the United States, English divides rather clearly into three grand dialect areas. They reflect the settlement of those areas by early migrants from England who brought their dialects with them. One such dialectal transplant from England is the vowel in words like *half, bath, aunt, glass,* and *laugh.* We easily recognize one way of pronouncing these words as a feature of cultivated speech in the East and of over-cultivated speech elsewhere. It is by no means uniform (in

Eastern Virginia, for example, the broad *a* will be heard in **master** and
aunt but not in many other words), and represents one side of a split
that took place in the eastern counties of England before the American
Revolution. The /a/ was transplanted from those counties as folk speech
by immigrants to New England, but it also took root in London and so
became established as fashionable speech in the parts of America that
maintained the closest ties with England.[30] Map 9–1 shows the three areas
(plus subdialectal sections) known, from their geographical position, as
Northern, Midland, and Southern.

Two metaphors describe the extremes of diffusion. One is the relay
race, the other the cross-country. In the first, a speaker picks up something from his neighbor to the east and runs with it as far as his neighbor
to the west, always staying between them. In the second, a speaker breaks
loose from the paternal neighborhood and travels far and near, picking
up pieces at each stop and dropping them all along the way. The latter
is the kind of diffusion that makes dialectology a hazardous business. As
Robert Louis Stevenson wrote in *The Amateur Emigrant,*

> I knew I liked Mr. Jones from the moment I saw him. I thought him
> by his face to be Scottish; nor could his accent undeceive me. For as there
> is a *lingua franca* of many tongues on the moles and in the feluccas of the
> Mediterranean, so there is a free or common accent among English-
> speaking men who follow the sea. They catch a twang of a New England
> port, from a cockney skipper, even a Scotsman sometimes learns to drop
> an *h*; a word of a dialect is picked up from another hand in the fore-
> castle; until often the result is undecipherable, and you have to ask for a
> man's place of birth.[31]

The compilers of the new *Dictionary of American Regional English*
are now publishing the most comprehensive survey ever made of recorded speech, covering dialects of the United States from Florida to
Alaska, for which they have tried "to collect the greater part . . . of the
words and phrases, pronunciations, spellings, and meanings used . . . up
to the present time."[32] Besides bringing to light the quantities of unreg-
istered written forms in obscure places, this project has rescued uncounted
expressions that would otherwise be lost as their users died because the
forms existed only in the spoken language. The estimated five million
entries have been processed by computers. (The compilers of the vast
Oxford English Dictionary assembled three and a half million entries by
hand.)

---

[30] Kurath 1965, pp. 239–40.
[31] South Seas Edition (New York: Charles Scribner's Sons, 1925), p. 9.
[32] Cassidy 1967, p. 14.

In Europe, dialect geography lacks much of the here-and-now flavor that it has in the United States. With a more stable population and with more radical linguistic as well as geographical and political barriers to surmount, European dialects are bound more tightly to their localities and have more to tell us about events long ago than about recent ones.

The most thoroughly investigated dialects anywhere in the world are those of the Romance languages, which are themselves, of course, just dialects of Latin that drifted apart in the early years of the Christian era. Since more is known about Latin—thanks partly to the very dialectal facts that it helps to illuminate—than about any other ancient language, dialectology in the Romance area has closer ties to historical linguistics than it has anywhere else.

The dialectologist who looked most consistently to geography as a key to the history of dialects was the Italian Matteo Bàrtoli. It should be possible, he thought, to correlate the past evolution of dialects with their positions relative to one another, and he expressed the correlation in a set of four "areal norms":

1. Norm of the isolated area: an area that is cut off and shielded from communication tends to retain older forms.

2. Norm of the lateral area: where a central area is wedged into the middle of a zone that presumably was once homogeneous, the edges of that area tend to retain older forms.

3. Norm of the principal area: if a zone is split into two segments, the larger one tends to retain the older forms. (This is in partial conflict with norms 1 and 2.)

4. Norm of the later area: an area that has been overrun—as by conquest—at a more recent date tends to retain older forms.

The norm of the lateral area is the most picturesque, with its suggestion of an adventurous dialect driving across the territory of a sedentary one and overspreading it everywhere except at the edges. Using the Romance languages in their present state as evidence of what probably happened while the speakers of Vulgar Latin were still more or less in touch with Rome, we can see in Table 9–2 the effect of continued contact in France and Italy as against interrupted contact, and hence the retention of older forms, in Spain and Romania.

The norm of the lateral area explains how it can happen that countries as far apart as Romania and Spain share forms and meanings that are missing in the areas that lie between. But why, if all these languages have a common source, should they be so different today? Mostly because the Romans, in their expeditions, made contact with speakers of

TABLE 9–2
Equivalent Terms in Four Romance Languages

Spain	France	Italy	Romania
hermoso	beau	bello	frumos
mesa	table	tavola	masa
hervir	bouillir	bollire	a fierbe
entonces	alors	allora	atunci
día	jour	giorno	zi
más	plus	più	mai

SOURCE: Adapted from Coseriu 1956, p. 38.

other languages and for a time spoke some form of mixed language with
them. This raises the question of a special kind of areal community mentioned earlier in connection with Black English, that of contact languages,
or pidgins. Wherever speakers of different languages are thrown together,
whether at trading posts or slave stations or on the battlefield, they devise
a compromise language to deal with the essentials. African pidgin was
one such. Another, often mixed with it in North America, was the pidgin
used to communicate with Indian tribes. The Portuguese in their trades,
travels, and conquests established pidgins around the world, including an
African pidgin of their own that influenced the language of blacks in
both English-speaking and Spanish-speaking America.[33] The English-
based pidgin of Melanesia was important enough in the Second World
War for the United States Armed Forces Institute to publish a manual for
its use.[34] Examples: *Bimeby leg belong you he-all-right 'gain* 'Your leg
will get well again'; *Sick he-down-im me* ('sickness downs me') 'I am
sick'; *Me like-im sauce-pan belong cook-im bread* 'I want a pan for cooking bread.'

A pidgin may continue as a mere trade language and vanish when trade
is cut off, or events may cause it to survive as the only language its users
have available to them.[35] This happened with the pidgin ancestor of
Gullah, and also with the French-based pidgin in Haiti. The result
then is that the pidgin is learned as a native language, and the process

---

[33] Granda 1970.
[34] Hall 1943.
[35] Hall 1962. See also Todd 1974.

of *creolization* begins: the children do their work, and the creole evolves like any other language. Haitian was a pidgin that has become a creole; so is Gullah, and so is Police Motu, a pidgin in the early stages of creolization in the neighborhood of Port Moresby in New Guinea, which is based not on English but on Motu, a Malayo-Polynesian language.[36] In a broad sense we all speak creoles, for all languages are mixed.

The variety of data in this section reveals why linguists for years resisted tackling problems of sociolinguistics and why many still do. Once the gate is open an uncontrollable flood of issues, questions, and controversies comes pouring in, many of them having little or nothing to do with language as a reasonably well-defined object of study. The difficulty is the same as with meaning, only on a larger scale. We saw how hard it is to tell when we have laid hold of the meaning *of* a term rather than a meaning that is a hanger-on and may be valid for some, invalid for others, present on one occasion, absent on another. Linguists ought to be able to occupy themselves with what is *in* a language, not with everything else in the world. The American who sees a sign in an Aberdeen shop window reading **Cook by gas** assumes that this is a dialectal difference between Scots and American English. But is it? Suppose that **by** and **with** in both dialects retain their normal ties to the meaning of 'agency' and 'means' (or 'accompaniment'), and the difference is due to a different *attitude* toward the operation of certain mechanical things (the American **It is run by electricity** perhaps reveals the same animistic viewpoint toward a source of power). Is **cook by gas** then a linguistic question or a cultural one? The nature of language makes it an uncomfortable field for people who like precision.

REGISTERS, REPERTORIES, ROLES, AND REPUTATIONS

A *register* is a variety that is not typically identified with any particular speech community but is tied to the communicative occasion. It would be odd to think of people-at-home as a community, yet speech-at-home may be as different from speech-with-strangers as a local dialect is from the standard. One cannot be dogmatic about this because registers can easily become identified with particular groups. Speech-with-one's-friends is a register midway between speech-at-home and speech-with-formal-acquaintances; but if one's friends all belong to Hell's Angels the register acquires community ties.

A speaker's *repertory* is the set of linguistic varieties that he has at his

---

[36] Hooley 1965.

command, each of which enables him to play a *role* defined within a speech community or a social situation. He may play the sycophant to a superior—a socially determined role that will lead him to use ingratiating mannerisms and flattering language; he will choose words from a particular register. Or he may meet with members of his union to discuss a strike; the language he uses will be that of his occupational community.

The *reputation* of a variety is the value placed on it by society. Not all roles are freely played. Some are forced on their users. One variety may capture the schools. Another may be actively campaigned against and marked for extinction.[37]

Registers

> What the [New York] *Times* calls *a reproof* or a *remonstrance,* the *News* calls a *belch* or a *beef.* A rash of strikes is described by the *Times* as a *plethora,* by the *News* as a *bellyful.* When the *Times* becomes *indignant,* it *deplores;* when the *News* gets *sore,* it says, *Nuts.*[38]

This quotation makes it clear that everyone is conscious of the appropriateness, or lack of it, between language on the one hand and occasion, audience, or channel on the other. Mostly it is a question of various degrees of formality, at least some of which can be found in any community, areal or non-areal. Even though Manchester or Chicago English may not consider itself in the prestige class of Southern British, there nevertheless are more formal or less formal varieties of each, with the formal varieties tending to be more alike from place to place than the informal ones.

For convenience one may divide the up-and-down continuum of formality and familiarity into levels, as two linguists have done, recognizing the following five: (1) oratorical, or frozen; (2) deliberative, or formal; (3) consultative; (4) casual; (5) intimate.[39] The oratorical register is used by professional speakers; it is a self-conscious form of public address. The deliberative register is aimed at any audience too large for effective interchange with the speaker. Both oratorical and deliberative tend to be monologs, though deliberative is not polished as an art form. Consultative is typically dialog, at the level where words still have to be chosen with some care; most business is transacted in this register. Casual implies the absence of any social barriers—the relationship, for example, between fellow students. Intimate adds kinship or close friendship.

---

[37] See Gregory and Carroll 1978.
[38] *The New Yorker* (31 May 1947), p. 31.
[39] Joos 1967, and Gleason 1965, pp. 357–61.

Most writing is addressed to audiences that cannot talk back, and accordingly tends to be upgraded to the deliberative level (the written counterpart of oratorical is poetry or poetic prose). This is true even in narrations. Raymond Chandler recorded the impression that Dashiell Hammett made by breaking with this tradition: "A rather revolutionary debunking of both the language and material of fiction had been going on for some time. . . . Hammett applied it to the detective story, and this, because of its heavy crust of English gentility and American pseudo-gentility, was pretty hard to get moving." It was hard to put people down on paper as they were, and "make them talk and think in the language they customarily used."[40]

The relative formality of writing of course reflects the fact that it is always more or less grafted onto the language that we learn first as children and that always remains for us the warmest and most interior part. The bookish overlay is cold and unexpressive, as one inner-city schoolchild revealed in the following interchange with the teacher:

> STUDENT (reading from an autobiographical essay): This lady didn't have no sense.
> TEACHER: What would be the standard English alternate for this sentence?
> STUDENT: She didn't have any sense. But not this lady: *she didn't have no sense.*[41]

Since registers are social phenomena, they are manifested in other ways besides the strictly linguistic: by deferential or respectful or domineering mannerisms, gestures, and tone of voice. But linguistic behavior shows them most unmistakably, and there are forms of speech that are clearly identified with particular registers. The example most often cited is that of forms of address. In most if not all societies the ways of saying 'you' must be watched with care; it is the word that most intimately *hits* the person, next to his own name, with which it shares some of the same taboo character (see pages 264–65). Even in the English of the United States, to address someone with *Hey, you!* is insulting by comparison with the familiar *Hey, bud!* Most if not all European languages have, or have had, two or more forms of 'you' for different registers—in French *tu* and *vous,* in German *du* and *Sie,* familiar and formal respectively. The formal maintains a certain social distance, for whatever reason—newness of acquaintance, respect, hostility; the familiar is used when the distance has been bridged. English no longer requires that a formal *ye, you* be dis-

---

40 *Pocket Atlantic* (New York: Pocket Books, 1946), pp. 209–10.
41 Grimshaw 1973, p. 33, quoting John J. Gumperz.

tinguished from a familiar *thou, thee; you* has been generalized. But at the top register we still address a judge as *your honor* and a cardinal as *your eminence,* with the added courtesy of the third singular form of the verb instead of the form directly associated with *you.* Another way of avoiding the threat of *you* is to use an exclusive *we* ('you and I'), which nurses in hospitals have the reputation of favoring. An example is the following, said by a nineteen-year-old American student to her five-year-old Japanese tutee, who was delaying things by insisting on tying his shoes: *Why don't we not worry about your shoes, OK?*[42] Besides the dodging of *you,* we see here three other components of courtesy behavior: a negative, to suggest rather than to command; a question, likewise; and the addition of a question tag, leaving acceptance of the suggestion open to the hearer.

The French *tu–vous* distinction, informal versus formal, is the prevailing type in Europe, but there are more complex systems. One that is more complex by just one step is that of Uruguay, where a once-snobbish *tú* (from standard Spanish) has wedged itself between the familiar *vos* and the formal *usted,* so that nowadays a young man is apt to call his closest male friends *vos* but use the *tú* as a casual form with women friends; women may respond in the same way, though they tend to generalize *tú* for both intimate and casual.[43] Italian and German had a similar three-point system, which is declining now as it has in standard Spanish, but Catalan maintains it: the middle term, *vós,* is used "among equals who have known each other for a long time, as a sign of respect; and also to speak with peasants."[44] Japanese has a much more complex scheme in which four levels of formality intersect with two levels of respect, the latter expressed by forms of the verb. The levels of formality, which are identified as *informal, polite, superpolite,* and *formal writing,* can be illustrated by the ways of expressing 'yes': *un, ee, hai,* and *sikari,* respectively.[45]

The ways of saying *yes* in English are not so strictly formalized as in Japanese, but even more delicate distinctions can be drawn with intonation. As for *no,* it is particularly sensitive to register, and is regulated not only by intonation but by a wide choice of expressions. If a person is being served at table, rather than *No more, please* it may be considered better manners to say *Thank you* with a headshake or a gesture of the hand. In expressing disbelief it is often better to start with *Well* and then

---

[42] Videotape shown at Stanford University, 4 December 1973, to Language Teaching Study Group from the People's Republic of China.

[43] Ricci and Ricci 1962–63. The *vos* is better known as an areal problem.

[44] Corominas 1954; see the entry "Vos."

[45] Kuno 1973, pp. 19–22.

hesitate than to use an outright negation. Instead of *I disagree* it is usually preferable to say *I don't know* and then state one's own opinion.

It is not unusual for syntax to be affected as well. In Chinese, the idea
that one group of officials (A) is more numerous than another group (B)
is expressed in a lecture as

A	*dwō*	*yú*	B
A	numerous	than	B

and in a conversation as

A	*bĭ*	B	*dwō*
A	compared to	B	numerous[46]

Syntactic differences in English are to be found at one extreme in the
dropping or contraction of words at the beginning of utterances (*Taste
good?* for *Does it taste good? Nat a good orange?* for *Isn't that a good
orange?*) and at the other extreme in special writing styles—for example,
the substitution in newspaper headlines of the present tense for the present perfect (*Heath Resigns* for *Heath Has Resigned*).[47] Vocabulary, however, is where the richest spread of differences can be found. The following scale gives some approximations:

Intimate	*Casual*	*Consultative*	*Formal*	*Frozen*
cute	pretty	attractive		comely
to guzzle	to swig	to drink	to imbibe	to quaff
nutty	crazy	insane	demented	mad
	scared	frightened	apprehensive	affrighted
slanted	catercorner	diagonal	oblique	
on the ball	smart	intelligent	perceptive	astute
to play like (he was dead)	to act like	to pretend		to feign (death)

It is not easy to fill out a chart of this sort because other meanings besides
those of register usually intervene. *Intelligent* and *perceptive,* for example, are not exactly as shown here, but differ also in terms of a feature of
sensitivity that attaches to *perceptive;* and the levels may switch. All the
same, *perceptive* tends to be a shade higher than *intelligent.* Another

---

[46] De Francis 1951, p. 50.
[47] Greenbaum 1975.

interfering factor is that of slang, which always belongs in the two bottom levels but does not define them. Thus *tipsy* and *crocked* are equally casual but *crocked* would be considered more slangy.

Register distinctions in pronunciation are more apt to show themselves as "misses" rather than "differences"—that is, the speaker takes less care or more care to articulate distinctly, but the phonemes are the same. Where there are phonemic differences they tend to attach themselves to particular words; thus a person who always refers to his *mother* when talking outside the family may refer to her as *muvver* to a close relative, retaining an infantile pronunciation that is sanctioned in the family. The supposed cultural preeminence of Britain and later of Boston and environs has led to many socially marked pronunciations: [áyðər] for [íðər], [vázəz] for [vésəz], [ánvəlop] for [ɛnvəlop], [əsyúm] for [əsúm], and so on; many of these are modeled on French.

The register levels are complicated by overlappings from various speech communities. A street gang almost by definition uses forms from the casual register, though it has forms that set it apart from other communities at whatever register. A society of chemists would for the most part hold its meetings and transact its business using consultative or formal. Here again we find socially marked forms. In everyday usage *iodine* is pronounced [ayədayn] by most Americans, but a chemist may call it [ayədin], to match the pronunciation of the other halogens, *fluorine, chlorine, bromine,* and *astatine.* A sailor's *below* is a landlubber's *downstairs.*

Repertories and roles

A speaker's repertory typically includes varieties of a single language, but one or more of the "varieties" may be in some additional language. This does not mean that problems of speech community—German versus Czech, or English versus Italian, say—supersede those of register. In parts of the world where conquest has imposed a language from outside, after a time the older and the newer languages may achieve a modus vivendi that is termed *stable bilingualism,* with one language serving in one capacity and the other in another, often with register distinctions. In Paraguay the majority of urban families are bilingual, using Spanish for official purposes and Guaraní among equals in the home and with friends; in some families "it is considered lacking in respect for a child to address an older person in Guaraní," though the child normally uses it with playmates.[48] Even where two rival varieties represent the "same

---

[48] Morínigo 1931, p. 30.

language" they may differ quite radically, as happens with the standard
language and the local dialects in Norway: two students home for a
vacation will use the standard when talking about school matters but will
switch to dialect to talk about other topics.[49] This illustrates another
point: how difficult it is to separate attitudes toward speakers from attitudes toward subjects. Even though the students may be close friends,
their academic identity submerges their relation of intimacy, and they
choose their roles accordingly.

The kind and degree of bilingualism reflects the nature and organization of society. If speakers of various languages or dialects are brought
so closely together that they have to intercommunicate, and yet no group
yields to any other, the result is some form of common speech that is not
native to anyone. This is the case of modern standard Arabic, which is
taught in the schools and is used in communicating across dialects. It was
also the situation in Europe for several hundred years after Latin had
ceased to be a colloquial language but was maintained for high-level
communication.[50] (A pidgin is also a non-native shared language, but
results from inter-societal rather than intra-societal contacts—see pages
210–11.) At the other extreme there have been societies so rigidly strati-
fied linguistically as well as socially that bilingualism was the exception—
the elites used one language for their intra-group communication, the
masses another; this was true of several pre–First World War European
countries.[51]

The more usual situation with bilingualism is that only a part of the
population—generally a minority with little power—is obliged to play a
role in more than one language. The majority speech is compulsory, with
compulsion often backed by law, but the minority one is kept up, with
varying success. This has happened repeatedly in the United States as
waves of Germans, Italians, Poles, Swedes, and others have immigrated
and created their own close-knit settlements. In time the minority is usually absorbed and its language disappears. At present the minority that
has attracted the greatest attention is the Chicano population in the
American Southwest, along with its Puerto Rican counterpart in the
Northeast. In Chicano bilingual speech one finds several kinds of language
mixing, including, of course, code switching. Thus if both speakers know
both languages, one of them may say one sentence in Spanish and the
next in English and then switch back; one language may simply be more
convenient for a particular topic than the other.

If the minority wields political power or possesses the outer size and

---

[49] Cazden 1972, p. 152.
[50] Kaye 1972.
[51] See Fishman 1967.

inner strength to maintain an ethnic identity, the community may remain bilingual indefinitely, or even reassert its own native speech. That is the situation in French Canada. In other parts of the world—Switzerland, for example—bilingualism is a natural consequence of a federation of minorities. One has to interact with speakers of other languages and learns to switch codes with relative ease.

If one does not have to shift to a second language but only to another variety or another register, code switching is just one of many aspects of normal, painless communication.[52] But sometimes it is coerced, and if the difficulties are not understood the social consequences can be serious. As we have seen, the differences between Black English and the standard taught in the schools are not numerous but do lie in some of the fundamentals. The black child might be better off if he spoke with a foreign accent, for then allowances would be made; but since others generally understand him they think he ought to "know better" than to talk the way he does, and if he uses forms that are not understood, he is blamed for his hearer's ignorance. What happens in the schools is that a white teacher who is faced with white pupils who do not use the standard and black pupils who do not use it, more often than not can understand the non-standard of the white but not that of the black (see Figure 9–3). The result is that the black child has the choice of being misunderstood or of being constantly on guard to use the standard in all communication with whites. If in addition the black non-standard has a low reputation, the child is "disadvantaged" in the worst sense of the term.[53]

Conflict between one register and another is usually less painful, but just as real. Two speakers may operate across essentially the same range, but one with home base, so to speak, closer to casual and the other with home base closer to formal. When they communicate they are liable to exaggerate the distance between them. Hearing A's average formal-like speech, B will interpret it as affectation; hearing B's average casual-like speech, A will interpret it as condescension—assuming, of course, that he regards B as an equal and does not put the whole thing down to vulgarity. The farther apart the home bases are, the wider the imagined distance and the greater the potential for misunderstanding—so long as they remain on shared ground (see Figure 9–4). If the two speakers do not share the same range of socially interpretable language and behavior, this particular source of conflict is absent. So one gets the paradox of misunderstanding growing out of understanding. A human being can accept

---

[52] Inability to switch registers in a second language often betrays the foreign learner. See Gregory and Carroll 1978, pp. 91–93.

[53] See Arthur 1971, pp. 5–8.

FIGURE 9–3
The American Teacher's Acquaintance with Non-standard English

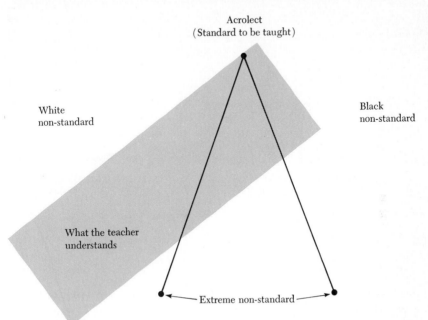

Acrolect
(Standard to be taught)

White
non-standard

Black
non-standard

What the teacher
understands

Extreme non-standard

SOURCE: Based on Arthur 1971.

a horse as a horse, however unlike a person; but something that pretends to be human had better be human, like me. As Jim puts it in Twain's *Huckleberry Finn,*

> "Is a Frenchman a man?"
> "Yes."
> "*Well,* den! Dad blame it, why doan' he *talk* like a man?"[54]

Reputations

The social status of words such as ***shanty, hooligan, shebang, slug*** (of liquor), ***slew*** (of stuff), ***gob*** (as in ***shut your gob***), ***puss*** ('face'), ***shindig, dornick,*** and ***shenanigans*** provides us with a record of socially devalued

---

[54] Chapter XIV, conclusion.

FIGURE 9–4
Cross-Perceptions of Repertory Ranges

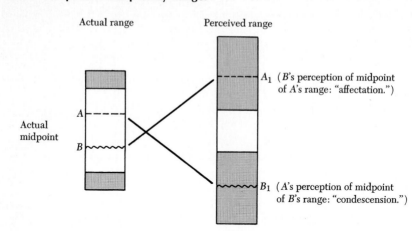

SOURCE: Adapted from Grimshaw 1973, p. 32.

* The unshaded area is the range controlled by all members of the speech community. The actual range shared (*left*) is wider, and the range not shared is narrower, than either seems to be when viewed from an off-center position (*right*).

speech, that of Irish immigrants in the nineteenth century: all are either from, or influenced by, the Gaelic second language of the English-speaking Irish who were the original occupants of ghettoes—called *shanty-towns*—in large Eastern cities. Where a community is looked down upon, its speech is likewise, and the speakers themselves may accept the devaluation and try to exchange their old ways for new: "When Mrs. Murphy became Mrs. Murfree, she left the distinguishing mark of her earlier dialect to the Irish of shantytown, and branded their use as below her or her children."[55]

Every immigrant group has to contend with linguistic hostility. As the group is assimilated the problem disappears, but with other speech communities it remains, as a class stigma. We have seen that the technical jargon of scientists and literary people tends to be seen at the level of formal register, hence looked up to. But the technical talk of farmers and mechanics is not, even though some of it may be as esoteric to the average speaker as terms from physics or canon law. It is not the language that is primarily devalued, but the speakers, and the language is a handy way of telling which individuals to consider inferior to oneself.

---

[55] See Hutson 1947.

One reaction to linguistic conflict is submission, usually after a period of resistance on the part of older speakers; this has been the fate of most ethnic minorities in the United States. Another reaction is a reassertion of the native variety and an attempt to purge it of influences from outside. When the influx of tourists into Martha's Vineyard threatened to submerge the local community, the response of the latter was to speed up certain changes in the pronunciation of the vowels, to make the local speech distinct from that of the mainlanders.[56] In either case—submission or resistance—the cohesive force is that of *purism*. A dominant group, whose children are not as choosy about their companions as they ought to be and start importing forms from "below," senses a threat to itself in the threat to its language and takes arms against Franglish, Spanglish, slanguage, or whatever corruption appears. A minority group, building resistance from within, does the same, claiming preeminence for its writers and speakers and warding off the infiltrations from above as best it can. This has been the history of Czech "closure" to German, Flemish to French, Afrikaans to English, Catalan and Basque to Castilian, with the less prestigious standing up to the more prestigious, and with every national language opposing the popularizing trends that emerge along with the shifting loyalties of young speakers.[57]

What has to be appreciated in this is the close identification of language with self. The advocate of the "let 'em learn English" philosophy displays a monolithic monolingual ignorance of the sacrifice. It is asking a millionaire to give up his fortune and start again without a penny in his pocket. Our language is part of us—far more than a symbol of ethnic identity, it is the warp of a fabric whose weft is our innermost being and our hold on reality. Our idiolect—including the range of our registers—is as it were our "self." For an adult speaker to surrender it is to put himself at the mercy of others who comprehend his handicap far less than if he were crippled or blind.

Less out of charity than practicality, the efforts of the dominant society to preserve the standard are therefore aimed at the young. The aims are seen as humanitarian, "to give every child an equal opportunity"—to acquire a standard that a few have acquired at no cost by choosing the right parents. Even so, this may be the best way out of a dilemma. Two concepts of linguistic democracy are in potential conflict. One, fostered by social activists and aided by sociolinguists who properly emphasize that every code has its excellencies and one has as much right to attention as another, is that linguistic variety should be encouraged. The other, the

---

[56] Labov 1963.
[57] See Wexler 1971.

traditional melting-pot view, is that every *individual* in the society has a right to his share, which he can only get by demanding it in fluent Standard—and it is therefore the duty of the schools to teach it to him. Indeed the traditionalist fears that bilingualism will lead to political tension and disunity, as in Belgium or Eastern Canada. There is a compromise, for which linguists can claim credit, largely through what has been learned in the initiatives taken by the Summer Institute of Linguistics in bringing literacy to various parts of the world. Those missionary linguists realized years ago that for speakers of a non-standard the schools had to represent a period of transition in which the child was first taught to read and write in the language or dialect native to him. Then, with literacy established, the standard could be learned and literacy transferred to it, with the child's own cultural heritage all the while respected and maintained. This kind of enlightened bidialectalism is coming more and more to be official policy.

Language devalued to the point of complete suppression comes under the heading of *taboo*. For the most part taboo is fragmentary, affecting words that relate to behavior that is not approved of. This will be dealt with in the next chapter. But a more sweeping kind of taboo is found where an entire segment of society is required to use a special language, which differs in lexicon or grammar, though rarely (and only superficially) in phonology, from that of the rest of the society. Among certain native Australian languages until recently there were two forms of speech, *guwal* and *dyalŋuy*, the latter having the same grammar and phonology as the former but a completely different vocabulary. It was required to be used with and in the presence of certain taboo relatives; in the Dyirbal tribe these included mother-in-law, father-in-law, paternal aunt's daughter, and maternal uncle's daughter (but not maternal aunt's daughter).[58]

ANALYSIS

A celebrated definition of the central aim of linguistics, which has guided a generation of researchers, is the following, by Noam Chomsky:

> Linguistic theory is concerned primarily with an ideal speaker-listener, in a completely homogeneous speech community, who knows its language perfectly and is unaffected by such grammatically irrelevant conditions as memory limitations, distractions, shifts of attention and interest, and errors

---

[58] Dixon 1972, pp. 32–33, 292–93.

(random or characteristic) in applying his knowledge of the language in actual performance.[59]

With minor qualifications the latter part of Chomsky's definition is still valid, but as the material covered in this chapter implies, the first part is no longer generally accepted. It is not merely that there is no idealized person or community (there is no ideal gas either, but idealization is basic to kinetics and thermodynamics), but that such an assumption obscures our understanding of natural language. The condition of a gas can be stabilized experimentally to allow for observation; a language cannot. It exists only in converse with an environment and can be studied only in connection with it. The study of variation, properly conceived, "adds to our knowledge of linguistic structure, and simplifies the situation."[60]

At the same time, not all parts of language are equally affected by its dynamics, and a shift from an idealized to a social point of view does not necessarily invalidate work already done. In particular, techniques of handling data have been developed that are too valuable to be cast aside. We have seen how at least one such technique, that of positing underlying forms, turned out to correlate with historical change. How make the best use of practices already in vogue?

One procedure that sociolinguists have adopted is to take older generative rules and rewrite them as *variable rules* that are sensitive to social contexts. Originally, transformational rules applied either categorically or optionally; in the one case speakers had to follow the rule, in the other they might or might not—but nothing was said about the conditions under which the "might or might not" applied. Sociolinguistics elected itself to make that condition explicit. An example of an optional rule is the following, applied to contraction in such forms as *He's there, I'm going, You're right:*

$$\mathrm{\vartheta} \longrightarrow (\emptyset) \ / \ \# \# \ [_____, +T] \ C \ \# \#$$

The parentheses mean 'optionally,' so that the interpretation up to the diagonal means 'shwa optionally goes to zero.' After the diagonal, the double double-crosses mean 'word boundary,' the $+T$ means a positive tense feature (that is, the word in question is a verb in either the present or the past tense), and the C means a single consonant. The underlined blank space is where the segment under consideration—that is, the shwa —would go if it were there. So altogether we are told that an auxiliary

[59] Chomsky 1965, p. 3.
[60] Labov 1969, p. 737.

whose only vowel is a shwa, which has no initial consonant, and which has a single end-consonant, may lose its shwa. This applies to *am, are, is,* and also to *have, had, will,* and *would* when they lose their initial conso-nant—for example, *She had been there* may be expressed with a full *had* /hæd/, or with *had* without its initial /h/ and /æ/ reduced to shwa /əd/, or with this last form changed by the rule to /d/: *She'd been there.*

It remains now to see if the "optional" can be defined. What condi-tions induce the speaker to exercise his option? One is the presence of a pronoun rather than a noun preceding the verb. We are more apt to say *I'll do it* than to say *The boy'll do it,* and we would not say *The data're compiled* at all. Another is having the verb followed by another verb rather than by a noun or an adjective: *She's going* would almost always be contracted, *He is wise* less necessarily so. These facts can be in-corporated in a variable rule to show that the presence of the preceding pronoun and that of the following verb affect the outcome:

$$\text{ə} \longrightarrow (\emptyset) \; / \; [\beta\text{Pro}] \; \#\# \; [\text{_____}, +\text{T}] \; \text{C} \; \#\# \; [\alpha\text{Vb}]$$

The Greek letters allow for the pronoun (Pro) and verb (Vb) features to be plus or minus without destroying the rule—they indicate that if the value is plus, the rule is more apt to apply, but if it is minus, it still may apply.[61]

A variable rule implies something for the form to vary *from.* The basis for variation, like that for other transformations, is some real or posited style or form of the language that will best explain all the variations. In the rule just cited, there is a form *with* shwa that is the springboard for the one without. Similarly there is a form with a full vowel that is the springboard for the one with shwa: we would "derive" *Who'd gone?* from *Who 'ad gone?* /hu əd gɔn/ and that in turn from *Who had gone?* The most conservative, deliberately pronounced form is used as the basis. We saw earlier in this chapter how the listener's grammar probably sorts out all the variants and ties them together under some such relationship as this, with something that approximates the most conservative variety sub-tending the others. So it happens that a given dialect, alive or dead, can be seen as basic to the description of an entire language. The researcher feels fortunate to find such a dialect actually preserved. An instance of this kind of lucky survival, matching that of Latin in the West, is that of Kannada in India, the literary form of which has been preserved for prestige purposes and can be used for generating the colloquial dialects.[62]

---

[61] Ibid., pp. 737, 739.
[62] Bright 1969.

Key terms and concepts

synchronic and diachronic
 linguistics
lect
  idiolect
  dialect
areal linguistics
standard and non-standard
 dialects
sex and age dialects
code
  occupational code
  professional jargon
diffusion

pidgin
creole, creolization
sociolinguistics
register
repertory
role
reputation
bilingualism
  stable bilingualism
bidialectalism
variable rule

Additional remarks and applications

1. The following is one of the worksheets used in preparing the *Linguistic Atlas of the Gulf States*.[63] See what your own choices would be. If you have others, state them. (The asterisk indicates a possible choice, not an incorrect form.)

   a. She likes to) dress up, *rig up, *slick up, *prink up, *doll up, /different terms for men? different terms for women putting on make up?/

   When a girl goes out to a party, in getting ready, you say she likes to _____.

   If a girl likes to put on her mother's clothes, she likes to _____.

   If a girl spends all her time in front of a mirror making herself look pretty, you say she likes to _____.

   If a woman likes to put on good clothes, you say she likes to _____.

---

[63] Pederson, McDavid, Foster, and Billiard 1972, pp. 128–29.

b. *purse* /for coins/ *pocketbook
What do you call the small leather container with a clasp on it that women carry money in?
Small thing you take to church to carry coins?
What do you put your money into in your pocket?
Something you would carry your money in is a _____.
If it was small and had a clasp on it for carrying coins, you would call it a _____.

c. *bracelet*
What does a woman wear around her wrist?

d. *string of beads* *pair of beads
Suppose there are a lot of little things strung up together and used to go around your neck as an ornament, what would you call these?

e. *suspenders* *galluses, *braces
What do men wear to hold up their trousers?

f. an old) *umbrella*
What do you hold over you when it rains?

g. *bedspread* *coverlet, *coverlid, *counterpane
What is the last thing you put on a bed? The fancy top cover.

h. *pillow* *piller, *pillow slip, *pillowcase, *pillow bier
At the head of the bed you put your head on a _____.

i. *bolster* /a large pillow/; it goes) clear (across the bed *clean, *plum, *slam, *jam
Do you remember using anything at the head of the bed that was about twice as long as a pillow?
That bolster didn't go part way across the bed; it went _____.

2. Test your reactions toward some other dialect of English. If you are a Northern (or Southern) speaker do you find a Southern (or Northern) accent irritating? How do you react toward a speaker of British Standard (Southern British, or "Received Pronunciation")? Does it make a difference whether the other speaker is of the same sex as you, or the opposite sex?

3. If you are a native speaker of American English, see if you can classify your own dialect by the following list of words:

Northern	Midland	Southern
cherry pit	piece 'distance'	corn shucks
pail	green beans	you-all
comforter	wait on 'wait for'	snap beans
stoop 'porch'	quarter till	pallet
clapboards 'siding'	want off 'want to	chitlins 'hogs'
angleworm	get off'	intestines'
swill 'slop'	blinds 'shades'	light bread 'white
brook 'creek'	poke 'sack'	bread raised
hadn't ought	all the better	with yeast'
teeter-totter	(That's all the	tote 'carry'
eaves troughs	better he can	jackleg 'untrained
fried cake 'dough-	do it.)	person'
nut'	you-uns	clabber cheese 'cot-
johnnycake 'corn-	spouts 'gutters'	tage cheese'
bread'	snake feeder	mouth harp
spider 'skillet'	'dragonfly'	'harmonica'
darning needle		croker sack 'burlap
'dragonfly'		bag'
Dutch cheese 'cot-		carry (someone
tage cheese'		home) 'escort'
		branch 'small
		stream'
		pulley bone
		'wishbone'
		hants 'ghosts'

SOURCE: Adapted from Babington and Atwood 1961. Used by permission of The University of Alabama Press. © 1961.

If you are like many other speakers of American English, you may find that you use words from all three lists. Try to relate them to different contacts during your life—residence in particular areas or close association with certain speakers.

4. Are there dialect problems among minority groups in your public school system? If so, see if you can identify some of the forms used. They may be phonological (*house* pronounced [hʌws], *pen* pronounced like *pin*), morphological (verb forms like *dove* or *might could,* or switching of preterit and participle forms like *He done it, He seen them, They had went, Somebody had stole it*), or syntactic (adjectives used as adverbs, as in *He did it easy;* non-standard

clauses, as in *This is a recipe that if you don't do it right you won't like it;* interchange of cases, as in *Him and me don't like it,* or its opposite, by overcompensation, *It's for he and I).* Where are the speakers from? Are the forms they use standard in those areas? Do you use similar forms sometimes (for example, *Whom shall I say is calling,* an overcompensation)?

5. Discuss the Spanish expression *Allá voy,* literally 'There I'm going,' which translates the English *I'm coming* in answer to a summons. Which language has the more complicated rule for the use of the verb meaning basically 'to proceed to a point other than the locus of the speaker' (compare *He comes here, He goes there, °He goes here*)?

6. A pidgin exists to be understood with the least possible effort. See if you can interpret the following from Melanesian Pidgin:

   a. Suppose man he-die, alltogether man he-make-im sing-sing 'long em.

   b. Cut-im grass belong head belong me.

   c. Bone belong dis-fellow man he all-same water.[64]

7. A caller on a radio talk show said *It's laid out so perfectly that you can do so much work with it!* Do you think the caller was a man or a woman? On a television program, the actor playing the role of a policeman was given the line *Jeannie's blossomed into such a lovely lady!* Comment.

8. Note some instances of slang in your speech and that of your friends and see if older speakers know what the slang means and also how they react to it. How would you feel about older speakers using such expressions?

9. If it is understandable that technical fields such as physics and surgery require a technical jargon, is the same true of technical fields dealing with the public, such as law and social services? If so, do these fields require a special effort to achieve clarity? Discuss.

10. Classify the following for register, and make any comment you con-sider relevant:

    a. *Broad and Alien Is the World* (title of a book by Ciro Alegría)

---

[64] These examples are from Hall 1943.

b. "How Stands Our Press?" (title of a pamphlet by O. G. Villard)

c. The same goes for him and his ideas.

d. How fatigued I am!

e. I gottagetoff.

Find an equivalent for each of the above in a different register.

11. What are some of the syntactic and lexical marks of oratorical or frozen register in the following passage?

> And myth is . . . ? For me, it is a story, a story of epic proportions in which natural and preternatural forces join to symbolize the essential realities of man in his world. In such a story, man's world of sight merges with his world of insight; the impalpable of his world of imagination becomes as real as the feel of the sword in his hand. Here, then, is narrative partaking of philosophy, and therefore containing within it the seeming mutually-exclusive elements of the magical and the mundane, the sense of immediate reality and the apocryphal, the social discord and the harmony, destruction and—the phoenix.[65]

12. Is there anything wrong with either of the following two sentences? If so, explain:

a. Let's show 'em.
b. Let's reveal 'em.

Are the following two acceptable? If not, what would you do to make them right?

c. Let's pray. (minister at a church service)
d. All seniors will please get up. (college president about to confer degrees)

13. Rate the following as casual or consultative:

a. He grew steadily worse.
b. He grew worse and worse.
c. She's all the time complaining.
d. She's constantly complaining.
e. I told him right there.
f. I promptly told him.

Do your decisions suggest anything about a register distinction for the *-ly* adverb standing before the verb?

---

[65] Kenneth Lash in *The New Mexico Quarterly Review* (Spring 1947).

14. One reason for the esteem in which consultative or formal register is held is that more people understand it than understand casual or intimate. What causes this? Relate your answer to social factors such as the media, mobility of speakers, and so on.

15. Discuss the problem that a schoolchild has in class on first being required to present something in deliberative register, when all his previous experience in communication has been in more intimate registers where there is immediate feedback from hearers.[66]

16. Do all three of the following compounds exist in everyday English: *child-abuse, wife-abuse, husband-abuse?* If not, comment.

For further reading

Allen, Harold B. (ed.). 1971. *Readings in American Dialectology* (New York: Appleton-Century-Crofts).

Bentley, Robert H., and Samuel D. Crawford. 1973. *Black Language Reader* (Glenview, Ill.: Scott, Foresman).

Dillard, J. L. 1972. *Black English* (New York: Random House).

Dohan, Mary Helen. 1974. *Our Own Words* (Baltimore: Penguin Books).

Gregory, Michael, and Susanne Carroll. 1978. *Language and Situation: Language Varieties and Their Social Contexts* (London: Routledge & Kegan Paul).

Hymes, Dell (ed.). 1971. *Pidginization and Creolization of Languages* (Cambridge, England: Cambridge University Press).

Joos, Martin. 1967. *The Five Clocks* (New York: Harcourt Brace Jovanovich).

Key, Mary Ritchie. 1975. *Male/Female Language with a Comprehensive Bibliography* (Metuchen, N.J.: The Scarecrow Press).

Labov, William. 1973. *Sociolinguistic Patterns* (Philadelphia: University of Pennsylvania Press).

Marckwardt, Albert H. 1958. *American English* (New York: Oxford University Press).

Reed, Carroll E. 1967. *Dialects of American English* (Cleveland and New York: World Publishing Company).

Scargill, H. M. 1973. *A Survey of Canadian English* (Toronto: Canadian Council of Teachers).

Todd, Loreto. 1974. *Pidgins and Creoles* (London: Routledge and Kegan Paul).

Trudgill, Peter. 1974. *Sociolinguistics: An Introduction* (Harmondsworth, England: Penguin Books).

---

[66] Gleason 1965, p. 361.

VARIATION IN TIME 10

Alively but often short-lived segment of any language is its slang. Currently one may hear *crash* 'to collapse into sound sleep'; *pig out* 'to eat to excess'; *programmed* 'predisposed'; *turkey* 'an awkward and dumb person'; *rip off* 'to steal (from)'; *zilch* 'none, nothing.' The last of these—*zilch*—has been around for forty years without being taken seriously enough to gain acceptance in the standard lexicon. For overeating, *pig out* has replaced the earlier *eat like a horse* and *hog it down*. Some expressions like *turkey* may soon be as obsolete as *noodle* or *booby*. Whatever the ultimate fate of these terms (*rip off* at least appears to be here to stay—it fulfills a need for a term for any sort of theft), it is clear that they temporarily increase the bulk of English words. One of them—*programmed*—points to another area that expands almost as fast as slang: the vocabulary of science and technology.

A language *grows* in the number of its words as the societies that use it create new entities that have to be named. Some of the ways of building new words were summarized in Chapter 4. There we saw that newness is relative: neologisms almost never result from a random combination of sounds that nonetheless satisfies the phonological requirements of the language; instead they are built of partially formed old morphological material. All the same, they are new configurations that stand for fresh concepts.

A language also *dies* bit by bit as words grow obsolete and pass from use. But obituaries are harder to write than birth notices. Old words can be revived—a historical novel reaches into the past and brings back not only archaic terms but also, for flavor, some hint of archaic grammar. Short of social collapse, vocabularies show a net increase over the years.

But expansion in the number of word forms is only one kind of change. Most speakers hardly know more than a fraction of the total anyway, and not the same fraction that other speakers know; yet they communicate on all matters of common concern. Differences in vocabulary become important for describing variation in space—dialects and codes can be largely delimited by them. But for variation in time, the dense core of sound and grammar is a better index.

The two great approaches to language are the descriptive and the historical, technically the *synchronic* and the *diachronic*. The content of all the chapters up to this one has been largely synchronic. Yet the two cannot really be pulled apart; the separation is mainly for convenience. With old speakers and young speakers coexisting and communicating, both the past and the future are with us in the present. Synchrony is a two-dimensional picture that flattens out the dimension of change and commands the sun to stand still. We fail to see the stirrings going on around us because change is seldom noticeable on the scale of a human lifetime. Besides, we can ignore it and still make ourselves understood.

Now and then we do notice a shift of grammar or pronunciation within our lifetime. Perhaps we see a rule taking shape as individual words drift into a new category. Notice the following adjective forms based on names of states:

*Virginian peanuts.	Hawaiian pineapple
*Californian earthquake	Alaskan earthquake
*Iowan landscape	New Mexican landscape

The forms in the first column are no longer in use, having been replaced by the growing trend toward using the noun form as adjective: *Iowa landscape.* We are witnessing a gradual restriction of the derived adjectives to mean the inhabitants: an Iowan, a Californian, a Virginian. The process is not complete for the newer states, and hardly affects other political entities. Just as we once spoke of **Californian gold** we still refer to **Puerto Rican rum.**

Another example is the changing rule for the possessive. Some older speakers still avoid expressions like **the college's president, the garden's fertility,** and few of any age would say *Spanish's words* or *Italian's derivations.* The old rule limited possessives to persons or to what could be easily personified; the new rule admits them for purely relational purposes, where an *of* phrase would have been used before: **the president of the college, the fertility of the garden.** This change has been going

on for a long time. It also illustrates a reversal of historical trends. The
-'s form was the only one in Old English, but was gradually replaced by
of phrases in Middle English until by the time of Chaucer most remaining
instances were found with personal nouns,[1] even though inanimate *its*
holds its own to this day: we may not be able to say °*German's words*
but *its words* is perfectly normal.

More often the only visible change is a gain or a loss in some already
existing rule. This can be seen for English in a tendency for verbs of
more than one syllable to be marked by having their last syllable more
prominent than the last syllable of corresponding adjectives and nouns—
for example, *supplement* pronounced /sʌpləmɛnt/ and /sʌpləmənt/. That
process continues to affect more and more words. Those ending in *-ate*
are typical. A speaker who still pronounces the ending as -/et/ with the
noun *candidate* may already have shifted to -/ət/ with the nouns *graduate, associate,* and *affiliate;* but will have retained -/et/ for the verbs.

Many changes slip by unobserved—often simply because our spelling
habits keep our minds in the old groove. For example, if someone were
to ask, "Is there such a word as *maybe?*" we would answer yes. The
process that converted *It may be* to *may be, may-be, maybe,* and *mebbe*
took a couple of hundred years, but it is finished. If someone were to ask,
"Is there such a word as *could-be?*" the answer would come harder, for
there is no such spelling. Yet we readily drop the *it* from *It could be*
and assign a definite intonation,

could be ⌣

and we say *Could be, he smokes a pipe. Could-be* is a word in the making.[2]

There are structural changes in progress too. The verb *see* of course
refers to vision. But it also long ago became a function word in causative
constructions like *I saw him home, See that he is taken care of.* And now,
almost on the sly, it has become a complementizer in constructions like *I
hate to see you work so hard,* which is in the same family as *I hate to
have you work so hard* and *I hate for you to work so hard.*

Change becomes visible only after long underground development.
Every alteration that establishes itself had to exist formerly as a choice.
And this means that the seedbed for variation in time is simply the whole

---

[1] The proportion of -'s to *of* with inanimate nouns in Chaucer is 137 to 531 in verse but
only 2 to 564 in prose, which reflects everyday usage more faithfully. See Mustanoja
1960, p. 74.
[2] See Greenbaum 1969, p. 109.

landscape of variation in space that we traveled over in the last chapter. When speakers migrate from one community to another they adopt the ways of the new community, and those of the old fall into partial disuse. If political upheavals abolish certain class distinctions, the vocabularies of superiority and submission vanish along with the roles they served. If religious ties are weakened, certain old forms will no longer be reverenced and will be forgotten. But no social revolutions are necessary for linguistic change, though of course they speed things up; it is enough for speakers to decide that one variant is worth adopting instead of another.[3]

How variants first appear is another question. Some are the result of mistakes, such as slips of the tongue. Or the mistakes may be logical ones. Children are given models to imitate that do not represent a genuine sampling of the grammatical competence of their elders. They build a grammar to account for what they *hear,* which may be slightly different from the grammar that their parents *know.* Consider the preposition *for* in *for free,* which was originally a non-standard blend of *free* and *for nothing.* Many speakers, partly because *free* alone is slightly ambiguous and partly to be humorous,[4] adopted the two-word phrase, until by the mid 1940s more and more children who only heard the form and could not appreciate the joke were adopting *for free* as their standard. The grammar of *for* with adjectives *(for good, for certain, for sure)* was thus extended.

Some innovative forces are within the language mechanism itself; the speaker makes mistakes, but they are due to complexities in the system. In every act of speech a number of things go on at once. We organize our sentences into patterns of sound that signal to the hearer how he is to decode them to represent the individual words and their connections in his mind. To this we add an intonation contour, with peaks of accent, to convey our feelings and our sense of the important. Around this we wrap a gestural envelope: a facial expression is often our only clue to the difference between a statement and a question. Sometimes these levels interfere with one another. The [p] of *yep* and *nope* is the result of shutting the mouth in self-satisfied finality at the end of an utterance. The gesture affects the word. Someone who says *Now wa-a-it a MIN-ute!* makes the sentence more spirited by putting an extra accent on *minute* even though there is no question of 'minute, not second'—the normal way of saying *Wait a minute* is with only one accent, on *wait.* Since most

---

[3] See Householder 1972.

[4] A humor that for its effect depends on the change being felt as deviant. See Fónagy 1971, especially pp. 209–15.

English words have a fixed or lexical stress, this example illustrates a certain amount of friction between the lexical level—the forms of words —and the intonational level. The result is like what happens when someone tries to eat and speak at the same time; the same organs are involved in both activities and each must yield a bit. One characteristic of intonational rhythm in English is that of placing a major accent close to the end of a sentence. Sometimes this leads to alternating pronunciations of the same word or even—with words most often used at the end of a phrase—to a permanent change. Take the suffix *-able.* Though normally when added to a verb it does not shift the stress *(permít, permíssible; cúltivate, cúltivatable; mínimize, mínimizable),* a good many speakers tend to move the stress to the right in longer forms, especially those with *-ize,* or *-fy: réalize, realízable; vérify, verifíable; idéntify, identifíable.*

These are cases of interference in the act of speaking. Other kinds of interference go deeper. There is a psychological interference that stems from the mere existence of more than one choice for roughly the same purpose; the result is that two get confused and produce a third, called a *blend.* And in a language such as English there is a conflict between written and spoken language that has led to countless changes in pronunciation.

Often the precipitating cause is imposed from outside. Any social change brings a new mix in the elements of language. When the Norman invasion brought to English many words containing the phoneme /v/— *vile, very, vale, vain, venial, venom*—English altered its phonemic system just enough to turn the sound of [v], which it already had as an allophone of /f/, into a new phoneme. The same thing happened with /z/.[5]

WHERE THE VARIANTS COME FROM

It is impossible to enumerate all the forces of change, whether they reside in the language or impinge from outside. Variation is infinite and its causes likewise. We are limited to the conspicuous and the typical. And we must keep in mind that the thousands of deviations are only raw material. Most of them come to nothing—mispronunciations, mistakes in grammar, artificial coinages, attempts at verbal humor, poetic distortions —the majority pass unnoticed, or are noticed and disregarded, or are briefly taken up but soon dropped. It is only by being noticed, appreciated, and adopted that a few make their way in to stay.

---

[5] Vachek 1965, pp. 53–54.

Speakers' errors

The most commonplace of all mistakes, in speech as well as in writing, are those caused by some malfunctioning in the neural commands that tell our vocal organs or our finger muscles what to do. A command may not be fully carried out. Or it may be carried out, but in the wrong sequence. Or it may trip another command that replaces it or is added to it. The trouble may be either at the coding end (for example, the commands are issued in the wrong order) or at the receiving end (the muscles try their best, but get in one another's way). Back of it there is usually a higher failure: the speaker is in a hurry, or feels that under the circumstances he can afford to be careless, and he neglects to pay close attention to what he is saying.[6]

Loss   A command is not fully executed. This is often a matter of timing. Carefully pronounced, the word *temperature* has four syllables, but the second, being a syllabic /r/, can be speeded up to the point that it forms a cluster with /p/ and one syllable is lost. This happens usually next to a stressed syllable, which robs its neighbors of some of their length. The initial loss may materialize as the reduction of a vowel, as when *schirreve* (the *reeve*, or king's officer, of the *shire*) had its second vowel reduced to shwa, giving the modern *sheriff*, which in turn many of the younger generation are pronouncing [šɛrf].

For most Americans *laboratory* is *lábratory* and for most Britishers it is *labóratry*, but both have lost a syllable (as happened also in Portuguese, giving us *Labrador*). The loss of the /t/ in *postpone* and of the /t/ and one /s/ in *postscript* is due to muscular inertia—/s/ and /t/ have the same point of articulation. Not only whole syllables may go, as in *'Deed I do* for *Indeed I do* but whole words, typically unaccented function words. *You like it?* is perfectly acceptable for *Do you like it?* Very young speakers carry this kind of pruning to an extreme; with less speech control than adults, they tend to hit the stressed syllables of a word and let the rest go: *'pression* for *expression* and *'raff* for *giraffe*.[7] Most of our nicknames—*Fred* for *Frederick, Angie* for *Angela, Chris* for *Christopher*—are the result of childhood's reduction of unnecessary syllables. We tolerate a great deal of such telegraphic reduction so long as it does not interfere too much with sense. The words *and, in, than,* and

---

[6] "Slips of the tongue are predictable natural processes introduced in the absence of close monitoring" (Bailey 1974, p. 19).

[7] Examples are from Brown and Bellugi 1964.

an are all reduced to /n/ in rapid speech: *The pen 'n' pencil 'n' the drawer are better 'n a typewriter to copy 'n easy thing like that.*

Ultimately such loss of syllables may leave us a much shortened form: *mob* from *mobile (vulgus)* as well as colloquial *lab, math,* and *hippo.* Such *stump words* have increased our stock of monosyllables.

Addition   Not only may a phoneme or syllable be lost, but the reverse may occur. An additional sound or sounds may intrude to make a word easier to articulate. Consonant clusters are difficult to articulate with speed, and so vowels may be added. In the Romance-speaking area that now covers France and Spain the Latin initial clusters with /s/ were unacceptable to the pre-Roman population, which split them into two syllables by adding an initial /e/. So we get Old French *estudie* (modern *étude*), Spanish *estudio,* and Portuguese *estudo,* where Italian has *studio,* all from Latin *studium.* Japanese does an even more thorough job of breaking up clusters, as can be seen in the words that it borrows—a *strike* in baseball is *sutoraiku.* The substandard forms *ellum* for *elm* and *athalete* for *athlete* are sometimes heard in English, where the clusters /lm/ and /θl/ have been broken up by the insertion of shwa.

Assimilation   A command (or its execution) is improperly timed. It comes too early or too late. The result is that a feature belonging to one phoneme is carried over to another, that is, it is changed to be more like the other: it is assimilated. In rapid speech, expressions such as *tin box, manpower, gunboat,* and *in place* are apt to become *timbox, mampower, gumboat,* and *implace:* the bilabial feature of the /b/ or /p/ is anticipated and converts the /n/ to /m/. This is what operated in Latin to change the *in-* prefix to *im-* and, in reverse, the *com-* prefix to *con-,* as can be seen in many English borrowings: *indent* and *intend* but *impress* and *immense; compel* and *commence* but *condense* and *contend.* One common type of assimilation is the voicing of voiceless consonants when they occur between vowels. Vowels are practically always voiced, and the speaker fails to shut off the voicing when he gets to the consonant or begins it too soon before he reaches the next vowel. This is one of the reasons why a voiced flap replaces [t] in American English in such expressions as *latter, better, atom, get 'im.* One even hears a /ǰ/ in place of a /č/ now and then—for example, *congratulate* pronounced as if it were spelled *congradulate.* Assimilation often creates an intrusive sound that may later show up in the spelling. In pronouncing the word *gamel* speakers tended to raise the velum a little too quickly in pronouncing the /m/, with the result that the latter half of the /m/ was pronounced with the velum up, automatically creating a /b/ and producing the modern form *gamble.* The same process inserted the /d/ in *thunder* and *tender* and the /b/ in the substandard pronunciation *fambly* for *family*. If the following sound is not only non-nasal but also voiceless, two features may be anticipated. The word *youngster* is often heard as *younkster:* the velum is raised too soon, and this would convert the /ŋ/ to /g/ except that the voicelessness of the /s/ also jumps the gun and changes the still unpronounced /g/ to a /k/. The same process inserted a /p/ after the /m/ in *empty* and *Thompson.*

There are also cases of reciprocal assimilation. Two adjoining sounds borrow features from each other. In the words *seven* and *eleven,* many speakers carry the labiodental articulation of the /v/ over to the /n/, which becomes a labiodental /ɱ/; but that is felt as an /m/, which then reacts on the /v/ to produce /b/. The result is *sebm, elebm.* Mutual assimilation of this sort has been responsible for the creation of new sounds that have become phonemes in their own right. Palatals are typical. In the word *cordial* the /d/ was drawn toward the position of the /y/, and the /y/ picked up the tighter closure of the /d/; the blending of the two resulted in /ǰ/. Related processes gave us the modern pronunciations of *capture, righteous, pinion, million, fissure, mission, Asian,* and the high-speed pronunciations *gotcha* for *got you, hadja* for *had you,* /mɪšə/ for *miss you,* and so on.

All the examples up to this point have been of *contact* assimilation— that is, the segments affected stand side by side. There is also *distance* assimilation, which is most apt to occur when two sounds not too far separated happen to have most of their features in common. A speaker coding an utterance preparatory to speaking it may misplace a feature. A college teacher intending to say *discussing shortly* came out with *discushing;* the palatal feature in the initial sound of *shortly* was anticipated in the second /s/ of *discussing.* A distance assimilation is more apt to be spotted as a lapse and corrected on the spot. But not always. A kind of distance assimilation involving vowels is common enough to have given rise to the phenomenon of *vowel harmony* in a number of languages. In Finnish there is a case ending *-hen,* whose vowel *e* assimilates to the preceding vowel: *pää-hän* 'heads,' *puu-hun* 'tree,' *maa-han* 'land,' *suo-hon* 'bog,' *kyy-hyn* 'viper,' *yö-hön* 'night,' *tie-hen* 'road.'[8] This assimilation involves lag: the feature is prolonged when it should be cut off. Most assimilation involves anticipation: the feature is turned on too soon.

Old assimilations are sometimes evidence of the former presence of sounds that have since disappeared. For example, we expect a /z/ to result when an /s/ comes directly before a voiced consonant in the same word, as happens with *cosmic, Moslem, lesbian;* but *isthmus* has /s/,

---

[8] Example from Anttila 1972, p. 73.

and the spelling confirms that the /s/ formerly stood before a /t/ and has not yet taken on the new voicing assimilation to the /m/.

Dissimilation   When a pianist has to hit the same key twice in succession he gets around the difficulty by using one finger one time and another the next. It is hard to get the same neural assembly to fire twice in quick succession. Since speech has nothing so handy as two different tongues to execute the same maneuver, it sometimes avoids the trouble by changing or dropping one of the repeated sounds. The opposite of assimilation, this differentiating of like sounds, is *dissimilation.* In the sentence *Our time is up in five minutes* we have no difficulty pronouncing the first word as /awr/, though we tend to prefer the simplified /ar/. But in *Our hour is up in five minutes,* we would be sure to say /ar/ to avoid the repetition of /aw/. Some sounds are more susceptible than others. In many languages dissimilation affects /r/ and /l/ especially. The word *grammar* has two /r/'s; for some speakers in Middle English times this was unsatisfactory, and they changed it to *glamor,* which has survived with a different meaning. The word *purpre* was changed to the modern *purple,* though *purpure* survives in heraldry. In the word *February* the first /r/ is simply dissimilated out for most speakers at least part of the time.

Metathesis   Sometimes whole segments are moved around, a kind of wholesale assimilation that involves not a change but an exchange. We call this *metathesis.* The resemblance to assimilation can be seen in errors like *I slaw Sloane* for *I saw Sloane;* as a pure metathesis this would be *I slaw Soane,* with the /l/ moved from one position to the other, rather than a mere borrowing of its features, with the cluster /sl/ replacing /s/. The same physiological processes are involved in both metathesis and assimilation: articulations are shifted about, whether because of miscoding or of mistiming. Since metathesis is on a larger scale than assimilation, it is usually caught and corrected—one can easily tell that *snop-shats* for *snap-shots* is a mistake. But some cases of metathesis survive, especially with difficult combinations of sounds, where many speakers tend to make the same adjustments. The word *uncomfortable* is commonly pronounced *uncomfterble,* with the /r/ moved to the following syllable. The clusters /ks/ and /sk/ are typical shifters. Many people say *asteriks* for *asterisk,* and the standard pronunciation *ask* goes back to a former *aks* that still survives dialectally. The two words *tax* and *task* come from the same source and still show a certain similarity in meaning.

A special kind of metathesis that usually involves coding at a higher level than mere sounds is the *spoonerism,* named after William A. Spooner, an English divine whose slips of the tongue were legendary: *Is the bean dizzy?* for *Is the dean busy?,* *Let me sew you to your sheet* for *Let me show you to your seat.* They are among the funniest of lapses because they involve more than an interchange of sounds. The typical spoonerism is not *Dend a spollar* for *Spend a dollar,* but such things as *Blake the grass* for *Break the glass.* The switches tend to be into well-worn grooves—more often than not at least one of the altered forms already exists as a word. That is true of all such lapses, whether they make a perfect spoonerism like *the beery wenches* for *the weary benches (of Parliament)* or an imperfect one like *an assign assailum* for *an insane asylum.* The set phrases and function words, however, are seldom involved in spoonerisms: *Hold my books* would probably never be said as *Mold high books* or *Hold by mooks.* Spoonerisms are the results of higher-level coding falling back on lower-level coding—the less habitual is snared by the more habitual. The mixup is at two or more levels,[9] unlike other metatheses, which are only at the level of sound, and unlike blends (to be discussed shortly), where the confusion is at the level of meaning (though they too result in a new configuration of sound). Since spoonerisms almost always yield utterances that are ludicrously inappropriate, they have little or no historical effect.

Many of the observations in this section are a restatement of facts already discussed in Chapters 2 and 3. In a broad sense most allophones of the phonemes are the result of assimilation. They are "conditioned" by neighboring sounds or neighboring events, which is to say that they pick up one or more features from their surroundings. Allomorphs too—those that are "phonologically conditioned"—are mostly traceable to assimilation. The plural endings in English (and the possessives of nouns and third-person-singular endings of verbs)—/s/ in *cats* but /z/ in *dogs* and *toys*—retain these features because of assimilation to the preceding sound. The /v/ of *wives,* the first /z/ of *houses,* and the /ð/ of *paths* are assimilations too. In Old English the sounds [f v], [s z], and [θ ð] were allophonic pairs. The plural ending caused the consonant to fall between two vowels, and it became voiced by assimilation. Thus the singular *hlāf* 'loaf' had the plural *hlāfas* 'loaves,' where /f/, with a vowel on either side, was sounded as [v], as shown in the modern spelling.

But allophones have little importance in themselves. They become important for historical change only when they are *chosen* for a communicative purpose, and by that time they have ceased to be mere allophones and are on their way to becoming phonemes in their own right. We have seen how the influx of Norman French words, in which /f/ and /v/ were distinct phonemes, helped to raise the status of the two sounds in English.

---

[9] Syntax is probably involved also. *Sold my hocks* for *Hold my socks* is a more likely spoonerism than *Bold my hooks* for *Hold my books* because the latter replaces a verb with an adjective.

In that case the "phonetic split" was the result of a foreign invasion. Just as often it comes about through some accidental loss in the language itself. In the word *stronger*, the old /n/ phoneme already had a velar allophone [ŋ] through assimilation to the following /g/. But in the base form *strong* the /g/ was lost, as it has been in all such words still spelled with -ng. Had the /n/ reverted to its alveolar pronunciation, there would have been nothing to distinguish *sung, king,* and *fang* from *sun, kin,* and *fan;* a host of homonyms would have been created. Probably to avoid this confusion speakers held on to the velar allophone, which by definition then became a new phoneme.[10]

The regularity of historical changes in sounds is due to more or less consistent behavior of the human speech mechanism. Speech is a code, expressed by means of sound-units integrated into a steady flow; and since the process is automatic, it causes certain predictable effects of unconscious planning, timing, and inertia.

But not all the problems of turning out a well-rounded sentence stem from a misalignment of automatic behavior. Nor are the automatic errors always purely so. Intellectual choices have to be made and intellectual confusions may be incurred. Mistakes at this level are from a wide range of faculties and their interaction often produces whimsical results. "Sporadic changes" is what they used to be called. Three of them will be treated here: blends, malapropisms, and spelling pronunciations.

Blends   Suppose someone is about to say *A spurious scarcity of goods led to high prices:*

A spurious (a) scarcity of goods . . .
          (b) shortage
          (c) sparseness
          (d) lack
          (e) dearth
          (etc.)

If he says a *curious spaircity of goods* we know that he has confused two things, both of which he intended to say: *spurious* and *scarcity.* This is little more than a metathesis (it is a *little* more because he has said *curious* and not *scurious*—an existing word is always favored, even if

---

[10] That, at least, is the linguistic way of describing the events. Psychologically listeners were probably already paying as much attention to the velar [ŋ] as to the /g/ in distinguishing between *sung* and *sun;* but since it makes for a more economical description to say that the /g/ was what counted and the velarity of [ŋ] was only an automatic consequence of the /n/'s being where it was, that is how the facts are represented.

wrong in sense). But if he says *a spurious sparsity of goods* he is probably confusing two things, only one of which he would want to say in a single breath: *scarcity* and *sparseness.* Enough speakers have made this confusion over the years so that *sparsity* is recognized (*sparseness* appeared in the early part of the nineteenth century, *sparsity* in the latter half). *Sparsity* is a *blend.*

The column (a) to (e) shows the dimension in which blends occur: it is paradigmatic, involving sets within the language (in this case, sets of synonyms), rather than syntagmatic, involving the horizontal axis of items in the spoken chain. It is also at a high cognitive level: the speaker is making one of the freest choices that a speaker can make, between two words that are nearly the same in meaning.

Blends do not necessarily result in new configurations of sound—the speaker who meant to say either *She was on the verge of a crackup* or *She was on the verge of a breakdown* and came out with *She was on the verge of a crackdown* did not create a new word—but when they do, the creation frequently sticks—speaker and hearer seem to think alike and the new form is accepted as freshly appropriate. *Glob* combines *gob* and *blob* in a nice union of form and meaning. *Riffle* is semantically a blend of *ripple* and *shuffle,* although the word form existed previously in another meaning. These creations are in the standard dictionaries, though other less common ones are not, such as *protruberant (protuberant + protrude).* Others with a promising look but no currency are *to slag (to lag + to sag* or to *slacken,* with a suggestion of *laggard* and *sluggard);*[11] *to stample (to trample + to stamp on);*[12] and *spinwheels (pinwheel + spin).* Since blends are drawn from paradigms with multiple members—usually a word has more than one synonym—it is nothing unusual for three or more alternatives to contribute. A speaker was heard to say *He plays the straight-pan type,* combining *straight man + straight face + dead pan.* Another was heard to say *The department is underhandicapped* meaning *understaffed* and *handicapped,* but also *underhanded* in the unusual sense of 'having too few hands,' where *hand* means 'worker.' Trade names and advertising words are often deliberately created blends: the *Wiltern Theater* is located at Wilshire and Western in Los Angeles; a *fishwich* is a sandwich of fish. At least one of Lewis Carroll's creations—*chortle (chuckle + snort)*—has been added to the dictionary.

The kind of blend that is most apt to persist is the one built of loose elements—phrases rather than single words; we tend not to monitor them

---

[11] *Their French work slagged all week,* from a report by an instructor reporting on a Harvard class.

[12] *If they spread their nets there people would stample them,* heard on a San Francisco radio station.

quite as carefully. A good many set phrases in fairly common use are composites of this kind. It is not easy to be sure, but the following are probably as represented:

rarely ever = rarely + hardly ever

most everywhere = most places + almost everywhere

twenty-some-odd = twenty-some + twenty odd

There's no use getting there before eight = It's no use getting there before eight + There's no use in getting there before eight

prices from $6.50 and up = prices $6.50 and up + prices from $6.50 up

equally as good = equally good + just as good

Blends like these occur constantly and for the most part die aborning, but the syntactic blends that have the greatest potential for linguistic change are the ones that alter the relations in highly productive patterns. It is commonplace to hear sentences like *He is one of those who does it best*, where the plural *those* is left high and dry as a result of blending *He is one who does it best* with *He is one of those who do it best*. In a sentence such as *It's been nine hours since I've eaten anything*, the tense relationships are disrupted by a blend between *It's been nine hours since I ate anything* and *It's been nine hours that I've not eaten anything.*[13] Such syntactic blends are the gravitational result of a vast submerged bulk of constructions that do not appear physically in utterances but reveal their existence by the changes they cause.

Malapropisms   A malapropism is a special kind of uneducated blend. It is named for a character in an eighteenth-century play, Mrs. Malaprop, who was afflicted with chronic word trouble (her language was *mal-apropos*). Instead of two (or more) expressions, either of which would be appropriate under the circumstances and both of which appear physically in the result (this is the ordinary blend), there is a confusion between two, and the inappropriate one is spoken. The result is not a new word form but a shift in meaning. The late Mayor Richard Daley of Chicago was a celebrated modern practitioner: "*harassing* the atom," "rising to higher *platitudes* of achievement" (probably blending *plateaus* and *altitudes*). A political writer says: "A man *aggregates* to himself the right," intending *arrogates*. A weatherman predicts: "Five below zero, *nominally* a safe temperature for driving," intending *normally.*

---

[13] See Long 1959, p. 124.

The mental twists that underlie a malapropism are often quite intricate. Senator Alan Bible of Nevada, announcing that a parcel of land had been put in trust for the Washoe Indians, said, "I hope this action *harks* a new era in stability and prosperity for those fine people."[14] This creates a kind of °*hark forward* on the basis of *hark back,* but the correct verb is *herald,* which probably made the leap to *hark* by way of the line from the Christmas hymn "*Hark,* the *Herald* Angels Sing," helped out by the verb *to mark* in *to mark a new era.* The pathological malapropist has been described as follows: "He is sure that *acumen* means 'omen,' that *bucolic* means 'colic,' that *cupidity* has to do with love, . . . that *hybrid* means 'aristocratic,' that *incongruous* means a time when Congress is not in session, that *frugal* means 'fruitful.' "[15] The odds against widespread acceptance of any of these pieces of false coin are high, but where the terms confused are more or less synonymous, chances of survival are better. *To comprise* means almost the same as *to be composed of,* and many say or write *to be comprised of. To careen* for *to career* meaning 'to rush headlong' is another example: a vehicle careering down a road is apt to careen—lurch from side to side; for most American speakers of English, *careen* has replaced *career.*

Deliberate malapropisms show up in literature and advertising. A tailor in New York City displays a sign reading *As you rip, so we shall sew.*

Spelling pronunciation   When someone pronounces *pulpit* to rime with *gulp it,* it is a fair inference that he did not acquire the word from hearing it (though ten years from now, as others imitate his pronunciation, this may no longer be true). Learning words from the oral tradition offers the opportunity, though not the guarantee, of saying them as they are customarily said. Guessing at them from reading, in a language that uses an alphabetic system of writing, provides as many chances of breaking with this tradition as there are unreasonable spellings. Left to guesswork, *hypocrite* will come out sounding something like *cryolite,* and *epitome* like *metronome.* This is the penalty for not spelling them *hippocrit* and *epitomy.* Of course, if the writing system is not alphabetic—if it is divorced from sound as it is in Chinese—false associations of precisely this kind do not occur. English spelling is just remote enough from pronunciation to ensure a good deal of interference.

The influence of spelling on pronunciation is twofold. First, there is the initial encounter: our introduction to a new word is probably more often through print than by ear, especially as a word we do not already know

---

[14] *The Valley Journal,* Sunnyvale, California (24 July 1970). Conceivably the senator said *marks,* and the transformation occurred in the brain or finger of a reporter or a typesetter.

[15] Downes 1957, p. 203. This reference thanks to William Perry.

is most apt to be of a literary or scientific or other specialized sort that
is written more often than spoken. We then may want to say it, and
we guess at what the letters represent. Second, there is the continual impression of visual images of words on our minds, the familiar ones as well
as the unfamiliar ones. A spelling may make us question an authentic
pronunciation if the latter is not very firmly established in the first place.

The influence of writing on the spoken language is a hazard of literate
societies. One linguist ventures the opinion that "it has probably been the
greatest single cause of phonological change in modern English, both
British and American."[16] Universal literacy is too recent a phenomenon
to reveal long-range effects, but it seems reasonable to suppose that one
such effect will be the slowing down of change. Reading is more widely
shared over a longer period of time than any form of listening: we "hear"
an author of a hundred years ago as clearly as we hear one today, if we
read him, and the cultivation of classics ensures that we will. Words,
images, and turns of phrase that might otherwise pass from the scene
acquire a firmer hold, and become the property of all who share the
culture.

Within this broader tendency toward uniformity, spelling pronunciations are both a confirmation and a contradiction. When spellings serve
as reminders of how things are pronounced today, pronunciation is less
apt to change: when we see *policeman* we are not so inclined to say
pleeceman. Here spelling is merely conservative. When spellings lead to
the revival of a pronunciation long since given up, their force is not conservative but reactionary. In Southern Britain the word *often* is coming
more and more to be pronounced with a [t] and with the *o* of *odd.* When
a spelling leads to a pronunciation that never existed, its influence is
neither conservative nor reactionary but subversive. Many words that
had long been spelled and pronounced with simple *t* were respelled with
th by writers who enjoyed showing off their etymological erudition. One
by one such words have taken on a pronunciation that they never had,
suggested by the *th: theater* (originally Middle English *teatre*), as also
Catholic, author, Theodore. The latest addition for many speakers is
thyme. Somehow *Thomas* managed to escape, but not *Anthony.*[17]

Nicknames are often an indication of older pronunciations—*Tom* for
Thomas, Kate for *Katherine, Dick* for *Richard* (which, besides the [k],
suggests an earlier apical flap for /ɾ/, the only /r/ sound apt to be imitated by a child as [d]). A large family of words spelled with *o* traditionally pronounced [ʌ] has been changing the [ʌ] year by year to [a].

---

[16] Householder 1971, p. 69. See also his Chapter 13, "The Primacy of Writing," pp.
244–64.

[17] Jespersen 1909, para. 2.622.

The older pronunciation survives in *ton, honey, money, company, stomach,* and *onion;* the new one is triumphant in *combat, common, honest,* and *astonish. Constable* can still be heard with [ʌ] among conservative speakers. A radio announcer recently said [kampəs] for *compass.*

Other influences may reinforce a spelling pronunciation. A broad *a* seems more elegant to some people, and a safer guess if the word looks at all like something imported from Continental Europe, such as *caviar.* Likewise we get *Mazda, plaza, patio, Copenhagen, Bahamas,* and many others pronounced with /a/ instead of the traditional /æ/ or /e/. An *i* also sometimes gets a Continental pronunciation: one persistent guesser on a San Francisco radio station was heard to say /fləbitəs/ for *phlebitis* /fləbáytəs/. *Capri* is pronounced as if spelled *Capree* instead of /kápri̵/; *Fatima* becomes /fətímə/ instead of /fǽtəmə/. These cases attest to our having in English "two subsystems of correspondences between phonemes and graphemes, one characteristic of the synchronically domestic, the other for synchronically foreign lexicon."[18]

Overgeneralization   It takes children a long time to learn restrictions on usage, many of which have little logic, and during their period of happy innocence they say many things that adults avoid saying. Two terms— *overgeneralization* and *analogical creation*—have been used for this special source of variant forms; the first views them as mistakes, the second as something delightfully inspired.

Overgeneralization is characteristic of the third and fourth grammars described in Chapter 8 (pages 173–74). The use of °*goed* instead of *went* is an extension, by analogy, of the past tense of regular verbs: *go* is to *goed* as *play* is to *played.* Past-tense forms such as °*drinked,* °*falled,* °*feeled,* and °*hurted,* and plurals such as °*dirts,* °*milks,* °*knifes,* and °*childs* are commonplace in children's speech.[19] Historically, overgeneralization has given us *worked* for *wrought* and *beseeched* for *besought.* Today *slayed* is threatening *slew; dived* vies with *dove.*

Applied to morphology, overgeneralization is often termed *leveling.* There is a "paradigmatic pressure" toward conjugating all the verbs the same way, having a uniform declension for nouns and adjectives, and bringing all other such tightly compacted sets—such as numerals, calendar periods, and points of the compass—into close alignment. The change is not always in the direction of the most regular overarching pattern. There may be an irregular pattern with more local influence, either because it is attached to some highly frequent form or because through meaning or some other association it is more closely related to the form

18 Vachek 1973, p. 55.
19 See Brown 1973, pp. 325–26.

that undergoes the change. The fairly new verb *to fit*[20] with its past *fitted* has such a close resemblance to *put* (past *put*), *set* (past *set*), *bite* (past *bit*), *spread* (past *spread*), and other one-syllable verbs with one-syllable past forms that for many speakers it has taken on the irregular past *fit:* "Gabrielle . . . shook her head No to everything we asked, whether the answer *fit* or didn't."[21] The same happened much earlier to the verb *to spit,* which now has *spit* (as well as *spat,* actually from another verb) as standard; we would regard *spitted* as a mistake. A final *-t* or *-d* is a temptation to drop the *-ed.* A hardware store in Los Angeles displayed a sign reading *Pipe cut and thread.*

The local influence is more in evidence where no paradigm is involved, only some powerful grammatical analogy or synonymy. The modifier *close* is not properly speaking a preposition, yet the association with *near* is such that it is sometimes used prepositionally if an adverb follows: *close home, closer there.* An adolescent speaker was heard to say *It's up to how much time I have. To be up to* and *to depend on* are close synonyms: *Whether I can accept the job is up to* (or *depends on*) *my mother.* But *to be up to* refers to a decision and is normally restricted to human objects: *It's up to you, It's up to the President,* not *It's up to the weather* or *It's up to how soon they get married.*

Hearers' errors: reinterpretation

The raw material for building a grammar and a vocabulary are what a child hears, or thinks he hears, and what an adult hears or reads, or thinks he hears or reads. If our hearing were flawless and we could read the minds of those who speak to us and around us, no language would change as a result of channel noise. But children and sometimes adults often mishear and occasionally misinterpret.

A child cannot seek out the facts from which she constructs her grammar and vocabulary. She depends on others to supply them for her. If they neglect to give her some important bit of evidence, her vision of the language at that point is bound to be different from theirs. We saw this with *for free* (page 234): when adults played with it, the child took it seriously and drew the only conclusion she could. A freshman class is assigned to write a theme in response to a story called "The Petrified Giant," about a large rock formation and how it affected the people nearby. One student complains: "This story doesn't make sense because a giant is bigger and stronger than anybody so why should he be petrified."

---

20 It probably dates from the late sixteenth century.
21 Dashiell Hammett, *The Dain Curse* (New York: Pocket Books, 1954), p. 150.

The teacher asks her what *petrified* means. She replies, "Scared—you know, petrified; like when you're petrified."[22] Her parents and at least some of her friends undoubtedly knew the literal meaning of the word, but never favored her with an example of it. Again, she draws the only inference possible.

More often the evidence is there, but is ambiguous. English has a great many compound nouns ending in an adverbial particle: *runoff, turn-around, shootout, playback, shakedown.* It also has numerous verbs made up the same way. A child comes into a store on an errand for his mother, buys something, and asks, "Will I get any change back?" apparently using the verb *to get* (something) *back.* The storekeeper says yes and completes the transaction, unaware that the child understands *changeback* as a compound noun, and that he is asking, essentially, "Will I get any change?" He is unaware, that is, until one day the child asks, "Will I get any changeback back?"[23] The reinterpretation gets by because it does not interfere with communication.

Folk etymology   Niccolo Tucci writes of his childhood:

> What the priest had told them was that my mother was an **Orthodox** Catholic. The Italian word for 'Orthodox' is **Ortodosso**, which in its feminine form, **Ortodossa**, sounds rather ominous to illiterate ears, because **un orto d'ossa** means a yard full of bones. This phonetic coincidence was enough to make the peasants connect my mother with some diabolical cult, and the feud dividing us from the people of Albiano became even deeper.[24]

A folk etymology is a kind of auditory malapropism. The hearer encounters an unfamiliar term, assumes it ought to be familiar, and proceeds to associate it with something he already knows. The confusion may lead to a mental change in the grammatical construction, as with *orto-dossa.* It may change the form of a word, as when a sixteen-year-old girl writes, "It's the *upmost*," meaning 'It's tops, it's the best,' reinterpreting the *ut-* of *utmost* as the more familiar *up.*

It is not necessary that the new interpretation make sense, only that it be somehow more plausible than what it replaces. This is especially clear in the folk etymologies invented by children. One child was convinced that *bakin' powder* was *bacon powder,*[25] another that *ice cream cone* was *ice cream comb.* But as a rule the substitute form is more intelligible as well as more plausible. A speaker was heard to say, referring

---

[22] From Morse 1974, p. 545.
[23] Example from Richard Siegel.
[24] *The New Yorker* (14 January 1950), p. 29.
[25] Example from Fred W. Householder, Jr., personal communication.

to a tree that had blown over, "We could have saved it by using *guide wires.*" The term is *guy wires,* but *guide* is more obviously meaningful than *guy.* Many who heard the term *renegade* applied to some sort of outlaw and who lacked the verb *to renege* as part of their vocabularies established instead a connection with *run* and *gate* ('road, way'), be- cause renegades were generally fugitives; *renegade* became *runagate.* The past-tense form *shined* was once looked upon as substandard, but enough people have assumed that it ought to be related to the noun *shine* (as in 'to give a *shine* to') so that now it is respectable to dis- tinguish between *The sun shone* and *He shined his shoes.* Evidence for folk etymology is sometimes roundabout. When someone calls for a *slam* or *belt* of liquor we can guess that he has thought of *slug of liquor* as if *slug* were the *slug* of boxing and not from the Irish *slog* 'swallow.'[26]

There may be a change in form so slight that it passes unnoticed. So much confusion already exists between *wh-* and *w-* (most Southern Brit- ishers, and many others, drop the /h/ in *where, which, while,* and so on) that when some speakers heard "He's a *wiz* (= wizard) at math" they thought it referred to intellectual quickness, to whizzing through a prob- lem; *wiz* became *whiz.* The extreme case is found where there is no dif- ference in form at all and we are unaware of any change until we see it written. There is no audible difference between "to give something *free rein*" and "to give it *free reign,*" but the latter, rather common, spelling reveals what has happened in the writer's mind.

Fusion and downgrading   A doctoral candidate consistently writes *thusfar* for *thus far* in her thesis. Obviously *thus* and *far* have ceased for her to be separately meaningful, and *thusfar* has joined the ranks of *whatso- ever, nevertheless, underway,* and many others.

All that it takes to create a fusion is two or more meaningful elements side by side and a disposition to take them as a unit rather than separ- ately. The disposition may be a certain degree of unfamiliarity of one of the elements; this was true of *thus far,* where *thus* is now a low-frequency word and is virtually restricted as a modifier to this one phrase (we now say *this much* and *this bold* instead of *thus much* and *thus bold*). Or it may be the clear-cut singleness of the meaning plus high frequency. A woman offers a child a *little bit* of candy. For her, a *little bit of* is ana- lytically clear. For the child it is a unit, and soon the adjective *little-bitty,* or *itty-bitty* or *itsy-bitsy,* is established as a synonym of *tiny.* When we say *Yes, truly* we make a clear comma break between the words; but when we say *Yes, indeed* we run them together in spite of the comma, and playful variants such as *yes indeedy* show what has happened.

---

[26] Hutson 1947, p. 20.

Fusion is a much more pervasive phenomenon than these examples suggest. It underlies the whole process of compounding. One can detect its work in the relative speed with which certain compounds are pronounced. We say *borderline* faster than we say *border zone.* We can detect it in vowel reduction: *fireman* is more fused for most speakers than *trashman;* the first has /mən/, the second /mæn/. And it shows up in the regularizing of inflections, as in *broadcasted* as the past tense of *broadcast*—if we did not feel that *to broadcast* is a fused verb we would not treat it differently from *to cast.* No matter how a compound is written, if it is truly a compound it will be fused to the point where there is some reluctance, however slight, to break it up. Many expressions that we still write as separate words are really compounds, fused in pronunciation and meaning. *Ill at ease* embodies a use of *ill* rarely encountered anywhere else. *Nice and hot, good and tired* show by their occasional spelling how *nice'n* and *good'n* have been converted to adverbs.

Fusion is even more. It is the unifying principle of collocations (see pages 53–57). Whenever a combination of words comes to be used again and again in reference to a particular thing or situation, it develops a kind of connective tissue. Sometimes we can tell a collocational fusion by the fact that it shelters words or constructions that are no longer current. *He gave of himself* contains an old partitive, also preserved in *partake of* but obsolete in *They ate of the meat. He is to blame* contains an old passive that is still found occasionally elsewhere (*These jobs are still to do* for *still to be done*). Other collocations can be seen by some unusual feature of their construction. The verb *is* has become fused to preceding expressions using *what* in such a way that *is* may be said twice. The basis is probably sentences like *What I want to know is, is he really like that?* where each *is* has its own function; but now one often hears *What he says is, is that nobody is like that.*

Fusion results in what is sometimes termed *opaqueness.* The opposite, *transparency,* is supposed to be the quality of expressions that speakers can easily "see through." For a speaker of English, *getatable* is transparent, *accessible* opaque, though a Roman would have penetrated *accessible* with no trouble. German is said to be more transparent than English because it builds more of its words out of native material: *vorzeigen* reveals the verb *zeigen* 'to show' whereas English *exhibit* reveals nothing. In a psychological sense it is doubtful that speakers often penetrate these associations. We are more apt to pass them over unconsciously —*to be tied up* and unable to keep an appointment, *to have one's hands full* with a job to do, *to keep one's shirt on* when there is cause for impatience—these are clear enough if we stop to think about them, but we seldom do and are often surprised when their literal meaning suddenly strikes us. It is enough for an expression to be semantically and functionally fused for it to be psychologically opaque.

It is fortunate that we can forget, that it is no longer necessary to think of *chilblains* as 'blains caused by chills,' of *How do you do?* as an inquiry about how one does, of *never mind* as an injunction not to notice something. New associations create new meanings, and language continues to build level on level.

Metanalysis   Though fusion is the normal direction of change as words are hammered together, sometimes the opposite takes place. A division is made where there was none before. The following exchange was heard between an uncle and his nine-year-old nephew:

> UNCLE: No, she's never ridden one.
> NEPHEW: I've never rid on one either.

In this example the false division has created an extra word. More frequently there is just a slippage in where an already existing separation ought to go. Otto Jespersen, who coined the term *metanalysis*, gives many examples of both kinds from the history of English, including the following:[27]

> *a nadder* → *an adder*
> *a napron* → *an apron*
> *richesse* → *rich-es*
> *pease* (mass) → *pea-s* (count, plural)
> *cherris* → *cherr-ies*
> *bod-ice* (old plural of *body*) → *bodices* (new word, new plural)

As the examples suggest, the division between the *an* form of the indefinite article and the noun that follows, and the one between a plural or fancied plural ending and the noun stem that precedes, are where such false divisions are most apt to be made. *Richesse, pease,* and *cherris* were originally mass nouns (like *wealth, corn,* and *fruit*) that just happened to have what sounded like a plural ending.

The *nadder–adder* type of change could occur with scarcely a ripple elsewhere, but the reformulated plurals—*cherries, peas,* and so on— required a new conception of the things named. One would no more pluralize *pease* than one would say *°corns* or *°wheats* (unless to refer to several species of corn or wheat). But *pease* was being pulled in another direction. A pea is about the size of a bean and as easy to think of individually as a bean is; and *bean* is a count noun: *bean, beans.* So children drew the obvious analogy: *pease* is to X as *beans* is to *bean.*

---

[27] Jespersen 1914, paras. 5.6–5.7.

A special kind of metanalysis which has its own special name is *back formation.* The "singularizing" of *pease* is a back formation created by analogizing *pease* with *beans* and clipping off the end of *pease* to make the singular *pea.* Back formation is metanalysis combined with over-generalization. The hearer makes a false division and associates part of it with a morphological element—usually a genuine suffix but sometimes a spurious one—which seems to be more or less independent. The reasoning goes like this: if a *seller* is a person who *sells,* then an *usher* should be a person who **ushes* and a *proctor* should be a person who **procts.* So, on the basis of the adjective *sedative* we have formed the verb *to sedate,* analogizing with *relative–relate, denotative–denotate,* and other such pairs. (The reverse process then gave *calmative* based on *to calm.*) The verb *to televise* is based on *television,* with a strong push from the suffix *-ise, -ize.* Often a sort of fusion has to precede the back formation. Sometimes the result of a back formation shows up not in the independent creation of the shorter form but in something else based on it. When people began using the term *motorcade* it was apparent that they had back-formed *caval-* from *cavalcade* in the process of splitting *-cade* off from it. This was easy to do, since we already had *cavalry.* Similarly the existence of a word *ham* referring to meat made it easier to split *-burger* off from *hamburger* and create the suffix-like element found in *nutburger, meatburger, Gainesburger, cheeseburger,* and many other recent coinages.

Reinduction   The subclassifications used in this section have somewhat artificially distinguished between errors typical of speakers and errors typical of listeners. There is no clear division between the individual's two roles when he blunders. Speakers monitor by ear everything they say, so a mistake in speaking is also a mistake in hearing. And no mistake in hearing is observable until someone gives evidence of it by speaking.

Reinduction is where we see the two roles most evenly balanced. The individual takes in the evidence by ear, digests it, forms a rule by abduction (a plausible guess on the basis of evidence), applies it by deduction, produces an utterance, sees what the reaction of hearers is, and by alternately testing and correcting, *induces* a final form of his rule that works. This is no different from what happens when he produces a *correct* rule. Reinduction figures in this section only because a resulting rule may deviate in some respect from the norm and produce a variant.

Suppose we hear someone say *Them ain't no good.* This outrages our grammatical sensibilities and we assume that it is simply wrong, a manifestation of unsystem and ignorance. Our prejudice is confirmed if we then hear him say *They ain't here.* "This person simply mixes things up; he has no idea of a distinction between *they* and *them,*" we think. But if we listen a little more closely we may realize that he is using ***them*** to refer to things and ***they*** to refer to people.[28] Given the model sentences heard as a child, this may be a perfectly reasonable induction. The correct rule (by our present standards) of course is that ***they*** is a subject pronoun and ***them*** is an object pronoun, without regard to things and people. But at one point in the singular the situation is exactly reversed: ***it*** refers to things, and now it is the question of subjects versus objects that makes no difference: ***It is useful, I need it. He*** and ***she*** as subjects are matched by ***him*** and ***her*** as objects. So we get the following realignment:

	Subject	*Object*
Human	he, she	him, her
	they	them
Non-human	it	it
	they → them	them

The non-human pronouns are regularized to have ***them*** uniformly for things plural, agreeing with ***it*** for things singular. The special treatment for humans creates no problem, for they get special treatment in many other ways. And if it seems puzzling that the same pronoun ***them*** should be used for human objects, that can be sensed as reflecting the fact that when human beings are objects of verbs, most of the time they are not in a typically human role—they are being pushed around, treated like things, especially in the plural, where individuality tends to disappear. Of course not all sentences that the learner hears will conform to his induction. ***They're no good*** can be said for things. So he may feel that he needs a special rule, perhaps "Use ***they*** when things somehow count as just as important as humans." He does not have to sacrifice his fundamental rule, only watch out for special occasions. He may even catch on to what the "correct" fundamental rule is and use it when dealing with certain people —to that extent he is bidialectal; but he will not use it when he is relaxed, at home, being taken as a model by his children.

The transition from model grammar to reinduced grammar can be seen in Figure 10–1. Grammar 1 is inaccessible—it is in the mind of whoever is speaking. Only what the learner hears—Output 1—is available for processing through his innate capacities (Laws of Language). From this, by abduction and deduction, he formulates his own grammar and produces his own output, which is available as a model for the next generation of learners.

---

[28] Example thanks to J. P. Maher, personal communication.

FIGURE 10–1
Abduction and Deduction in the Acquisition of Language

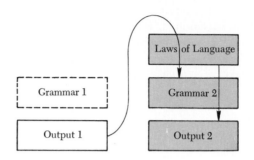

SOURCE: Adapted from Andersen 1973, p. 778.

The combination of fundamental rules and special rules (exceptions) explains how changes in grammar can be both sudden and gradual at the same time. The new grammar that children form is discontinuous with the grammar of their parents; this is a sudden change. But the discrepancies are masked—and hence escape detection and correction—by the concessions made with the special rules. And these, like all burdensome exceptions, tend to be eliminated with time. Basically all linguistic change is of this kind, and it bears a more than accidental resemblance to other changes in our social habits. The new generation forms its own convictions about politeness and rudeness and virtue and vice, but conforms outwardly—perhaps even unconsciously—by going through the old motions when survival or comfort demand it. Only later, when the lid is off, are we aware of what has happened.[29]

Inductions and special rules are able to coexist because together they make up the filing system that brings order to the endless supply of model sentences that come our way. The extreme of the special rule is the collocation (Chapter 4), which is a rule unto itself. The two extremes, rule and collocation, are in a tug of war. The collocation represents what we are used to. The rule represents our freedom to invent. Each is carried in our minds as a criterion of correctness. We may reject an expression because it is ill-formed according to our rules—an impulse to say *°better enough* on the analogy of *good enough* is throttled because our rule does

---

[29] The discussion is based on Andersen 1973.

not permit **enough** to follow a comparative. Or we may accept or reject on the basis of sheer familiarity. The peculiar grammar of many idioms does not bother us because we are accustomed to them: **to know better, to come a cropper, to make no bones about something.** On the other hand, we may reject a perfectly well-formed expression if it is very low in frequency; we readily say **all day, all week, all year,** but **all hour** seems wrong and is apt to be replaced by **the whole hour.** We certainly reject *°all minute.*[30]

Word meanings are reinduced too. The example **for free** was mentioned earlier—not being able to read their parents' minds (where **for free** is labeled "joke"), children took it as a sober, ordinary equivalent for plain **free.** One area in which meaning is constantly changing by reinduction is that of explicitness, especially explicitness leaning toward exaggeration. In place of **disliking** spinach we **hate** it. The child sees no real evidence of strong emotion and concludes that **hate** represents something less than abomination. The common practice of adding unnecessarily specific or emphatic modifiers puts a parasitic growth on otherwise healthy nouns and verbs. A flight attendant advises passengers to check for their **personal belongings;** belongings are normally personal, and become something less by this process, just as **unique** has been robbed of its uniqueness by speakers who habitually say **very unique.** This is why the professional exaggerator is unable to wield an influence much beyond his own generation. The child, inducing the meaning from what she sees, quite innocently and correctly reads the word in the light of the evidence, not the evidence in the light—or the dark—of the word.

The changing world

Language is not the only thing that moves. Sometimes it stands still, relatively speaking, and the world moves. This is the source of most collocations. The clearest examples are the compounds that start out as syntactic constructions. There is a grammatical rule in English that allows us to build sub-sentences by attaching an **-ing** verb to a noun. We can say "I couldn't sleep because of the incessant **horn-blowing** going on next

---

[30] The prerequisites seem to be two. First the unit has to be great enough for its duration to seem long. *°All minute* is excluded because hardly anything we might do in just a minute's time would seem to be worth a remark about how long it took. On the other hand, *°all century* has plenty of duration, which brings up the second prerequisite. Units of time function in two separate ways: one is to express measurement, the other to express an established period for an activity. We schedule particular days, weeks, and years for things we do (this is the context where **all** is used with a unit of time and no article), but not particular centuries and certainly not particular minutes.

door," or "What was all that *dirt-throwing* about?" In the middle years
of the American Civil War, General John H. Morgan was operating in
Kentucky before he made his famous raid into Indiana and Ohio. The
success of the raid depended in part on intercepting enemy telegrams.
One of Morgan's officers gave the following account: "Without delay we
passed through Springfield and Bardstown, crossing the Louisville and
Nashville at Lebanon Junction, thirty miles from Louisville on the 6th.
. . . Tapping the wires at Lebanon Junction, we learned from intercepted
despatches that the garrison at Louisville was much alarmed, and in expectation of immediate attack."[31] *Tapping the wires* is a grammatical
construction. So, *at that time,* would *wiretapping* have been. Over the
years, as the custom of tapping wires became established, *wiretapping*
was infused with a specific content and became "a word." *Horn-blowing*
is not a word in this sense; *firefighting* is.

We see the most typical effect of a changing world in the constellation
of meanings around a word, where lights flicker out and others brighten
as energy is cut off from one or more senses and flows elsewhere. Most
people would be puzzled today at the expression *rickety children,* failing
to make the obvious connection with rickets. As the disease became less
and less prevalent, the transferred sense of 'shaky, tottering, feeble' was
left without its home base and became the central meaning of the word,
as in *a rickety chair.* The variant *rachitic* has taken over the original
meaning.

Among the names of tools and appliances, a change in material culture
often widens a split that is always latently present in such words. An
icebox is a box for ice—that is its material side. It is also a place to
keep things cold—that is its function. With the advent of mechanical
refrigeration ice became superfluous, yet many people kept the name,
preserving the function but ignoring the material. Nowadays we drink
through *straws* often made of glass, from *glasses* sometimes made of
plastic, and wipe our mouths afterward on *napkins* made of paper (*nappe*
'linen cloth').

Sometimes a material change is matched by a material change in language. As more and more women have taken up activities formerly reserved for men, languages that make gender distinctions in their nouns
have had to accommodate their occupational titles. As long as it was
unthinkable for anybody but a man to be a doctor, the word for 'doctor'
could remain comfortably masculine. But the new state of affairs forced
a decision: either feminines had to be coined to match every masculine,
or the gender of the noun had to become a formality. The languages

---

[31] From Tamony 1973, pp. 1–2.

facing this problem—Polish, for example—are still trying to decide in each case which of two variant forms to adopt.[32]

Changes in the material world can be sudden. The semantic reactions can be equally sudden. So change in meaning is more unpredictable than any other kind of change.

Bilingualism

The most revolutionary cause of change is the forced encounter between one culture and another. It need not be violent. It may well be cooperative, as when seamen from various lands man a single ship, or mixed armies fight a common foe. Whatever brings two speakers of different languages into contact and makes them communicate with each other counts as a force for change. In Chapter 9 we saw this manifested in pidgins and creoles. But the proliferation of variants as a result of bilingualism need not be on quite so grand a scale in order to effect quite considerable changes in either or both of two languages in contact. There may be an inpouring of commercial goods with their inventories, assembling instructions, and service manuals packed with terms that have no equivalents in the native language but must be adopted if the goods are to be put to use. The "foreign" language may be old rather than new: religious tradition often preserves a contact that otherwise would have faded, as when Latin was maintained in the Western church and Church Slavonic in large parts of the Eastern, as ritual languages. Fashion may be responsible, as when Paris established itself as arbiter in the nineteenth century and poured its genteelisms into all the languages of Europe. Whenever for any reason a person learns or half-learns a second language, he will mix some of it with the language he already knows, and others who are not bilingual, or are less so, will follow him if doing so seems to lead them where they want to go.

Borrowings are concentrated in the areas where contact is most intense. So it is not surprising that science and technology lead the field nowadays, with sports and tourism close behind. In Hungarian, for example, English sporting terms were taken in wholesale for half a century—four or five hundred of them, even including some numerals, especially in tennis.[33] But contacts have grown so close in recent times, with press, radio, television, and international travel, that a kind of universal diffusion is taking place.[34]

---

[32] See Nalobow 1971.
[33] Csapó 1971.
[34] See Peruzzi 1958.

Typically the flow is greater in one direction than in the other. The speaker of a language regarded for any reason as socially or culturally superior does not feel under any compulsion to learn a language regarded as inferior, though he may condescend to pick up an occasional word that saves him the trouble of inventing one himself. That is often the fate of contact languages that have been brought low by conquest. English shows little trace of the dozens of Indian languages that were once—and in many cases still are—spoken between the Atlantic and Pacific, except for the numerous geographical names such as *Mississippi, Oklahoma, Topeka,* and *Shawnee,* and a few names for material objects like *tobacco, chocolate, hammock, potato, skunk, raccoon*—and even these were often taken by way of French or Spanish, which had borrowed them first. On the other hand, borrowings *from* English in the lands under British and American rule have been vast, if not devastating. Words have been taken in by the hundreds, and here and there the deeper levels have also been affected. In Chamorro, the language spoken on Guam, the phoneme /r/ has been introduced from English, as have certain consonant clusters that were not previously permitted and shifts of accent to vowels that could not formerly carry it.[35] Naturally, other politically or economically dominant languages have made equally deep inroads into the native languages of the areas they overran. Tagalog, one of the languages of the Philippines, adopted so many Spanish loanwords that it had to augment its vowel system from three to five.[36]

Enforced bilingualism can be disruptive. In the Swiss village of Bonaduz, where speakers went from Romansh to German in a relatively short period of time (in 1900, 63 percent classified themselves as Romansh-speaking, 37 percent as German-speaking; ten years later the proportions were reversed: 31 percent and 69 percent), the German that was learned was picked up from several different dialects and resulted in such a conglomeration that speakers differed widely in the rules of their grammar.[37] But more commonly the defenses are stronger, a single language is held on to, and what is accepted from outside is rather carefully filtered. Borrowing is made as painless as possible. Words are affected first, grammar last. The borrowing language often develops a kind of grammatical receptacle whereby foreign words can come in and cause the least trouble. An example is the two frames in which Chicano Spanish admits English verbs. One is *Hizo* _____ *mucho,* as in *Hizo improve mucho* (literally, 'She did [made] improve a lot'). The other is *Está* _____ *-ing mucho,* as in *Está improving mucho* ('She is improving a lot').[38] The on-

[35] Topping 1962.
[36] See Bowen 1971, especially pp. 946–47.
[37] Moulton 1971, pp. 942–43.
[38] From Reyes 1975. See also Pfaff 1979.

going system of the borrowing language is always reckoned with. It can reject a sound or a word form as quite indigestible. Or it can assimilate it quickly and easily. An example of the latter is the word *mandarin,* ultimately from Sanskrit *mantrin* 'counselor' (and akin to English *mind*—a counselor is a person who makes one think). It was taken into Portuguese as *mandarim,* and from there spread to other Western languages. In English it connotes a bureaucrat, usually a reactionary one, and it has overtones of supposedly oriental pretentiousness. But in Portuguese it immediately attached itself to the verb *mandar* 'to command' and came to signify a 'bossy person.'

The simplest lexical borrowings are those where a language adopts both form and meaning, as English *chic, blitzkrieg, tea.* Continued use may further adapt the phonology, as English *depot* from the French. Subtler borrowings sometimes blend native and borrowed morphemes, or translate the foreign word into native morphemes.[39] In this way *gospel* was an early English loan translation of Latin *evangelium* ('good news' = in Old English *gōd spel*).

Less spectacular (and less noticed) than bilingual borrowing is bidialectal borrowing. A loanshift of sorts occurs whenever we "learn a new meaning for a word"—the meaning had to be part of someone else's speech for us to acquire it, and our acquiring it is to a certain extent learning just so much of another dialect. In fact, the whole process of language learning is one of bringing our personal ways of talking and comprehending in line first with those of other individuals at close range and then with expanding circles of speech communities outward to the limits of our reach in society.

But dialect borrowing is generally thought of as the picking up of items that have been identified as typical of some speech community other than the one to which the speaker most intimately belongs. In North Carolina, a region where some Northern pronunciations have found their way in, along with Northern perceptions of some Southern pronunciations, the local variety remains with one meaning and the new comes in with another. (The spellings of the last two examples represent what a Northerner thinks he hears.)

> One who is *ruined* is verily so; one who is *ruint* is trivially so.
> One who is *poor* is moderately so; one who is *real pore* is poverty-stricken (often used ironically).
> One who is *fired* can be rehired; one who is *farred* is out.[40]

---

[39] For the classification and further examples see Haugen 1972, pp. 79–109.

[40] Examples thanks to Walter Beale and David Moore, personal communication. What is called "eye dialect" may be involved in *pore* and *farred.* The Northern comic strip artist thinks he hears *pore,* and puts it in the mouth of his illiterate characters; the Southerner reads the comics, and exaggerates *pore* for effect.

The schools are often responsible for splits of this kind. They try to suppress an undesirable variant, but the miscreant almost always escapes by putting on a disguise. Not that contrariness is necessarily involved—any variant from another dialect may gain acceptance just as easily:

> "He's an igernut, durn fool," said the mountaineer when my sister mentioned a local character.
>
> "He certainly sounds ignorant," she agreed, thinking to correct his pronunciation diplomatically.
>
> "Oh, he ain't ignorant," the man retorted. "Lotsa folks is ignorant and can't help it. But he's just plain igernut. He don't want to learn nothin'. Them's two different words, you know."[41]

Devotees of westerns never confuse a *pardner* with a *partner,* a *critter* with a *creature,* or a *greazer* with a *greaser.*

Invention

There is some originality in every act of speech. Language in action is the fitting of linguistic material to aspects of reality, and the fit is one that has to be improvised in however slight a degree. In referring to something as a *dog* we assume that the token animal we see is covered by the previously learned term. Most of the time the utterance comes automatically; it is not a *logical* assumption because we do not think about it. But now and then we are confronted with something for which our automatic responses do not suffice, and then we have to cast about for a form and a meaning that will come sufficiently close, given a bit of paraphrasing and a dash of imagination on the part of our hearer.

A three-year-old girl does not know the word *to dream.* In reporting a dream she tells of what she *saw in her pillow.* A four-year-old, unable to manage a phrase such as *to look seriously at someone,* says she will *make her face mad at someone.* This is familiar material used to cope with a new situation. Its motivation is the same as when Sir Humphrey Davy in 1807 needed a name for a new element he had discovered, and called it *potassium,* inventing a Latinized form of *potash,* originally *potashes,* from which the hydroxide was extracted. Some form of analogy is always involved. The speaker looks for a relatedness in language that

---

[41] *Reader's Digest* (April 1947), p. 90.

corresponds to the relatedness in the real world. Ordinarily the machinery of language gives it to us quickly, but sometimes the problem has to be addressed deliberately. And in between are the times when we are just a little bit unsure—perhaps there is exactly the right expression for our needs out there somewhere, but we forget it. Such was probably the case with the speaker on a talk show who referred to the *wiseness* of doing something (instead of the *wisdom* of doing it) by analogy to *foolishness.* When an airline promises to "make your flight as smooth and quiet and *on time* as possible," we recognize an improvised adjective replacing *punctual,* which in this context would have too personal a ring. The hearer has no trouble interpreting these flashes of linguistic insight because he makes the same analogies. When he hears a medical association warning about "the amount of unburned particles *exhausted* in the air" he knows precisely what the intention of the verb is because he relates it to the noun *exhaust* (of a car) and is familiar with the thousands of cases in English where noun and verb are the same in form.

When the analogy in the real world is striking enough to be noticed, we call the result a *metaphor.* A couple of hundred years ago some sailor likened long-winded storytellers to spinners of yarn. This is how a figurative *He likes to spin yarns* was reinterpreted as meaning literally *He likes to tell yarns,* and *yarn* became a synonym of *story.* Countless present meanings are embalmed metaphors: *to lie low, to walk out on something, to raise the roof, to go ahead full steam.* Most of our abstractions are borrowed metaphors from Greek or Latin: *to insult* means 'to jump on,' *eccentric* is 'off center,' a *hyperbole* is 'a throwing beyond.' The "vague reference" principle (pages 110–11) is a way of saying that every time we speak we metaphorize. "Metaphor," says one linguist-stylistician, "is not a figure of speech among the others, but a basic grammatical category."[42]

HOW THE VARIANTS ARE REACTED TO

Summing up all the hazards and speculations that we have touched on so far, we can appreciate the retort of a certain public figure on being advised to "watch out" when he expressed himself in language. "When I speak," he said, "let the language watch out."

The profusion of variants would have no effect if other persons besides their originators did not take them up. What fate lies between the source

---

[42] Valesio 1974, p. 17.

and the mainstream? The answers take us into the field of *historical linguistics*.[43]

Resistance

Most resistance to change is passive. The variant serves an immediate purpose, but there is no continuity between the first occasion and a next occasion when it might be useful, and it is lost. Or it is recognized as a lapse, mentally (or actually) corrected, and ignored thereafter.

Some resistance is deliberate. Conservative speakers in every culture feel called upon to defend the bastions of purity and propriety—just as well perhaps, because too much change within a lifetime could interfere with communication. As long as old and young have to live together the checks are as important as the changes.

Resistance can also be active but unthinking. Something about a variant disqualifies it for adoption. Speakers may feel that a form that is otherwise all right (it fits, say, the phonological drift of the language) is unacceptable because it leaves too little meat in a word. In Castilian the Latin word *foedu* 'ugly' gave *feo* by one of the series of changes that nearly all words underwent, and would have given *°eo* by a succeeding step; but "speakers shied away from the total stripping of an already meager sound structure."[44] Resistance to overly stripped-down forms may even lead to compensation in the other direction: *expanding* a form. We see this in the **Abel, Baker, Charlie** substitutes for **A, B, C**. Or speakers may have a dim awareness of some meaningful morphological element and avoid disfiguring it, in spite of the tendency of other words of similar shape to lose certain of their component sounds. In Portuguese, if Latin **regula** 'straightedge' had followed the line of least phonological resistance it would have ended up as *°relha* (as **tegula** gave **telha** 'tile'), but instead it clung to a portion of its suffix and gave **régua**.[45]

---

[43] For brief histories of the English language the reader is referred to the following, in recent editions of three popular dictionaries: W. Nelson Francis, "The English Language and Its History," in *Webster's New Collegiate Dictionary* (Springfield, Mass.: G. and C. Merriam, 1973), pp. 20a–29a; Kemp Malone, "Historical Sketch of the English Language," in *Random House Dictionary of the English Language* (New York: Random House, 1971), pp. xv–xxi; Morton W. Bloomfield, "A Brief History of the English Language," pp. xiv–xviii, and Calvert Watkins, "The Indo-European Origin of English," pp. xix–xx, both in *The American Heritage Dictionary of the English Language* (New York: American Heritage, and Boston: Houghton Mifflin, 1969). A good brief treatment is also to be found in Chapter 8 of Margaret Schlauch's *The Gift of Language* (New York: Dover, 1955).

[44] Levy 1973, p. 206.

[45] Malkiel 1972, pp. 325–26.

Sometimes what is preserved may be an iconic value of the word. The sound symbolism that we saw earlier in connection with the high front vowels—*chip* versus *chop* and *freep* versus *frope* (page 10)—probably accounts for the form *peak* alongside of *pike* in reference to something pointed: a point is manifestly small. And there are a number of other such pairs, including *peep* for the *peeping* (also *piping*) of a bird and *teeny* alongside of *tiny.*

Changing attitudes may diminish the value of a form, and then the older variant suffers. The verb *to discriminate* basically refers to making careful distinctions, but it came to be used more and more in connection with distinctions of the wrong kind, and now it would be a little chancy to call someone of refined tastes a *discriminating person.* Much the same has happened to the verb *segregate.* A degraded term may pass out of use entirely (see page 149) or only be restricted more narrowly in its use.

A more general and inclusive reason for resistance is conflict of homonyms. This is merely an acute form of the loss of contrast, a violation of the first law of language, which is that distinct functions are carried by distinct forms. If forces tend to deflect two or more forms toward each other so that they look or sound too much alike, speakers will try to reestablish the contrast. If the distinction makes little or no difference, they will give it up: this is happening with the phonemic contrast between /a/ and /ɔ/ (page 24); it happened earlier in English with the two forms of the plural object pronoun, *hem* (surviving as *'em*) and *them* (of Scandinavian origin): they did not merge formally, but we now regard *'em* as a shortened form of *them.* If the contrast is important it will be strengthened. This is accomplished in various ways. A speaker may simply use a trick such as extra emphasis. A punster was heard to say, "He'll [*he* = 'the other fellow'] get the business, and *you'll* get the *business*"—one will be helped and the other ruined.

With words, there is a kind of trade-off between form and meaning. The less resemblance there is in meaning between two forms, the more phonological resemblance there can be without creating a conflict. The words *to, too,* and *two* are phonologically identical, yet there is little conflict because they have completely different functions. (There is *some* conflict, however: we can say *her very happy children* but not °*her too happy children*—it sounds too much like *her two happy children*). On the other hand, too much resemblance brings anguish to the sensitive stylist: *The painter succeeded in painting the pain on her face all too plainly.* We obviously can't solve this kind of problem by abolishing one or more of the words from the language, but we can banish them from the immediate context by using a synonym or a paraphrase.

Sometimes a conflict is so serious that it results in the total loss of a form. The most famous example is the French word for *cock.* In southern France, the normal development of the expected Latin word, *gallus,* would have been *gat.* But in the same area the word *cattus* produced *gat.* Had *gallus* been retained, the result would have been two meanings of *gat* ('cat' and 'cock'), both apt to occur in similar contexts where they would have caused confusion. One had to go, so speakers substituted other words for *gallus:* one meaning 'chicken,' one meaning 'pheasant,' and a third meaning, literally 'priest.' In English the phrase *to wax and to wane* is common and causes no trouble, since *wax* coupled with *wane* is clear. But while we readily say *It waned* or *It is on the wane,* we avoid *It waxed* and cannot say *It is on the wax* at all. Conflict of homonyms forces us to say *It is on the increase.*

Fundamentally, there is no difference between collisions like these and one between antagonistic senses of a single word. A century ago a *saloon* was any large room, especially one for receptions. But the proprietors of grog shops in the United States began to call their establishments saloons to raise them in the public esteem. The effect on the word, of course, was the opposite—it was lowered. As a result, one sense of the word was relegated to history (including television westerns) and the other was replaced by the French cognate *salon.*

There are other circumstances than being a stylist that create an aversion to forms that are too much alike even though not necessarily identical—the need for clear directions on board ship, for example. The Old English word for the left-hand side of a ship looking forward was *backboard,* but there was also another: *ladeborde,* possibly meaning 'lading or loading side.' In time the latter was reinterpreted to eliminate any reference to loading, and the two words became rivals. *Ladeborde,* transformed into *larboard,* became a perfect mate for *starboard.* But the neat semantic analogy soon turned into a nuisance. *Starboard* and *larboard* were too easily confused and eventually a newly reinterpreted word, *port,* entered the competition and eliminated *larboard.*

A negative force even stronger than homonymic conflict is *taboo.* This we met before in connection with degradation (page 149), with the threat of *you* (page 213), and with family rules and their special vocabularies (page 222). If society regards something as unmentionable, and yet is forced to mention it, the name becomes the scapegoat for the thing. It has its "real" name, and that of course we secretly know, but never say. A substitute, termed a euphemism (see pages 149–50), is adopted to indicate the forbidden object without naming it. Of course, if the name is never, never said, the next generation has no opportunity to learn it. Then, since the object itself (which can be as sacred as Jahweh or as profane as human excrement) is still taboo, the substitute word is learned as the name, and in turn becomes taboo. The result is a continual succession of words marching to oblivion (or converted to other uses). The threat of *you,* for example, can extend to a personal name. In aboriginal Australian cultures, when a person died, his name was buried with him and could not be exhumed for a certain length of time; not only his name but other words closely similar to it were temporarily abolished. The solution adopted by some tribes was to borrow substitute words from the language of a neighboring tribe.[46]

Acceptance

Like most resistance, most acceptance of change is also passive. Unconsciously we assume that *everything means something* and *everything different means something different.* If our interlocutor uses an expression that sounds strange to us, our first impulse is not to accuse him mentally of talking nonsense but to assume that he has merely missed his aim. We may even fail to hear the error.

But if the variant is conspicuous enough so that we cannot avoid noticing it, the tendency then is to assign it a value. The cheapest such added value is "his way of talking rather than mine." Hiking the price a little gives "their way of talking" or "the way of talking on *X* occasion," leading to the many restrictions of code and register. At the same time we are likely not to be satisfied with such a low level of contrast; we either abolish it or make something of it. The passenger on an airplane finds it superfluous to talk about *port* and *starboard* instead of *left* and *right,* and the old navigational terminology falls into disuse. We may for a time be willing to accept two pronounciations of *vase* (/ves/ or /vez/ in everyday parlance and /vaz/ in polite society), but we are not content to let it go at that indefinitely: an imaginative speaker is heard to say, "These small ones are my /vezəz/ but these big ones are my /vazəz/."[47] The word *rear* may be more elegant than the word *back,* but *rear door* and *back door* have shifted from a mere register distinction to a technical one: the rear door of a building or institution or vehicle but the back door of a house. Luxury distinctions tend to become practical distinctions.

The same is true of dialect differences, as we saw earlier with *ignorant–igernut, poor–pore,* and *partner–pardner.* It is equally true of the differences that grow out of the variant grammars that result from reinduction. Suppose there comes a time when you are using *burnt* as the past of *burn* and I am using *burned.* Our conversation turns on the subject of something charred and you use your variant *burnt.* I suspect that you are in possession of a formula that I lack, whereby a thing gets burned and ends up burnt. Anything can tip the scales in the direction of a split like this— perhaps just the fact that *burned* takes longer to say and hence sounds like something going on, while *burnt* is short, like something finished.

---

[46] Lamb 1974, p. 22.
[47] Labov 1970, pp. 77, footnote.

This differentiation occurs with other paired expressions that supposedly have the same grammatical status. There is only one singular form *antenna,* and consequently it has to carry all the meanings of that word; but there are two plurals, *antennas* and *antennae,* and their meanings have tended to split. The word *staff* and its plural variants is a mosaic of bifurcations:

$$\left.\begin{array}{l}\textit{staff–staves} \\ \textit{staff–staffs}\end{array}\right\} \text{ 'cudgel'}$$

staff–staffs   'official personnel'

stave–staves   'barrel slats'

$$\left.\begin{array}{l}\textit{staff–staves} \\ \textit{stave–staves}\end{array}\right\} \text{ 'lines for writing music'}$$

At any moment there are probably dozens of latent distinctions in the back of our minds, ready to crystallize by reinduction into unmistakable bifurcations once enough speakers develop similar leanings.

CUMULATIVE CHANGE

There is no question that language changes. But does it *evolve?* Evolution implies more than innumerable heterogeneous collisions, most of them canceling one another out. It implies a drift, a direction, almost a purpose. If we look only at meaning, the metaphorical leaps seem to take us in all directions. The ancestral form that gave the Greek word for 'fire,' *pyr* (which we have in *pyromaniac* and *funeral pyre*), also gave a Latin word *burrus,* 'fiery red.' This led to Romance forms meaning 'dark red' (Provencal *burel* was 'brownish red') and, in turn, Old French *buire,* with a variant *bure,* meaning 'dark brown.' The color was extended to a material of that color, baize, which was the sense that the word came to have in the Modern French form, *bureau.* This baize was used for covering writing desks, which in turn appropriated the name, extending it to articles of furniture. The writing desks were used in government offices, and our modern bureaucracies are a fitting climax to this bit of semasiological vagrancy. (*Semasiology* is the semantic history of word forms.)

But while such deflections of meaning would have been as hard to predict as the direction of a ricocheting bullet, the bullet itself—the bit of phonological stuff containing an initial bilabial stop and an /r/—remains more or less intact, flattened a bit but identifiable. Forms, unlike meanings, are stable enough to be projected backward into prehistory. Figure 10–2 shows the probable ancestry of the English words *hammer* and

FIGURE 10–2
Probable Evolution of the Words Related to <u>Hammer</u> and <u>Heaven</u>

SOURCE: Adapted from Maher 1973, p. 451.

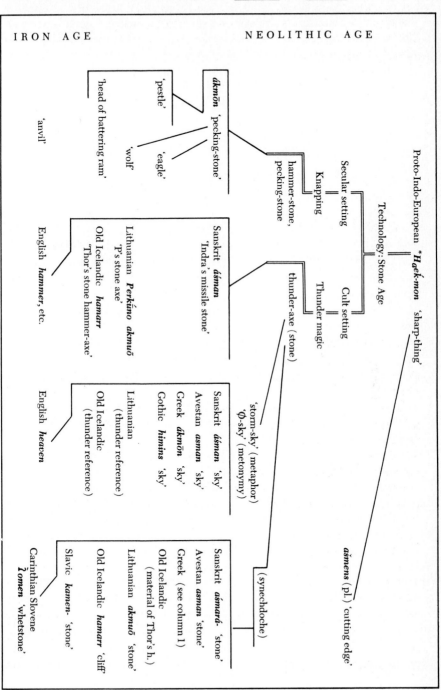

heaven, traced back to a Stone Age form meaning 'something sharp,' and transformed semantically by a series of bold images that include interpreting the sharp thing as an ax, the ax as the source of the crash of thunder, the thunder as the sky, the sky as the abode of gods, and so on. The semantic shifts have to be treated with respect, for otherwise there would be no assurance that the similarity in form was not due to accident, but the form gives the historical linguist something to build on.

Progress

All languages get better to the extent that they get worse. That is, when something happens to upset the equilibrium at some point in the vast system of contrasts that constitutes a language, something else happens to restore it. But that, if it can be called progress at all, is progress chasing its tail.

One of the great linguists of a generation ago, Otto Jespersen, felt that one sign of progress—particularly marked in languages like English and Chinese—is the discarding of "reminders." When we say **Mary is the sweetest, dearest, loveliest girl I know,** we express the one superlative idea three times in the suffix *-est,* as can be seen by factoring it out and saying instead **Mary is the most sweet, dear, lovely girl I know.** In the latter construction, supposedly typical of a later stage of language growth, we do not require an explicit superlative each time, but get the same results through the larger organization of the sentence. Jespersen was really reversing the older argument that Latin was a superior language because it was highly inflected.[48]

Jespersen did not have the benefit of recent thinking about redundancy, which holds that reminders are necessary. If a particular bit of information is expressed only once, it will not be intelligible unless all channels are functioning perfectly, free of noise and with undistracted attention on the part of the hearer. Still, it may be that we need less redundancy than we needed before; there seldom are clean breaks in language change and perhaps this one is coming gradually. Unquestionably we depend as no civilization ever has before on communication in writing, and there redundancy can be cut to a minimum—if the reader misses the point, he goes back and re-reads. A tape recording can be replayed. And for centuries now it has been getting physically easier to communicate; speakers are less separated in space, they depend very little on hunting for a livelihood, and a shouted command in battle could probably not be heard above the din anyway. It is not so much that we have lost the

---

[48] See Jespersen 1894.

power of communicating under adverse conditions as that we seldom need to and have developed easier ways of reaching one another that allow more information to be transmitted. Our sensitivity to contrasts is undoubtedly greater than that of our ancestors, and the tones need not be quite so sharp—more of them can be packed into a narrow space. Besides cutting down on the need for reminders this has probably subdued the fortis quality (characteristic of sounds produced with strong muscular tension) that earlier speech sounds may have had.

From the standpoint of a more complex civilization, there has been progress. Not all would agree that there can ever be progress in any absolute sense.

Key terms and concepts

slang
change in sound of words
  loss
  addition
  assimilation
  dissimilation
  metathesis
  spoonerism
blend
malapropism
spelling pronunciation

interpretative change
  overgeneralization
  analogical creation
  leveling
  reinterpretation
  folk etymology
  fusion
  downgrading
  metanalysis
  back formation
reinduction
loan words and borrowing
invention
metaphor
historical linguistics
change
  resistance to
  acceptance of
conflict of homonyms
taboo
cumulative change and/or
  progress

Additional remarks and applications

1. How do you pronounce the following expressions? Discuss any differences between the first column and the second in the sounds

represented by the italicized letters:

a. brea*d*	brea*d*th
b. *k*eel	*c*ool
c. in*f*inite	in*t*imate
d. mi*s*ter	mi*s*chief
e. th*r*ee	ag*r*ee
f. We've go*t* *t*wo runs.	We've go*t* *t*o run.

2. *Webster's Third New International Dictionary* records **coppice** and **copse** as identical in meaning. Account for what appears to have happened phonologically.

3. A speaker is heard to say *I would never let my membership lasp.* What has happened?

4. What is the term for the change exemplified in **liberry** for **library?** In making **hors d'œuvre** rime with **nerve?**

5. Trace the series of changes that reduced the pronunciation of *government* to **gubment.**

6. Identify the phonetic alterations in the following: *pram* for *perambulator; sprite,* a form of *spirit; bird,* from Old English *brid; number,* related to German *Nummer;* dialectal *fillum* for *film; tremble,* ultimately from Latin *tremulus.*

7. Analyze the following blends, then check your answers with the footnote. (Your solutions may be better than the ones suggested.)

    a. Are we going to stand still and be laughed at as overgrown, stupid *clouts?* (from a foreign language magazine)

    b. *a skull and dugger* program (referring to a Disney television program)

    c. They'll *bustle* him off to a mental hospital.

    d. Now that you *rub around* with those people. . . .

    e. The singer had a *sachrymose* voice.

    f. Give them the tone with your *pitchfork.*

    g. They made up after their little *spiff.*

    h. The test will include *both* speaking *as well as* reading.

    i. It will go down *in posterity.*

    j. I've *gone through a lot of expense* to do this.[49]

---

[49] a. *clod* + *lout;* b. *skulduggery* + *cloak and dagger;* c. *hustle* + *bundle;* d. *run around with* + *rub elbows with;* e. *saccharine* + *lachrymose;* f. *tuning fork* + *pitchpipe;* g. *spat* + *tiff;* h. *both X and Y* + *X as well as Y;* i. *in history* + *to posterity;* j. *to go through a lot* + *to go to a lot of expense.*

8. Identify the correct forms to replace the following malapropisms:

   a. The issue would be more quickly enjoined.
   b. I made them a sincere offer but they flaunted it.
   c. He lives in Pepsi-Cola, Florida.
   d. She couldn't get into that college because they refused to waver the requirement.
   e. The prisoner asked the judge for a hideous corpus.

9. Check your own pronunciations of the following words. Then look them up in an older dictionary (say one published between 1900 and 1910) and in as recent a one as possible. If you discern a pattern of change, account for it: *gynecology, conjurer, hover, dour, thence, chiropodist, chaise longue.* What further complication is there in the last example?

10. If you heard *That is a deadly poison* and *That is a very deadly poison* which would you take more seriously? What about *The wreck was a disaster* and *The wreck was a serious disaster?* What do these instances illustrate?

11. If any of the following occur in your speech, what are they probably instances of?

   a. I'm beat—I can't go another foot.
   b. Well I'll be blowed!
   c. I like reading whodunits.
   d. It's cold outside—I'm plumb froze.
   e. What are you all het up about?
   f. He just sort of snuck up on us.

   Give the standard forms of the verbs.

12. Look up the etymologies of the words *rogue, scamp, jerk, mischievous, naughty,* and *rascal.* Do they have something in common in the way of change of meaning? Has something similar happened more recently to the expression *far out?*

13. Mixed metaphors *(The idea was no sooner born than it faded; The dark corners of their ignorance fell before her eloquence; As you go down the path of life, drink it to the full)* are condemned as bad style. What change have the expressions undergone that encourages speakers and writers to mix them?

14. Look at the following doublets that are the result of dialect borrowing and explain the differences in meaning, if any: *girl, gal; curse, cuss; burst, bust; parcel, passel; vermin, varmint; saucy, sassy; ordinary, ornery; hoist, heist; rearing, rarin'; shaken up, shook up; slick, sleek; stamp, stomp.*

15. In what way do the social meanings affect our use or avoidance of the following terms?—*undertaker, mortician; wolf, Don Juan; cop, pig, officer; servants, help.* Think of other examples, especially those involving occupations.

For further reading

Baugh, Albert C. 1957. *A History of the English Language* (New York: Appleton-Century-Crofts).

Jespersen, Otto. 1964. *Language, Its Nature, Development, and Origin* (New York: W. W. Norton).

Lehmann, Winfred P. 1973. *Historical Linguistics: An Introduction* (New York: Holt, Rinehart & Winston).

McKnight, George H. 1968. *The Evolution of the English Language* (New York: Dover).

Sturtevant, Edgar H. 1942. *Linguistic Change* (New York: Stechert).

Traugott, Elizabeth Closs. 1972. *A History of English Syntax* (New York: Holt, Rinehart & Winston).

Wolfe, Patricia M. 1972. *Linguistic Change and the Great Vowel Shift in English* (Berkeley and Los Angeles: University of California Press).

WRITING
AND READING
11

While human beings have walked the earth and talked to one another for over a million years, their talk died with the sound waves that carried it until—a mere 6,000 years ago—some genius or geniuses invented writing. Before that, as in preliterate societies even today, the records of human culture—religious rules of conduct, social laws, treaty rights to territory—were as fragile as the elders' memories, for these things had to be transmitted by word of mouth. With writing, history begins; humans reflect on themselves and philosophy is born. All knowledge as we know it today is built on writing. Writing holds empires together by enabling them to be governed centrally. Writing indeed effected a full-scale revolution of culture.

But the process took thousands of years. It is as if writing was fated to repeat—on a foreshortened time scale—the history of spoken language, starting with iconic signs similar to those of gesture (and, like gesture, *visual*), evolving through stages of greater and greater arbitrariness, and finally coupling itself to the fully arbitrary units that had already crystallized in speech. To understand the past of writing we must begin with the present, which we know best.

WRITING AND SPEECH

Convergence of writing and speech

Speech is prior to writing not only historically but also genetically and logically. Genetically we know that speech comes first because children who are blind have no difficulty in learning to speak but children who are deaf have great difficulty in learning to read[1]—shutting off the channels of sight has little effect on acquiring language, but shutting off those of sound is almost fatal to it. The take-off point for reading is located somewhere in the recursive grammar stage, the last of the four grammars described in Chapter 8 (pages 173–75). The child must not only be talking with a fair degree of fluency but must have an awareness of what he is doing, must be able to form an internal image of an utterance, especially of sounds and their relationships to word shapes. Until he has a sense of what a word is, a feel for such things as syllables and rime, a child is not ready to read. Readiness comes only when the child is able to recognize word segments and store them in short-term memory, in a kind of phonetic notation that matches what is stored when listening to speech. Interpretation and comprehension proceed from there, using the same mechanisms as language in general.[2]

As for learning to write, that comes much later, when the child has the power to coordinate other muscular activities as skillfully as her genetic equipment permitted her to control her speech organs while she was still an infant.

The logical primacy of speech can be seen in the form taken by all well-developed writing systems. Without exception they "cut in" at some point on the stream of spoken language. Some of them key their primary symbols to distinctive sounds; those systems are *alphabetic*. Others key them to syllables, and are accordingly *syllabic;* still others to words: these are *logographic* ('word-writing'). Psychologically the effect of cutting in at a lower level is to gain the advantage of the higher levels. Thus English writing is alphabetic, and we can, if we have to, assign values almost letter by letter and "sound out" words as we read or write. But—especially in reading—we see the letters in assemblies as well as one by one: we know what the syllable *Mc* in proper names looks like and react to it as a unit. At the level of words, whatever success the "whole word" method of learning to read may have had is due to our appreciation of visible word-shapes; 'languorous' is stored in our minds as ***languorous***

---

[1] Mattingly 1971.

[2] Mattingly and Kavanagh 1972.

and does not have to be reconstituted from *l-a-n-g-u-o-r-o-u-s* every time we read it.[3]

With these advantages it is no wonder that alphabets have become the most widespread of all forms of writing. They use symbols that with more or less refinement correspond to individual sounds, and the degree of refinement is measured by how close the correspondence comes to being one-to-one. A perfect correspondence, with each letter symbol standing for one and only one distinctive sound, would of course be a form of phonemic writing. Some modern writing systems come very close to this ideal: Spanish, Czech, Finnish. Even the much-maligned English system allows us to interpret most spellings with confidence: we are safe in inferring that *sline,* if there were such a word, would rime with *fine,* not with *fin,* and that *wip* would rime with *rip,* not with *ripe.*

An alphabetic system has the capacity to become completely phonemic, and if it has failed to do so the reason is that writers have other needs and interests than that of making writing a perfect copy of sound. The needs are practical and the interests are both practical and esthetic. Among the needs are the functions that writing has fulfilled since its beginnings: communication across time (which until the invention of sound-recording devices was impossible for speech), communication across great distance (which likewise was impossible for speech until the appearance of the telephone), and communication to great numbers of people (which was closed to speech until the invention of radio). In modern times, the vastly greater size of the readership—for many publications, embracing readers of English from Tacoma to Calcutta—has made it necessary for writing to transcend local dialects and adhere to a standard that can be widely understood. A Southerner's *The poor roof bulged* would (in some areas) be transcribed /ðə poə rʊf bʊljd/, and a Northerner's /ðə pʊr ruf bʌljd/; with both of them agreed on standard spellings, trouble is avoided. Almost all major languages—those that have succeeded in bringing within their fold great numbers of speakers over wide areas of the globe—tend to have greater uniformity in spelling than in pronunciation.

This uniformity reflects tradition, of course, and inertia. Adults have learned the system and see no need to change it. But it also reflects much of the real uniformity that underlies the comparatively superficial differences of pronunciation. It is no coincidence that the underlying forms described in Chapter 3 have traits that are preserved in spelling: the *g* of *resign,* the *n* of *damn,* the *t* of *dissection,* which emerge as phonemes in *resignation, damnation,* and *dissect.* If the history of words is in some way recapitulated in these derivations, then a spelling that was frozen at an early date and embodies the history will have some value in revealing

---

[3] Tzeng et al. 1977, p. 623.

the relationships between cognates.[4] It unquestionably helps to have all the regular plurals in English spelled with s regardless of whether the pronunciation is [s] or [z]. The word *news* is spelled the same in *The news is good* and *I read the newspapers,* even though for many speakers the latter has /nus/ rather than /nuz/. We have to choose which level of language we want to represent most faithfully with our written symbols: distinctive sounds or morphemes. English spelling takes the first alternative, but with no great conviction: it is morphophonemic as well as phonemic.

Esthetic considerations, too, prevent a writing system from becoming fully phonemic and may even interfere at the morphophonemic level. Countless establishments bear some such name as *Ye Olde Antique Shoppe.* Common English names are sometimes regarded as too common, and ambitious parents dress them up with exotic spellings: *Alyce* for *Alice, Bettye* for *Betty, Edythe* for *Edith.* Some spellings are almost systematically prestigious—for example, the agentive suffix spelled *-or* rather than *-er: advisor,* not *adviser; expeditor,* not *expediter.* One esthetic attitude in particular has deflected writing away from speech and even created a counter-evolutionary trend: the deference that is felt in all societies, including our own, to the authority of the written word. For the Hindus, the Sanskrit writings embody "the language of the gods," and knowledge of Sanskrit and use of Sanskrit words has long been a prestige symbol in India.[5] In our society a respect for standard spellings is a requirement for social and economic advancement; the person who writes words with bad spellings in a letter of application will find it almost as hard to get a job as the one who has been caught writing bad checks. As a result, all spellings are locked in place and shielded from reform. Long after pronunciations have changed, the old spellings live on, including some that did not exist historically but were introduced by pseudo-scholarship: the *h* of *rhyme,* the *c* of *indict,* the *g* of *feign.*

The convergence of writing and speech virtually stops at the level of morphemes. Ordinary writing does not show syntactic structure either by tree diagrams or by labeled bracketing—even though the latter is easy enough to set up typographically: [s[NP *The stuff that they served* NP] [VP *was awful* VP]s]. What writing failed to do here was to provide for the *prosody*—the accents, rhythm, and intonation that help to mark the syntax of speech. Writers do sometimes use italics for accent (**This is for me, not you**), but this must be done sparingly. Rhythm and intonation

---

[4] Samuel Johnson in his great *Dictionary* (1755) established this "morphological spelling" by consistently preferring, when there was a choice of two or more forms, the one that retained the largest number of root letters, thus preserving the etymology.

[5] Sjoberg 1962, pp. 276–77.

are roughly indicated by punctuation and capitalization, but too much is left out and what is put in suffers from a confusion of two aims: the representations of the breaks that we *hear* and the divisions that logical-minded persons sometimes insist that we *write*—the two usually agree, but not always. Consider the following sentence: ***It is common knowledge that, if we are to learn to speak another language well, we must spend a great deal of time practicing it.*** There is no comma after ***knowledge,*** where a pause would normally come, but there is one after ***that,*** where most speakers would not pause at all.[6]

In all this we can detect the hand of an ancient tradition: that writing never fully symbolizes speech but serves as a prompter to what we want to say. The result is that writers have to make many choices that are not forced on them as speakers. The lack of markers for intonation is seen in the faux pas of the person who felt so warmly toward an invited speaker that in his later thank-you letter he wrote ***You would have been welcome if you had said nothing at all,*** neglecting to note that what he intended as

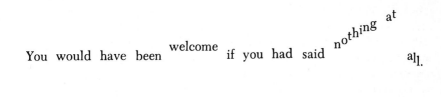

could be taken as

wel

You would have been

come if you had said nothing at a ll.

In writing we must put ***even if*** in the first of these, to signal the intention.

The jockeying necessary to overcome the lack of accent and intonation markings calls for a high degree of skill, which is part of the equipment of every good writer. Sometimes nothing can remedy the defect. Lord Acton's phrase ***Compromise is the soul if not the whole of politics*** remains ambiguous; we shall never know whether he meant 'is the soul, nay, more, possibly the whole,' or 'if not the whole, at least the soul.' Sometimes a simple repetition—unnecessary in speech—will clear things up. So with the phrase ***more or less.*** The question ***Are you more or less***

[6] Scott 1966, p. 540.

satisfied with the way things went? is ambiguous and one of the meanings can be pinned down in writing by repeating a word: *Are you more satisfied or less satisfied . . . ?* The accommodation most often called for is a change in word order, with or without a change in construction. A speaker wishing to reprove someone for shouting can say *Is shóuting necessary?* and be clearly understood if he puts the main accent on *shouting* and de-accents *necessary;* but if the sentence is written, the regularity with which main accents fall at the end will lead the reader to interpret it as *Is shouting nécessary?* A good writer will change the wording to get *shout* at the end: *Is it necessary to shout?* There are certain syntactic patterns that are more or less standard cues to placement of accent. One such is the "cleft sentence":

SPOKEN: The cát (not the dóg) caught the rat.
WRITTEN: It was the cat that caught the rat. (cleft)

Another is the passive voice:

SPOKEN: The néighbors (not the police) caught the thief.
WRITTEN: The thief was caught by the neighbors.

Now and then we can make capital of a deficiency. Just as a piece of writing can—to advantage—span two or more dialects and so gain in universality, so by its very ambiguity it can at one and the same time embrace two or more actual utterances that we do not care to distinguish, and thereby gain in generality. At check-out counters in stores there used to be containers of free samples with a sign reading *Take one.* Ordinarily this would represent the utterance *Táke one.* But if customers were to help themselves to several, the storekeeper could point out that the sign read *Take óne.*

So we see both primary and secondary divergences between speech and writing: primary ones that are simply the lack on one side of some device that is present in the other—a graphic sign such as the apostrophe in writing, or a distinctive sound such as an accent in speech; and secondary ones that are the result of having to make alternative choices or arrangements in order to remedy a primary lack. There are vested interests in both.

Writing and speech as partially independent systems

The great nineteenth-century linguist Wilhelm von Humboldt expressed what he felt to be the true relationship between writing and speech: "language intrinsically lies in the act of its production in reality; . . . even its preservation in writing is only an incomplete mummified repository which needs, for full understanding, an imaginative oral reconstruction."[7] Most linguists over the years have agreed. Written language could never have come into existence and could not exist today without speech. But to say that it is *only* a mummified repository is not quite true; this is like the *only* of another famous reductionist claim that we saw earlier, that the speech organs are only organs of digestion: in the latter case we are saying that speech is only an overlaid function, and in the former we are saying the same about writing, when the fact is that both have branched off to some extent and achieved a new level of integration.

Writing speaks words to the mind in a voice of its own, sometimes more clearly than words spoken aloud. It is almost impossible, without help from written signs, to unravel the last line of the Carolyn West limerick:

> But I'd hate to relate
> What that fellow named Tate
> And his tête-a-tête ate at 8:08.

Everyone has had the experience of misunderstanding something heard and not getting it straight until seeing it written: *Peace Corps* interpreted as *P-Score, youth rehabilitation* as *U-3 habilitation.*[8] In one frustrating encounter a librarian spent the better part of an hour rounding up materials on *youth in Asia* for a high-school student who finally showed his assignment sheet with the word written out: *euthanasia.*[9] Many puns depend on an interference between visible and audible signals: the estate called *Belleigh Acres* and the *Akimbo Arms,* a Japanese motel. There are other intentional misspellings besides the *olde* and *Edythe* mentioned earlier: *goddamit* is softened by being written that way. We even find a visual symbolism resembling the sound-symbolism of Chapter 6 (page 130). Readers asked to match 'pleasant' and 'unpleasant' to the spellings *grey* and *gray* tend to do it in that order, and to make such associations as *her lovely grey eyes* contrasting with *a gray gloomy day.* The *gh* of *ghastly, ghoulish, aghast,* and *ghost* marks—like a phonestheme—a kind of semantic constellation.[10]

Punctuation, too, may be short-circuited directly to meaning. The four expressions *my sister's friend's investments, my sisters' friends' investments, my sisters' friend's investments,* and *my sister's friends' investments* all sound identical but are clearly distinguished by the position of

---

[7] In Salus 1969, pp. 184–85.

[8] Example from Lee Hultzén, personal communication.

[9] Example from John Algeo, personal communication.

[10] Bolinger 1946, p. 336.

the apostrophe. Likewise quotation marks are useful in writing but demand the awkward reading aloud of "quote . . . unquote."

There are also structural correspondences, not sharply defined but statistically unmistakable. The most striking is the shortness of function words. Many of them have homonyms that are not function words, and if there is a difference in length, the function word is shorter.[11]

I–eye	to–two
so–sew	by–buy
be–bee	in–inn

Capitalization marks proper nouns and proper adjectives. But it is still used or omitted occasionally for other purposes that are directly related to meaning—omitted in e. e. cummings's verse for a kind of playing-down effect, added here and there in verse or prose to dignify or exaggerate: in Shakespeare's First Folio the tragedies consistently had more capitalization of common nouns than the comedies—a register distinction in writing.[12]

Linguists used to think of the relationship between writing and speech as a simple substitution of a visual symbol for an oral symbol: grapheme for phoneme.[13] But the relationship is not necessarily one to one, although it is expressible by rules. (*F* matches /f/, but so does *ph;* the *i* of *fine* matches /ay/, but the rule for this must take account of the presence of *e,* in view of what happens with *fin.* And so on.) The phonemic correspondences are the entry into the language system. A written message is interpreted phonemically and from there on the processing is the same as for speech.

Figure 11–1 shows the conception of speech and writing as more or less independent systems that tend to run parallel but converge more and more and finally intertwine. At the right and left extremes are elements that go directly to meaning without the intervention of arbitrary units such as phonemes and graphemes—one example on the graphic side is the numeral *2,* one on the spoken side a raising of the eyebrows for questioning. In the center each step along the graphic course marks an upward progression and at the same time a sidewise link to the concurring steps in speech. If we encounter the spelling *slough* we may have to sound out the word to tell which of the homographs is intended— /slʌf/, /slu/, or

---

[11] Vachek 1973, p. 54, footnote 26.

[12] Tritt 1973, p. 47.

[13] The grapheme, like the phoneme, is a set of variants all of which have the same value. Thus the graphs **A,** *a,* and a are all allographs of the grapheme that represents the first letter of the alphabet.

FIGURE 11–1
Speech and Writing as Semi-Independent Systems

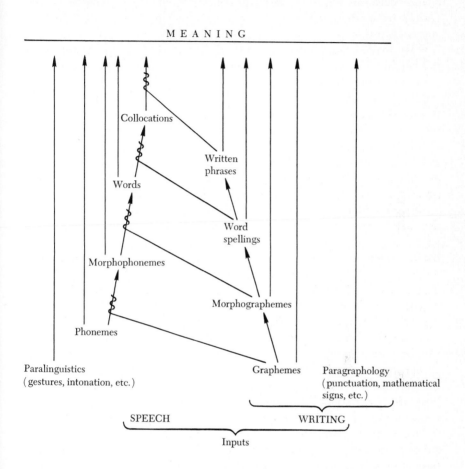

M E A N I N G

Collocations

Written
phrases

Words

Word
spellings

Morphophonemes

Morphographemes

Phonemes

Paralinguistics   Graphemes   Paragraphology
(gestures, intonation, etc.)   (punctuation, mathematical
                                                                    signs, etc.)

SPEECH   WRITING

Inputs

/slaw/; and if we find the word **read** with no indication of tense we may
have to puzzle it out in terms of its morphophonemic makeup. But each
graphic step likewise has the potential of going directly to meaning. The
spelling *-que* just before a space tells us that the word of which it is a
part is probably of French origin, just as an initial *ph, ps,* or *xy* indicates
'Greek,' along with connotations of learnedness. There are even graphs
that carry register distinctions: some forms of letters are more elegant
than others.

Each system, spoken and written, contributes its part. A speaker in-
fected with literacy is no longer the same person. His brain is full of
visual and auditory interminglings. Aware that a word may be misinter-
preted, he may spell it out, as one TV interviewee did with the sentence

You just feel e-x-o-r-c-i-s-e-d. He has become an expert *translator* from one mode to the other, as adept at interpreting from writing to speech and from speech to writing as he is in shifting from one register or spoken variety to another, with full awareness of the matching values in both systems.[14]

If we look at this difference between the two systems we see that from the beginning it has been a question of *translation*. From the time of the earliest literacy till the nineteenth century, reading and writing were taught through models that used a language differing in important ways from the vernacular of the learners. Homer was already antiquated at the time he was taught to Greek schoolboys. Understanding him meant translating his idiom to theirs—only, since it was "the same language," the differences were put down to style. The use of archaic models was unavoidable in cultures where written documents were few and the only assuredly respectable ones were those that had stood the test of time.

Universal literacy has partially closed the gap between the language of the models and the language of the learners; the more *they* have been able to write, the more up-to-date the writings have become. But the gap has not been closed completely and may never be, for two reasons: first, writing necessarily reaches toward the past; second, writing is writing. The first has to do with who our readers are, the second with the fact that writing is not speech.

Obviously we need not concern ourselves with one class of readers, the relatives and intimates to whom we write informal letters. They forgive us our misspellings and read our meanings between the lines because they know us. It is the unknown reader or the half-stranger who is the problem. He owes us nothing and probably speaks a different dialect from ours. He is impatient with a writer who cannot execute a meaning in the form that he has come to expect.

That form is usually nothing other than our friend the Standard, which roughly embodies the forms that underlie all dialects and accordingly is best able to speak to all of them. The correspondence is not perfect. There is much that is preserved for the sake of preservation. But the core tends to correspond to an older phase of the language, from which the current ones have evolved.

---

[14] For the concept of translation applied to writing and speech, see Haas 1973. Actually the translation, for all of us excepting a few professional transcribers (such as court reporters and biographers), nearly always goes in just one direction: writing → speech. Writing has always been more a device for noting down what is to be spoken later than for recording what has already been said. This may well be why—as one linguist has pointed out—it is simpler to set up rules for converting spellings to phonemes than the reverse. He argues that writing, for literate societies, serves as the backup to the standard, the master form to which all other forms are referred. See Householder 1971, Ch. 13, "The Primacy of Writing."

The second reason for the persistence of the gap is the nature of writing as a medium for language. We have described the literate person as "an expert *translator* from one mode to the other"; or, as one linguist puts it, "In being required constantly to pass from sounds to letters, and from letters to sounds, we are in the situation of a truly bilingual interpreter."[15] But though bilingual in this sense, the writer is not *natively* so. He learns the basics of his language before he can read a single word, and the learning process itself is partly one of translating what he already knows into a new medium. Furthermore, as best we can tell he is not programmed genetically for reading and writing as he is for hearing and speaking; that may come some day, but meanwhile writing is more truly an overlaid function than speaking is. And being learned comparatively late, it depends more on precepts and less on examples.

The efficiency of English spelling

No other spelling system in the world has been the occasion of so much amazement, frustration, irritation, sarcasm, and cold fury as that of English—a reflection as much of the large numbers of non-English-speaking people who have tried to learn it as of its own inherent refractoriness. British place names are the butt of the following riddle:

> *Problem:* How do you pronounce **athvrenzavce?**
>
> *Answer:* You don't pronounce it at all because they are all silent letters: **ath** as in **Strathaven; v** as in **Milngavie; ren** as in **Cirencester; z** as in **Culzean; av** as in **Abergavenny; ce** as in **Leicester.**[16]

The tributes to other, more ordinary spellings have been just as heartfelt. Here is part of a poem composed by Richard Krogh:

> Beware of heard, a dreadful word
> That looks like beard and sounds like bird.
> And dead; it's said like bed, not bead;
> For goodness sake, don't call it deed!
> Watch out for meat and great and threat
> (They rhyme with suite and straight and debt).
> A moth is not a moth in Mother,
> Nor both in bother, broth in brother.

---

[15] Haas 1973, p. 1.
[16] Example from J. D. McClure, personal communication.

Reviewing these protests and experiencing the pain even as a native speaker of trying to learn how to spell a word and remember it afterward, one is astonished to read the claim, in a serious study of English sounds and spellings, that "conventional orthography is . . . a near optimal system for the lexical representation of English words."[17] It is necessary to consider this endorsement of the status quo in the light of the two sound-systems discussed in Chapters 2 and 3. From the standpoint of the *picture* stage, English orthography is a fright. From that of the *picture–pictorial–depict* stage, as we have seen, it has its points, for it gives a common spelling for words that stem from a common source.

The educational problem is obvious. The child beginning to learn to read still has a leg and a half firmly planted in the *picture* stage. She has learned some important morphophonemic alternations, probably including *fight–fought, bring–brought, think–thought* (but not *seek–sought*—she will not have learned *seek,* and when she does she may go on saying *seek–seeked* to the end of her days). These provide some justification for a uniform spelling for the past tense of those verbs, though a very weak justification for this particular spelling, which is both redundant and inconsistent with *teach–taught* and *catch–caught.* As for the alternations in *fine* and *finish, decide* and *decision, reside* and *residence,* the spellings are more consistently relatable but the words themselves are either not in the learner's vocabulary or are there but unrelated: a six-year-old is not ready to see a connection between *fine* and *finish,* even though he probably knows both words.

To try to teach the words and connections in addition to the rules for reading is the same bad educational practice, though on a smaller scale, as trying to teach literacy in a foreign language (a Navaho child, for instance, being forced to learn to read in English, which he knows only imperfectly); each task is difficult enough by itself without mixing it with the other. What the child needs is the quickest possible entry for written symbols into the part of his language that he knows well, and the easiest match is through a writing system that is fairly close to the autonomous phonemes of the *picture* stage. In other words, if we consider only the problem of learning to read and leave other questions aside, including other educational ones, the best writing system is the one that comes closest to being ideally phonetic. Something of the kind is the basis for most styles of teaching beginners today. Even the Dick-and-Jane readers used reduced lists of words that had reasonably consistent spellings. The differences are mainly in where the entry into the spoken system is to be made. The whole-word method makes it at the level of words. Another

---

[17] Chomsky and Halle 1968, p. 49. The same idea is paraphrased on page 184, footnote 18.

method, not yet tried on any considerable scale, advocates making it at the level of the syllable.[18] The Initial Teaching Alphabet is a modified phonemic approach.[19]

There remains the question, when the gates are opened to the flood of other considerations—the preservation of documents, the different pronunciations in different dialects, the direct spelling-to-meaning relationships diagrammed in Figure 11–1, the vested interest of the millions who already know the existing system—of whether English spelling is efficient enough to be worth keeping as it is or should be mildly or drastically reformed. Reform is hardly unthinkable—the Dutch have done it every forty years or so.[20] The problem is one for society as a whole.

With spoken language, the sound-system, the words, and the syntax are under daily pressures of change, and a language at any given moment is probably the best communicative instrument its culture can have. But writing lives in a cocoon. It is controlled by schools and copy editors. There is no competition from millions of inventive writers who in the give-and-take of correspondence might attain something approaching the same kind of consensus that speakers attain in speech. A real written *language* has never existed; what we have is a code watched over by a priestly caste.

So for every argument that we ought to live with the system we have, there is a counter-argument that we ought to tear it down and build it up again. The reader can imagine this argument extending far into the night.

THE GROWTH OF WRITING[21]

Long before writing itself was invented, primitive man had looked for aids to memory, and the predecessors of writing systems were just such *mnemonic devices*. Almost every community of people at one time used *tallies* of some kind, most often sticks that could be notched to indicate number. The Western gunman who notched the handle of his gun was following a primitive custom of keeping count of his victims. Debts could be notched into tallies, or a piece of wood could be scored and then cut in halves with the lender and debtor each retaining matching halves. The later joining of the pieces would ensure that the memory of neither one "defaulted."

---

[18] Gleitman and Rozin 1973.

[19] See Pitman and St. John 1969.

[20] Pointed out by Robert S. Kirsner, personal communication.

[21] This section is drawn for the most part from Gelb 1963.

Among the Incas of Peru as well as among peoples in Persia and China knotted cords served to record facts and messages. The *quipu,* as it was called, was a thick main cord with many slender cords attached to it. Different meanings were carried by different colors, types of knots, distance of knot from main cord, and so on. Although the quipu served for numerical information, it seems to have been used also for more complex matters such as soothsaying and astronomy. The North American Indians used *wampum,* woven designs in bead work to recall important events such as treaties. These memory aids were useful, but mainly limited to numerical data. A more complete way of recording speech was yet to be found.

One step was the *rebus.* Most of us remember how as children we looked at a row of pictures and discovered that their names were clues to the meaning of the puzzle. For example,

meant, 'I can see you.'—***eye*** is a homophone of ***I, can*** ('container') of ***can*** ('be able'), and so on. Hans Jensen in his *Sign, Symbol, and Script* tells how the Yorubas of West Africa developed rebus messages using material objects. Cowrie shells were used as tallies—six of them stood for the number ***six,*** for which the Yoruba word is ***efa.*** But ***efa*** also meant 'be attracted to,' and a boy would send six cowries to a girl to say 'I love you.' To return his love, she might send eight cowries—the word for ***eight*** was ***ejo,*** which was also a form of the verb ***jo,*** 'to be in agreement'—"I love you too."

But most languages have too few homophones for the rebus to be very useful, even when pictures are used. Still, pictorial writing marked an advance over tallies by making it possible at least to describe concrete objects. The *pictogram,* a stylized drawing of an object, was the earliest form of picture writing. But it was not yet writing as we understand it, for it spoke to the mind through the eye alone, not through the eye as stimulus to the ear.

Among the American Indians, pictures, by their nature—representing meaning directly and not through verbalization—were able to surmount the barriers of tribal languages. But the disadvantages matched the advantages: since picture writing did not actually record words, different "readings" were possible, and this led to ambiguity.

The real gift of picture writing was that it formed the basis of Chinese characters and Egyptian hieroglyphs. To convey more complex and abstract concepts, one pictogram could be combined with others to form an *ideogram.* If  = 'house' and  = 'woman,' the two can be put together as ⟨⟩ to mean 'home.' Doubling the 'woman' sign yields ⟨⟩⟨⟩ , a possible ideogram for 'bigamy.'

Chinese has continued with character writing down to the present, though reforms are being fostered by the present regime in China. To read a book in Classical Chinese, one must know some 3000 characters; to be a real scholar, one must learn as many as 40,000. The difficulty of learning to read this system outweighs any advantages that the suggestive shapes of the symbols have to offer.

Hieroglyphics took the road that eventually led to the alphabet. There were three main steps: the writing of words, the writing of syllables, and the writing of distinctive sounds. Each stage overlapped the following one. Even Modern English writing has a few remnants of word signs and syllable signs: in *IOU* the letters stand for words; the symbol ¶ means 'paragraph' and § means 'section.' (We also use the primitive device of pluralizing symbols by doubling them: ¶¶, §§.) *Bar-b-q* uses *b* and *q* to stand for the syllables /bi/ and /kyu/, as *OK* stands for the syllables /o/ and /ke/.

Archeology enables us to estimate the dates of the three steps and credit their first appearance to particular societies, though we cannot be sure that some later archeological find will not reveal that the style was borrowed from a near neighbor who invented it a century or two earlier.

Word writing

While the interpreter of a pictorial message was usually free to ad-lib, a few of the signs must always have referred to individual persons or things that could be mentioned in speech by just one name. A drawing of a small bear could have been verbalized as *small bear, little bear,* or *bear cub,* but if it designated a person known as *Little Bear* only that reading would have been admissible. This would have supported a tendency to associate the drawing with a particular *name* rather than with an idea that might be variously named.

Something similar must have happened with pictorial messages where the interpreter was theoretically free to ad-lib. If the message was to himself—a series of reminders—a timid person no doubt did as he would do today and memorized the text. When he came to deliver it, using his notes for added confidence, each symbol for a particular meaning would also have stood for a particular word or phrase. It is not difficult to imagine almost from the first a tendency to link a written sign to its meaning, not directly, but via a particular word or words. Any such tendency must have taken hold quickly, for it put all the resources of language at the command of the writer and reader. For the first time writing was *phonetized:* a given sign represented a given complex of sounds.

When this step was first taken is impossible to determine. One cannot tell by looking at the earliest pictorial messages whether they were interpreted idea by idea, with the words ad-libbed, or word by word. The signs might have been direct representations of concrete objects, or figurative representations of one notion through another (the sun for 'bright, brilliant, blinding'), or diagrams (an empty circle for 'empty, vacant, hollow')—nothing would prove that a word rather than a meaning was intended.

But somewhere in the word-writing stage an event took place that proved the word-by-word interpretation beyond a doubt. The pictorial stage would have found it very difficult to express abstract notions like tense and mood in the verb; so if we find *would be* symbolized by a drawing of a piece of wood and a drawing of a bee, we can be certain that the figures no longer stand for ideas. This is the *rebus,* which we have already seen.

Now nothing stood in the way of applying the same phonetic principle not just to whole words but to parts of words. Most languages contain words of more than one syllable, and often the syllables are the same in sound as certain one-syllable words. A slight extension of the rebus game enabled writers to use double characters for two-syllable words. In a modern rebus, *fancy* can be depicted by a fan and a sea. At first the sign-to-syllable relationship would not have been pure—a three-syllable word like *loggerhead* could have been represented by two signs, one for logger and one for head—but the basis for syllabic writing was laid, and the whole period of word writing was a mixture of word and syllable writing.[22]

The earliest developed form of word-syllabic writing was that of the Sumerians in Mesopotamia at the end of the fourth millennium B.C. The Egypti: s had their own system within a century or so of this, but were probably influenced by the Sumerians.

A sample of a well-known syllabary is shown in Figure 11–2.

Syllable writing

Even after the knack of writing by syllables had been acquired, pure syllable writing was rather long in coming. The older word-signs were kept through tradition and inertia, and often a given word could be represented either by its own sign or by signs for its syllables. The second historical step—the discarding of all the word-signs and the adoption of a straightforward system of syllable writing—had to be taken by disre-

---

[22] Gelb 1963, pp. 99–105.

FIGURE 11–2   The Cherokee Syllabary*

a	e	i	o	u	ʌ
D a	R e	T i	ꭳ o	Ơ u	i ʌ
f ga	ꮁ ge	y gi	A go	J gu	E gʌ
Oʮ ha	? he	A hi	Ⱶ ho	Γ hu	ꭸ hʌ
W la	ꮈ le	P li	G lo	M lu	ꮑ lʌ
ꮊ ma	Oꮉ me	H mi	3 mo	ꭹ mu	
Θ na	ꮄ ne	ꜰ ni	Z no	ꮔ nu	ꭴ nʌ
I gwa	ꮺ gwe	ꮆ gwi	Ñ gwo	ꮝ gwu	Ɛ gwʌ
Ⴗ sa	4 se	b si	ꮼ so	ꭲ su	R sʌ
ꮧ da	f de	ꮧ di	Λ do	S du	ꮫ dʌ
ꮿ dla	L dle	G dli	ꮬ dlo	ꭿ dlu	P dlʌ
G dza	V dze	ꮒ dzi	K dzo	d dzu	Cꭷ dzʌ
G wa	ꮾ we	Ө wi	O wo	ꭵ wu	6 wʌ
ꮃ ya	ꮹ ye	ꮽ yi	ꮢ yo	G yu	B yʌ

ꜣ	ka
ꮏ	hna
G	nah
ꮝ	s
W	ta
ꮤ	ti
Ɩ	tla
ꮦ	te

SOURCE: Adapted from p. 414 of *An Introduction to Descriptive Linguistics*, Revised Edition, by H. A. Gleason, Jr. Copyright © 1955, 1961 by Holt, Rinehart and Winston, Publishers. Reprinted by permission of Holt, Rinehart and Winston, Publishers.

* This syllabary was invented between 1809 and 1821 by Sequoya (George Guess) and used by the Cherokee people and missionaries working among them. It is partly an adaptation of Roman letters.

spectful foreigners who had no romantic attachments to the old signs and merely borrowed what was practical.[23] These were the Phoenicians. Other borrowers of other systems did the same, but the Phoenicians are most important to us because they stand in direct line with the later development of the alphabet.

The Phoenicians, around the middle of the second millennium B.C., imitated the one-consonant syllabary of the Egyptians, throwing out the rest. By about 1000 B.C. they had developed a completely syllabic form of writing with no word signs and no signs for more than one syllable.

---

[23] Ibid., p. 196.

The vowels were still omitted, though where needed to avoid ambiguity they were often added in the form of consonants whose features resembled those of the desired vowel. For example, Semitic writing—including Phoenician—had syllabic signs for the semiconsonants /w/ and /y/ (plus a vowel), and used them as makeshifts for the simple vowels /u/ and /i/. There were other such makeshifts. The glimmerings of alphabetic writing were already visible.

Sound writing: the alphabet

It is a bit presumptuous of modern phonology to appropriate the term "distinctive sound" for its phonemes, as if the users of language would never have supposed at each new and successive refinement of the relationship between sound and symbol that they had at last hit upon the phonetic atom. This is dramatized for us now with the theory of distinctive features; what we had thought was the atom, the phoneme, turns out to be a rather complex molecule. Words and syllables must have been felt to be just as distinctively irreducible in their time. So if phonemes continue to be called distinctive sounds—and the phrase is too firmly entrenched to be got rid of easily—we should remember that the term refers to a set of phonetic features, at a certain level of refinement, which actually came into consciousness with the growth of alphabetic writing. For that we can thank mainly the Greeks of some three thousand years ago.

The Phoenicians were the seafaring traders of the ancient world and carried their writing wherever they went as one of the tools of their trade. It was probably in the ninth century B.C. that the form of Phoenician writing that was to become the Greek alphabet was planted along the western shores of the Aegean.[24]

The Greek innovation—and it was gradual, like all the others—was to do consistently what the Phoenicians had done sporadically: to add the interpretative vowel signs to all their syllables. What they themselves must have regarded still as a syllabary thus became an alphabet by accident. A sign signifying /mu/ (as well as /mi me ma/) would not have needed any /u/ after it if the context made it clear that /mu/ was intended. An English sentence written *Y mst b crfl wth sch ppl* would give us no trouble—*mst* here can only mean *must.* But when the symbol for any *m*-plus-vowel syllable was consistently accompanied by a sign for a particular vowel, it was natural for the next generation of scribes to forget that it stood for the syllable and take it for the consonant alone. Now

---

[24] Ibid., pp. 178–81.

it was possible to go on to a full specification of all the phonemes. This was the form of writing that captured the greatest number of languages around the world, including—with modifications—the Semitic itself, from which it was derived. We can never guess how far the progress and power of the Western world may have been due to the speedup of communication and the accumulation of recorded experience that was made possible when a quasi-phonemic writing that could be quickly learned took literacy away from a select priesthood and put it within reach of the general public.

A number of scholars believe that letters—the distinctive signs of writing—may have undergone an evolution similar to that of the distinctive sounds of speech: that is, to have begun as gestural designs that were eventually formalized, "phonemicized." The most obvious designs would be those imitating the various shapes the mouth takes during articulation (the "roundness" of *o*, for example). We know that at least one alphabet was deliberately invented in this way: the Korean alphabet promulgated in 1446 by King Sejong. And Alexander Melville Bell devised his similar "visible speech" four hundred years later. But there are hints that other systems used the same idea—Devanagari (India), Arabic, and possibly Japanese.[25]

The stages of development of writing are summarized in Table 11–1.

DECIPHERMENT

One of the most fascinating chapters in the recovery of the past is the interpretation of ancient writings on scattered, fragmentary, and often fragile artifacts that have come down to us.[26] Much of our ability to read them is due to the continuity of certain cultures that developed a writing system at an early date and have kept their tradition sufficiently alive to our own day to give us a basis of comparison with earlier systems related to them. Foremost among these traditions are the Chinese, Hebrew, Sanskrit, Greco-Roman, and Persian, the last having been carried on in India by the Parsees, who fled there during the Mohammedan invasion of Persia in the eighth century. Now and then some precious bit of bilingual or multilingual evidence comes to light—a document such as the Rosetta stone, on which identical messages appear in two or more languages, at least one of which could already be read. The Rosetta stone contained

---

[25] Data from Peter Mayer, in press release dated Nov. 27, 1977 and entitled "Are Letters Mouthshapes?"

[26] The story can be read in Cleator 1959 and Doblhofer 1971.

TABLE 11–1
Stages of the Development of Writing

NO WRITING: *Pictures*

FORERUNNERS OF WRITING: *Semasiography*

1. Descriptive-Representational Devices
2. Identifying-Mnemonic Devices

FULL WRITING: *Phonography*

1. *Word-Syllabic:*	Sumerian (Akkadian)	Egyptian	Hittite (Aegean)	Chinese
2. *Syllabic:*	Elamite Hurrian etc.	West Semitic (Phoenician) (Hebrew) (Aramaic) etc.	Cypro- Minoan Cypriote Phaistos? Byblos?	Japanese
3. *Alphabetic:*		Greek Aramaic (vocalized)° Hebrew (vocalized)° Latin Indic° etc.		

SOURCE: Adapted from Gelb 1963, p. 191.
° Tentatively classed as alphabetic.

inscriptions in two varieties of Egyptian writing, plus Greek. The most impressive multilingual record of all was the Persian inscriptions done at Bisutun by order of King Darius, with parallel texts in Persian, Elamite, and Assyrian (Babylonian).[27] The Persian empire embraced peoples speaking these three principal languages, and other Persian inscriptions likewise are written in all three.

---

[27] Pedersen 1962, p. 155.

Today there are some four hundred different writing systems in use around the world. Besides the Roman letters of our own alphabet, most of us recognize those of Greek, if only from their use by fraternities and sororities. The Russian alphabet is based on the Greek. Much of the Near East and Africa employs the Arabic script, beautiful in its decorative applications to Persian miniatures and to the designs of Oriental rugs. There are hundreds of others besides these more or less familiar examples, but all modern writing systems together are only a small fraction of those used at some time in the past. Certain of these ancient writings have left remains that have been deciphered, but others still await a key that will unlock the language they recorded.

Deciphering a written language that is no longer spoken is an almost insuperable task. First the type of writing must be identified: is it phonetic like our alphabet, pictorial as Mayan seems to be, or is it some combination like Egyptian hieroglyphics? Even if mainly phonetic, is the correspondence to speech phonemic or syllabic? And what of the order of the signs? The system does not necessarily proceed like ours. It may read from top to bottom like Chinese or from right to left like Hebrew. Or it may be placed into a pleasing design within a cartouche (oblong figure), as in Egypt. It may even spiral into or out from the center of a disc, as on the Phaistos Disc from Crete.

The problem for the decipherer is further complicated by the fact that there is no consistent relationship between writing systems and language families. Persian is a good example: it is related in word stock and grammar to the Indo-European languages, but it borrowed its scripts from the Semitic languages surrounding it in the Near East. Thus Persian looks like Arabic because it uses a related system of writing, but there is no corresponding structural relationship. In the same way, there is no necessary reason for English to be written in Roman letters; properly adapted, Russian or Arabic would have been just as feasible.

The more the puzzles, the harder the decipherer's job. It is fairly easy to decipher a system of writing if the language corresponding to it is known, but extremely difficult otherwise. This is the case of Etruscan, the riddle of which is still unsolved.

The most famous decipherment of all was the reading of the Egyptian hieroglyphics by Jean François Champollion, using the Rosetta stone with its parallel inscriptions in hieroglyphics and forms of Greek. Other scholars before Champollion had pointed the way to a reading, but he was the first to break the entire code. In 1824 he published his proof that the hieroglyphics were neither wholly phonetic nor wholly pictographic, but a combination—contrary to what earlier scholars had wrongly assumed.

Cuneiform came next. Here, the stumbling block had literally been a block. Most scholars worked from an inscription that went around a rectilinear arch—up one side, across the top, and down the other side. It was long assumed that the position of the cuneiform letters in relationship to the vertical was immaterial. Actually, the letters were positioned in much the way an inscription running around the edge of a coin might be. After this was cleared up, yet another puzzle faced the scholars: the script turned out to be a syllabary. Eventually, by the middle of the nineteenth century, all the problems were solved.

Other inscriptions have only been decoded within recent times. Hittite is one such. Not until 1917 had the decipherment of Hittite gone far enough to show that it was not an Oriental language but an early branch of the far-flung Indo-European family.

A more recent triumph was the decipherment—announced in 1952— of Linear B, a form of writing used on the island of Crete and on part of the Greek mainland. It opened the door to that part of the ancient world that pertained to the legendary King Minos and his capital at Knossos. This time the solution depended largely on statistical techniques.[28]

There are still mysteries awaiting some scholar or some talented amateur. Mayan is still spoken in the Yucatan peninsula of Mexico, but the Mayan glyphs have defied all attempts at reading. They can hardly be phonetic, or they would have been unlocked by now. And contemporary speakers, the Mayan Indians themselves, are unable to match the symbols to their native speech. Another puzzle comes from the Indus Valley, a form of writing very similar to the *rongo rongo* script of Easter Island— itself still a mystery.

Decipherment has its counterpart in the breaking of secret codes. In fact, early writing must have been felt by the illiterate to be a secret code itself—the word *rune*, which signifies a character of the Germanic alphabet, originally meant 'secret'; and in Egypt, writing was the jealously guarded property of a priestly caste. The art of making and breaking codes—cryptography and cryptanalysis—has reached a high level of proficiency, largely under the impetus of war. One demonstration was the breaking of the Japanese "Purple Code" early in World War II by a U.S. team under Colonel William Friedman.

THE FUTURE OF WRITING

Literacy programs are expensive, and a third of the world's population is illiterate. Of the world's adult population in 1970 (between 2 and 3 bil-

---

[28] For a rehearsal of the way in which the talented amateur Michael Ventris broke the code, see Chadwick 1960.

lion), almost 800 million were illiterate—and though the percentage was being reduced, in absolute figures illiteracy was gaining because of high birth rates. In the modern world an illiterate society is an uneducated one. How is the wisdom locked in print to be released if books and periodicals cannot be read?

Audiovisual technology might seem to be the answer, but unfortunately, we are a long way from a television or even a radio that will establish genuine two-way communication. The ham radio operator enjoys it, but if all who now exchange letters were to exchange the same number of radio messages, there would not be enough frequencies to go around—to say nothing of the cost.

Suppose the difficulty could be hurdled by some great advance in technology. Would reading and writing then go the way of the horse and buggy? Probably not, for there are other costs that are higher still. Consider four, which can be labeled archives, speed, symbols, and fact, just for convenience.

Archives   The record of civilization is in print. To make it accessible to everyone by ear might well cost more than all literacy programs for a century. Besides, who is to interpret it? How easy would it be for politicians to revise the past?

Speed   The average speaking rate is six syllables per second. A listener can comprehend somewhat faster than that—which makes it possible to speed up a recording slightly—but cannot approach the rate of the average reader. Another side to the question of speed is freedom to scan and skip: by noting just a word here and there readers can decide whether there is anything on a page that interests them.

Symbols   Ordinary speech is not the only medium of communication embodied in writing. The whole edifice of science and logic is built on a tight system of mathematical symbols. It is possible of course to verbalize an expression such as $\sqrt{\dfrac{(a^2 + b^2)}{c}}$ but next to impossible to manipulate it if words have to be used; the practical value of it is in avoiding words. Are we to forgo this kind of literacy too?

Fact   Writing is dispassionate. We saw this earlier as a liability: a great part of the emotional content of speech is lost when it is put on paper. Yet for transmitting *public* knowledge this can be an advantage, and it is precisely the truth values that are least affected by it. If you read **Caspar submitted his report** you know as much about what happened as if someone spoke the same words, and you are not swayed by any tone of enthusiasm or distaste in the voice of a speaker. And written agreements are secure agreements; oral ones are not. To dispense with literacy we would have to dispense with law and commerce, the areas where writing began in the first place.

There are cultures, not all of which are literate; but there is also a world-wide culture of which writing is a part. Literacy, for better or for worse, will have to be taught, for all of the foreseeable future.

But styles and systems of writing undoubtedly will change. Even as simple a matter as the shapes of alphabetic letters is open to criticism. Would-be readers who are dyslexic have great trouble with the letters *p, b, q,* and *d,* which are identical in shape and differ only in their orientation. Adopting characters with more contrast would be a great help for a substantial segment of the population and some help to every learner.[29]

If the past is any guide to the future, it will be events exterior to language that will lead to new experiments in writing, not efforts deliberately directed toward reform. The history of spelling reform in English has been the same as that of other piecemeal reforms where vested interests were at stake (such as Prohibition or truth in advertising): a long record of frustration. Shortly before and after the turn of the century, England and the United States witnessed a vigorous movement toward reform of spelling that enlisted many notable figures, including Charles Darwin, Alfred Lord Tennyson, and, more recently, George Bernard Shaw. For a time it even enjoyed an organization, the Simplified Spelling Board, with a subsidy of $25,000 a year from Andrew Carnegie and the official support of Theodore Roosevelt, who ordered the Government Printing Office to adopt some three hundred revised spellings. But today one hardly ever hears of it, and spelling reformers are regarded as cranks.

Key terms and concepts

reading readiness	rebus
logographic writing	pictogram
grapheme	ideogram
graph	syllabary
allograph	alphabet
mnemonic device	decipherment

---

[29] Barber 1973.

Additional remarks and applications

1. Interpret the following figure, pretending first that you are reading it as a pictogram, then as a word symbol or logogram, then as a syllable symbol or syllabogram. What words might correspond to it as a pictogram? Of what words might it form part if it were a syllabogram?

2. List four letters which are fairly consistent in their phonemic values in English and four which are highly inconsistent. By and large, is it the vowel letters or the consonant letters that are more consistent?

3. In Chapter 10, pages 265–66, we noted that bifurcations in pronunciation enrich the language with new words. Are there also sometimes bifurcations in spelling, in which a word with more than one meaning comes to be spelled in different ways, though remaining the same in pronunciation? Look up the etymologies of the following pairs: *errant–arrant, crumby–crummy, coin–coign, born–borne.*

4. The following sentences are from written sources. Each can be interpreted in two radically different ways. Read them aloud, adding the unwritten elements (accents or intonations) that will make the meanings clear:

   a. *Several cities have imported taxicabs propelled by light diesel engines.*

   Meanings: 'possess imported taxicabs'; 'have performed the action of importing cabs.'

   b. *Physics and biology surely provide basic stuff for the critical mind of the humanist. Only science, to its own misfortune, is presently out of bounds for him.* (Just the second sentence.)

   Meanings: 'but science'; 'science alone.'

   c. *Teixidor seems to feel that Ramirez himself would never have consented.*

   Meanings: 'Ramirez, as far as he himself was concerned'; 'not even as important a person as Ramirez.'

5. Contrast the stage at which a particular sign (something like Λ)

could be given the interpretation 'peak, apex, vertex, top, cap, summit' with the stage at which it could be given the interpretation 'peak, peek, pique, Peke.'

6. The units of writing, unlike those of speech, are often the creation of individuals. Consult any good encyclopedia, under **Cherokee** or **Sequoya,** for an account of the Cherokee syllabary (see page 289).

7. Do languages differ in the efficiency with which they can be written in syllables by contrast with distinctive sounds? Consider the variety of syllable types in English. Assume that each syllable (*ta, tab, tack, tam,* and so on) requires a separate and distinct symbol.

8. Young children must be taught to read, and they must also be taught words that they do not already know in their speech. Should these two things be combined in the initial steps of learning to read? Explain. How does your school system teach reading, by the whole-word method, by phonics, or in some other way? Are slow readers a problem? Does your school have a program for teaching rapid reading? What devices are used?

9. If you know a system of shorthand, explain and demonstrate what kind of writing it is.

10. Intending **Basque,** a typist writes **Bask.** Intending *weigh* the same typist writes *weight.* What two contrary tendencies do these misspellings represent?

11. Art Linkletter quoted someone as having written *He's such a good writer that he won the Pullet Surprise.*[30] Comment.

12. Make a list of homonymic pairs or sets such as *troupe–troop, review–revue, plum–plumb, use–ewes–youse–yews, seer–sear–cere–sere–Cyr,* and discuss the advantages and disadvantages of the spellings.

For further reading

Chadwick, John. 1960. *The Decipherment of Linear B* (London: Cambridge University Press).

---

[30] Credited to Linkletter by Leo Rosten, *Rome Wasn't Burned in a Day* (Garden City, N.Y.: Doubleday, 1972), p. 50.

Dewey, Godfrey. 1971. *English Spelling: Roadblock to Reading* (New York: Teachers College Press, Columbia University).

Diringer, David. 1968. *The Alphabet: A Key to the History of Mankind,* 3rd ed. (New York: Philosophical Library).

Doblhofer, Ernst. 1961. *Voices in Stone: The Decipherment of Ancient Scripts and Writings* (New York: Viking).

Gelb, Ignace J. 1963. *A Study of Writing,* 2nd ed. (Chicago: University of Chicago Press).

Kavanagh, James F., and Ignatius G. Mattingly (eds.). 1972. *Language by Ear and by Eye* (Cambridge, Mass.: M.I.T. Press).

Ogg, Oscar. 1971. *The 26 Letters* (New York: Thomas Y. Crowell).

Scragg, D. G. 1974. *A History of English Spelling* (New York: Harper & Row).

Smith, Frank. 1971. *Understanding Reading: A Psycholinguistic Study of Reading and Learning to Read* (New York: Holt, Rinehart & Winston).

LANGUAGE AND THE PUBLIC INTEREST 12

Since language is the property of everyone, everyone claims the privilege of holding opinions about it and defending the true faith. After all, the rules of language are rules of behaving in public; and like other forms of public behavior, the rights tend to be sharply culled from the wrongs. They may be justified by history or good taste or effective communication, sanctioned (like pornography) according to local or national standards, taught wisely or pedantically, enforced by persuasion or compulsion. What they always represent is some form of interference in ways of speaking and writing, with rewards for compliance and penalties for defiance. Effective interference expresses the will of some group or groups.

As there is scarcely any group in a society that is not affected to some degree by the way it uses language or the way language is used about it, the forces that would regulate usage are a tangle of clashes, temporary alliances, advances, and retreats. Every "ought" in language promotes an interest of some kind—the culture-imparting of education, the image-making of commerce and politics, the conflict-easing (or suppressing) of government, the fact-defining and truth-conveying of science, law, and political reform.

Each such interest develops a program of sorts, even sometimes a code of explicit rules, with which it confronts the rest of the world. But within its confines, which may be as narrow as a street gang or as wide as a whole society, it regulates its members covertly. A language or dialect is imprinted on an individual by the speakers with whom he identifies himself. Its authority is informal. It needs no formulated rules but serves as a model to follow and acts immediately—through the surprise, incomprehension, or amusement of its users—to drive offenders back into line.

Informal-internal authority is inseparable from the speech level or geographical or occupational dialect that enforces it. It may be oriented in any direction: a literary speaker may be ridiculed into being colloquial or a colloquial one into being literary. Until he learns the parlance every newcomer is made to feel out of place.

Formal-external authority, on the other hand, is self-conscious. Rules are its stock in trade. It comes into existence where informal authority cannot be exercised in the normal way. Informal authority depends on the overpowering effect of the many on the few. One newcomer in a community does not need a school to teach her how to speak; nor does the youngest child in a family where everyone else is more versed in the language than she is require more than their presence to keep her straight. But where large groups of aspirants are isolated from their models, the latter must assume artificial forms—codified rules and the means to transmit them, by schooling if the learning problem is complex, by mere publicity if it is simple.

THE IMPOSITION OF LANGUAGE

Imposing a dialect

Hell is for those who are offered the light but spurn it. The heathens are blameless if they ignore a gospel that they have never heard, but damnation awaits our neighbors who have been shown the way and refuse to take it. Speakers of a foreign language are like the heathens; they are forgivable because their only fault has been the lack of opportunity to learn to talk as we do. We resent the speakers of some unfamiliar dialect of our own language because they have had the opportunity—they prove this by the fact that we can usually understand them—but have obviously misapplied it. They don't get things quite right—something about their intonation or the way they drawl their vowels or gesture a shade too slowly or too fast fails to measure up.

So we do what we can to bring them into line, as we may once have been brought into line ourselves (if we were not lucky enough to be born to a family that already spoke Parisian French or Tuscan Italian or Received Southern British). The method is not necessarily crude or heartless and its human targets are not necessarily victims: there are always learners—outsiders moving in, younger generations moving up—and they may be as eager to take as we are to give. Especially when the gift is advertised as part of the "cultural heritage" with prestige at stake. The art object in question is an establishment dialect, the "standard," which nearly every society sees fit to impose in the schools and to promote through the great army of language wholesalers: the reporters of news, writers of stories, preachers of sermons, and pleaders of cases and causes. In most modern societies the teaching of the standard language—including writing—probably absorbs more educational resources than any other single effort.

To the extent that it is codified, the substance of what is taught is known as normative or prescriptive grammar. Textbooks embodying it—which are a mixture of description along traditional lines and comparisons of good and bad usage—make up the great bulk of writing on language, and go back to its very beginnings. In the ancient world they were mostly individual products, but with the Renaissance there came a change. An epidemic of learned societies swept Italy and spread across Europe—"academies," they were called, each with special interests ranging from meteorology to the study of Petrarch. Two of the later Italian academies were devoted largely to matters of language: the Florentine Academy, founded in 1540, and the Accademia della Crusca, founded in 1582 and still in existence. These two were influential in establishing Tuscan as the standard dialect of Italy, and served as models for similar bodies in other countries: the ones still active include the French Academy, founded in 1630 largely at the instance of Cardinal Richelieu; the Spanish Academy, founded in 1713; and the Swedish Academy, founded in 1786. The academies were a reaction to the collapse of Latin, and had as their aim the "defense" and "purification" of the new vernaculars. Attempts to establish similar bodies in Germany (1617), England (around 1712), and the United States (1821) were failures.

With their official charters, the academies represented the earliest intervention of governments in matters of language. The existing academy with the widest reach today is the Spanish Academy, with thirteen affiliated bodies in Latin America besides Puerto Rico and the Philippines, a permanent commission recognized by the governments of nine countries, and interests that include establishing leagues for the defense of the language even in certain cities of the United States that have a large Hispanic population.[1] For all the excessively pedantic tone of pronouncements by official bodies, the academies, through the dictionaries and grammars they have published, have supported a great deal of useful linguistic work.

---

[1] Guitarte and Torres Quintero 1968.

In America it has been up to the schools not only to implement the standard but up to a point to set it, for lack of any official body to make the decisions. For teachers secure in their knowledge of correct usage it was enough to say, "Do as I do." But for others it was a case of "Do as I say," and this demanded a code, embodied either as *lists* of things to say or not to say, or as *rules* to figure them out. The lists were easy to draw up. The rules called for an analytical understanding that too few teachers and textbook writers were capable of. Many misconceptions found their way into the code. Here are some examples (not, of course, subscribed to by those who knew better):

1. "A *pre*position is something that is put *before*. Therefore a preposition cannnot be used to end a sentence." Here the name supersedes the fact. If a man is called Paddleford, by definition he paddles a ford.

2. "The possessive must be used with the gerund when the subject of the latter is expressed: *John's saying that annoyed me,* not *°John saying that annoyed me.*" If obeyed to the letter and applied to pronouns (the other-than-personal kind) this would yield *°I don't approve of this's being done so carelessly, °Any fewer's voting that way would be a disaster.*

3. "A preposition cannot be compared. Therefore **nearer** and **nearest** in such expressions as *°nearer the front* and *°nearest home* should carry a *to: nearer to the front, nearest to home.*" Besides the fact that these forms have been used for over two centuries, the formulators of the rule seem to have forgotten that *-er* and *-est* are only one kind of comparison. The rule would also exclude *He was so near death,* in view of what happens with other prepositions when we attempt to combine them with *so: °so of,* and *°so under* are as bad as *°of-er, °under-est.*

Teaching usage by incompletely formulated and ineptly explained rules often *creates* mistakes: "Grammar mattered even more to Miss Mapes than to most teachers. She jumped Lloyd Furman so effectively for saying *He don't* and *It don't* that she drove him one day into a *They doesn't.*"[2] For a student who only half understands what a grammatical object is, it does no good to say, "Use *whom,* not *who,* when there is a verb or preposition that takes the form in question as its object." Hypergenteelisms such as the almost-standard secretarial *Whom shall I say is calling?* are the result.

---

[2] *The New Yorker* (24 May 1947), p. 61.

Since rules are hard to teach, good conduct in language is most often upheld by explicit prohibitions. If teachers cannot serve students as a model of what to do, they can at least memorize a list of things that the students are not to do and crack the whip if they do them. Guidebooks set forth the do's and don'ts of language, and some, such as Fowler's *Dictionary of Modern English Usage*[3] or Bernstein's *The Careful Writer*[4] are useful.

But all too often by the time an interloper makes the blacklist, the cause has already been lost. The "error" cannot be listed until somebody takes note of it, and that will not be until enough people are accepting it to attract attention. Once it wins a beachhead all the unconscious processes of adaptation get under way: it crowds into a bit of semantic territory and backs its rivals into their mountain fastnesses. From then on, when the special meaning comes to mind, it is hard to resist using the special expression. Take the phrase *part and parcel,* frowned upon as redundant: *part* alone is supposedly enough. Yet **Alaska is part of the United States** is a colorless geopolitical fact while **Alaska is part and parcel of the United States** is an assertion of sovereignty: the Alaskans had better not try to secede, and the Russians had better stay home.

Some additional examples, culled from high-school and college handbooks:

1. **"She claims that she was cheated.** Use **says, declares, maintains,** etc." But *claim* connotes skepticism on the part of the speaker. The other verbs cannot substitute for it.

2. **"Dont blame the accident on me.** Say **Don't blame me for the accident."** The value of **blame on** is that it enables the speaker to maneuver *me* to the end of the sentence, a more effective position for emphasis.

3. "Avoid **the reason is because;** say **the reason is that."** It is odd that, of all adverb clauses, this one should be singled out for reprobation. No one objects to **the time is when, the place is where,** or **the question is why. Is** has the same linking function in all of them.

Concentration on errors is like the concentration on sin in an old-time religion. The list of thou-shalt-nots is somewhat longer than the Ten Commandments but still brief enough so that one can substitute learning them by heart for the more arduous task of acquiring a command of a second dialect of English.

---

[3] Fowler 1926 and 1965.
[4] Bernstein 1965.

If drawing up a grammatical Baedeker of places to avoid as a way of not having to teach when to visit them and when to stay away is not a sound educational practice, why is it tolerated? Perhaps one reason is the same as why students study for exams instead of studying a course. When the men of Gilead took the passes of Jordan after defeating the Ephraimites they tested those who tried to filter back by asking each one to pronounce the word *shibboleth.* Whoever said *sibboleth* was killed—betrayed by his dialect. The penalties in modern societies are not that severe, but a simple language test with answers that can be marked by rote suffices to tell whether one comes from a proper background. For some social purposes, knowing the correct answers is as good as knowing what the course is about.

This is distressing to linguists with a social conscience. They complain that language should not be downgraded "to the level of table manners," and point out that children often bring to school a richer conception of language than that of many of their teachers. For children it is instrumental (a way of getting things done), regulative (a vehicle for rules of behavior), interactional (a means of keeping in touch with others), personal (an expression of the self), heuristic (a key to learning about the environment), and representational (a channel for imparting information). The teacher's insistence on the ritual function is unfamiliar and disaffecting.[5] Here is where linguistics can help teachers play their authoritarian role more effectively by giving them a breadth of appreciation to match the child's and the understanding necessary to intellectualize it.

The teacher needs to be thoroughly familiar with the regional standard in addition to the universal written standard and to be aware of other dialects and their scales of acceptability, especially the ones that are native to the students. Beyond that, the chief requirement is an ability to make the students see their language objectively. This means overcoming the "tertiary response," the defensiveness of those who regard their way of talking as an extension of their personalities and any criticism of it as a criticism of themselves. It also means disarming the notions of superiority cherished by other students who already command the regional standard. It is ethically correct and linguistically sound to instill an equal respect for all dialects as forms of language that one puts on and takes off at the behest of the community. One device is the enlightened bidialectalism suggested in an earlier chapter (pages 221–22). Another is the capsule lecture that justifies a fault—on all grounds except those of convention—before proceeding to correct it, thus wiping out any stigma that it may carry. For example, if the teacher is working with a newly

---

[5] Halliday 1973, pp. 9–21.

arrived group that habitually uses *workin'*, *sellin'*, and *playin'*, he might explain the situation like this:

> Of course everyone around here says *working, selling,* and *playing,* and that is the way we must do it except at home and on the playground, but if you slip up and someone smiles at you just remember—and keep it to yourself—that the joke is really on him, because *workin'* is historically correct. Some members of the upper classes in England still use it. What happened is that there were two rival forms of pronunciation, just one of which was favored by the schools and became the standard about two hundred years ago. But they never could drive out the other form and I'd bet that if you listened closely to the people here you'd notice that they use it sometimes. They would probably never say *Whatcha composin'?* to a composer, but it wouldn't surprise me at all to hear them say *Whatcha cookin'?* to a cook.

An example or two like this is enough to break the ice. Such a constructive approach takes imagination, sympathy, and a little more knowledge than the ordinary, but it achieves a justifiable educational objective, which no fanatical hunting of grammatical scapegoats can do.

Imposing a language

Formal attempts to impose one dialect as standard on all the speakers of a language are usually superfluous, because the conditions that make it desirable—closer communication and greater economic and political interdependence—are already at work in informal ways to bring about a kind of standardization. Yet for various reasons and in numerous places people have felt that attaining a standard by unpremeditated accommodation would be too slow a process, and reformers have stepped in. The impulse may come from a burgeoning nationalism that seeks identity in a common language, or from a centralization of government with the rising need to communicate with all citizens quickly and efficiently, or from a technological or commercial interdependence that must no longer be hobbled by a division of tongues.

During the nineteenth and early part of the twentieth centuries the typical kind of interference was that which promoted the spread of literacy, a consequence of the democratization that followed the American and French revolutions. Its mechanical genius was the printing press, which demands standardization: a single dialect and a uniform spelling. Its scope was usually confined to a single language; the speakers all more or less understood one another already and reforms were relatively painless.

Take the standardization undertaken in Norway by Ivar Aasen a century ago. Norway was emerging from domination by Denmark, and the Norwegian peasantry had become a political force. Aasen sought an authentic Norwegian language with which to replace the Danish that was still used by the ruling classes, and he found it by synthesizing Norwegian dialects in a language that all patriotic Norwegians would feel was natural and right. The result was the New Norse, or *Landsmål,* which is still extensively used.[6]

Another example is the re-Latinization of Romanian at about the same time.[7] Though Romanian was originally a Latin language, over the centuries it absorbed a great deal from Turks, Greeks, and neighboring Slavs, especially by word borrowing. As in Norway, the upsurge of nationalistic feeling brought with it a desire for an authentic Romanian, free of non-Latin elements. The other Latin languages, especially French, were imitated, and not only was much taken over in the way of vocabulary, but even the syntax was modified to some extent—with such changes as the simplification of the verb system, the dropping of the neuter gender, and the strengthening of the infinitive at the expense of the subjunctive.

An example from this century is provided by Turkey, among the sweeping reforms carried out by the dictator Kemal Atatürk. In 1932, after he had abolished the traditional Persian script and replaced it with Roman, he created a Turkish Linguistic Society, to which he appointed party members and school teachers, and gave it the job of revamping Turkish.[8]

More typical of the problems faced by language planners now is the rise not of submerged classes but of submerged peoples. It is no longer dialect against dialect but language against language, and easy adjustments are impossible. Most of the new nations that have emerged and consolidated themselves since the Second World War—about forty in Africa alone, besides Indonesia, Israel, Pakistan, Malaysia, the Philippines, and many more—contain segments of population that speak mutually unintelligible languages. The same problem confronts some political entities of long standing, such as India and China, whose loosely federated parts the new nationalism has pulled more closely together. It is difficult to make any one of the native languages official. At the same time, nationalistic fervor demands that the language of the colonial power be thrown off. The upshot is that these nations have had to decide what language to adopt and then seek ways to have it accepted by persons who do not speak it natively.[9]

Conditions around the world are so diverse that no two countries face

---

[6] See Haugen 1972, pp. 191–214.
[7] Pointed out by Professor Dumitru Chitoran of the University of Bucharest.
[8] Haugen 1972, p. 170.
[9] See Ramos 1961.

identical problems and no one typical case can be cited. Two examples will show how wide the range of solutions can be.

First, Israel. In less than thirty years this small country accomplished the most remarkable feat of linguistic engineering in history. No one vernacular language existed among the far-flung Jewish people who were migrating to the new homeland; but Hebrew, which died out as a spoken language more than two thousand years ago, still lived in the Jewish liturgy—as Latin did in the Roman Catholic Church. Here was enough of a unifying force to be the best candidate for adoption. The schools took on the job, and immigrants from all over Europe and the Near East, as well as the older generations of settlers, were taught what could almost as easily have been an artificial language. One thing that eased the transition somewhat was that the former languages of the immigrants were nearly all of a pan-European type, so that the remodeled language was essentially European in its lexical representation of the world, though Hebrew in its sounds and grammatical structure.[10]

Second, the Philippines. Over three hundred years of Spanish rule and forty years of American rule failed to establish either Spanish or English as more than rather widely accepted trade languages. Just after independence in 1946, the census showed six languages spoken by at least half a million people each, the chief one being Tagalog with about seven million speakers. The question of which one should be adopted had been officially posed a decade earlier with the creation of an Institute of National Language. With its preponderance in numbers and its strategic position in central Luzon, Tagalog was favored from the first and in 1937 was proclaimed the basis of the new National Language to be taught in all primary and secondary schools beginning in 1940.[11]

Of the other countries formerly under colonial rule, some have elected, officially or unofficially, to stay with the language of the colonial power, either as the dominant language or as an equal partner with the native language or languages. Malay was legally established in 1967 in Malaysia, but English continues to be recognized in the courts and in Parliament; the ties with England are close, and anyway only 15 percent of the population is Malay, the rest being mostly Indians and Chinese who would rather stay with English.[12] The constitution of India decreed that in 1965 Hindi was to become the official language, with other languages,

---

[10] For example, the Hebrew word *taḥana* 'station' in the sense of a stopping place was still semantically close to the root meaning of stopped movement. But when terms were needed for 'radio station,' 'police station,' 'gas station,' 'service station,' and 'first aid station,' the newly formed compounds used *taḥana* in this extended sense just as in most European languages, along with the equivalents for 'police,' 'gas,' 'service,' and other 'stations.' See Rosén 1969, especially pp. 95–96.

[11] See Frei 1959, and Villa Panganiban 1957.

[12] New York *Times* (16 April 1967), p. 10.

including English, accorded a special status; but opposition from non-Hindi-speaking Indians was so strong that English has kept its dominant position. Indonesia, like Malaysia, adopted Malay as its official language, and has enjoyed much more success in promoting its use; competition from the colonial language (Dutch) was lighter, and Malay was already in extensive use as a lingua franca. In Algeria, which became independent of France in 1962, French continued to be the language of the law courts till 1971. Algeria brings us to Africa, where south of the Sahara the linguistic situation in many areas is chaotic. Niger, formerly under French rule, was still groping for a single national language in 1973. The exclusive official status still enjoyed by European languages in countries such as Guinea (French), Senegal (French), Nigeria (English), and Sierra Leone (English) testifies to the difficulty of getting agreement on which of the many native languages to adopt. The Sudan closed the Christian mission schools because they were making it more difficult to nationalize Arabic in a country one part of which was already split among more than a hundred different languages.[13] The psychological problems are acute and painful; language loyalty competes with efficiency, and tribal conflicts are inflamed by the lack of a common medium of communication. Kenya, with over sixty tribal languages and both Swahili and English officially recognized, has just such problems of national cohesion. As the Nairobi *Times* commented, "The moment we all acquire a national language, all suspicion between us will disappear and we will talk, think, act, dress and see like one giant—one big Kenyan."[14]

In firmly established societies the imposition of a language generally takes a more tranquil course. The Soviet Union has allowed its constituent republics to keep their own languages and encouraged them to develop regional literatures,[15] while promoting Russian as the national language. In Canada an accommodation has finally been reached between English and French whereby both languages are official and both are required in schools. The situation in China is somewhat like the one described in Norway, on a vastly greater scale. Though numerous mutually unintelligible dialects are tolerated, the schools teach all subjects from the first grade on in a conventionalized variety of the Peking dialect and use a Latinized alphabet to help children with the pronunciation. Here the great advantage of the regular Chinese writing has proved itself: not being tied to any one of the dialects, it is used throughout the country and is understood in other areas as well, such as Japan, which have adapted it as their own system.[16] Nevertheless the goal is eventually—

---

[13] Knappert 1968, p. 66.
[14] Reported in the Los Angeles *Times,* January 11, 1978.
[15] Fodor 1966, p. 22.
[16] See Wang 1973 and 1974.

when the standard language is in general use everywhere—to shift to the Latinized alphabet.

In the United States, minority languages have had a somewhat harder time owing to racial attitudes. The Indian languages were submerged along with their speakers. Immigrant groups have managed to maintain their languages for a time, but the communities where French or German or Swedish was formerly spoken have gradually given them up, with church services in the old language usually the last vestige to go. English has imposed itself not so much through official policy as by simply swamping the competition. But in twenty-one of the fifty states there were laws sitting quietly in the background to ensure the swamping. In seven states a teacher who tried to teach bilingually was subject to legal punishment. With the rise of conscious ethnicity, minority languages are getting more consideration from federal, state, and local governments. In 1972 New York City invested heavily in a new bilingual education program to help its quarter of a million Puerto Rican children, and Massachusetts enacted a law requiring instruction in any foreign language wherever a certain minimum of its native speakers were enrolled in a given school; this was mainly designed to help the Portuguese- and Spanish-speaking minorities. A similar act in California the same year was broadened by the Bilingual-Bicultural Education Act of 1976 to aid the 250,000 school children whose primary language was other than English. The Federal Government has funded bilingual projects through the Bilingual Education Act of 1968. The Supreme Court in 1974 interpreted the 1964 Civil Rights Act to require bilingual instruction.

Even in countries with fairly stable governments, attempts to impose a single language can be both a cause and an effect of social unrest. China seems to be the exception; the shoulder-to-the-wheel philosophy of that country has extended even to language, and teams of students are to be found visiting workers and other segments of the society to encourage them in learning and using the standard—there is very little resentment of the fact that those who already speak the standard have an advantage, and the eventual disappearance of the local languages is faced without apparent concern.[17] But in other countries any such program is likely to have explosive consequences. In Spain the Basques and Catalans were the backbone of resistance to Franco during the Civil War of 1936–39 and still fight for autonomy. In Belgium the resentment toward the compulsory extension of French is high, and though it has not led to any armed insurrection, it has led to the fall of more than one government.[18]

[17] Charles A. Ferguson, "Language and Linguistics in China." Lecture at Linguistic Colloquium, Stanford University, 21 November 1974.
[18] Murray Seeger, "Language Split Bedevils Belgian Politics," Los Angeles *Times*, October 18, 1978, Part 1–A, pp. 1, 4–5.

In Great Britain there are the Welsh and Scottish national movements and in Ireland the attempts at literary resurgence of Gaelic. In Italy five separatist groups—identified by a language or dialect—clamor for independence from Rome: Sicily, Sardinia, Aosta Valley (French-speaking), Alto Adige (South Tyrol—German), Friuli-Venezia (near Trieste).[19]

The division of tongues, with the resulting cultural and political divisiveness, is one of the greatest problems facing the human race. And the attempts to liquidate it by force are an equal problem.

Constructed languages

What governments have tried to do with the whip, a few intellectuals have tried from time to time to do with the carrot: achieve a common tongue by inventing one so easy to learn that all would be eager to adopt it. Some proposals have been sheer romanticism; one of the most recent is Lincos, a "language for cosmic intercourse," brought forth in 1960.[20] The best known is Esperanto. It was invented by a Russian physician, Ludwig Zamenhof, and first appeared in print in 1887. Zamenhof made the sensible decision to keep words as European-looking as possible; Esperanto succeeded because it had the appearance of a natural language and a familiar Western feel about it, in striking contrast with unlikely-looking and highly abstract predecessors. Among the latter was Volapük, actually the first interlanguage to gain widespread attention. Some of the erstwhile followers of Volapük then set out to devise a system that would be free of the artificialities that plagued even Esperanto. They took their cue from Mundo Lingue (1889) which survived only in its master concept, which was that a pan-European language already lay hidden in the common features of the languages of Western Europe, and needed only to be coaxed out. The result was a succession of undertakings all along similar lines: Idiom Neutral in 1902, Occidental in 1925, Novial in 1928, Mondial in 1943, and Interlingua in 1951. Idiom Neutral was the most serious rival of Esperanto in its day, and Interlingua, the product of the International Auxiliary Language Association, has inherited the mantle. An advocate of Interlingua describes it as follows:

> [The interlanguage] is the international vocabulary of the contemporary European languages, largely technical terminology of latinate origin, reduced to the most neutral forms and using a grammar which recognizes features that are shared by all the source languages, but rejects those

[19] Wendy Owen, "5 Italian Separatist Groups Gain Strength," Los Angeles *Times*, July 8, 1979, Part 1–A, pp. 10–11.
[20] Freudenthal 1960.

which are idiosyncratic. It is not surprising then that the interlanguage is
. . . readable at sight to any educated individual who knows one or two
of the languages of Western Europe.[21]

Neither Esperanto nor Interlingua is a *universal* language on logical
principles as conceived in the first attempts that were made in the seven-
teenth century. They are European, and what makes them possible and
useful as standby languages in the Western world is a European quality
that sets them apart. The gulf between this world and other worlds is
portrayed by an eminent Sinologist:

> . . . With his initiation into the [Chinese] language, the student enters a
> world of unfamiliarity. He early finds that . . . the assumptions he thought
> were universal prove to be Western, idiosyncratic and confined in space
> and time to his own heritage. Every basic assumption he has been accus-
> tomed to make needs re-examination and reformulation in the Chinese
> mold before it becomes applicable or useful.[22]

The problem is the broadly Whorfian one of conceptual structures and
their embodiment not so much in the superficialities of grammar and
morphology as in the lexicon. Instead of Chinese, any native language
of Australia, South America, or Central Africa would have served for
comparison. There is no basis yet for a world-wide auxiliary language
that would not be almost as hard to learn as a totally unfamiliar language.
By the time the basis is laid, the need may have passed—a prediction
that can be taken in either a hopeful or an ominous sense.

The dictionary

In a country without the language controls of a government policy, an
academy, or a prestige dialect, a social drive for "authority" in establishing a standard language may yet arise. In the United States the dictionary
became a force of control, with *Webster's New International Dictionary*
once dubbing itself the "supreme authority." But in 1961 the third
edition departed from the traditional role and adopted a new objective
policy in recording the language. The controversy that raged for several
years after the appearance of the *Third* testified to the deep-seated attitudes of the public toward what a dictionary is supposed to represent.[23]
That traditional role deserves examination.

Lists of words are both easier to make and easier to understand than

---

[21] Esterhill 1974.
[22] Dobson 1973, p. 8.
[23] Sledd and Ebbitt 1962 provide a rich sampling of the controversy.

grammars. The first overt linguistic interest that the average person acquires is in words; he has learned the framework of his speech and forgotten how he did it, but all his life he is confronted with new terms. So he finds a dictionary a prime necessity in trade, profession, and pastime (word games are almost the only point where linguistics and entertainment meet—crossword puzzles rival schools as promoters of dictionary sales). Few people need a grammar, but involve a man in a lawsuit over the meaning of a word in a contract and he craves authority fast. What importance the publishers of dictionaries have attached to this may be seen in a blurb for *Webster's Second* that appeared in 1940, citing testimonials from the supreme courts of six states.

But the real key to the authoritative position of the dictionary in American life lies in our history as a colony of England. Cut off from English-speaking cultural centers during the first decades of their national existence and insecure in their own ways of speech, Americans looked for written standards, like people who lack confidence in their social graces and turn to Emily Post and her sister columnists.

With such a background, it is not surprising that word lists were compiled earlier and have attained wider circulation than any other books about language. The following concerns the influence wielded on pronunciation by the dictionary of John Walker, published in 1791:

> Not only does Walker's pronunciation prevail today in many individual words (. . . his recommended pronunciations of *soot, wreath, slabber, coffer, gold, veneer, cognizance, boatswain, construe, lieutenant, nepotism,* although all admittedly not general usage in his time, are now standard American pronunciation); but also Walker's efforts to secure an exact pronunciation of unstressed vowels have had a tremendous effect on modern American pronunciation.[24]

Something of the same authority was granted to the spelling in Noah Webster's *American Dictionary of the English Language* (1828). (Webster was already the author of the *American Spelling Book*—80 million copies sold to the schools during the nineteenth century.) His preference for simplified forms laid the foundations for the differences between American and British orthography down to the present day:

-ize for *-ise* as in *civilize*
-ter for *-tre* as in *theater*
-or for *-our* as in *honor*
-k for *-que* as in *check*
-s for *-c* as in *defense*
jail for *gaol*

---

[24] Sheldon 1947, p. 145.

So great was the impact of Webster's work that "Webster's" became virtually synonymous with "dictionary."

The content of a dictionary is determined not only by what words and idioms are extant in the language (and of course the resources of the publishers) but also by the need the dictionary is intended to serve and the amount of information available to satisfy it. Dictionary-makers rely heavily on other published studies of words, but the real shapers are the people who use the book and the kinds of information they want. Here is where the craving for authority has left its mark.

The standard dictionary gives five items of information: spelling, pronunciation, part of speech, derivation, and meaning, usually in that order except that the last two are about as often reversed. Leaving out the part of speech for the moment, we can say that the remaining four are where the average user looks for final pronouncements. If she needs to write a word but has forgotten how to spell it, or sees a word and is unsure of its pronunciation, the dictionary fills her wants. If she is curious about the word as a word, she will probably look for its origin; etymology is the branch of linguistics that has been with us long enough to arouse a bit of popular interest. And if the word is new to her, she will want it defined or illustrated.

The order in which the four items are given has had certain consequences. Putting the spelling first has abetted the tendency of the average person to take the written word as primary and the spoken form as an unstable sort of nuance attached to it. In this and other ways the four-way order emphasizes externals. Spelling is the written trace of a word. Pronunciation is its linguistic form, like the shape that a die puts on a coin, but has little or nothing to do with value. Derivation is a snatch of history, sometimes without relevance. The value system, or meaning, comes last, and in reality includes so much that what the dictionary offers is hardly more than a sample, a small reminder that generally suffices only because the average user already knows the language and can guess at what the dictionary leaves out.

Webster's Third did not escape these shortcomings, but it did break with the authoritarian tradition and follow undeviatingly a trail dear to the heart of linguists that was blazed in 1947 by the *American College Dictionary*—still one of the best of the desk-size volumes—with the announcement that "no dictionary founded on the methods of modern scholarship can prescribe as to usage; it can only inform on the basis of the facts of usage."[25] In pronunciations and definitions, and above all in the words it included, the *Third* abandoned the pretense of standing as a lexical canon. If a term was pronounced in a certain way by a sub-

_____

[25] *American College Dictionary*, p. ix.

stantial portion of the population, the *Third* recorded it, and it did the same with meaning. Of course, *any* up-to-date dictionary is bound to give this impression when it first appears—even of the *Second* it was said that it "went to the street" for its new words and meanings. But in the two areas of pronunciation and meaning the *Third* discarded all the trappings of purism. One criticism fairly leveled at it was that, having decided to cover the spectrum, it ought to have labeled the colors more carefully, as the *American College Dictionary* did; it became harder than before to tell when a term was regarded as respectable and when it was not, or what level of speech it belonged to: extreme vulgarity was marked, as for **piss** or **fart,** but most other degrees of formality and informality were not, as for **jerk** or **gripe.** Reacting to this omission, the *American Heritage Dictionary* (1969) employed a "usage panel" whose votes appear as part of the entries of disputed items (for example, 92 percent of the panel oppose **infer** in the sense of 'imply').

In one area the *Third* remained almost as authoritarian as ever: spelling. To be consistent, if everyone's pronunciation everywhere was to be used in striking statistical averages, everyone's spelling everywhere—in informal notes and personal correspondence as well as in things intended for print—ought to have been collected and digested before deciding what spellings were to be recorded. Many people "carelessly" write **principle** for **principal, lead** for **led,** and **kinda** for **kind of,** just as they "carelessly" say /pʌlpət/ for /pʊlpət/ or /kanstəbəl/ for /kʌnstəbəl/, but the careless pronunciations are recorded and the careless spellings are not. In spelling, the dictionary is not a dictionary in the modern sense but a style manual, an authoritative guide.

But a dictionary that is supposed to return a profit for its publisher can carry analysis only so far. Thus users of the *Third* cannot tell, if they look up **afire,** that they are not permitted to say °*an afire house.* Nor can they find the opposing categories of temporal-spatial made clear between **long, lengthy, short,** or **brief** visit, but only **long** or **short** pencil. And what of a dim category of sex in the fact that a man can have **children** but only a woman can have **babies?** As of 1979, only one English dictionary—with a reduced vocabulary and a special aim—had attempted to make up for these deficiencies: *The Longman Dictionary of Contemporary English* (1978).

There is a similar problem with definitions. A substantial part of them fail to define carefully enough to exclude gross errors. Take the verb **to wage.** *Webster's Third* defines it as 'to carry on actions that constitute or promote,' and this is followed by a series of typical objects: war, campaign, battle, filibuster. *The American Heritage Dictionary* says 'to engage in (a war or campaign).' The question is, can one wage an election, a seance, a conversation, or a seduction? Or even a fight? The *Third* does include **farmers still waging a losing fight with poor, stony land** among its examples, but while that is normal enough, there is a difference in acceptability between the following:

> Last night Hogan waged a fight against his political adversaries.

> All summer long, Hogan waged a continuous fight against his political adversaries.

It needs to be stated that whatever is waged has to be aggressive and sustained. *Battle* and *fight* are aggressive but too brief (though one might wage a series of battles); an investigation is sustained enough but is not inherently aggressive. On the other hand, *to wage a conversation* might be an effective figure of speech to describe what goes on between two very uninhibited talkers. The examples in dictionaries suggest the semantic range but fail to close it in. It does not take a perfectionist to see how much room there is for improvement in our dictionaries, even if the linguist's ideal is unattainable.

LANGUAGE AND EMPATHY

We often turn to dictionaries to settle a dispute about the appropriateness of a word or pronunciation, but we have few arbiters for language itself. And even though language has its ethic, for some reason we seldom pose it to ourselves in the ordinary terms of power and prestige or of good conduct and bad. We feel that we have a right to regulate the use of money in ways that will spread its benefits, for it is a creature of society and must respond to society's needs. But language is no less a medium of exchange, and like money was created by and for society. And like money it is subject to abuse and debasement.

The exchange of language is the sharing of experience. If we regard as the highest mark of civilization an ability to project ourselves into the mental and physical world of others, to share their thoughts, feelings, and visions, to sense their angers and encounter the same walls that shut them in and the same escapes to freedom, we must ask how language is to be used if we are to be civilized.

Though laws forbid the undue concentration of economic power, the only laws against the misuse of language have to do with the content of messages: obscenity, perjury, sedition, defamation in its various forms of libel and slander, and, recently, truth in advertising and lending. There are no laws against the unfair exploitation of language as language, in its essence. People may carry as many concealed verbal weapons as they like and strike with them as they please—far from being censured for it, they will be admired and applauded.

In a small, unstratified society the rule of equal access perhaps applies. No one is excessively rich in either material or verbal goods. In more complex societies it does not apply, because language, like wealth and color, is a weapon of *de facto* segregation. With the disappearance of the less visible tokens of birth and breeding, language has in some areas taken over their function of opening or closing the doors to membership in a ruling caste. There is no question that the Received Pronunciation of Southern British has been just such a badge of admission—this was the theme of Bernard Shaw's *Pygmalion* and its musical version, *My Fair Lady*. The lines are not so clearly drawn in America, but a rustic accent is enough to preclude employment in certain jobs.

Society recognizes the problem of equal access only through the unequal efforts of the schools. They are unequal because alongside of schools striving for an ethic of equality there are others striving for an ethic of charity that, for all its good intentions, only deepens class lines. The *public* effort for equal access must be toward the elimination of every sort of verbal snobbery. There is nothing intrinsically bad about words as such, and to exclude a form of speech is to exclude the person who uses it. The task of democratizing a society includes far more than speech forms, of course, but headway will be that much more difficult if we overlook the intricate ties of speech with everything else that spells privilege.

Public cures may be long in coming, but meanwhile some of the ills of unequal access can be avoided if we recognize our personal responsibility toward the sharing of experience through language. We can discharge it by trying as hard to meet our neighbors on their dialectal terms as we would try to meet foreigners on the terms of their languages. This means never using our superior verbal skill, if we have it, or our inheritance of a prestige dialect for which we never worked a day, to browbeat or establish a difference in status between our neighbors and us. It means remembering that language is the most public of all public domains, to be kept free at all costs of claims that would turn any part of it into the property of some exclusive club, whether of scientists, artisans, or the socially elect. The virtue of language is in being ordinary.

Key terms and concepts

informal-internal authority
formal-external authority
"standard" language
academies
national language

imposing a dialect
bilingual education
constructed languages
dictionary
ethical use of language

Additional remarks and applications

1. How do you react to a person who says *He don't, I won't go there no more, Who did they see? Me and Suzy don't like it.* If you react unfavorably, what is the basis for your disapproval? How does one strike a balance between two opposing demands: the need for uniformity in language and the equal right of each dialect to consideration and respect?

2. A study of *shall* and *will*[26] showed that *will* has always predominated in sentences of the *I will go* type, with *shall* only in recent times gaining a special favor in England. The effort to impose *shall* when the subject is *I* or *we* is now seen as a classic instance of pedantry. See if you can describe the ways in which you use *shall* and *will,* and compare them with the recommendations of any reference grammar or handbook that you can readily consult.

3. One scapegoat achieved fame in the slogan for a brand of cigarette: *Winston tastes good like a cigarette should.* This way of using *like* has long been common among English writers, including Shakespeare, but nowadays stirs feelings of guilt in many speakers. For those who would also feel uncomfortably formal if they replaced *Do it like I do it* with *Do it as I do it,* what is the two-word substitute for *like?* Can you think of another compromise expression that speakers or writers use in order to avoid both the "incorrect" expression and the uncomfortably formal "correct" one?

4. Would you regard the following as mistakes? *Tell him to kindly leave; a more perfect union; I'll explain whatever you ask about; Whenever Mary or John is at home, they answer the phone.* Decide how you would reword any that you would consider incorrect.

5. What is the fundamental difference between computer "languages" (which are of course constructed) and a constructed language such as Interlingua? What are some of the linguistic applications of computers?[27]

---

[26] Fries 1956–57.
[27] See, for example, Winograd 1974.

6. Look up *distrustful* in *Modern Guide to Synonyms and Related Words*[28] and study the discussion of *distrustful* and *mistrustful*. What does it reveal about the inadequacies of the definitions in most dictionaries? Is there any general meaning in the prefixes *dis-* and *mis-* that carries over into the contrast between *distrustful* and *mistrustful?*

7. *Webster's Third* defines the transitive sense of the verb *to hop* as 'to get upon by or as if by hopping: climb aboard.' The following fit the definition, but would you use them?

    a. The bus won't start until you hop it.
    b. I hopped the plane but got right off again because there was a bomb scare.
    c. The engineer hopped the train and we were soon in motion.
    d. The kids used to hop the old locomotive that stood in the park.

How about these?

    e. The best way to get there is to hop a plane.
    f. You can hop a freight without its costing you a nickel.
    g. I hopped a ride to Los Angeles.

Since you can't "climb aboard" a ride, there must be something that the dictionary has missed. See if you can figure it out, then consult the footnote.[29]

8. In July of 1974 the undersecretary of the treasury was on the point of warning the oil-producing countries that any new cutbacks in production would be regarded by the United States and other oil importers as an "unfriendly act." The State Department objected strongly and the wording was changed to a "counterproductive measure." Is the dictionary of any help in telling what the trouble was? Discuss.

For further reading

Connor, George Allen, and others. 1959. *Esperanto: The World Interlanguage*, 2nd ed. (New York: Yoseloff).

---

[28] New York: Funk and Wagnalls, 1968, p. 171.

[29] First, only a passenger does the hopping. Second, there has to be a journey with a destination. *Hop* shares some of the characteristics of *by* plus the name of a conveyance: *I hopped a plane = I went by plane;* that is why it is a bit unusual to have *hop* followed by the definite article except to refer to some regularly scheduled line *(I hopped the 9:45 and got there early).*

Fishman, Joshua A. (ed.). 1973. *Advances in Language Planning* (The Hague: Mouton).

Gerli, E. Michael, James E. Alatis, and Richard I. Brod (eds.). 1978. *Language in American Life* (Washington, D.C.: Georgetown University Press).

Giglioli, Pier Paolo (ed.). 1972. *Language and Social Context* (Harmondsworth, England: Penguin Books).

Gove, Philip B. 1967. *The Role of the Dictionary* (Indianapolis: Bobbs-Merrill).

Ohannessian, Sirarpi, and others (eds.). 1975. *Language Surveys in Developing Nations* (Arlington, Va.: Center for Applied Linguistics).

Rubin, Joan, and Roger W. Shuy (eds.). 1973. *Language Planning: Current Issues and Research* (Washington, D.C.: Georgetown University Press).

Schneider, Susan Gilbert. 1978. *Revolution, Reaction or Reform: The 1974 Bilingual Education Act* (Arlington, Va.: Center for Applied Linguistics).

REFERENCES

INTRODUCTION

Bateman, Donald Ray. 1966. "The Effects of a Study of a Generative Grammar upon the Structure of Written Sentences of Ninth and Tenth Graders," Ph.D. dissertation, Ohio State University, 1965, abstracted in *Linguistics* 26:21–22.

Carmichael, Leonard. 1966. "The Early Growth of Language Capacity in the Individual," in Eric H. Lenneberg (ed.), *New Directions in the Study of Language* (Cambridge, Mass.: M.I.T. Press).

Gleitman, Lila R., and Henry Gleitman. 1970. *Phrase and Paraphrase* (New York: W. W. Norton).

Lamendella, John T. 1975. *Introduction to the Neuropsychology of Language* (Rowley, Mass.: Newbury House).

CHAPTER 1

Arango Montoya, Francisco. 1972. "Lenguas y dialectos indígenas," *América Indígena* 32:1169–76.

Birdwhistell, Ray L. 1970. *Kinesics and Context* (Philadelphia: University of Pennsylvania Press).

Bruneau, Thomas. 1973. "Communicative Silence," *Journal of Communication* 23:17–46.

Jakobson, Roman. 1970. "Linguistics," in *Main Trends of Research in the Social and Human Sciences,* vol. 1 (The Hague: Mouton)

Lamendella, John T. 1975. *Introduction to the Neuropsychology of Language* (Rowley, Mass.: Newbury House).

Lehmann, W. P. 1973. "A Structural Principle of Language and Its Implications," *Language* 49:47–66.

Makkai, Adam. 1973. "A Pragmo-ecological View of Linguistic Structure and Language Universals," *Language Sciences* 27:9–22.

Sapir, Edward. 1921. *Language* (New York: Harcourt Brace Jovanovich).

Sebeok, Thomas A. 1962. "Coding in the Evolution of Signaling Behavior," *Behavioral Science* 7:430–42.

Wittmann, Henri. 1966. "Two Models of the Linguistic Mechanism," *Canadian Journal of Linguistics* 11:83–93.

CHAPTER 2

Anderson, Lambert. 1959. "Ticuna Vowels with Special Regard to the System of Five Tonemes," *Serie Linguística Especial,* No. 1 (Rio de Janeiro: Museu Nacional), 76–127.

Bolinger, Dwight. 1963. "Length, Vowel, Juncture," *Linguistics* 1:5–29.

Bullowa, Margaret. 1972. "From Communication to Language." Paper read at International Symposium on First Language Acquisition, Florence, Italy, manuscript p. 2.

Fillenbaum, Samuel. 1971. "Processing and Recall of Compatible and Incompatible Question and Answer Pairs," *Language and Speech* 14:256–65.

Fischer-Jørgensen, Eli. 1967. "Phonetic Analysis of Breathy (Murmured) Vowels in Gujarati," *Indian Linguistics* 28:71–139.

Fromkin, Victoria. 1973. "Slips of the Tongue," *Scientific American* 229: 110–17.

Lehiste, Ilse. 1972. "The Timing of Utterances and Linguistic Boundaries," *Journal of the Acoustical Society of America* 51:2018–24.

Lenneberg, Eric H. 1967. *Biological Foundations of Language* (New York: Wiley).

Sigurd, Bengt. 1963. "A Note on the Number of Phonemes," *Statistical Methods in Linguistics,* No. 2.

CHAPTER 3

Pak, Tae-Yong. 1971. "Convertibility Between Distinctive Features and Phonemes," *Linguistics* 66:97–114.

Thomas, David D. 1962. "On Defining the 'Word' in Vietnamese," *Van-hoa Nguyet-san* 11:519–23.

CHAPTER 4

Adams, Valerie. 1973. *An Introduction to Modern English Word Formation* (London: Longman).

Cazden, Courtney B. 1972. *Child Language and Education* (New York: Holt, Rinehart & Winston).

Greenbaum, Sidney. 1970. *Verb-Intensifier Collocations in English* (The Hague: Mouton).

————. 1974. "Some Verb-Intensifier Collocations in American and British English," *American Speech* 49:79–89.

Marchand, Hans. 1969. *The Categories and Types of Present-day English Word-Formation* (Munich: C. H. Beck).

Mitchell, T. F. 1971. "Linguistic 'Goings On': Collocations and Other Lexical Matters Arising on the Syntagmatic Record," *Archivum Linguisticum*. New series 2:35–69.

Van Lancker, Diana. 1979. "Idiomatic versus Literal Interpretations of Di-tropically Ambiguous Sentences," Manuscript.

CHAPTER 5

Algeo, John. 1972. *Problems in the Origins and Development of the English Language*, 2nd ed. (New York: Harcourt Brace Jovanovich).

Boxwell, Maurice. 1967. "Weri Pronoun System," *Linguistics* 29:34–43.

Friedrich, Paul. 1972. "Shape Categories in Grammar," *Linguistics* 77:5–21.

Longacre, Robert E. 1970. "Paragraph and Sentence Structure in New Guinea Highlands Languages," *Kivung* 3:150–63.

Osgood, Charles E. 1971. "Explorations in Semantic Space: A Personal Diary," *Journal of Social Issues* 27:5–64.

Pavel, Thomas G. 1973. "*Phèdre:* Outline of a Narrative Grammar," *Language Sciences* 28:1–6.

Powlinson, Paul S. 1965. "A Paragraph Analysis of a Yagua Folktale," *International Journal of American Linguistics* 31:109–18.

Ross, John R. 1970. "On Declarative Sentences," in R. Jacobs and P. Rosen-baum (eds.), *Readings in English Transformational Grammar* (Boston: Ginn).

Smith, Barbara Herstein. 1968. *Poetic Closure* (Chicago: University of Chicago).

Tervoort, Bernard Th. 1968. "You Me Downtown Movie Fun?" *Lingua* 21: 455–65.

van Dijk, Teun A. 1972. *Some Aspects of Text Grammars* (The Hague: Mouton).

Welmers, William E. 1950. "Notes on Two Languages in the Senufo Group," *Language* 26:126–46.

CHAPTER 6

Barber, Charles. 1964. *Linguistic Change in Present-day English* (University, Ala.: University of Alabama Press).

Durbin, Marshall. 1973. "Sound Symbolism in the Mayan Language Family," in Munro S. Edmonson (ed.), *Meaning in Mayan Languages: Ethnolinguistic Studies* (The Hague: Mouton).

Hill, A. A. 1973. "Some Thoughts on Segmentation of Lexical Meaning," *Annals of the New York Academy of Sciences* 211:269–78.

Jespersen, Otto. 1921. *Language: Its Nature, Development and Origin* (Reprinted 1964. New York: Norton).

———. 1924. *The Philosophy of Grammar* (Reprinted 1965. New York: Norton).

Kirsner, Robert S., and Sandra A. Thompson. 1976. "The Role of Pragmatic Inference in Semantics: A Study of Sensory Verb Complements in English," *Glossa* 10:200–40.

Locke, Simeon; David Caplan; and Lucia Kellar. 1973. *A Study in Neurolinguistics* (Springfield, Ill.: Charles C. Thomas). Reviewed by P. G. Patel, *Canadian Journal of Linguistics* 20 (1975).

Maher, J. P. 1975. "The Situational Motivation of Syntax and the Semantic Motivation of Polysemy and Semantic Change," in Mario Saltarelli and Dieter Warner (eds.), *Studies in Romance Diachronic Linguistics* (The Hague: Mouton).

Quirk, Randolph. 1970. "Taking a Deep Smell," *Journal of Linguistics* 6:119–24.

Weir, Ruth Hirsch. 1962. *Language in the Crib* (The Hague: Mouton).

CHAPTER 7

Berlin, Brent, and Paul Kay. 1969. *Basic Color Terms: Their Universality and Evolution* (Berkeley and Los Angeles: University of California Press).

Bolinger, Dwight. 1972. *Degree Words* (The Hague: Mouton).

———. 1973. "Objective and Subjective: Sentences Without Performatives," *Linguistic Inquiry* 4:414–17.

Bull, W. E. 1960. *Time, Tense, and the Verb* (Berkeley and Los Angeles: University of California Press).

Coseriu, Eugenio. 1958. *Logicismo y antilogicismo en la gramática*, 2nd ed. (Montevideo: Universidad de la República).

Furugori, Teiji. 1974. "Pass the Car in Front of You: A Simulation of Cognitive Processes for Understanding," in *Proceedings of the Association for Computer Machinery*, Annual Conference, November, pp. 380–86.

Geis, Michael L. 1973. "*If* and *Unless*," in Braj B. Kachru et al. (eds.), *Issues in Linguistics: Papers in Honor of Henry and Renée Kahane* (Urbana: University of Illinois Press).

Greenfield, Patricia M., and Jerome S. Bruner. 1971. "Learning and Language," *Psychology Today* 5:40–43, 74–79.

Hayakawa, S. I. 1978. *Language in Thought and Action*, 4th ed. (New York: Harcourt Brace Jovanovich).

Hays, David G. 1973. "Linguistics and the Future of Computation," *National Computer Conference*, pp. 1–8.

Hjelmslev, Louis. 1961. *Prolegomena to a Theory of Language*, trans. by Francis J. Whitfield. (Madison: University of Wisconsin Press).

Kučera, Henry. 1969. "Computers in Language Analysis and in Lexicography," in *The American Heritage Dictionary of the English Language* (New York: American Heritage, and Boston: Houghton Mifflin).

Lakoff, Robin. 1972. "Language in Context," *Language* 48:907–27.

———. 1975. "Contextual Change and Historical Change: The Translator as Time Machine," in Mario Saltarelli and Dieter Wanner (eds.), *Diachronic Studies in Romance Linguistics* (The Hague: Mouton).

Landar, Herbert J.; Susan M. Ervin; and Arnold E. Horowitz. 1960. "Navaho Color Categories," *Language* 36:368–82.

Marchand, Hans. 1966. Review of Karl E. Zimmer, *Affixal Negation in English and Other Languages. Language* 42:134–42.

Mathews, Mitford M. 1961. *The Beginnings of American English* (Chicago: University of Chicago Press).

Mencken, H. L. 1945. *The American Language,* suppl. I (New York: Alfred A. Knopf).

Minsky, Marvin L. 1967. *Computation, Finite and Infinite Machines* (Englewood Cliffs, N.J.: Prentice-Hall).

Oppenheimer, Max, Jr. 1961–62. "Some Linguistic Aspects of Mind-Conditioning by the Soviet Press," *Journal of Human Relations* 10:21–31.

Osgood, Charles E. 1971. "Exploration in Semantic Space: A Personal Diary," *Journal of Social Issues* 27:5–64.

———; George J. Suci; and Percy H. Tannenbaum. 1957. *The Measurement of Meaning* (Urbana: University of Illinois Press).

Prator, Clifford H. 1963. "Adjectives of Temperature," *English Language Teaching* 17:158–64.

Quine, W. V. 1960. *Word and Object.* (Cambridge, Mass.: Technology Press of M.I.T., and New York: Wiley).

Silverstein, Michael (ed.). 1971. *Whitney on Language.* (Cambridge, Mass.: M.I.T. Press).

Smith, Donald. 1975. "Experiencer Deletion." *Glossa* 9:182–201.

Stanley, Julia P. 1972 (1). "Syntactic Exploitation: Passive Adjectives in English." Paper read at meeting of Southeastern Conference on Linguistics VII, 21 April.

———. 1972 (2). "The Semantic Features of the Machismo Ethic in English." Paper read at meeting of South Atlantic Modern Language Association, 3 November.

Watson, John B. 1919. *Psychology from the Standpoint of a Behaviorist* (Philadelphia and London: J. B. Lippincott).

Weinreich, Uriel. 1958. "Travels Through Semantic Space," *Word* 14:346–66.

Whorf, Benjamin Lee. 1941. "Languages and Logic," *Technology Review* (April).

———. 1949. "The Relation of Habitual Thought and Behavior to Language," in *Four Articles on Metalinguistics* (Washington, D.C.: Foreign Service Institute, Department of State).

———. 1957. "Science and Linguistics," in John B. Carroll (ed.), *Language, Thought, and Reality* (Cambridge, Mass.: The Technology Press of M.I.T.).

CHAPTER 8

Bellugi, Ursula, and Edward S. Klima. 1973. "Formational Constraints on Language in a Visual Mode." Proposal to National Science Foundation from the Salk Institute for Biological Studies.

Bender, M. Lionel. 1973. "Linguistic Indeterminacy: Why You Cannot Reconstruct 'Proto-Human,'" *Language Sciences* 26:7–12.

Britton, James. 1970. *Language and Learning* (Miami: University of Miami Press).

Brown, Roger W. 1973. *A First Language: The Early Stages* (Cambridge, Mass.: Harvard University Press).

Chafe, Wallace. 1970. *Meaning and the Structure of Language* (Chicago: University of Chicago Press).

Chang, Nien-Chuang T. 1972. "Tones and Intonation in the Chengtu Dialect," in D. Bolinger (ed.), *Intonation* (Harmondsworth, England: Penguin).

Darwin, Charles. 1873. *The Expression of the Emotions in Man and Animals* (Reprinted 1965. Chicago: University of Chicago Press).

Engel, Walburga von Raffler. 1970. "The Function of Repetition in Child Language," *Bollettino di Psicologia Applicata* 97–98–99:27–32.

Flavell, John T.; Ann G. Friedrichs; and Jane D. Hoyt. 1970. "Developmental Changes in Memorization Processes," *Cognitive Psychology* 1:324–40.

Fónagy, Ivan. 1972. "A propos de la genèse de la phrase enfantine," *Lingua* 30:31–74.

Gardner, R. Allen, and Beatrice T. Gardner. 1969. "Teaching Sign Language to a Chimpanzee," *Science* 165:664–72.

———. 1978. "Comparative Psychology and Language Acquisition," *Annals of the New York Academy of Sciences* 309:37–76.

Gleitman, Lila R., and Elizabeth F. Shipley. 1963. "A Proposal for the Study of the Acquisition of English Syntax." Grant proposal submitted 1 March to National Institutes of Health.

———; Henry Gleitman; and Elizabeth F. Shipley. 1973. "The Emergence of the Child as Grammarian," *Cognition: International Journal of Cognitive Psychology* 1:137–64.

Hebb, D. O.; W. E. Lambert; and G. R. Tucker. 1971. "Language, Thought, and Experience," *Modern Language Journal* 55:212–22.

Hewes, Gordon W. 1971. *Language Origins: A Bibliography*. Department of Anthropology, University of Colorado.

———. 1973. "An Explicit Formulation of the Relationship Between Tool-Using, Tool-Making and the Emergence of Language," *Visible Language* 7:101–27.

Hockett, Charles F., and Robert Ascher. 1964. "The Human Revolution," *American Scientist* 52:71–92.

Jakobson, Roman. 1968. *Child Language, Aphasia, and Phonological Universals*. Trans. Allan R. Keiler (The Hague: Mouton).

————. 1969. "Linguistics in Its Relation to Other Sciences," in *Actes du Xe Congrès International des Linguistes, Bucarest, 28 Août–2 Septembre 1967* (Bucarest: Editions de l'Academie de la République Socialiste de Roumanie).

Krashen, Stephen D. 1973. "Lateralization, Language Learning, and the Critical Period: Some New Evidence," *Language Learning* 23:63–74.

Kuipers, A. H. 1968. "Unique Types and Typological Universals," in *Pratidānam: Indian, Iranian and Indo-European Studies Presented to Franciscus Bernardus Jacobus Kuiper on His Sixtieth Birthday* (The Hague: Mouton).

LaBarre, Weston. 1954. *The Human Animal* (Chicago: University of Chicago Press).

Lamendella, John T. 1973. "Innateness Claims in Psycholinguistics." Preprint.

————. 1975. *Introduction to the Neuropsychology of Language.* (Rowley, Mass.: Newbury House).

Langer, Susanne K. 1948. *Philosophy in a New Key* (New York: New American Library).

Leakey, Richard E., and Roger Lewin. 1978. *People of the Lake: Mankind and Its Beginnings* (Garden City, N.Y.: Anchor Press).

Lenneberg, Eric H. 1966. "A Biological Perspective of Language," in Eric H. Lenneberg (ed.), *New Directions in the Study of Language* (Cambridge, Mass.: M.I.T. Press).

————. 1967. *Biological Foundations of Language* (New York: Wiley).

————. 1973. "The Neurology of Language," *Daedalus* 102:3.115–33.

Lieberman, Philip. 1967. *Intonation, Perception, and Language.* Research Monograph No. 38. (Cambridge, Mass.: M.I.T. Press).

————. 1972. *The Speech of Primates* (The Hague: Mouton).

Luria, A. R., and L. S. Tsvetkova. 1970. "The Mechanism of 'Dynamic Aphasia,'" in Manfred Bierwisch and Karl Erich Heidolph (eds.), *Progress in Linguistics* (The Hague: Mouton).

Mattingly, Ignatius G. 1971. "Reading, the Linguistic Process, and Linguistic Awareness." *Haskins Laboratories Status Report on Speech Research* (July–September), 23–24.

————. 1973. "Phonetic Prerequisites for First-Language Acquisition." *Haskins Laboratories Status Report on Speech Research* (April–June), 65–69.

Nichols, Johanna. 1971. "Diminutive Consonant Symbolism in Western North America," *Language* 47:826–48.

Pines, Maya. 1973. *The Brain Changers* (New York: Harcourt Brace Jovanovich).

Premack, Ann James, and David Premack. 1972. "Teaching Language to an Ape," *Scientific American* 227:92–99.

Sagan, Carl. 1977. *The Dragons of Eden: Speculations on the Evolution of Human Intelligence* (New York: Random House).

Scholes, Robert J. 1969. "On Functors and Contentives in Children's Imitations." Communication Sciences Laboratory Quarterly Report, Department of Speech, University of Florida 7:3.

Sebeok, Thomas A. 1969. "Semiotics and Ethology," *The Linguistic Reporter,* Suppl. 22, October, 9–15.

Shipley, Elizabeth F.; Carlota S. Smith; and Lila R. Gleitman. 1969. "A Study on the Acquisition of Language: Free Responses to Commands," *Language* 45:322–42.

Stokoe, William C., Jr., Dorothy C. Casterline, and Carl G. Croneberg. 1965. *A Dictionary of American Sign Language on Linguistic Principles* (Washington, D.C.: Gallaudet College Press).

Swadesh, Morris. 1971. *The Origin and Diversification of Language* (Chicago: Aldine Atherton).

Tanz, Christine. 1971. "Sound Symbolism in Words Relating to Proximity and Distance," *Language and Speech* 14:266–76.

Ultan, Russell. 1978. "Size-Sound Symbolism," in Joseph H. Greenberg (ed.), *Universals of Human Language,* vol. 2, *Phonology,* 525–68. (Stanford, Calif.: Stanford University Press).

Van Lancker, Diana. 1975. *Heterogeneity in Language and Speech: Neurolinguistic Studies. UCLA Working Paper in Phonetics,* No. 29.

Weir, Ruth Hirsch. 1962. *Language in the Crib* (The Hague: Mouton).

Wescott, Roger W. 1967. "The Evolution of Language: Reopening a Closed Subject," *Studies in Linguistics* 19:67–81.

CHAPTER 9

Agard, Frederick B. 1971. "Language and Dialect: Some Tentative Postulates," *Linguistics* 65:5–24.

Allen, Harold B. 1973–76. *The Linguistic Atlas of the Upper Midwest,* 3 vols. (Minneapolis: University of Minnesota Press).

Arthur, Bradford. 1971. "The Interaction of Dialect and Style in Urban American English," in *UCLA Work Papers in Teaching English as a Second Language* 5:1–18.

Babington, Mima, and E. Bagby Atwood. 1961. "Lexical Usage in Southern Louisiana," *Publication of the American Dialect Society,* No. 36, November, pp. 1–24.

Bailey, Charles-James N. 1974. *Old and New Views on Language History and Language Relationships.* Manuscript.

Bright, William. 1969. "Phonological Rules in Literary and Colloquial Kannada," *Working Papers in Linguistics,* University of Hawaii, 11:75–90.

Bross, I. D. J. 1973. "Languages in Cancer Research," in Edwin A. Mirand et al. (eds.), *Perspectives in Cancer Research and Treatment* (New York: Alan R. Liss).

Cassidy, Frederic G. 1967. "American Regionalism and the Harmless Drudge," *Publications of the Modern Language Association* 82:12–19.

Cazden, Courtney B. 1972. *Child Language and Education* (New York: Holt, Rinehart & Winston).

Chomsky, A. N. 1965. *Aspects of the Theory of Syntax* (Cambridge, Mass.: M.I.T. Press).

Conklin, Harold C. 1959. "Linguistic Play in Its Cultural Context," *Language* 35:631–36.

Corominas, J. 1954. *Diccionario crítico etimológico de la lengua castellana* (Bern: Editorial Francke).

Coseriu, Eugenio. 1956. *La geografía lingüística* (Montevideo: Instituto de Filología).

De Francis, John. 1951. "Aspects of Linguistic Structure," in *Georgetown University Monograph Series on Languages and Linguistics* 1:48–51.

Dillard, J. L. 1972. *Black English* (New York: Random House).

Dixon, R. M. W. 1972. *The Dyirbal Language of North Queensland* (London: Cambridge University Press).

Engel, Walburga von Raffler. 1972. "Some Phono-stylistic Features of Black English," *Phonetica* 25:53–64.

Fickett, Joan G. 1972. "Tense and Aspect in Black English," *Journal of English Linguistics* 6:17–19.

Fishman, Joshua A. 1967. "Bilingualism With and Without Diglossia; Diglossia With and Without Bilingualism," *Journal of Social Issues* 23:29–38.

Gleason, H. A. 1965. *Linguistics and English Grammar* (New York: Holt, Rinehart & Winston).

Granda, Germán de. 1970. "Cimarronismo, palenques y hablas 'criollas' en Hispanoamérica," *Boletín del Instituto Caro y Cuervo* 25:448–69.

Greenbaum, Sidney. 1975. "Grammar and the Foreign Language Teacher," in *On TESOL 74* (Washington, D.C.: Teachers of English to Speakers of Other Languages).

Gregory, Michael, and Susanne Carroll. 1978. *Language and Situation: Language Varieties and Their Social Contexts* (London: Routledge & Kegan Paul).

Grimshaw, Allen D. 1973. Review of John J. Gumperz, *Language in Social Groups,* ed. by Anwar S. Dil (Stanford, Calif.: Stanford University Press, 1971). In *Language Sciences* 27:29–37.

Haas, Mary R. 1964. "Men's and Women's Speech in Koasati," in Dell Hymes (ed.), *Language in Culture and Society* (New York: Harper & Row), 228–33.

Hall, Robert A., Jr. 1943. *Melanesian Pidgin Phrase-Book and Vocabulary.* (Linguistic Society of America, Special Publication).

———. 1962. "The Life Cycle of Pidgin Languages," *Lingua* 11:151–56.

Hall, William S., and Roy O. Freedle. 1973. "A Developmental Investigation of Standard and Nonstandard English Among Black and White Children," *Human Development* 16:440–64.

———. 1975. *Culture and Language: The Black American Experience* (Washington, D.C.: Hemisphere Publishing).

Hannerz, Ulf. 1970. "Language Variation and Social Relationships," *Studia Linguistica* 24:128–51.

Hewes, Gordon W. 1973. "An Explicit Formulation of the Relationship Between Tool-Using, Tool-Making, and the Emergence of Language," *Visible Language* 7:101–27.

Hooley, Bruce A. 1965. Review of S. A. Wurm and J. H. Harris, *Police Motu:*

An Introduction to the Trade Language of Papua (Canberra, Australia: Linguistic Circle of Canberra, 1963). In *Language* 41:168–70.

Hutson, Arthur E. 1947. "Gaelic Loan-Words in America," *American Speech* 22:18–23.

Hymes, Dell. 1962. "The Ethnography of Speaking," in Thomas Gladwin and William C. Sturtevant (eds.), *Anthropology and Human Behavior* (Washington, D.C.: The Anthropological Society of Washington).

Joos, Martin. 1967. *The Five Clocks* (New York: Harcourt Brace Jovanovich).

Kaye, Alan S. 1972. "Remarks on Diglossia in Arabic," *Linguistics* 81:32–48.

Keller-Cohen, Deborah. 1973. "Deictic Reference in Children's Speech." Paper read at Linguistic Society of America, San Diego, 29 December.

Key, Mary Ritchie. 1972. "Linguistic Behavior of Male and Female," *Linguistics* 88:15–31.

———. 1975. *Male/Female Language with a Comprehensive Bibliography* (Metuchen, N.J.: The Scarecrow Press).

Kuno, Susumu. 1973. *The Structure of the Japanese Language* (Cambridge, Mass.: M.I.T. Press).

Kurath, Hans. 1949. *A Word Geography of the Eastern United States* (Ann Arbor: University of Michigan Press).

———. 1965. "Some Aspects of Atlantic Seaboard English Considered in Their Connections with British English," in *Communications et rapports du Premier Congrès International de Dialectologie Générale*, Louvain, Belgium, pp. 236–40.

Labov, William. 1963. "The Social Motivation of a Sound Change," *Word* 19:273–309.

———. 1969. "Contraction, Deletion, and Inherent Variability of the English Copula," *Language* 45:715–62.

———. 1970. "The Study of Language in Its Social Context." *Studium Generale* 23:30–87.

———. 1972. "Negative Attraction and Negative Concord," *Language* 48:773–818.

Lakoff, Robin. 1973. "Language and Woman's Place," *Language in Society* 2:45–79. Reprinted 1975 (New York: Harper Colophon Books).

Maurer, D. W. 1955. "Whiz Mob," *Publication of the American Dialect Society*, No. 24.

Morínigo, Marcos A. 1931. *Hispanismos en el guaraní* (Buenos Aires: J. Peuser).

Moulton, William. 1963. Review in *Journal of English and Germanic Philology* 62:828–37.

O'Neil, Wayne. 1970. "Comes the Revolution," *Harvard Graduate School of Education Bulletin* 14:3.2–3.

Orton, Harold, Stewart Sanderson, and John Widdowson (eds.). 1978. *The Linguistic Atlas of England* (London: Croom Helm).

Pederson, Lee. 1971. "Southern Speech and the LAGS Project," *Orbis* 20:79–89.

Ricci, Julio, and Iris Malan de Ricci. 1962–63. "Anotaciones sobre el uso de los pronombres *tú* y *vos* en el español de Uruguay," *Anales del Instituto de Profesores Artigas* 7–8.

Stewart, William A. 1968. "Continuity and Change in American Negro Dialects," *The Florida FL Reporter* (Spring 1968), 3, 4, 14–18.

Teeter, Karl V. 1973. "Linguistics and Anthropology," *Daedalus* 102:87–98.

Todd, Loreto. 1974. *Pidgins and Creoles* (London: Routledge & Kegan Paul).

Turner, Lorenzo. 1949. *Africanisms in the Gullah Dialect* (Chicago: University of Chicago Press).

Wexler, Paul. 1971. "Diglossia, Language Standardization, and Purism: Parameters for a Typology of Literary Language," *Lingua* 27:330–54.

Williams, Robert L. (ed.). 1975. *Ebonics: The True Language of Black Folks* (St. Louis, Mo.: Institute of Black Studies).

Wolfram, Walt. 1973. Review of William J. Samarin, *Tongues of Men and Angels* (New York: Macmillan, 1972). In *Language Sciences* 27:37–40.

CHAPTER 10

Andersen, Henning. 1973. "Abductive and Deductive Change," *Language* 49:765–93.

Anttila, Raimo. 1972. *An Introduction to Historical and Comparative Linguistics* (New York: Macmillan).

Bailey, Charles-James N. 1974. *Old and New Views on Language History and Language Relationships.* Manuscript.

Bowen, J. Donald. 1971. "Hispanic Languages and Influence in Oceania," in Thomas A. Sebeok (ed.), *Current Trends in Linguistics.* Linguistics in Oceania, vol. 8 (The Hague: Mouton).

Brown, Roger. 1973. *A First Language: The Early Stages* (Cambridge, Mass.: Harvard University Press).

——— and Ursula Bellugi. 1964. "Three Processes in the Child's Acquisition of Syntax," *Harvard Educational Review* 34:133–51.

Csapó, József. 1971. "English Sporting Terms in Hungarian," *Hungarian Studies in English* 5:5–50.

Downes, Mildred J. 1957. "The Unreader," *Language Arts* 32:202–04.

Fónagy, Ivan. 1971. "Double Coding in Speech," *Semiotica* 3:189–222.

Greenbaum, Sidney. 1969. *Studies in English Adverbial Usage* (London: Longmans).

Haugen, Einar. 1972. *The Ecology of Language* (Stanford, Calif.: Stanford University Press).

Householder, Fred W., Jr. 1971. *Linguistic Speculations* (Cambridge, England: Cambridge University Press).

———. 1972. "The Principal Step in Linguistic Change," *Language Sciences* 20:1–5.

Hutson, Arthur E. 1947. "Gaelic Loan-Words in American," *American Speech* 22:18–23.

Jespersen, Otto. 1894. *Progress in Language, with Special Reference to English* (London: Swan Sonnenschein, and New York: Macmillan).

———. 1909. 1914. *A Modern English Grammar on Historical Principles,* Parts I and II (New York: Barnes and Noble).

Labov, William. 1970. "The Study of Language in Its Social Context," *Studium Generale* 23:30–87.

Lamb, David. 1974. "Linguists Find Twists in Aborigines' Tongue," *Los Angeles Times* (4 February), p. 22 (account of work of Summer Institute of Linguistics).

Levy, John F. 1973. "Tendential Transfer of Old Spanish *hedo* < *foedu* to the Family of *heder* < *foetere*," *Romance Philology* 27:204–10.

Long, Ralph B. 1959. *A Grammar of American English* (Austin, Texas: University Co-op).

Maher, J. Peter. 1973. "*H_aekmon: '(stone) axe' and 'sky' in I-E/Battle-Axe Culture," *The Journal of Indo-European Studies* 1:441–62.

Malkiel, Yakov. 1972. "The Rise of the Nominal Augments in Romance," *Romance Philology* 26:306–34.

Morse, J. Mitchell. 1974. "Race, Class, and Metaphor," *College English* 35:545–65.

Moulton, William G. 1971. Review of Pieder Cavigelli, *Die Germanisierung von Bonaduz in Geschichtlicher und Sprachlicher Schau* (Frauenfeld, Germany: Huber, 1969). In *Language* 47:938–43.

Mustanoja, Tauno F. 1960. *A Middle English Syntax*. Pt. 1: *Parts of Speech* (Helsinki: Société Néophilologique).

Nalobow, Kenneth L. 1971. "The Gender of 'Professor Nowak' in Polish," *Polish Review* 16:71–78.

Peruzzi, Emilio. 1958. *Saggi di linguistica europea* (Salamanca, Spain: Consejo Superior de Investigaciones Científicas).

Pfaff, Carol W. 1979. "Constraints on Language Mixing: Intrasentential Code-Switching and Borrowing in Spanish/English," *Language* 55:291–318.

Reyes, Rogelio. 1975. "Language Mixing in Chicano Bilingual Speech," in J. Donald Bowen and Jacob Ornstein (eds.), *Studies on Southwest Spanish* (Rowley, Mass.: Newbury House).

Tamony, Peter. 1973. "Wiretapping and Bugging, 1863—Watergate 1972," in his *Americanisms: Content and Continuum*, No. 33, May.

Topping, Donald M. 1962. "Loanblends: A Tool for Linguists," *Language Learning* 12:281–87.

Vachek, Josef. 1965. "On the Internal and External Determination of Sound Laws." *Biuletyn Polskiego Towarzystwa Językoznawczego* 23:49–57.

———. 1973. *Written Language: General Problems and Problems of English* (The Hague: Mouton).

Valesio, Paolo. 1974. *Alliteration and the Grammar of Rhetoric*. Manuscript.

CHAPTER 11

Barber, E. J. W. 1973. "The Formal Economy of Written Signs," *Visible Language* 7:155–66.

Bolinger, Dwight. 1946. "Visual Morphemes," *Language* 22:333–40.

Chadwick, John. 1960. *The Decipherment of Linear B* (London: Cambridge University Press).

Chomsky, A. N., and Morris Halle. 1968. *The Sound Pattern of English* (New York: Harper & Row).

Cleator, P. E. 1959, 1962. *Lost Languages* (New York: New American Library).

Doblhofer, Ernst. 1971. *Voices in Stone: The Decipherment of Ancient Scripts and Writings,* transl. Mervyn Savill (New York: Collier Books).

Gelb, I. J. 1963. *A Study of Writing,* rev. ed. (Chicago: University of Chicago Press).

Gleitman, Lila R., and Paul Rozin. 1973. "Teaching Reading by Use of a Syllabary," *Reading Research Quarterly* 8:447–501.

Haas, William. 1973. *Phono-graphic Translation* (Manchester, England: Manchester University Press).

Householder, Fred W., Jr. 1971. *Linguistic Speculations* (Cambridge, England: Cambridge University Press).

Mattingly, Ignatius G. 1971. "Reading, the Linguistic Process, and Linguistic Awareness." *Haskins Laboratories Status Report on Speech Research* (July–September), 23–24.

————, and James F. Kavanagh. 1972. "The Relationship Between Speech and Reading," *The Linguistic Reporter* 14:5.1–4.

Pedersen, Holger. 1962. *The Discovery of Language,* tr. John Webster Spargo (Bloomington: Indiana University Press).

Pitman, Sir James, and John St. John. 1969. *Alphabets and Reading: The Initial Teaching Alphabet* (New York: Pitman).

Salus, Peter (ed.). 1969. *On Language: Plato to von Humboldt* (New York: Holt, Rinehart & Winston).

Scott, Charles T. 1966. "The Linguistic Basis for the Development of Reading Skill," *Modern Language Journal* 50:535–44.

Sjoberg, Andrée F. 1962. "Coexistent Phonemic Systems in Telugu," *Word* 18:269–79.

Tritt, Carleton S. 1973. "The Language of Capitalization in Shakespeare's First Folio," *Visible Language* 7:41–50.

Tzeng, Ovid J. L., Daisy L. Hung, and William S.-Y. Wang. 1977. "Speech Decoding in Reading Chinese Characters," *Journal of Experimental Psychology* 3:621–30.

Vachek, Josef. 1973. *Written Language: General Problems and Problems of English* (The Hague: Mouton).

CHAPTER 12

Bernstein, Theodore M. 1965. *The Careful Writer: A Modern Guide to English Usage* (New York: Atheneum).

Dobson, W. A. C. H. 1973. "China as a World Power," *American Council of Learned Societies Newsletter* 24:3.1–10.

Esterhill, Frank. 1974. "Reversing Babel: The Emergence of an Interlanguage," *The ATA Chronicle, Newspaper of the American Translators Association* 3:3.6–9.

Fodor, István. 1966. "Linguistic Problems and 'Language Planning' in Africa," *Linguistics* 25:18–33.

Fowler, H. W. 1926 and 1965. *Dictionary of Modern English Usage* (Oxford and London: Oxford University Press); 2nd ed., rev. by Sir Ernest Gowers (New York and Oxford, England: Oxford University Press).

Frei, Ernest J. 1959. *The Historical Development of the Philippine National Language* (Manila: Institute of National Language).

Freudenthal, Hans. 1960. *Lincos: Design of a Language for Cosmic Intercourse* (Amsterdam: North-Holland Publishing).

Fries, C. C. 1956–57. "The Periphrastic Uses of *Shall* and *Will* in Modern English," *Language Learning* 7:38–99.

Guitarte, Guillermo L., and Rafael Torres Quintero. 1968. "Linguistic Correctness and the Role of the Academies," in Thomas A. Seboek (ed.), *Current Trends in Linguistics*. Ibero-American and Caribbean Linguistics, vol. 4 (The Hague: Mouton).

Halliday, M. A. K. 1973. *Explorations in the Functions of Language* (London: Edward Arnold).

Haugen, Einar. 1972. *The Ecology of Language* (Stanford, Calif.: Stanford University Press).

Knappert, Jan. 1968. "The Function of Language in a Political Situation," *Linguistics* 39:59–67.

Ramos, Maximo. 1961. *Language Policy in Certain Newly Independent States* (Manila: Philippine Center for Language Study).

Rosén, Haiim B. 1969. "Israel Language Policy, Language Teaching and Linguistics," *Ariel, a Review of the Arts and Sciences in Israel*, 25:92–111.

Sheldon, Esther K. 1947. "Walker's Influence on the Pronunciation of English," *Publications of the Modern Language Association of America* 62:130–46.

Sledd, James, and Wilma R. Ebbitt, 1962. *Dictionaries and That Dictionary* (Chicago: Scott, Foresman and Company).

Villa Panganiban, José. 1957. "The Family of Philippine Languages and Dialects" and "A Filipino National Language Is Not Impossible," *Unitas* 30: 823–33 and 855–62.

Wang, William S.-Y. 1973. "The Chinese Language," *Scientific American* 228: 2.51–60.

———. 1974. "Notes on a Trip to China," *Linguistic Reporter* 16:1.3–4.

Winograd, Terry. 1974. "Artificial Intelligence—When Will Computers Understand People?" *Psychology Today* 7:12.73–79.

INDEX

This Index includes names, subjects, words, and morphemes. Certain entries refer to concepts rather than to terms. For instance, *mother-in-law language* is not mentioned by name on page 222, but an example of such language is given on that page. Similarly *hesitation sound,* which is named and defined on page 6, is illustrated without specific identification on page 43.

Words and morphemes that are given some discussion in the text appear in the index in bold-face italic type. Thus *boy,* discussed on pages 112–13, is included; but *adolescent,* which is merely listed as a partial synonym, is not.